D1276196

To Natasha,
I hope you enjoy
my book and C.D.
"How Sweet It Is"
Bob Harris
Thanksgiving 2015

How Sweet It Is!

FROM THE COTTON MILL TO THE CROWS' NEST

By Bob Harris

Forward by Coach Mike Krzyzewski

HOW SWEET IT IS
FROM THE COTTON MILL TO THE CROWS NEST
THE STORY OF BOB HARRIS
THE VOICE OF THE DUKE BLUE DEVILS

By Bob Harris
Design by Debra Davis Rezeli
and Bonnie B. Roberson

Library of Congress Control Number: 2010915988
ISBN 978-1-4507-4303-7

FIRST PRINTING

"HOW SWEET IT IS"
IS DEDICATED TO PHYLLIS

SHE HAS BEEN WITH ME NEARLY EVERY STEP OF THE WAY ON
THIS WONDERFUL JOURNEY, AND HER SACRIFICES
MADE MY CAREER POSSIBLE. THE BOOK WAS HER IDEA.
AT FIRST I RESISTED,
BUT I'M SO GLAD SHE PERSISTED.

Foreword by Mike Krzyzewski

For the past 30 years, I have been so fortunate to be a part of one of the greatest families in all of sport: Duke Athletics. And, no one is a prouder or more devoted member of that family than the long-time "Voice of the Blue Devils," Bob Harris.

When my wife, daughters, and I first arrived in Durham in 1980, Bob made an immediate impact on us as someone who knew Duke Basketball inside and out. In getting to know him, I also got to know Duke, its Athletics program, its rich history, and the many players and coaches who have made it great. Bob's knowledge and guidance were invaluable as we adjusted to our new home in a place where college sports is an integral part of the social fabric.

In the more than three decades that Bob has been a part of the Duke family, he has made some of signature games in the history of college basketball come to life, including each of Duke's three national championships and, perhaps most memorably, the 1992 Duke-Kentucky Regional Final that some believe was the greatest college basketball game ever played. Though I don't get to hear him call Duke Basketball games live, his voice is inextricably linked in my mind to these moments in time – part of the soundtrack to the countless memories I have of this place. His is the voice that Duke fans have learned to trust and I mean it when I say that Bob Harris has played a prominent role in helping Duke establish one of the top programs in sport.

Bob is Duke Blue through and through and it shows in his work. At Duke, we're fortunate that many of our games are televised nationally. But, despite the availability of coverage, many of our fans actually turn down the volume on their televisions and up on their radios to listen to Bob call the games on the Duke Radio Network as they watch the action on TV. That is a testament to the loyal following Bob has built throughout his storied career.

Twice on each game day – once before and once after -- Bob and I spend some time together to discuss that night's opponent and help tell the story of Duke Basketball. Between games during the season, we also tape a brief daily show that airs locally. Undoubtedly, Bob and I have conducted thousands of interviews the past three decades, usually in one take. For me, he's prepared every time. He is consistently enthusiastic, informative, and most importantly, positive about the young men who've represented Duke so well through the years. Because of our relationship and the rhythm we have established, I am able to be completely honest and forthright in these interviews – when I am excited, when I am worried, when I am in good spirits, and even when I am angry, this comes through in my conversations with Bob and the listeners benefit from knowing truly where the coaching staff stands.

Always willing to lend his help to worthwhile causes, Bob invests so much of his time and energy in community service and charitable events. The Duke Children's Hospital, Brad Johnson Celebrity Golf Classic for the Eblen Foundation, Brenner Children's Hospital, Children's Charities of the Bluegrass, Children's Miracle Network, Coastal Classic for New Hanover Medical Center, Hebron Colony Ministries, 'Me Fine Now' Foundation, the Ronald McDonald House of Durham, Special Olympics of North Carolina and the Durham Rescue Mission are just a few of the events/charities Bob works with each year. A native of North Carolina, he is deeply committed to his local community, his state, and as evidenced by the list above, to making children's lives better. We have a phrase we use a lot in our program: "A person is not complete until he becomes a part of something bigger than himself or herself." Bob does not only understand this concept, he lives it.

Now entering his fifth decade in broadcasting, Bob has been the recipient of several awards including the North Carolina Sportscaster of the Year twice, the Robert Marlowe Award for Sports Broadcasting, the Ray Reeve Award for Sports Broadcasting, and induction into the Stanly County Sports Hall of Fame. He was also deservedly inducted into the

North Carolina Sports Hall of Fame in 2006.

Perhaps Bob's most fitting honor came at the ACC Tournament in March of 2009 when was presented with the prestigious Marvin "Skeeter" Francis Award. This honor recognizes individuals for distinguished service and promotion to the Atlantic Coast Conference. Bob joined the likes of media legends Billy Packer, C.D. Chesley, Mary Garber, Ron Green, and Furman Bisher as a recipient of that award. One day later, Bob joined us on the court again, this time as an ACC champion following our victory over Florida State in the 2009 ACC Championship Game. He is as much of a part of our team as anyone – and no one tells the story of the Duke Blue Devils better.

In addition to forming a wonderful friendship with Bob over the past 30 years, we've been able to establish a great relationship with his wife, Phyllis, as well. Phyllis, daughter Bobbi, granddaughter Meredith and grandson Tripp are all a huge part of Bob's personal and professional life and we're fortunate to count each of them as friends of our program.

What follows on these pages are the memories and anecdotes that have shaped the life of a man who I consider to be a dear friend. Bob's been terrific for us for three decades – here's hoping for three more.

Acknowledgments

To acknowledge and say 'thank you' to everyone who has had anything to do with this book would be to acknowledge every person that I have ever come in contact with. In some way, they are all a part of who I am and what I have been able to accomplish.

First of all, I want to thank Johnny Moore, President of Moore Productions, and a man I have known for well over thirty years. We first worked together when he came to Duke in 1977 after graduating from Guilford. He was Tom Mickle's assistant in the Sports Information Department. In 1991, Johnny left Duke to publish 'Devilirum.'

Johnny has always had the best interests of Duke University and those who are a part, large or small, of the big picture. I worked for Johnny as host of the Duke coaches' television shows before joining him on a full time basis in 1998. Johnny has always been a person who never put limits on an employee. He always encouraged those around him to be more than just a job title. We have the kind of relationship that creates dialogue both ways. He has been the only person in a supervisory position to offer me constructive criticism, and an honest appraisal of the job that I was doing. Some people in those positions feel that they should only give positive feedback. I have always looked to Johnny to be totally honest with my 'end product' and to give me an honest assessment of my broadcasts and all other aspects of my job. He has always done that. His right-hand-man, John Roth, deserves a huge 'thank you' for making my job so much easier. His willingness to handle so many of the things helps me more than he knows.

Rusty Helser is a wonderful human being. He has compassion for everyone he comes in contact with, and passion for everything he does.

I have been blessed to work with him since the early 1980s. Thanks to Rusty for the many hours of work and thought in processing the CD. To the people at George's Grill, American & Efird Mills, Goodyear Tire and Rubber Company, Albemarle Shoe Center, Western-Southern Life Insurance, WZKY, WEGO/WPEG, WDNC, WDBS, WTIK, Moore Productions and ISP for allowing me to earn a living for my family while pursuing my life's work. Some days were tough, but the overwhelming majority were wonderful.

I thank every teacher and instructor I had at Central Elementary, Albemarle High and N.C. State College for their efforts and guidance in my education. The same goes for the Sunday School teachers at North Albemarle Baptist Church. To pastors and good friends, W.B. Holmes, Leroy Caulder, O.H. Bolch, Dr. John Huff, Ken Gibson, and David Alexander, thanks for trying to keep my feet on the right path. Coaches have always played a huge part in my life. Beginning with my Little League coach, Cobb Talbert, and continuing to AHS where Toby Webb, Don and 'Bear' Knotts, Bob Gantt, Ken Frazier and Tom Maultsby taught me life-lessons along with offense, defense, the 2-3 zone, and the squeeze bunt.

The Duke coaches have been invaluable. Our interactions have been more than professional relationships. They allowed me to learn even more so I could perfect my craft. Mike McGee, 'Red' Wilson, Steve Sloan, Steve Spurrier, Barry Wilson, Fred Goldsmith, Carl Franks, Ted Roof, David Cutcliffe and all 104 of their assistants gave me the benefit of their football expertise. Bill Foster and Mike Krzyzewski and their aides improved my basketball knowledge. From Pfeiffer, there was Joe Ferebee, Francis Essic and Tom Childress. Thanks to Duke athletic directors Carl James, Tom Butters, Joe Alleva and Kevin White for their direction and the opportunity to be associated with one of the greatest universities in the world.

That learning experience hasn't been limited to just the coaches of the teams that I broadcast for. It includes coaches like Charlie English, George Whitfield, Clyde King, Dean, Lefty, Pete, Gary, Dave, Roy, Bobby, Frank, Bill, Terry, Bo, Al, Dick, Monte, Carl, Norm, Les, Mack, Steve, David, Seth, Jerry, George, Chuck, John, Mike, Danny, Tommy and Rick.

Another special group has been all of the student-athletes that have dotted the rosters of the teams that I have broadcast for. More than wins and losses, the guys and gals who had a wonderful time during their careers have made my experience so much more rewarding. Those relationships with Little Leaguers to high school to university student-athletes continue today.

I want to thank every member of the Duke Radio Network crews and those who have made the TV shows so much fun for a 'non-TV guy.' Whether it was Donnie Tuck, who was an engineer for one year, or Wes Chesson, who has been with me for over thirty years, or my 'extra eyes' for forty years, Clyde Cupples; I thank you all for your loyalty and professionalism and always trying to make the Duke Radio Network the best in the country, and making our Duke fans proud. The individuals will be discussed throughout the book.

I must thank all of the fans. You wore the green and gold of West Stanly, the Blue and White of AHS, the red and grey of South Stanly and the red, white and blue of North Stanly. You wore the black and gold of Pfeiffer and the various combinations of Little League and City League teams. You are Duke Blue, through and through. And many others who just listened because it was a ballgame and you were a fan. I hope you have had half the enjoyment of listening that I have had in broadcasting the games. Ain't we had fun???

I would add another 200 pages to the book if I named every advertiser who helped pay my bills by buying airtime on my stations. There would be that many more who were my customers in the retail stores where I worked. Good friends are hard to come by. I have so many, and for so many reasons. Folks who are always there for me, and my family, are good friends. I have talked about so many of the people who have become good friends through my professional life. There are others like Chip Chesson, Coy Clayton, Mike Ray, Jim Elkins, Crae Morton, K.D. Kennedy, Lynn and Dave Travis, Charles Brown, Gene Starnes, Eric Hinshaw, Gene Edmundson, Jim Hardin, Drs Richard Ferro, Jeff Bytomski, Mel Berlin, and Michael Cuffe, who are mentioned for reasons known only to them and my family. All of them are treasures to the Harris family. I have told them all, privately, for many years, but I wanted to say 'thank you' publicly.

As you can see, there have been thousands of people who have played a part in my life. For some, there are no words that will express my love and appreciation for your impact on my life. Those people are my family.

Daddy gave me a love of, and appreciation for, sports. Momma made sure I was in church. Paul and Wilma Shoe gave me their beautiful daughter, who gave me two beautiful daughters. Bobbi gave us two fantastic grandchildren, Tripp and Meredith. I've always been told that coaches must have special women for their wives because of all the time demands on them. Broadcasters must have them too. I've seen too many peers in the industry who didn't have the same good fortune I did in picking a mate. We are a lot alike in some ways, and a lot different in others. That, and commitment, are what makes it work.

There are many others, and I would love to list all of you individually, but I would certainly leave out someone. I wouldn't want to hurt anyone's feelings. So to all my friends, thank you!!

Preface

What's in a Name?

More than just the title of my book, these words have become my signature call. Since 2000, Duke fans know something spectacular and very significant has just happened when they hear me shout, "HOW SWEET IT IS!" Plays that change the emotion and outcome of the game normally come just after long struggles; whether it's a guard having a shooting slump or a quarterback without a completed pass, football and basketball games have times of great challenges. This is also the case in the game of life. And as I began writing this book it became very clear to me that it, too, is about moments of struggle and great changes, which altered the course of my life. HOW SWEET IT IS!

Life is also a journey, and like so many people, my life has taken some interesting routes. 'From the Cotton Mill to the Crows Nest' is more than a catchy subtitle. It is the culmination of more than 60 years of journeys, some of which propelled me forward and some that set me back a little, but all of which have made me who I am today. I was born and raised on a 'cotton mill hill' and I was, and will continue to be, a 'mill hill boy' for the rest of my life. In some circles, that term is used to differentiate social levels. In Stanly County in the 1940s and '50s, it seemed that most folks only used the term for house location, not for an inference of lesser financial or educational levels.

This is the story of my life. I hope you will enjoy my reminiscing, and will laugh a little at the stories, and perhaps, even get a bit misty as you recall your own history. Most of all, I hope, as you are going through life's challenges and successes, you will remember "HOW SWEET IT IS!"

CHAPTER ONE
The Foundations

Life is a series of choices. Some are small and have no direct effect on our lives. The color of the shirt I want to wear today, the kind of shoes; they might seem important at 7:00 am, but by 8:30, you have forgotten all about that decision. Some choices can influence the rest of our lives. What choices will I make in my career? How will I prepare for adulthood? Who will I marry? Am I making the right career move? Many of my choices led me to exactly where I am today.

We have no choice in many things; God sets some. We don't determine our parents, or our siblings. He gives us the family we need. My parents were both in their mid-thirties when I was born, and my only sibling was already fourteen. My parents had to endure the Great Depression and all of its hardships. Daddy was 25 at the beginning of that era and worked in the cotton mill in Albemarle, N.C. It wasn't a glamorous job by any stretch of the imagination. It did keep him gainfully employed and able to raise his young family. His outlook on life was always, "We'll make it through somehow." And we did. Through the Depression, World War II, the Korean War and the fluctuations of the textile industry, this outlook on life enabled him to persevere.

One of the best examples of this is etched vividly in my memory. In the mid-1950s, the mills would produce the yarn as needed by industry. One summer he worked forty-nine consecutive days in the mill. Forty-nine days without one single day away from American & Efird Plant #5, where he 'ran' drawing machines. He did okay financially during that period, but a few months later, when the mill went on 'short time' he was working only three days a week. I remember seeing one of his paychecks for $27.50 after taxes. TWENTY-SEVEN DOLLARS AND A HALF!!

When I was eight years old, our rent for the four-room mill house we lived in was $8.00 per week. Milk was 92 cents a gallon, bread was 18 cents a loaf, eggs were 61 cents a dozen, and you could get a ten-pound bag of potatoes for 53 cents. Sunday's pot roast was 43 cents a pound, and the leftovers might last until Tuesday night's supper (dinner was what you ate at noon around our house). Gas was 23 cents a gallon, but we didn't worry about that. We didn't have a car. We walked almost everywhere we needed to go. Albemarle wasn't that big, and vacation week was when Daddy didn't have to go to work and could work in our garden or maybe go fishing with neighbors who DID have a car.

My Daddy didn't have many choices in those matters. His formal education consisted of a couple of weeks at the beginning of the school years when he was six and seven years old. He then quit to help on the farm. He was eventually a mill hand, and would be for the rest of his working life. Some folks referred to all who worked in the cotton mills and lived in the company houses as 'lintheads.' Daddy was one, and so was I. And I am STILL a 'linthead' at heart. It gave me a firm, realistic background on which to build my life. Looking back now, I realize just how poor we really were.

It is a little more than 114 miles from my boyhood home at 236 Wilson Street in Albemarle, North Carolina to historic Cameron Indoor Stadium, the home of the Duke University 'Blue Devils.' It takes about two hours today, but it took me a great deal longer than that, more than 30 years in fact. It was an adventuresome odyssey, but it was an interesting one. My journey took some very interesting turns, and consisted of a number of roadblocks and detours.

As a kid, I never had a nickname. I have been called by several versions of my true, full given name, Bobby Gene. By the time I got to high school, the Gene was dropped and I was known as Bobby. After Phyllis and I had dated a while, she began to call me Bob. Our daughters called me Dad, and our grandchildren call me Poppaw. Some refer to me as Robert. A name I have been extremely proud to be known as for thirty-five-plus years is the 'Voice of the Duke Blue Devils.'

My 'second family' gave me this title, and I am so proud of it. The 'family' I am referring to is comprised of the folks who are ardent supporters of Duke University. This moniker is not unique to me. Most every school in the country refers to their radio announcer as 'The Voice of…' It can be one of esteem, respect, admiration or simply identification. I just hope I fall into one of these.

I really never thought of a career in broadcasting while I was growing up. Oh yes, I did my share of 'pretend' announcing when playing ball by myself. I've been involved with sports most of my life. I wanted to catch for my team, the Brooklyn Dodgers. So did about a million other kids playing ball on vacant lots everywhere in America in the late-1940s and 50s. Could I ever hope to play in Brooklyn? I thought so. Was it my top priority? No. BUT, I had always been told that anything was possible. So why not believe I could make the roster in 'Flatbush.'

Back in the '50s, Albemarle's North Depot Street was a traffic jam every eight hours as bus- and carloads of textile workers rode in from the countryside for their turn at drenching sweat, replenishing salt pills, tobacco-covered spittoons and dope-wagon meals on the hardwood floors of American & Efird and Wiscassett Mills. From the outside looking in, life looked justifiably tough for these trojans of the hardwood; but beyond the oppressive heat, strained muscles and six-day work weeks, life was a joy for these textile workers, who relished in their children's every success and persevered daily for their ultimate goal… a better life for their children.

As children growing up on North Depot during these glorious days, Bobby Harris, my two brothers and I had a neighborhood full of boys that enjoyed nothing more than a baseball or football game on 'The Big Field' or a basketball game on the dusty spot behind our house. Many a fly ball was snagged on that grassed, sloping knoll we loved and many a running bank-shot bounced off that swaying, wooden backboard and found only the bottom of the net. The love of the games were planted on these fields of our youth and nurtured with the tradition of excellence of Stanly County American Legion and Wiscassett baseball and the Albemarle Bulldog football program of Toby Webb.

Jim Lisk, Editor Stanly News & Press May 2009

I was born Albemarle in 1942. The town of about 11,000 was like so many others in North Carolina, and all over the southern United States in that era. It was a community that probably looked like all the rest of the 'mill-towns' of that era. Looking at old black and white pictures of Piedmont North Carolina during World War II, it would be hard to distinguish one from the other. A lot of the community-related activities revolved around the mills' employees.Textiles didn't just provide a good portion of the jobs for the town, but a large share of the revenue for the merchants. The employees' taxes helped fund the five elementary schools and two high schools. The industry provided sustenance for those families that lived in the various mill villages that populated the town. Our family was included in that vast group.

There were two cotton mills in Albemarle, the Wiscassett and the American & Efird. Wiscassett was a part of Cannon Mills headquartered in Kannapolis. A&E was a part of a larger company with a number of locations in the Mt. Holly area on the west side of Charlotte. Both plants in Albemarle did the same things. They received bales of raw cotton and turned out spools and spindles of yarn that were then sold to other companies that made either sewing thread or materials for clothing and other cotton fabric uses. The other mills were Wiscassett Hosiery Mill and Lillian Knitting Mill. Wiscasset Hosiery made nylon hose for ladies. Pantyhose had not been developed in the 40s. Cannon was one of the nation's leading manufacturers of stockings. There were those with seams running from heel to the top of the stocking, and there were the seamless stockings that gained popularity in the 50s. Even though I had relatives and church families who were 'hosiery mill' folks, the cotton mill life was what I knew more about.

My Daddy worked in the Efird Manufacturing Company plant #5 in Albemarle from 1916, when he was 12 years old, until he retired in 1971 at age 67. I can't remember him ever missing a day of work. If he did, it was for a family funeral. He walked seven blocks to work each morning and then back home seven blocks again every afternoon, regardless of the weather. He always had cotton lint on his bib-overalls and in his hair when he got home. In later years he would use an air hose to 'blow off' the machines, then turn it on himself before walking out the door to come home. He ran (operated) the same type of machine, drawing frames, from the first day he was employed until he punched out for the last time 55 years later. He always said that he wore out four models of drawings. Daddy's work ethic and his love of sports drive me to this day.

John Efird Harris was born in 1904 on the point of land in Montgomery County where the Uwharrie River joins the Pee Dee River just across the river from Morrow Mountain State Park. That "home place" was just a good piece of farmland that his family 'tended' for the owner. In return for all their work, the Elihue Harris family got a small percentage of the crops and foodstuffs raised on the farm to live on. Daddy never learned to read or write much, having attended only a few weeks of the first grade and a few more of the second. It didn't take Daddy long to see that, when you went to school, you not only received an education, you also received various vaccinations from the school nurse. Daddy was a wiry man. He was all of five-foot-six and weighed 135 pounds all through his adult life. As tough as he was, he had no use for vaccinations of any sort. So that, was one of the reasons he quit school so early.

I never saw Daddy read very much. Momma read aloud stories that might interest him. I only saw him write his name on a check or a legal document. He didn't talk very much about his lack of education. It probably bothered him some, but in the early 20th century, lots of rural America didn't have a lot of formal education. He had a job, which was an accomplishment during the Great Depression. He had a loving family, and loved helping other people. It didn't matter to Daddy whether he could read and write, he was comfortable in his surroundings. He slipped into eternity, quietly, sitting in his favorite chair, at the age of 86.

Daddy's first experience at hard work was on the farm. By the time he was ten, he was helping the cooking crew for the surveying crew of

Carolina Power and Light Company as they set the boundaries for Lake Tillery. As a second job, Daddy helped out on Will Lowder's flat-bottom ferries bringing wagons and supplies back and forth across the Pee Dee River. The ferry worked the river from Montgomery County to the foot of Morrow Mountain in Stanly County. Daddy believed in loyalty to his employer, and thanks to him, so do I.

I don't know exactly how my mama met my daddy. One of them said that they first met at a corn shucking. That was a farming AND social affair of that day. The other said they met at church. It didn't really matter, they dated for a proper period and were married in 1927.

Nora Gertrude Harris was born in 1906 in Moratock, not far from the area were Daddy was born. There were three or four non-related Harris families in western Montgomery County, where numerous Scotch-Irish immigrants had settled many years before. Two of my four great-grandfathers fought in the Civil War.

When I was born on August 22, I came into the world in Yadkin Hospital. Two of my friends and I were born within a twelve-hour period. One friend, Gary Whitley was born on Friday night. Ted Russell was born about five minutes after I was. Not much of a claim-to-fame, but the three of us still tell the story. The next time we met was early summer of 1953. We were at the Little League baseball tryouts at Efird Park. American & Efird Mill wanted the 10-12-year old kids in town to have some organized baseball. The three of us were never teammates. Gary was on the Red Sox team, Ted played for the Yankees, and I got to play for the Dodgers, coached by my neighbor, Cobb Talbert.

Gary and I email quite often and I certainly remember a frightening incident that almost took his life. I had always heard that Gary and a couple of buddies were in a pear tree one night and the lady who lived there shot at them with a .22 rifle. Gary was hit in the thigh and we all thought his athletic career was over. Gary sets the record straight.

I celebrate July 3rd every year instead of the 4th. If you can remember that far back, I got shot on July 3rd, 1956 around 10:15 PM. I was 14 years old, and had just been to a "Spinners" baseball game with Pep Mabry, Jerry Burleson, and Butch Helms. I never left the sidewalk, and was never in the tree. We had a pear tree in our front yard, and I didn't even like pears. BUT, Pep and Jerry were in the tree.

Three years later, during our senior year, you also wrote an article in the "Full Moon" (our school paper) about me getting shot, and later becoming all-conference. I really appreciated that writing. What most people don't know about me was how proud I was to receive the school sportsmanship award our senior year. I was told that I was the 1st non-football player to win that award in a long, long, time.

Fourteen months after this event, around the 3rd weekend of September 1958, Jerry Burleson was tragically killed in an auto accident. He had just turned 16 that July. We were sophomores at AHS.

Even though Daddy worked at the mill, Momma earned money at home by 'taking in sewing.' She really enjoyed being a seamstress and was a very good one. She always had a stack of work around the sewing machine. She did alterations and made dresses, skirts and blouses for ladies. Since we lived right across the street from the Wiscassett Hosiery Mill, a lot of those ladies brought their clothes to her to be altered, or to have a new dress made.

Our family was physically and emotionally close. My invalid maternal grandmother, and two of Momma's five sisters lived about six blocks from us. A brother lived across the street from them. While the two aunts worked in the hosiery mill each day, Momma stayed with Grandma. We all visited a lot, and made trips across the river to see Daddy's relatives.

I had only one sibling, my sister, Maxine. She was fourteen when I was born, and naturally we weren't really close when I was young. That didn't mean I didn't love her, but you know how aggravating little brothers can be to teenagers, especially if they have to baby sit.

I was three when Maxine graduated from high school. Until the 50s, twelfth grade wasn't mandatory. She worked across the street in the Wiscassett mill for about five years, and met her future husband on a blind date. C.T. Owens was stationed in Norfolk, Virginia after the war. He had a shipmate who was from Stanly County, and was dating Maxine's

MY SISTER MAXINE & ME 1947

friend. C.T. was born Olathe, Kansas, just outside Kansas City. His Navy time missed the war but he was in the post-war cleanup after the U.S. took back Guam, Saipan and Tinian. C.T. received his discharge in 1949, and they married that fall and moved near our apartment on Fourth Street. He went from meat-cutter to selling feed for All Star Mills. C.T. became an auctioneer during this time as well as selling real estate. I even helped out at the auctions as the 'money man' for the sales in the late 60s. Maxine 'wrote' the sale as the items were sold, and I was the cashier as the winners paid for the items they had bought.

Discipline is different in each family. In some, the father does it, and in others it's the mother. Both did it in my family. One event concerning discipline sticks in my memory to this day. I was outside and my mom called me. I knew I was in trouble by the tone of her voice. She came out the front door toward me and I took off running around the house. I knew, in my five-year-old mind, that I could out-run her. Looking over my shoulder, I knew she had given up. Oops! I ran smack dab into her. She went around the house the opposite way. I don't know if it was a coincidence or not, but we always had hedge bushes where we lived, and they made the best "switches" or "hickories" you've had applied to your backside. The "switching" I got was worse because I ran from her.

I remember what Santa Claus brought on many Christmas Eves, but my first recollection is the Christmas of 1947. I was five years old and on Christmas morning, I found a pedal car under the Christmas tree. It was a sleek, burgundy 1941 Chrysler. It had silver headlights on each fender, a silver hood ornament and hubcaps. After breakfast, we always walked the four and a half blocks to my grandmother's house to exchange presents. That morning, I pedaled my car all the way. One of my aunts made several pictures of me in the car.

MY PEDAL CAR CHRISTMAS 1947

I rode that car up and down 4th Street until I got too big to fit into the seat and get my feet on the pedals. Thankfully, we didn't throw it away. I have kept it all these years, and it was always in a storage area wherever we lived. In the 70s, I spray-painted it blue to keep it from rusting.

I really wanted to restore the car, because of the sentimental value, not the dollar value. I searched the Internet and found a company in Texas that stocked every part you could imagine, for every model of pedal car you could imagine. The prices were very reasonable.

In 1999, on a sales call to one of my best sales accounts, Elkins Chrysler in Durham, I told Jim Elkins about the car. He asked if I'd bring it in. I did and he made a proposal. He would restore the pedal car to "showroom-new" if I'd let him display it in his showroom. I bought the two 'headlights' and the hood ornament from that company in Texas. I bought some cream-colored vinyl and covered a piece of plywood and a piece of foam rubber to re-make the seat. Everything else was intact.

Jim showed it to his paint and body shop guys, and they were confident they could replicate Christmas morning 1947 except for one thing, ME!!! They did it just as if it belonged to the President of the United States. There was enough of the original burgundy paint under the fenders that they could run it through a machine that matched the paint exactly. They took off the old paints and painted my car just like any regular-size vehicle that was brought in. I showed them the picture from 1947 and they even matched the white stripes on the rear fenders.

I couldn't believe my eyes when they rolled that car out into the sunshine. I was five years old again. OK, it was all in my mind. My 57-

THE REFURBISHED PEDAL CAR WITH
ELKINS CREW 11/99

year old body dared me to even put a LEG inside that car, much less anything else. Everyone in the shop who had touched the car in the process came out for the 'unveiling' and were all beaming at the results, as you can see in the 'after' photo. Ah, the 'ghost of Christmas past.'

We made about a dozen pictures for posterity. I gave each one of the men a copy. The car was on display in the Elkins showroom from Thanksgiving until Christmas.

Speaking of Elkins and Christmas, I was the TV spokesman for the dealership in the early 90s and we did a multitude of 'thematic' commercials. None as 'thematic' or traumatic as the Christmas spot in 1997. I appeared on camera as an elf, wearing green spandex tights!

The following fall I was checking out the Christmas ornaments at the Hallmark store in South Square and Hallmark had issued a new line of pedal cars for ornaments and displays in sizes from one inch to eight inches long. I told the manager about my car, and she asked if I would like to have it on display in her store in November and December. She offered me a complete set of the Hallmark miniatures to put it in their store. While it was on display, a man saw it and told her to offer me $3,000.00 for it. I turned him down. It is now sitting atop the armoire in our master bedroom.

I can't say enough about Albemarle in that era. It was a great town to grow up in. My family spent most evenings sitting in the living room around an Atwater-Kent upright radio listening to The Jack Benny Show, Mr. & Mrs. North, Amos & Andy and Mr. Keane - Tracer of Lost Persons. Momma always enjoyed Ma Perkins and Our Gal Sunday in the afternoons.

ELVES BOB &
RONNIE McMANNEN TAPE
ELKINS TV SPOT

'SANTA' JIM LOWE & 'ELF' BOB @
ELKINS CHRYSLER CHRISTMAS
PARTY 1977

Daddy and I enjoyed the ball games most of all. We would listen to football games on Saturday afternoons, and baseball games whenever they were on. In fact Daddy really hoped I would become a major league baseball player. He was a big Boston Red Sox fan. Momma cared NOTHING about 'old ball' and wanted me to be a preacher. I tried to please both of them. I became a sportscaster.

I loved listening to the radio. It was magic for me. I got to listen to all of the greats of that era, Bill Stern, Graham McNamee, Add Penfield and others. They 'put me in the seats' with their eloquent descriptions of the games. I knew what was going on in the games because they were 'my eyes.' Television was just 'a passing fancy' to some folks. The radio sports-casters painted a word picture in my mind. Radio was the theater of the mind, way before people ever heard that term.

One particular Saturday afternoon, I heard my Daddy all the way from Charlotte. When I was six or seven, Daddy and my uncle Charlie Doby went to the North Carolina-South Carolina High School Shrine

Bowl football game in Memorial Stadium. I was really hurt that they didn't take me with them. Daddy told me to listen to the game on the radio and listen closely. He promised to yell to me. I sat in right there the whole game waiting to hear my dad yell 'hello' to me. And sure enough, I really did hear him yell out,"Hey, Bobby." I was positive I did. It sure sounded like his voice.

BOB AT 7

It is amazing what was important enough to remember from your childhood. When I was about five years old, Daddy had a co-worker make a two-foot-long bat for me. Roy Talbert made it out of a chair leg in his wood-working shop. I carried that bat every-where, and even tried to sleep with it. I think I had a ball or a bat in my hands most of my childhood.

If there was anything that linked small towns throughout America in the 1940s, 50s, and 60s, it was baseball. The smaller communities in the south, especially the mill-towns, really included the 'Grand Old Game' in the very fabric of their collective lives. Inexpensive entertainment? You bet! Thrills and excitement? Absolutely! Just as much as grandstands of Ebbets Field and other big league parks.

There were different levels of baseball to watch. It might be the local mill team. It might be a minor league or semi-pro team. The semi-pro team in Albemarle was the Wiscassett Spinners. They got their name from the sponsoring mill, and the fact that the company spun cotton yarn into thread. The teams in their league were from other mill towns like Kannapolis, Burlington, Concord, Asheboro, Salisbury, and Landis. We made sure to get to the ballpark while the teams were having batting practice. Several of us positioned ourselves beyond the outfield fence to chase down homerun balls and the others stationed themselves behind the grandstand to grab foul balls. The ticket takers would let us in free if we brought them a ball. Money was tight for them TOO.

There seemed to be a game every night at Wiscassett Park in the summers. I only lived about 2 miles from there, and it was easy to walk to the park when the Spinners or our American Legion team was in town. We always stopped at a little snowball stand about four blocks from the house to make the walk easier. The Albemarle High School Bulldogs played there in the spring too. I was so proud to get to play on that field.

A BALL IN MY HAND
EARLY 1947

Baseball seemed to be in the blood of everybody who grew up in my hometown. I was fortunate to have had a sports heritage like I did. Albemarle had a legacy of championship American Legion teams, a Class D minor league franchise in the late 40s, the Spinners, and outstanding high school teams.

Wiscassett Park was built on company land in the northwest section of Albemarle in the early 1950s. The park's dimensions were longer than some major league stadiums. Ebbets Field was 343 feet in left field, 393 to dead center, and 297 to right field. Wiscassett's big three were: 385 feet down the left field line, 410 feet to straightaway center field, and 365 to the right field corner. I never came close to hitting one out of that park. I hit thousands of balls out in my daydreams and those at night too. On my best effort my senior season, I rifled one down the left field line to the fence against Landis High School. That glowing achievement has an asterisk. I tried to stretch a sure double into a triple and was thrown out trying to get back to second base. Thrown out or not, it was still a great moment for me. It goes without saying that I wasn't the swiftest of foot. Tom Maultsby, the coach my senior year, waited until the season was over to tell me the ratings that a scout had given me while watching one of our games. The majority of the categories were about average, but on the subject of speed, he had written, "speed - deceptive --- slower than he looks."

Albemarle always had some pretty good baseball teams. In 1940, the American Legion team won the Little World Series (national championship). That Series was held at Efird Park in Albemarle. The city hosted the Series again in 1944, but they didn't win the title that year. The 'Depot Street Gang' had some of our greatest sports moments on that field from 1953 through '55. By then, it was our Little League field. Jim Lisk and I knew the names Lefty, Wheaties, and Boger way before we learned about Mantle, Aaron, Williams and Mays.

Every boy in Stanly County grew up hearing the stories of 1940 when pitcher J.W. 'Lefty' Lisk, third baseman Sam Andrew, catcher Hoyle Boger and their teammates defeated San Diego in the American Legion World Series at the Efird Ball Park. There had been 13,500 crazed fans cheering on Post 76 in their classic, 9-8 final game win, one that came when Lisk, Boger and Andrew combined to foil a suicide-squeeze play in San Diego's last at bat.

2005 DEDICATION OF A HISTORIC MONUMENT FOR 1940 ALBEMARLE AMERICAN LEGION BASEBALL NATIONAL CHAMPIONS - JOHN LITTLE, FRANK LITTLE, J.W. 'LEFTY' LISK, TOMMY RABE, BOB, CRAIG LISK & SHERRILL CRANFORD.

I started playing organized baseball when I was ten years old.I wanted to be a center fielder. The mill-sponsored teams were not as much for competition that first summer as they were for learning the fundamentals. The coaches took every kid who signed up to play and divided us into teams. That didn't matter; we were playing baseball, wearing a uniform.

The next year, we had tryouts and the managers of the teams then drafted the players they wanted for their teams. The four managers were volunteers who worked at American and Efird Mills, but they taught us how to hit, field and play the game like it should be played.

Cobb Talbert was the manager of the Dodgers, and our neighbor on Wilson Street. Our families were friends and since I watched him play with the Spinners for several years, I really wanted to play for him. He really knew baseball and treated us like 'players' and not just kids.

The afternoon of the draft meeting, I waited for Cobb to walk by my house. I couldn't wait to hear if I had been picked. I really hoped it would his team, but any team at all would have been okay. I think I ran a half a block to meet him on his way home. I was so excited that I could barely get the words out of my mouth. I finally blurted out, "Cobb, did I get picked?" "Yes, Bobby, you did. I picked you and James Lisk and Max Morgan and a couple more pretty good players on my team." As it turned out, we WERE a VERY good team, not for just that year but for my next two years. I had made the Dodgers. It wasn't Brooklyn, but it might as well had been. Here again, "HOW SWEET IT IS!"

Coach Talbert moved me from shortstop to catcher at the first game because the two other players who had any experience behind the plate were going to play other positions. Max Morgan would pitch and Lisk would play short. James was also a pitcher, and when it was his turn on the mound, Max went to short. I didn't miss an inning that summer. I found a home behind the plate. I never thought that I would catch into my 50's. With most positions, baseball is about anticipation. But as the catcher, I was involved in every play and the entire game was in front of me. I even called the pitches for the pitchers. Max had a good fastball, curve and had the best 12-year old knuckleball I ever saw. Lisk threw hard and had a wicked curve. We won the 4-team league championship that year and I made the All-Star Team as the #2 catcher. We played the Norwood All Stars at Wiscassett Park and to us; it was the 'Big Time'. The fact that fast-baller Frank Capel threw a two-hit shutout was of no consequence. We won the championship again in 1955. I was the starting All-Star catcher, but we lost to Norwood again. This time we played in their semi-pro park and they had Linwood Hurt, a lefty with an intimidating curveball. We did score some runs, but not enough.

Jim Lisk shares those same memories.

In 1953, American & Efird Mills started a Little League Baseball program on the same field where the 'Boys of '40' had put Albemarle on the map. It was then that Bobby and I joined in that inseparable bond of pitcher-catcher for Coach Cobb Talbert and our Dodgers teammates. While both Bobby and I cherished our baseball card collections and traded players often with the neighborhood gang, it was on that Little League diamond where we did our best impersonations of the Brooklyn Dodgers' battery of Carl Erskine and Roy Campanella that filled our youth with complete joy... while building a love of the game that will forever be ours.

CHAPTER TWO
The Fifties

Baseball wasn't the only pastime for the youngsters growing up in Albemarle at that time. There were many things that kept our minds, bodies, and imaginations busy and entertained in our formative years.

It was four blocks from my house to 'the square.' That was the middle of the business and entertainment area of Albemarle. I use that term loosely. There were two theaters, the Alameda and the Stanly. A good Saturday was heading to the Stanly Theater for a full day. We didn't actually say theater; we just said we were 'going to the show.' When we did use the word theater, we pronounced it 'thee-ate-ur.' The Alameda didn't show many 'shoot-'em-ups,' as my uncle Norman called them.

It was only two blocks away, so it didn't take long for us to get to 'the show.' Some days we would make it in record time. It just depended on how hot the sidewalks were in the summertime. Many times we were barefoot. Of course we would walk on the two-foot strip of grass between the curb and sidewalk as much as possible. When we had to cross the street, we had to run fast to make it to the next patch of grass or shade on the other side of the street. We weren't in Cub Scouts, but we WERE 'tenderfoots.'

For fifty-cents (which we had to earn by doing chores), we could have a day. First, we stopped at the Goody Shop to get a hot dog AND a Coke for 10 cents, or we could get a hamburger with mustard, slaw, chili and onion and a drink for only 15 cents. We NEVER called them sodas. A soda was the concoction you got when you mixed cherry or vanilla syrup with 'fizz' water at the soda fountain in the drug store. After the quick food stop, we walked up the hill a half block and got into the show for 7 cents. We would have just enough money for us to get a dime bag of popcorn, a nickel Coke, a nickel candy bar and a nickel box of Raisinettes to munch on during the movie.

Seven cents got us more than just one feature. For that hard-earned sum, we got to watch the newsreel of the week's news (pre-TV ----remember?), a 5-6 minute comedy such as the Three Stooges, two or three color cartoons, a chapter of the latest serial like The Dead-End Kids, Jungle Boy or Buck Rogers, previews of coming attractions, AND a double feature. Maxine took me to my first movie in 1948. I was 6 years old. It was "FRONTIER AGENT" starring Johnny Mack Brown. I kept wondering why it was always raining because the picture was pretty grainy. The sound was a bit muffled, but none of that mattered... we were at the movies.. It wasn't the Roxie, but I did get to meet "Whip" Wilson and Al "Fuzzy" St. John. They came to Albemarle on a publicity tour. I also got to meet the famous "Johnny" Roventini. He had been a real New York bellhop, a 47-inch tall man with a distinctive high-pitched voice. He was first used in radio cigarette commercials, sending out his "Call for Philip Morrrrriiss." They were popular in the 30s, 40s and 50s in their radio, TV and print advertising.

We would get to the show just before the 11:00 am start, then we'd head back out to the sunshine when we left just before 3:00 pm. We would get back home and grab an early supper and then head out to Wiscassett if there was a game that night. Some times we'd just stay in there and watch it all over again. It was OK. The management didn't care. They didn't clear out the people after every showing like now. One man took full advantage of this.

Larry Holt ran the elevator in the Hill Building, the only building over two-floors tall in town. He spoke to everyone who got in the car. When you returned his greeting, he recognized your voice. He was totally blind. He lived about six blocks from his work, and walked with his cane every day. He knew every step, every uneven spot in the sidewalk and every intersection. Of course, everyone in town knew Larry and watched out for him. If the weather was bad he took a taxi.

Larry would usually beat us to the show EVERY Saturday morning. He would get his drink and the biggest bag of popcorn they had, and settle in on the back row, in the seat farthest from the aisle. He would stay there all day and listen to everything over and over, until the theater closed.

Another colorful local man was Constable Bill Kearns. Bill was, to my knowledge, the only elected Constable in the county. He was a rather short, and very thin man. He wore a law enforcement-type cap and sometimes had a pistol and holster strapped to his waist. The end of the gun barrel struck him about the knee. The barrel wasn't that long, his legs were rather short and his gun belt was about six inches below his pants belt. He was a sign painter by vocation and usually painted most of the window signs in Albemarle's businesses. He was a terrific artist and printer. When he wasn't painting, you could find him sitting on 'Bill's bench' on the sidewalk on the south side of the courthouse at the square. Sometimes he was sleeping, other times he had that cigar stub bouncing up and down as he chatted with friends who came to enjoy the warm sunshine.

The finest school beneath the sun,
Central School our hearts have won,
With colors true of white and blue,
With pride we view. Loyalty is our motto,
Loyal we'll be wherever we go,
Our love we show, each day we go
To Central School.

It's amazing what the mind holds on to! I haven't remembered all the words to that little ditty in over 50 years. I can't remember what Phyllis told me to do thirty minutes ago, but I have retained this! Central Elementary School WAS one of the best anywhere. Mrs. B.C. Parker was the principal, and NO ONE wanted to be sent to her office for disciplinary action. Her brother-in-law was North Carolina Governor Luther Hodges. I can still remember walking into that red brick building in September of 1948, and meeting the sweetest first grade teacher a scared six-year old could ever hope to have. Miss Jean Winecoff got my educational process off on the right foot.

We always lived within walking distance of Central. Heck, we lived within walking distance to MOST of Albemarle. For the first two years of school, we lived on North 4th Street. It was all of two blocks from front door to front door. In September of 1950, we moved to Wilson Street, and that was a long three-and-a-half block walk. When I moved on to high school, it was just a three-block hike if I followed a path through the block between 2nd and 3rd Streets, using Mr. Rogers' and Mrs. Huneycutt's driveways. They never said a word about us using them. No, I wasn't the only one from my neighborhood to do that. At the beginning of my junior year, the new Albemarle Senior High was opened and it was about 2 miles away, much to far to walk. I rode to school with my next-door neighbor and several others for that year.

The summer days were not always sunny so we could play ball or cowboys and Indians. On days when it rained, we would spend the day on somebody's front porch with our baseball and football card collections (mostly duplicates) and play 'Who is it?' We would take turns asking statistical questions from the information printed on the backs of the Topps and Bowman cards. There were ONLY two companies in the fifties AND they had only one set each year. The questions were, "Which Brooklyn Dodgers player is from Anderson, Indiana, and won 21 games last season." Of course, we all knew it was Carl Erksine. If nobody got it with the first clue, we'd keep on giving more hints until someone answered it correctly, then we would move on to the next card. I am sure our parents wished we knew as much about world history as we did the backs of those baseball and football cards.

With all of the sports figures I had the opportunity to meet in my first years of sportscasting, I had never met a member of the Brooklyn Dodgers until the Duke Children's Classic golf tournament here at Duke. I almost flipped out when I found out that Carl Erskine and Clem Labine would be two of the celebrities in the 1991 event. I had been a volunteer and celebrity player since 1976 and was more excited to meet these two than Bob Hope, President Ford, Dinah Shore or dozens of others who had come to Duke. Perry Como was the Honorary Chairman for the first

23 years of the event. There'll be more on him later.

I made a bee-line for the two of them when they showed up at the parings party on Friday night. We established a good relationship right off the bat (no pun intended). Phyllis even got into the act by taking Betty Erskine and Barbara Labine shopping in Durham.

Fridays of the tournament are for practice rounds for the celebs and those paying $2,000.00 to play. In 1994, Clem and Carl came again. I had asked them to play their practice rounds with our new football coach, Fred Goldsmith. Fred was a Brooklyn fan of long standing. His father was a friend of Jackie Robinson. Jackie came to the hospital when Fred had polio as a kid. They wouldn't let Robinson in to see him because of his skin color. Jackie told the nurse that it was okay, and that he would visit Fred in his home later. Fred was happy to learn in our first meeting that I was a Brooklyn fan too. He was more excited than I when that Friday finally rolled around. Fred rode with Carl and Clem rode with me in carts.

On the 16th hole at Croasdaile Country Club, I hit my drive right down the middle of the fairway. It rolled down to the bottom of a depression and, since it had rained on Thursday night, the fairways were kind of soft so we couldn't drive in certain areas. I grabbed my three-wood and three-iron and headed to my ball. Clem waited in the cart. This was just after most courses had outlawed metal spikes and gone to the soft spiked shoes. As I started down the small slant of the fairway both feet shot out from under me and the back of my belt scraped up about a foot of mud. The first thing everyone does after a fall is what???Right, look to see if anyone was watching. To my embarrassment, Clem was. As I gathered my wits and my clubs, Clem hollered over, "Bob, are you OK?" I said yes, and he shot back, "SAFE" with his hands out like an umpire. Everyone had a big laugh and I didn't feel bad at all, because I was in Heaven with my two former Brooklyn Dodgers players.

I became friends with both Carl and Clem. Clem and I would talk by phone about every three months. I would talk to "Oisk" less frequently. At the Classic in May of 1993, Clem was talking about the Dodgers Fantasy Camps that he helped run, and told me I should come down for one of them. I told him that I couldn't devote a full week in February or November to travel to Vero Beach, Florida because of football and basketball seasons. He invited Phyllis and me to come for just a few days if we could, and just observe. Since Duke had two open Saturdays, back-to-back, we went that November. We spent time watching the camp activities and the games the campers played each afternoon, but the highlight of the trip was the interviews. In two afternoons, I interviewed Preacher Roe, Ralph Branca, Roger Craig, Carl Erskine, Clem Labine and "Duke" Snider.

I had the first five on tape and was waiting for 'The Duke of Flatbush' to complete the sextet. This was Friday afternoon and all of the campers were getting all of their memorabilia autographed before heading home. Clem showed me where to wait for Snider, and I did. He had the longest line of campers. Every so often Duke would look my way with a very apologetic expression. When he finished, he walked over and apologized TO ME. I told him that there was nothing to apologize for. Those campers were paying him and his obligation was to them, not some freeloader like me!

I told him I only needed three or four minutes of his time, but he said, "Take a half hour if you want to. I'm in no hurry." The next fifteen minutes were awesome. I asked him all the questions I would have if the interview had been 40 years earlier. I even asked about something I had picked up on while listening to the Brooklyn games as a kid. It seemed that a fan would yell out, "Atta boy Duke" every so often during the games. It wasn't just when Snider was batting or had made a good play. He chuckled and said that I was not the first to ask him about that. In the final years that the Dodgers were in Brooklyn, the play-by-play man didn't travel with the team. He got all of the information, pitch-by-pitch, from the old Teletype ticker and would re-create the game as if he was there. He had continuous general crowd noise that played all the time. He also had several 'excitement' tapes to use when a big play occurred. All of this had been taped at a home game. The fan yelling Duke's name just happened to be on the general noise segment, so it was heard a lot more often. Snider did a lot of great things for the Dodgers, but not that often.

When the interview was over, I thanked him and he, again, apologized for making me wait. Phyllis had been sitting outside the clubhouse, waiting for me to finish up. I was wrapping up my equipment as I walked out to her. We were going over to Holman Stadium for the final game of the camp and that was a walk of about a hundred yards or more. She asked me how the Snider interview went and I could not answer her for about 75 of those yards. I have NEVER been affected that much over one interview. Was this another "HOW SWEET IT IS" event? YES!!

Clem Labine even gave me his Dodgers cap that he wore at the camp. Yes, it has "LA" on the front, but it was his and it's still the Dodgers.

I received some sorrowing news in March of 2007. Clement Walter Labine died March 2, in Vero Beach. He would have been 81 on August 6th that summer.

When the Depot Street Gang got tired of baseball and football trivia off the cards, we would always find something to sing. One of the more popular songs of the mid-fifties was "Heart of my Heart." The Four Aces had a big hit with it in 1953 and we thought it was about us. The words, "When we were kids on the corner of the street. We were rough and ready guys, but oh how we could harmonize...." fit us perfectly.

The 'Depot Street Gang' came into existence in 1952 when I was eight years old. There were three Lisk brothers and five Caudle brothers who were the only ones who lived on Depot Street. W.C. Talbert lived through the block on North First Street, Jan and Mike Caudle lived out of the neighborhood on South Third Street, but came up quite a lot. I lived on Wilson, but the house was on the corner of Wilson and Depot. Our baseball 'diamond' and football 'stadium' was 'the big field' and was just a vacant, grass lot on the corner of Depot and West North Streets. The Stanly News and Press buildings cover that site now, and the Editor of the bi-weekly newspaper, ironically, is Jim Lisk, the oldest of the Lisk brothers. He became the editor in 2007 after several years as Sports Editor. Jim was a year behind me in school even though I was only four months older. He, too, was a Dickson Foundation Scholar at N.C. State and we roomed together for a year.

In the fall of 1961, I was off to Wolfpack Country and room 306 in Berry Dorm to room with my old battery mate while we cheered on All-American quarterback Roman Gabriel and our former Little

League competitor and outstanding Albemarle 3-sport athlete, Don Montgomery.

I shall never forget a defining moment when Bobby and I were returning to Berry Dorm from a pickup basketball at the gym. Just as we walked past the backside of Reynolds Coliseum, the Pack's amazing, rifle-armed QB stepped through the door. Once again seizing the moment, Bob jumped at the opportunity, and in a precursor of many days and years to come, Bob Harris began interviewing Gabriel.

Now, these many years later, Bob has distinguished himself as the "Voice of the Duke Blue Devils" and has been justifiably honored for his seizing the moments with elegance and candor.

All personality roots were defined in those formative years of our youth, in that wonderful era when textiles drove the economy of North Carolina and that wonderful place we called home - Albemarle. For all of us grew up in that era, it's always been a source of great pride that "The Voice of the Blue Devils" shared our youth.

We played basketball between the Lisk house and a small creek we referred to as 'the branch.' Right beside of it was a nice broom straw field and 'the Durango Kid, Wild Bill Hickock, Hopalong Cassidy and Jesse James' took over in that area when we played cowboys and Indians. Generals Patton, Eisenhower, McArthur and others' led their troops through the thickets when we played Army. This little group consisted of about thirteen or fourteen kids all about five years apart in age. We just called ourselves the 'Depot Street Gang' but it was a gang more like "Spanky," "Alfalfa," and the rest of the "Little Rascals." Today's gangs give guys like us a bad name!!

It was during this time that I was introduced to my first television. There weren't many TVs in Albemarle in the late 1940s, but our neighbors in the early fifties, Joe and Nell Avery, had one and their house became a gathering spot for the entire neighborhood. We would all sit around the television, like we did the radio, and watch our favorite shows. There was "I Love Lucy" on Mondays, "Uncle Miltie," Milton Berle on Tuesdays. On Wednesday nights we watched the fights presented by Pabst Blue

Ribbon beer, and Fridays when we saw the Gillette Cavalcade of Sports.

I can't let that reference to Pabst go by without mentioning a very embarrassing incident for the Burney family who lived up the street from us. 'Boots' Burney was Nell Avery's sister. She and her husband Harold attended First Presbyterian Church. 'Sal', as he was called, was a Deacon and usher of the church. Their son Bill was about three or four years old and watched the fights just like the adults. Information point here: Stanly County was a 'dry' county, meaning no alcohol was sold (legally) in the entire county.

On one particular Sunday morning, the Burney's were in church. Bill was standing on the back pew between them, and at the end of a hymn, he decided he wanted to sing. Which song did he favor the congregation with? "What'll ya have? Pabst Blue Ribbon, What'll ya have? Pabst Blue Ribbon." That was the jingle from the Pabst commercials played every Wednesday night when we watched the fights. The blushing Deacon grabbed Bill, put his hand over his mouth and headed out the door. Bill didn't get to watch the fights for a while.

Every Wednesday night we were invited into the Avery sitting room, and cheer on fighters like Rocky Marciano, Joe Louis, Jake LaMotta, Kid Gavilan, Jersey Joe Walcott. We loved to watch wrestling with the likes of Gorgeous George, Abe Jacobs, the Great Bolo, Johnny Weaver, Penny Banner and our favorite, George Becker.

BOB, ACC BASKETBALL REFEREE PAUL HAUSMAN, PRO WRESTLERS TIM "MR. WRESTLING" WOODS AND IVAN "THE RUSSIAN BEAR" KOLOFF

This made for good sporting entertainment and we had a seat better than ringside to watch. I had no inkling that one day I would be on the other side, describing sports action for listeners to enjoy. If Hollywood would have given me all best writers, they couldn't have come up with my story. Back then, I was just dreaming of playing for the Dodgers, hitting the winning home run in the bottom of the ninth, or scoring the winning touchdown as the final gun sounded, or making the winning basket against Carolina as the horn sounded. Sometimes we just don't dream about the right things. Just about my entire world revolved around sports. If I wasn't playing ball, I was near a radio, television, or in the bleachers. I didn't care about cars or many other things

During the summer I would be up before 7:00 am and down at the 'big field' by about 8. We played all day long, except for dinner (lunch), and then it was back to the bat and ball. Time was not important to us back then. Time, it seemed, was endless and we were spending as much of it playing baseball as we could.

Nobody wore a wristwatch. I don't remember very many of us even possessing one back then. We told time by watching the sun and sidewalks around the field. Crowell Talbert (Cobb's brother) was a great alarm. When he came down North Street on his way to start the second shift at the mill, we knew it was 3:30. A half hour or so later, at 4:05, Daddy would come up the short hill on his way home from the first shift and he would give a shrill whistle. When I heard that whistle, I knew Mamma had supper on the table at home.

I began the ninth grade at Albemarle High School in 1956. My love of sports certainly continued there. I knew I had to hit the books as much as I did the baseball, or I would be in the bleachers instead of on the field or court. For the first couple of weeks, I was concentrating on getting to my next class and hoping not to be harassed by the upper-classmen too much. My homeroom teacher was Mary Martin Hassell. She graduated from Durham High AND Duke in three years each. I had ninth grade chorus with Paul Fry. Next came Algebra I with Gerald Braswell, General Science taught by Louise Saunders, English with Paul Fry's wife, Willie, and PE, coached by Bill Robinette. This was a good beginning for me. I had chorus with Paul Fry for all four high school years. I was selected for Senior Mixed Chorus, which was the top-level choir, my sophomore, junior and senior years. I also earned a spot in Boys' Double Quartet my last two years. Mrs. Fry came back into my life my senior year for senior English. She was advisor for the Full Moon, the school paper, and I was its sports editor.

My basketball career was short. I got cut from the team after just a few practices. I knew I wasn't that good and, besides baseball season was not too far off, and I was better at that. I was one of the few freshmen to make the team. I was so happy to be on varsity and so was Daddy, but my dreams of starting for the Bulldogs were not to be realized in the near future.

The baseball coach was the B-Team football and head basketball coach. He felt that if you were not a football player, you couldn't be much of an athlete, if you were one at all. Since I didn't try to play football, I figured my playing time wouldn't be much. I was wrong. I didn't get into a game at all; not a single inning. I didn't get to pinch hit or pinch run. I did get to catch batting practice, every day.

My sophomore year was more of the same. I 'rode the bench' while the coach started five different players behind the plate. I didn't get a sniff. I would not be truthful if I said I wasn't furious over the fact I hadn't missed a practice or game for a year and a half, but never even got a chance to show what I could do. Midway through the season, I was ready to quit the team. We had a rainout of a Friday afternoon game and I thought that was the right time to do it. I went to the gym and told the coach I need the locker room key to get my practice gear. He thought I was going to take it home to wash before Monday's practice. I told him that I was quitting the team.

His response wasn't as surprising as it was hurtful. "Bobby, you go ahead and quit. But if you do, you will always be a quitter in everything you do. You'll never be a success at anything. I'm not surprised that you want to quit."

I couldn't believe my ears. This coach encouraged me to quit. I knew he didn't think very much of my athleticism, but to tell me to go ahead and quit blew me away. That afternoon, I told Daddy what he had said. He told me that if I quit, I couldn't go back. With my ego bruised and my confidence gone, I didn't go back. That coach didn't come back in the fall of 1958 either. He got out of teaching.

The spring of 1959 rolled around and I didn't try out for the team. The morning after the first practice, a couple of the guys on the team talked to me about trying it once more. Assistant football coach Don Knotts had agreed to coach and Ken Frazier was his assistant. I had a good working relationship with Don as student manager and trainer for the football team. He was my U.S. History teacher that year as well. The players told me that he said he would leave the decision to tryout up to me.

I told Daddy about the situation that night and asked him what I should do. He left it up to me, with one stipulation, "If you make the team, you will not quit, no matter what happens." My skills had not improved since the previous season since I had not picked up a bat or ball in that time. Coach Knotts offered me a chance, and I did my best not to let him down. Not only did I make the team, I earned the starting job that I wanted so badly as a freshman and sophomore. My junior and senior years I started every game and played just about every inning. "HOW SWEET IT IS!!"

I served as the Honorary Chairman of the Triangle Special Olympics Summer Games held in Chapel Hill in the mid-80s. I made the rounds and thanked as many of the wonderful volunteers as possible. While talking with a young volunteer from a county next to Stanly, I noticed that his name was the same as that baseball coach. He was a Jr. I found that he was born in Albemarle and his dad had taught and coached there. I inquired about his parents and asked him to tell his dad "Thanks" for giving me the impetus to do the things I have been able to do. Sometimes negatives can be turned into positives. I did with this.

Thankfully, every other teacher and coach that I had in my four years at AHS were wonderful. One of the best was my French teacher for my junior and senior years. I had to have two years of foreign language to get into college and French was the only foreign language taught there. Mildred Deese was a wonderful teacher and still is a great friend. Not only did she teach me how to conjugate French verbs, she taught me not 'to go to the well too often.'

All classrooms in the new high school buildings had individual desks, and my senior year, I sat on the front row, next to the door in her class.

Every room had transoms on the side next to the hall to allow airflow, and they could be closed with a long pole with a small metal hook on the end. It hung by the front door, right beside my seat. We picked at Mrs. Deese all the time, and she picked back. Every now and then, during one of those 'picking' moments, I would slide the pole from its hanger and sort of swing it toward her. I would then hang it up. The last week of school before exams, I 'went to the well once too often.' As I swung the pole in her direction, she grabbed it and yanked it out of my hand. She then got up and proceeded to crack me on the head with it. It wasn't vicious. It was playful, but embarrassing, because the entire class roared when she did it. "I've been waiting all year to do that," was her only comment. We still laugh about it to this day.

I told her after our first trip to Paris that I had used the French that she had taught me in ordering lunch in a Paris restaurant. She swelled with pride and wanted to know what I had ordered. "Deux Big Mac, deux pomme-frites, and deux Coca Cola." She wanted to take another swing at me!!!

The summer of 1958, after my sophomore year, was my first experience in the job market. A couple from North Albemarle Baptist Church had opened a drive-in restaurant just north of the business district in Albemarle. George's Grill was owned and operated by George and Fronnie Russell. George was an usher with Daddy and several other men. Fronnie was a very religious woman who had a bit of shrillness in her voice. As a six-year old, she had scared me to death on several occasions. In the late forties and early fifties, it wasn't all that uncommon for people who 'got full of the Spirit' in the church service to say 'Amen' or 'Praise the Lord.' Some even got so 'full' that they 'went to shouting' as the older folks said. Fronnie was one of those 'shouters' and would sometimes leave her seat and walk the aisles. That particular Sunday morning when she was sitting right behind me when she 'got full' I almost came out of my skin, but she WAS a good woman.

Fronnie was also one of the best cooks in the church. At Home-comings, people would find her food first. She made the best ham salad I ever ate. That was one of the most popular sandwiches on the menu at George's. They also served burgers and hotdogs, as well as several other sandwiches. In the summer, many drove in for ice cream. One flavor was called 'White House.' It was vanilla ice cream with bits of cherries in it. One afternoon I took an order for two cones of 'White House' and handed it through the little window to George to fill. He looked at the paper, adjusted his glasses, and tried to read it again. "What the heck is this order," he bellowed at me. I told him, and he said, "If your writing is that bad, just draw a cone and put a little white house on top of it." Fronnie looked at my order and chastised George for hollering at me. She told him, in no uncertain terms, to go and get his eyes checked.

This was not the same drive-in that 'American Graffiti' made popular. We didn't wear skates because the area around the building where all the cars parked to order and eat in their cars was gravel, not paved. There were no speakers for them to place their orders. When they drove in, they either honked their horns, or flashed their headlights. We would take the orders and deliver the food when it was ready. When the patrons were finished, or needed something else, they would repeat the 'honk' or 'flash.' We would then remove the tray that had fit over their rolled-down window.

That tray on the window caused me a lot of embarrassment one Sunday afternoon. A foursome pulled in and ordered four soft drinks. As I put the tray with four OPENED bottles of Coke on it, one of them started wobbling and fell off the tray into the car. That wasn't bad enough. The bottle went, top first, into the gap between the man's arm and ribs, and emptied all down his side, drenching his Sunday suit. I felt awful, George was mad, but the man acted as if it happened to him every day. He couldn't have been nicer about the whole fiasco. George offered to pay for the cleaning bill, but my customer said, "No." He STILL tipped me!!! Tips usually ranged from a nickel to a quarter.

The summer after my junior year in high school, I wanted to make more than the carhop job paid the previous year. Daddy was pretty sure he could get me a job at A&E. The pay would be double the restaurant money, so I went to work in the cotton mill. My parents were insistent that I was going to get a scholarship, ANY scholarship, and go to college some way.

I really wanted to go to N.C. State to study Textile Technology. I still had another year of high school, and I knew I needed to earn some money. In 1959, the mill's working conditions were significantly better than in 1916 when Daddy started there. Even so, there were several areas of the mill where it was still 120 degrees in the afternoons in August. The fact that the windows remained open during my entire eight-hour shift didn't help much. My job was to help a crew that cleaned the spinning frames of the built-up lint and sludge. It was messy, greasy, oily and noisy, but, hey, I was making $1.00 an hour!

That first summer I was sent to the spinning department. This area is the next to last part of the process that begins with the raw cotton and finishes with thread. Another reason I wanted to work at A&E, besides the money I was making, was the chance to learn the textile industry from the ground up. Because Daddy worked there, I was eligible to apply for a four-year academic scholarship, and that was the ONLY way I was going to college. American Yarn in Mount Holly bought the Efird Manufacturing Company in the early 1950s. Rush S. Dickson was their owner, and he merged it with his company to form the American and Efird Mills. He had set up the Dickson Foundation that handled his many philanthropic endeavors. Daddy said that he looked out for his employees and their families and had a good head for business.

He made eight scholarships available to the children of the mill workers to attend North Carolina State College every year. Girls could also apply for the scholarships. The guys chose between textile technology and textile chemistry. The girls could opt for nursing school if they didn't want textile studies.

Sometimes there were not eight children of employees who wanted to go to college or who didn't qualify. Then, kids of other textile company's employees could apply. Each scholarship was valued at $6,000.00. Basically, it was a half-scholarship because tuition, room and board totaled about $1,500 per semester. A big benefit of the scholarship was a job in one of the company plants during summer vacations. Most jobs were minimum wage types at $1.00 per hour. For a 40-hour workweek, for 15 weeks in the summer, the winners could make $600.00 per summer. The minimum wage did go up while I worked there, but there was still a gap.

Every student looks forward to that senior year for various reasons. Some can't wait to get out of school, and others see it as the plateau from which to reach the next level. Mine was what I hoped it would be. I saved enough money over that summer to buy my family's first car. It was a gray 1952 Plymouth. We didn't really need a car before then because we lived so close to town, work, church and family. We walked everywhere. In case of rain, there was always Mr. Charlie Mann of C & M Taxi. He owned part of the company but drove one of the cabs too. He was always there when we needed him.

The "Gray Ghost" replaced Mr. Charlie after August 1959. I learned to drive in a 1948 Dodge that belonged to a friend of the family, Lane Bowers. He taught me the basics of driving. Uncle Charlie Doby retired and moved to Albemarle that summer. He helped as well. I began to drive myself to the new Albemarle Senior High on the north side of town that fall. I needed a car since I was the senior manager of the football team, the 'Full Moon' Sports Editor, and had practice and engagements for the Boys Double Quartet and our music group, "The Staffs." And, being a senior and not having a car just wasn't cool!.

As school years had for the previous two, my senior year began on August 15th, the first day of football practice. The players and managers brought cots and rollaway beds to the gym and we held two weeks of preseason camp. The alarm clock was beside my bed and I woke up the other two student managers at 5:45 each morning so that we could get orange and grape juice for the team. I went back to the gym at 6 am and turn on the lights, to the blaring sounds of Little Richard's recording of "Oh, My Soul." The players put on their gear, gulped their juice and hit the practice field. After the morning practices we helped the cafeteria ladies fix and serve breakfast to the team. Two-a-days made good football teams, and the Bulldogs had a great program. Coach Toby Webb made Albemarle a winner.

My sophomore year, 1957, the Bulldogs went 12-0. We won the Western North Carolina High School Activities Association championship. One highlight of that season was the win over Charlotte Harding, the #1 AAA team in the state. They came to Albemarle in mid-October and the Bulldogs were ranked #1 in the state in the AA division. The Charlotte Observer built this game to gigantic proportions for two weeks. Thirteen busloads of Harding fans, along with hundreds more fans that drove themselves, came the 42 miles from the 'Queen City' down Highway 27 to the 'small town' of Albemarle. Thousands of fans sat and stood around the field that night to see an 'old-fashioned' butt-kickin' by Albemarle. We ran over, through and around the Rams, and threw a few times. Final -- the #1 AA team 54, the #1 AAA team 7.

BOB & AHS FOOTBALL COACH TOBY WEBB 2006

After a 10-0 regular season, the Bulldogs played at Lexington for the Piedmont Championship. It was supposed to be played on the first Friday night after the end of the regular season, but it rained, and rained, and RAINED. We thought we saw a man, a boat and a bunch of animals. The game was postponed to Saturday night, then to Monday night, and finally, to Thanksgiving Day. A week of rain had made the Lexington football field a quagmire. We kicked off at noon, and Albemarle scored on the first possession. The Bulldogs and Yellow Jackets slogged and slipped through the mud for the rest of the game. Albemarle won 7– 0, and advanced.

The WNCHSAA title game was supposed to be played the next night (Friday), and Marion High was waiting. The Association said the game would not be played the night after Thanksgiving, and with the Shrine Bowl game the next week, a cancellation was in the offing. Coach Webb persuaded them to let us play the game the next Wednesday night in Salisbury. Our 6'2"- 225 pound All-America fullback, Roger Whitley, got permission to leave the North Carolina Shrine team to play in the championship game. Rumor had it that a yellow football was sent to the

Bulldogs football office from Marion, suggesting that we were afraid to play them. Some folks thought Coach Webb or the assistants sent it to fire up the team. Coach has denied that to this day.

Whether the yellow football was real or not, the teams met in Salisbury on one of the coldest nights I ever experienced on a football field. One of my duties as a manager and trainer was to run to the huddle with a water bucket and dipper so the players could get some refreshment. Not on this night! The buckets were freezing just as quick as we filled them. We came up with the idea of using towels that we soaked when a time-out was called. Even with that strategy, by the time I got to the huddle, ice crystals had formed on the towels. The players didn't seem to mind, but my hands still hurt when I remember that night.

Marion scored on their first possession, but Whitley and Roger Smith scored three touchdowns each and Albemarle controlled the game and the scoreboard. Smith even completed a rare TD pass in the waning moments, and remembers some of the aftermath of that lopsided game.

> *In the days after the Marion game, there were bitter allegations from the Marion team that Albemarle had exhibited terrible sportsmanship by running up the score. In support of this claim, Marion pointed to a late-game touchdown Albemarle scored to make the final score 54 to 6. As I recall, the game was winding down, and this touchdown was scored on a play called, 418-W Pass. The play was designed for me to run to the right and pass the ball to our great tight end, Don Montgomery, was to run a down-and-out pattern: ten yards down the field and then break out to the sideline. It was supposed to put pressure on the defensive back to choose between treating the play as a run by coming up and stopping me, or treating the play as a pass by staying back and covering Don.*
>
> *On the face of it, the allegations that this play was an attempt to run up the score do not hold water – frozen or not. The fact is that I was such an erratic passer that it is far more likely this play was called in the belief that the pass would be incomplete and the margin of victory would not be increased. By pure intervention of the fates, it turned out differently, of course. I ran to the right with the ball*

and the defensive back came up to make a play on me -- just as Don made his break, running along the goal line toward the sideline. As soon as the ball left my hand, I knew it was going to be short, but it wobbled its way toward Don. It reached him at foot-level, but he made a miraculous shoe-top catch and touched the ball down just inside the goal line. Touchdown.

I would apologize for these seven superfluous points but, at this late date, I do not know to whom I should apologize. And, besides, I am really proud of this rare pass completion.

The Bulldogs offensive line averaged 190 pounds from end-to-end that season. That was HUGE for 1957. James "Jungle" Johnson, the six-foot-four, 270-pound left tackle who was right in the middle of the unbalanced line of our single wing offense, upped that average. Coach Webb insisted that he be listed at 235 in the program so as to not scare the opponents. All eleven starters graduated from college, and six of them earned football scholarships. Roger Whitley was Junior College All-America at Ferrum, and Little All-America at Lees-McRae.

Coach Webb learned the single wing offense from UNC's legendary Carl Snavely. Webb orchestrated the precision offense to near-perfection during his tenure at Albemarle. There's an old saying, "If you can't lick 'em, join 'em." That was so true in the South Piedmont Conference during the 1959 season. Six of the eight league teams were running completely single wing offenses or they mixed plays from it with their T-formation offense. Toby Webb's teams won the South Piedmont Conference title every year he was at the helm at Albemarle.

Roger Smith recalls the first team meeting of 'two-a-days' every year.

In the heat of mid-August, with the days growing shorter and the promise of autumn chill shimmering like a mirage in the distance, Albemarle High School Football Coach Toby Webb convenes an annual meeting. All the boys going out for the football team have been summoned and are gathering on the front steps of the high school, right there on Third Street across from Miss Caughman's house. Coach Webb is standing on the sidewalk before us.

'Men, I've been hoping someone would invent a pill or some kind of medicine that would get you in shape and turn you into great football players. Then, you could take those pills and spend the rest of the summer cruising around town, eating Harman-Burgers and What-A-Burgers, and drinking Pepsis and Coca Colas, skiing at the lake, and hanging around the swimming pool listening to the jukebox with Susie Belle. You could have a good time all through the fall, and the team could meet on Friday evenings to play the games.

But so far, nobody has invented such a pill or such medicine. So, I don't know anything for us to do but to say good-bye to Susie Belle and run, hit, and practice. The problem is that we've been hearing rumors that those fellows over at Thomasville and Kannapolis are planning to run, hit, and practice, too. I wish I were a better coach than the coaches at those places, but I am not. So, I don't know anything for us to do but run, hit, and practice longer and harder than they do. We will just outwork them!'

We did outwork them, of course, and we usually won. And with that, Coach Webb gave us the gift of a foundation stone for our lives: 'There is no substitute for persistent, hard work.

He left coaching in 1959 for school administration. He was principal of Albemarle Junior High School, then Albemarle Senior High, and finally Superintendent of Albemarle City Schools. He influenced the lives of more young men in Albemarle than anyone else in the late 1940's and 50s. As "Jungle" and Graham agreed recently, Coach taught his players trust. Johnson said, "All of us would have laid down on a railroad track with the train whistle sounding in the distance if Coach had asked us to do it. We knew that he had a purpose in everything he had us do." The players, and I too, thought he was teaching the team how to win football games, but that was secondary. Toby Webb taught all of us how to grow into men. Even though I never played a down of football for Coach, he still calls me 'one of my boys.' He uses that designation for his team. As Harwood recalled, "Coach didn't care whether you lived in Forest Hills, West Albemarle, on the mill hill or in the country. We were all treated the same. We were, and still are, family."

After Coach Webb stepped down, Bob "Goo Goo" Gantt replaced him. He had been our backfield coach for several years. With change came a new media approach to the Bulldog dynasty. Area newspapers assumed that the ownership of the SPC would change hands. They picked Albemarle to finish dead last. You know what happens when you assume. And they did just that! Gantt's squad didn't miss a beat. We were unbeaten in conference, but tied Kannapolis and Concord. In the Piedmont Championship game we faced undefeated, untied and UN-SCORED ON Children's Home. The Bulldogs pushed the Methodists all over the field but could manage only a 6-0 win. We moved on to the WNCHSAA title game again, but lost 34-13 to a great Hickory team. 8-2-2, not a bad season at all!!! For the three years I was with the team, the record was 28-5-2

My senior year was clicking on all cylinders. The Senior Mixed Chorus and Boys' Double Quartet both got Superior++ ratings, the top rating in the state, in those competitions. We were the only high school chorus invited to perform with nine collegiate choirs and a full orchestra in Raleigh's Memorial Auditorium just before Christmas. We sang Handel's "The Messiah." Paul Fry was to choral music what Toby Webb was to football. Both men helped me so much. Coach Webb schooled me in the fundamentals of football, how to be a winner, and, most importantly, how to be a successful man. Mr. Fry's advice to me was simple Reach for the stars and keep perceived limitations out of your way.

In high school, another common bond emerged for both of us as we came under the influence of a wonderful gentleman, Paul Fry, the AHS choral director. Dressed in our white dinner jackets and black tuxedo pants for the annual Christmas and spring concerts, we shared the same risers while giving the tenor section our best. Through all the rehearsals and concerts, it was Bob's impromptu taking the lead on "In the Still of the Night" that remains fresh to my memory. As the 100 choral members stood in the lobby of the old Albemarle Hotel, awaiting our turn to take to the risers in the hotel's smoke- filled dining hall to sing for the Albemarle Lions Club, it was Bobby that seized the moment and the lead while the rest of us joined with the backup.

Fellow-first tenor Jim Lisk

On February 28th, the Boys' Double Quartet went to Chapel Hill for the North Carolina Music Ensemble Contest. After lunch we went to the Pi Kappa Alpha fraternity house to visit with several Albemarle guys, with hopes of going with them to the UNC-Duke basketball game that afternoon in Woolen Gym. Enough of the PiKa brothers were not going that all eight of us were able to use their student tickets to get in. That was as close as I ever came to being a UNC student. Danny Lotz was the senior captain of the Tar Heels and Duke started five sophomores, Carroll Youngkin, Howard Hurt, Fred Kast, Doug Kistler and Johnny Frye. Remember that freshmen were not allowed on the varsity until 1973. That was my first college basketball game to see in person.

My first experience at the microphone came that year too, as I served as the P.A. announcer for the A.S.H.S Bulldogs' home basketball games. Neil McGeachy and his Statesville High School team came to play us in the last game of the season. It was the first year that Statesville played in our conference. Neil was quite an athlete and had gained a reputation in football, basketball, and track.

The game was close, and the lead changed hands too many times to count. With the final seconds ticking away, Albemarle was ahead. Neil put up a shot as the final buzzer went off. Nearly everyone in attendance was on their feet but the officials couldn't agree if the shot was good or not.

They, as all officials do in this situation, went to the scorer's table and ask the official scorer if the shot beat the buzzer. The home team is responsible for keeping the official book, but when the officials asked her if the shot made it in time, she honestly said she didn't know.

The officials then asked the second scorer, who kept the book for Statesville, if she had seen the shot go in before the buzzer and she, too, told them that she couldn't honestly say. Of course the Statesville crowd was saying the shot was good while the Albemarle faithful contended that it left his hands too late.

As the discussion continued on the floor with nearly everyone expressing their opinions, one of the officials looked to me and asked,

"Did you see the last shot?"

"Yes, sir," I responded

"Well, was it good or not?"

"It was still in his hands when the buzzer went off," I responded.

That was it. The officials waved off the apparent basket. For the next few moments I was probably the most loved AND hated person in the gym. But my response to the officials was true. Neil still had the ball in his hands when the buzzer sounded. It had nothing to do with who was the home team or where I went to school. It was disappointing for the Statesville team and their fans, but no one really said anything to me after the call. It was an exemplary show of sportsmanship from both sides.

Neil was the freshman coach at Duke for a year before being moved up to Bucky Waters' top assistant. When Bucky was not retained after the 1973 season, he was given a one-year contract as head coach, and even though he knew the odds were against the Blue Devils on the court that year, Neil had the courage to take the job and put all he had into it, but his only Duke team finished 10-16. He did preside over Duke's 1,000th basketball win when the Blue Devil's stunned Virginia. I still see and talk to Neil from time to time. I have always enjoyed his friendship, but I do have to say, he still gives me a hard time about that last call.

BOB HANDLES AHS BASKETBALL PA DUTIES 1960

Little did I know......

My senior year was moving rapidly. I was not trying to wish my life away, but February could not come quickly enough. February meant that base-ball practice would soon begin, and I was looking forward to that. Our team wasn't all that bad in 1959, but most of other conference opponents were better.We only won four or five of the fourteen gameswe played that season. We were determined to make our senior season one to be remembered. And remembered it was, for us anyway. The 1960 Bulldogs ended the season 7-7, the best record in nearly 10 years.

Friday the 13th is supposed to signify bad luck. Not so for me. I remember Friday the 13th, 1960 as one of the greatest days of my life. It all began that morning at the Senior Awards Day program. I was recognized before the student body as a winner of the Dickson Foundation Scholarship. Hey, this Friday the 13th was off to a big start!

We played our final baseball game of the season against Asheboro that afternoon, with the SPC title on the line for the Comets. Mickey Mantle, Stan Musial, and Ted Williams, on their best day couldn't have been happier than I was after that game. In the 4th inning, I doubled to drive in our first two runs and scored the third run later as we won, 3-1. Our win kept Asheboro from winning the conference championship.

I hurried home after we finished, cleaned up, donned my white dinner jacket and headed to school for our annual Spring Concert. The Senior Mixed Chorus, our Boys' Double Quartet, and 'The Staffs' performed. Next to baseball, I loved singing. 'The Staffs' consisted of Peggy Jordan, Harry Whitley, Terry Still, Steve Hill and me. Steve played a 'mean' bass guitar, Sherry Pegram played piano, and I was the lead vocalist. We played for several parties and local dances in the summer and during our senior year. We considered ourselves a

THE CATCHER 1960

'street-corner' Do-Wop group. We sang songs like, "In the Still of The Night," "Sixteen Candles," " Oh, Donna" and "Wiggle Wiggle."

At the concert 'The Staffs' sang "Wiggle Wiggle," and we begged Mr. Fry to let the Double Quartet depart from traditional 4-part Barber-shop music we usually sang, and do a little Rock & Roll. We sang "Sometimes (When I'm All Alone)." It was the 'B' side of Danny and The Juniors big hit of "At The Hop." I had the solo on both songs, and I always said that the reason that the evening was lucky was that 'I didn't forget any of the words or fall off the stage.' If any seventeen year-old ever had a more gratifying day EVER, I just can't fathom what it was like. I had the baseball game of my career, I had two solos in the concert, and was presented with a college scholarship, all in one day. That was a pretty special day for anyone, especially a kid from the cotton mill hill. I could have yelled, "HOW SWEET IT IS!!" It would have been very appropriate.

CHAPTER THREE

It's Off To State College

In September of the first year of the 60s, I left Stanly County for the 123-mile journey to N.C. State. We loaded up my sister and brother-in-law's car with everything I needed to be a college freshman. They, along with Daddy and Momma, drove me to Raleigh. Orientation week got my first semester off and running. I had visited the State campus in the spring of 1956. Our 8th grade from Central Elementary School took trip to the State Capitol every year as a part of the North Carolina history class. There were side visits to Duke and UNC. Eddie Lefler, my roommate-to-be, and I visited the School of Textiles the fall of '59 before we were accepted to school and before we had received our scholarships. I had followed State by listening to 'The Squire of Wake County,' Ray Reeve on the radio.

Ray Reeve was a character, and a very good broadcaster. He broadcast football and basketball games all over North Carolina before settling in with the Wolfpack Network. His big event was the Dixie Classic. State coach Everett Case came up with the idea soon after taking the job. He wanted to showcase the Wolfpack talent as well as that of the other North Carolina schools. The tournament was played on three days between Christmas and New Years, with the first round play pitting 'Big Four' teams against out-of-state teams. There was a winner's bracket and a consolation bracket, so every team was guaranteed to play three games, and Reeve broadcast ALL 12 games BY HIMSELF!!!

The Classic was extremely popular in its thirteen-year history from 1949 to 1961. The Classic's run came to a screeching halt after the N.C. State Wolfpack and the UNC Tar Heels were both caught up in a point-shaving scandal.

The Dixie Classic was so popular and meant so much to the student body of N.C. State that a large number of students, including me in the only protest I ever participated in, marched from the Bell Tower down Hillsborough Street to the Capital to show our 'civil unrest.' A picture of the protesters was in the Raleigh News & Observer the next morning, with a young Bob Harris near the top of one of the statues that adorns the Capital grounds, with his arm around the figure.

There was one scary thing to me about the State campus. It had as many students and faculty as Albemarle did residents. I felt that I had a good academic background from high school and I knew that I had to do well in the classroom to keep my scholarship. I really didn't want to let anyone down, especially my family and the Dickson Foundation.

A really good thing about my first year at State was rooming with Lefler, a classmate at Albemarle High. His grandparents lived in my neighborhood on Wilson Street, so I felt more comfortable, knowing that I wouldn't have to get acquainted with a strange roommate, and one that might not be compatible with me.

Eddie and I were in a group of twelve Albemarle High grads in that freshman class, so we had even more friends spread out over the campus. Because of different majors and classes, we all went our separate ways. The campus was rather large, and we didn't see each other all that much, except for an occasional class or in the cafeteria or at the Gateway Restaurant across the street from the Bell Tower, or Gino's Restaurant downtown.

When you're in new surroundings, you tend to look for familiarity. My home-away-from-home, Berry Dorm, was about 100 yards from the main line of the Seaboard Airline Railroad. I had always lived in sight of railroad tracks, and this was perfect. Their tracks ran right through the State campus, so I could hear the engines and their horns from my room. It was exciting to stand on the Pullen Road overpass and watch those mighty diesel engines pull 70-100 freight cars. When it snowed we tried to drop snowballs down the exhaust stacks. We had to watch out for the M&O, the campus police, in their little Studebaker Larks. Campus security came under the Maintenance & Operations Department, thus the name, M&O.

On the north side of the tracks was Riddick Stadium, where the Wolfpack football team played their home games. Broughton High also played there some Friday nights. We didn't have far to walk from the dorm to Reynolds Coliseum where we watched Jon Speaks, Kenny Rohloff, Russ Marvel and the Wolfpack basketball team play. The Army and Air Force R.O.T.C. units were headquartered in Reynolds. Classrooms were on the ground floor of the Coliseum floor, and the 'arms room' was in the basement. All of the M-1 rifles that the cadets used for drills and parades were housed in this area. I'll talk more about that later.

Reynolds hosted more than just athletics events. The Ice Capades brought their show to Raleigh each year. The Rock & Roll Caravans came to Reynolds each fall and spring with the biggest names in R&R. In the spring of 1961, I was inducted into Mu Beta Psi, a national honorary music fraternity, and any members who wanted to, could work as ushers and backstage security for these events. I worked backstage for three of them, and met and talked with Paul Anka, The Drifters, Sam Cooke, Dion (after he left The Belmonts), and a little-known singer named Tony Orlando (about 10 years before Dawn). Dion was the headliner for one particular show, but the group on stage right before him was the Drifters. They were called back for two encores. As they headed back to the stage for #2, Dion turned to me and disgustedly said, "That is the damnedest act I've ever tried to follow."

Then there was the man who set the music world on its ear, Chubby Checker. He was born Ernest Evans in Spring Gulley, South Carolina, but grew up in South Philadelphia. He attended South Philadelphia High School with his friend Fabiano Anthony Forte, who would become a teen idol himself, using the name Fabian. Chubby burst onto the Billboard charts in 1960 with his #1 recording of "The Twist." According to Checker's website, he is the only artist to have 5 albums in the Top 12 all at once, the only artist to have a song to be #1 twice - "The Twist", and the only artist to have 9 double-sided hits. I met him in 1961. It was just a brief "hello" and "I really love your music," but for years, I bragged that Chubby Checker gave me a personal Twist lesson that night.

Chubby's daughter, Mistie Bass, was a highly recruited basketball player out of high school and chose to attend Duke in 2002. Chubby was very proud of her and came to Cameron Indoor Stadium several times a year to see her play in person. Usually he had no trouble with fans crowding around him, mainly because the students, and most of their parents, weren't even born when he was topping the Billboard charts. Every now and then, fans of my age would come by just to shake hands or get an autograph. I sat with him several times behind the Duke bench and talked about the game more than his career. I asked him if he would mind signing two album covers and an original 45rpm of "The Twist" which I bought in 1960. Rather than taking them to a game, I left them with Mistie and he signed them 'out of the limelight.'

I did finally 'fess up' to my brag of 45 years about the personal Twist lesson. He laughed and told me that I wasn't the first person to admit to that. He said he was honored just to be remembered that long.

Mu Beta Psi members also had the opportunity to fill those roles for events at Memorial Auditorium downtown. I worked backstage for The New Glenn Miller Orchestra and a young comic named Bob Newhart.

I seriously thought about trying out for the baseball team that fall.I wondered if I could make the roster as a catcher. In no time flat, I realized that my chances of making the State team as a freshman were about equal to me making the Dodgers roster. State's starting catcher was back for his senior season and there were two other freshmen that I knew, vying for the back-ups. Football QB Jimmy Rossi, from Asheville, had been All-State in North Carolina, and FB Pete Falzarano had made All-State in Pennsylvania. Knowing that both were in West Raleigh on football scholarships let me know that they were better athletes than I was. I had dreamed of playing at State, but I also knew reality when I saw it.

Pete Falzarano was a better football player than baseball. We both lived in Berry dorm and got to be closer than I really wanted to get on one sunny, warm April afternoon. My room was on the third floor overlooking the quad that included Becton and Bagwell dorms, plus the snack bar. The quad was the site of some great tag football games in the fall and other activities the rest of the school year.

One of those activities was getting a tan when the weather first got warm enough in the spring. On this particular afternoon, the quad was crowded with sunbathers and I thought it might be fun to see how they would react to a little rain. I had a large plastic cup for drinking water at the sink, which was right beside the window of our room. I pulled the top section of the window down and was able to launch a full cup down on the guys and quickly duck so I wouldn't be seen. After the effects subsided, I would see if the coast was clear and unload another 'shower'. This went on for the better part of an hour. I made another toss and ducked. From behind me I heard, "Harris, you *#@*%#*." I turned to find my door completely full of Falzarano. I suddenly saw my body flying out that third story window to my death below. I began begging for my life. He just laughed and told me that nothing was going to happen ..... right then. "But, when you're not expecting it, I'll get you back." I spent several weeks in mortal fear because I was all of 160 pounds and Pete was a 230-pound fullback.

On the night of our Military Ball, I went to the common shower on our small hall. I finished showering and dried off, put on under-shorts and socks and walked out the door. There was Pete, leering, with a waste paper basket full of water. I got my payback, from head to toe.

If I had made the State baseball team, it would have kept me from singing with the Men's Glee Club, because both had late afternoon practices. Paul Fry knew my vocal abilities and went to bat for me. He convinced Perry Watson, the Director of the Glee Club, to allow me to audition for a spot, even though I never learned to read music, which was a requirement for membership. I never had a problem in Mr. Fry's choruses, or Double Quartet, or 'The Staffs,' or church choirs. I had been singing in all sorts of programs since second grade without the ability to read music. I 'sight-read' all of our choral sheet music and I had a 'good ear' for music that I listened to on records and radio. I must have been pretty good at it, because after Mr. Watson's tryout, I became a 1st tenor in the N.C. State Men's Glee Club.

State had no degree-offering music department but their marching and symphonic bands and Glee Club were really good. Our Glee Club practiced Monday through Thursday afternoons at 5. We held a Christmas Concert every December and a Spring Concert in May. I still have the two albums we recorded, and UNC-TV also taped a 30-minute special for their airing around the state. We sang a variety of music, from show tunes and popular selections to religious, traditional and Baroque. We even tuned up a guitar and did a couple of Western songs.

I would have traveled a lot if I had made the baseball team, but the Glee Club traveled each spring. We toured North Carolina, singing in towns like Greensboro, Roxboro, Burlington, Rockingham, Eden, and Concord. Around tour time my sophomore year, Phyllis and I had gotten pretty serious. For our concert in Concord, Daddy and Momma drove out to Phyllis' house and rode with her and her mom to Concord. We got to spend about 15 minutes together after the concert, and the Tour moved on.

When you talk about loyal and dedicated alumni groups, you have to put State people right up there with the most devoted. Wolfpack Clubs are in every state in the Union and every county in North Carolina. Some of the greatest memories that I have of those tours are from staying in the homes of the alumni, enjoying their hospitality and listening to the stories of their days on campus. We had so much fun traveling and singing all over the state.

I guess that my freshman year was not any different from that of other freshmen. All of us had to take English 101 and 102, Math and Chemistry classes, plus the few textile classes that were required for my major. To be quite frank, I was kind of bored with the textile classes. I'm not saying that I knew all of it, but it was pretty much of a review for me because I worked in the mill for two summers. You had to learn things quickly in the cotton mill, or you didn't have a job long. There were too many families that depended on the salaries that were earned there for anyone to mess up. It was a great education in itself.

I had good overseers at A&E, men who had spent most of their lives there. Having just that limited experience from those two summers, I felt that most things being taught were sort of old-hat, not just to me, but also to others who came to State by the same route I did. It was almost like being a freshman math major and being taught fractions for most of the year. All of the other classes I had were very challenging and I really had to study hard, but the textile classes were remedial.

The Morrill Act of 1862 provided for agriculture and mechanical Land-Grant colleges to be built around the country where the government had sufficient land. North Carolina State College was one of them. Because of federal funding, students had to be meet certain requirements.

One of those requirements was that every physically qualified male student had to take the Reserve Officers Training Corps program for two years. Two hours of classroom and a minimum of one hour of drill instruction were required each week. All of us freshmen were fitted with uniforms of the branch of service we had chosen. I picked the Army for no reason. We had the standard olive drab wool trousers, jacket and cover (hat), long and short sleeve tan shirts, black ties, black socks and black, plain-toe oxford shoes. Those shoes had to be 'spit-shined' so that you could see your face in them every time you wore them. We had to polish the brass buttons and 'adornments' with Brasso. In October, an officer (upper classman) came to our squad while we were in formation and asked if any of us were 'an even six feet tall.' I put up my hand, and before I could drop it he asked if we wanted to volunteer for the Color Guard. I was told to report to the Armory in Reynolds to draw my 16-pound M-1 rifle, then proceed to another location for more instruction. I had seen Color Guards in Armed Forces Day and Christmas parades in Albemarle, and on TV, but I had no clue what they did when not on parade. I discovered very quickly that I had made a good decision. I was given Corporal stripes on the spot and began learning the various commands that a Color Guard used in the performance of their duties.

The number one unit consisted of four upper classmen. The three other new recruits and I made up the second unit. That freshman year we didn't present the Colors at any games nor march in any parades. The first unit handled all of those. They had all moved on by the 1961-62 school year, and I assumed the duties of Color Guard Commander, and wore Staff Sergeant stripes. We made all of the appearances that year. Merits were dispersed for perfect inspections and performances.

The Commander, me, issued the merits, as well as demerits for less than perfect acts. For every two merits earned, an extra point was added to our classroom grade for the semester. I pulled up my letter grade from a 'C' to an 'A' both semesters, and I didn't just give myself the merits either, because an Army officer inspected and graded me.

We worked in tandem with the Pershing Rifles drill team several times for parades and such. The Commander of that unit was also a Textile major and was from a small town in eastern North Carolina. He was raised just outside the small town of Speed. We knew each other, but only casually. He was in the Advanced ROTC, meaning he was an upperclassman, and had obligated himself to military duty after graduation. Henry didn't mind that. He was looking at a career. And what a career he had.

He served two tours of duty in Vietnam with the 5th Special Forces. After the Gulf War, he came back to North Carolina and led the 82nd Airborne Division at Ft. Bragg. He led the Joint Task Force during Operation Uphold Democracy in Haiti in '94. Henry was promoted to General in 1996, and the following year he was appointed Chairman of the Joint Chiefs of Staff, and held that position for four years. Okay, you're wondering who this Henry really is. He is Four Star General of the U.S. Army, Retired, Henry Hugh Shelton. And here I am just a sportscaster. We've had a few chances to get together and reminisce about the days in West Raleigh. I had the privilege of emceeing the awards program at the Triangle Chapter of the National Football Foundation at Cameron Indoor Stadium in April of 2009. Hugh received the Distinguished American Award from the Foundation.

The Army Color Guard alternated with the Color Guard of the Air Force wing in Presentation of the Colors at football and basketball games. The presentation in Reynolds was really special. In those days, the house lights were off and a single spotlight was focused on the American flag when the Color Guard got to mid-court for the National Anthem. I had the distinct honor of carrying the American flag since I was the Commander. There were two very special nights that year, the game with Wake Forest, and the ACC Tournament, which was held in Reynolds from 1953 through 1966. During the Anthem of the Wake game I allowed my eyes to wander ever so slightly toward the Wake bench. There were Coach Bones McKinney, Len Chappell and Billy Packer, both All Americans. Slowly, I glanced over to the State bench, and saw Coach Everett Case, and several of my classmates who were on the team. My brain was telling my body, "Steady, DON'T drop the flag!!" Getting the opportunity to present the Colors at the opening game of the ACC Tournament that March was exciting. It was my first ACC Tournament game to see in person. It was 14 years before I saw my second one, and I had the pleasure of broadcasting that one.

Another stipulation of the Morrill Act that I spoke of earlier was that every physically qualified male had to take two years of P.E. and pass a swimming test before they could graduate. We were all given the swim test during orientation week, and were required to swim two laps in an Olympic-size pool as well as tread water for five minutes. I could play baseball, I could sing, and I knew hard work, but I couldn't swim. I had to learn or become the oldest freshman in N.C. State history.

I didn't even take the swim test. I told Bill Sonner, the instructor, that I could not swim at all, and he informed me that I would have to take beginning swimming, and learn to swim two laps without stopping in the Thompson Gym pool.

Even though I couldn't swim, I found a secret that I needed to pass the course with a higher grade. The mandatory two laps had to be done without stopping. If we couldn't do that, we took the course again. The grade for that SECOND six weeks was our SEMESTER grade. All P.E. classes were split with two different sports each semester. The grades were averaged for final credit .... except for repeating the beginning swimming class. An upper classman gave me the 'inside scoop' on this.

MY SOPHOMORE NC STATE PICTURE 1962

He had done the same thing.

On test day at the end of the first six weeks, I jumped in and began swimming at my 'fastest' pace. When I got to the halfway point I stood up and wiped the water from my eyes, and swam back to the starting point where Coach Sonner was waiting. He said, "You have to do it without stopping. You are going to have to take the class over." I put on my best 'disappointed face' and asked, "Are you sure, Coach?" I tried to hide the smile on my face from him as I went back to the dressing room. I really could have swam the two laps, maybe even three or four, without stopping, but I stood up on purpose. I guess you could say I 'threw the fight.' I did it because I needed a higher grade from this class to boost my overall grade point average for the semester. The math and chemistry classes were beating me to death. I knew that I had to maintain a 2.0 average to hold on to my scholarship and I was not making the grades I thought I would. Looking back, I believe that I wasn't all that interested in college after all. I still wanted to do my best and not let down the people who had given me this college opportunity. I met with the textile scholarship committee at the end of that first year, and told them I would try harder during my sophomore year. I wanted to bring my GPA to the level I knew it should be. Oh, I got an A in swimming that second six weeks. I swam ten laps without stopping in my final test.

During the summer of 1961, it was back to American & Efird Mill for another twelve weeks of cotton lint and sweating. I worked in the same building as my Dad that year. He was in plant #5 and I worked in the winding room of #4 as a helper to the overhauling crew. My pay jumped all the way to $1.65 an hour for this job. I had worked in plants 1 and 2 during the first two summers and the jobs there paid a little less.

Every summer at North Albemarle Baptist Church we observed Youth Week. The young people were selected for all of the positions of the church for that week. We were Sunday School teachers, Deacons, Ushers and the like. That summer, I was asked to be the Youth Week Pastor for the second straight year. The summer before, I just presided over the worship service and Rev. Leroy Caulder preached. But this summer Rev. Caulder asked me if I would like to have the sermon. I did a decent job with my sermon, entitled, "Wisdom Hath Builded Her House." Phyllis and her mom and aunt Nell came to hear me. That didn't add TOO much pressure.

I had prepared my 'sermon' on several note cards. As I came to the pulpit to begin, I pulled the cards out and began with, "As you see, I will be using some notes this morning. I hope I have a better start that one young seminary student who was delivering HIS first sermon on the Creation." One of his instructors told him to use a note card inside his suit coat pocket and just look down at the pocket for important names that he needed to remember. He started with, "In the beginning, God created the Heavens and the Earth. He created a man from the dust and called him..." (He looked to the note card) "Adam. He created a helpmate from Adam's rib and called her......." (He looked to the note card) "Eve. After a while a son was born to them and they called him...." (He looked to the note card but didn't pull it up enough) "and they called him J.C. Penney."

I got a great laugh, and it put me much more at ease. I've used that story dozens of times in speaking to various groups.

I had always been very active at North Albemarle. I was given speaking parts at all of the Christmas programs and Bible School programs since I was six years old. I was in Youth Choir before moving up to the Adult Choir when I went to high school. I became part of the church quartet with Charlie B. Smith, the choir director, his son Roger, now a successful lawyer in Raleigh, and Harold Hudson. I sang 1st tenor, Charlie B. was 2nd tenor, Roger was baritone and Harold sang bass. Charlie B. and Harold are singing with the Heavenly Choir now.

On the Sunday before July 4th, I was a part of a trio that had the special music for the service. I made it through the first verse just fine. On the second verse I saw yellow words on black paper. One sentence into the third verse, I fainted and fell straight back, right into Rev. Caulder's lap. When I woke up I was in the bathroom of the educational building with cold towels on my head. The two girls I was singing with, Nancy Smith and Pat Lawhon, finished the song like nothing was wrong.

Before I get too much farther along, I need to back- track and bring our history into focus. In the summer of 1961, I asked a lady that I had gotten to know in the mill, Wilma Shoe, if she might know a good, Baptist, Republican girl who might be interested in going out to eat sometime. There has never been any real doubt that I have always been a conservative Republican.

JIM BROYHILL BOOTH AT STANLY COUNTY FAIR 1962 BOB (V.P. YOUNG REPUBLICANS CLUB) & HAZEL BLALOCK (SECRETARY OF CLUB)

She said yes, there just MIGHT be a girl who just MIGHT want to go out... her daughter. She said that Phyllis had just broken up with her boyfriend and she probably would be interested in meeting me. She told me that she would talk with Phyllis that night and would give me an answer the next day. The next morning, I was nervous about getting her answer. Would I have a chance to date Phyllis, or not. Wilma gave me what I believe was the best news I would ever hear; Phyllis DID want to meet me and would go out with me. I called her that night and arranged a date for Friday night.

Just before I went to her house, I remembered that I knew who Phyllis was. Her picture was in the paper after she won a beauty contest. I saw her briefly at a cookout for the contestants earlier in the summer, and she was with her boyfriend. I had been asked to go by the second runner-up. Phyllis and I assumed the other was tied to the person we were with, and we both assumed wrongly. I was just accompanying the girl I was with.

Phyllis later told me that she had seen me earlier that same summer coming out of the mill. She was waiting to pick up her mother. The reason she remembered me was the bandage I had on my head. Bandage is not a good description. One-third of my head was wrapped in a LARGE gauze skullcap. The previous Sunday, July 30, 1961, my buddy Ken York and I hopped in 'the ol' Gray Ghost' after church and lunch, and headed to Morrow Mountain State Park and the swimming pool, just as we had done almost every sunny Sunday afternoon that summer.

We got there about 2pm and changed into our trunks in the pool house. In those days, you had to step into a small cement pool of disinfected water as you went out the door to the pool. This was a health precaution to prevent the spread of athletes' foot. The chemicals in the small pool made your feet kinda slick. I went to the side of the pool to jump in, just like always. Just as I was about to leap, a small boy pushed off from the side right below me. I had not seen him next to the wall of the pool. In an effort to stop so that I wouldn't land on him, my feet slipped out from under me. I went headfirst into three feet of water. Several people told me later that I made a perfect 'swan dive' into the pool.

My head made quick and severe contact with the bottom of the pool. It didn't give an inch. My body did. I went unconscious. Onlookers said that I stood up for a brief second with blood gushing everywhere and then fell back into the water. A lifeguard pulled me out and I was rushed to Stanly County Memorial Hospital where I received nine stitches to close the 'upside-down Y' in my hairline. I regained conscientiousness about 7pm, but had to stay overnight.

The lifeguard who pulled me out was a friend of mine since elementary school. Chip Cain was a year ahead of me and played football for the Bulldogs before going to the University of South Carolina. We were also in Mixed Chorus together.

Less than a month after rescuing me, Chip was dead. He drowned while water skiing on Lake Tillery .... near the base of Morrow Mountain.

Finally it was Friday night. I drove the 9.93 miles to Phyllis' home in the community of Finger to pick her up, and we headed back toward town. Not knowing Phyllis' likes and dislikes, I wasn't sure of what to suggest that we do on this first date. We didn't like either of the movies that were playing, so we just drove around for a while, trying to decide on something we thought we might like.

After a while she asked me, "Well, what do you want to do, Bobby?"

Jokingly, I said, "Well since we are just driving around, would you like to drive down to South Carolina and get married?"

In those days, South Carolina allowed 16 year-olds to marry without parental consent. I know that many, many young, love-struck North Carolina couples 'ran off' to Chesterfield or Dillon to tie the knot. They worried about telling their parents later. That's what my folks had done in 1927. I don't whether Phyllis knew if I was kidding or not, but she brushed off my 'proposal' by saying, "Maybe later."

I think I knew Phyllis was the girl for me after just one date. We talked about our families and I learned that her paternal grandmother, Margaret Julia Ann Shoe sold fresh vegetables from their farm to 'city folks' in my neighborhood. Phyllis got her first name, Margaret, from her. She told me also that her dad, Paul, sold watermelons and cantaloupes in town several years later and that she came with him a lot. I found out a couple of months into our courtship that she had asked one of our neighbors, who worked with her mom in the mill, about me. He told her what a swell guy I was. Neighbors do stretch the truth sometimes.

In just a few weeks I went back to State. We wrote each other every week. Around Thanksgiving I began coming home every weekend. We went out every Friday and Saturday night and Sunday afternoon. As the weeks passed, "Goodbye" became harder to say.

PHYLLIS IN MILLINGPORT HIGH BASKETBALL UNIFORM 1962

I am two years older that Phyllis and she was a senior at Millingport High School. It was the smallest of the ten high schools in Stanly County. With only four girls in her class, she played basketball all four years. She was the number two scorer in the county and made the all-county team her junior and senior seasons. She was a forward and averaged over twenty points a game. Beauty, brains, AND she could shoot a basketball with the best. We NEVER played 'HORSE.'

My second year at State was pretty much like the first. Phyllis and I were beginning to get a little more serious as the fall went on. I invited her to come to Raleigh to see her very first football game. Since her high school was so small, they didn't field a team. There were only ten students in her graduating class, six of them were boys. I rode home with a friend on Friday afternoon and very early Saturday morning, I drove to Phyllis' house and drove her car to Raleigh because I had an eight o'clock math class. The game was moved to a 10am kickoff so some of the fans could also see the Duke-Carolina game at 2 that afternoon. I made sure that Phyllis was properly adorned with a Homecoming Chrysanthemum corsage for the game with South Carolina. I spent most of the game explaining the rules and strategies to her, and we both loved it. The Wolfpack beat the Gamecocks 33-14.

The following spring, I invited Phyllis to a cookout for the members of Mu Beta Psi and their dates. There was also a dance at the Student Union that night, featuring the Paul Whiteman Orchestra. Again, I thumbed home on Friday afternoon and we drove her '58 Chevy back to Raleigh Saturday morning. It was more reliable than my '52 Plymouth.

The cookout at Umstead Park was 'lightly' attended to say the least. When Phyllis and I arrived, we were greeted by Ralph Daniels and Ted Halvorson, neither of whom had a date. The grill was hot and the hamburgers and hot dogs were cooking. We waited, and waited, and waited. No one else showed up. The four of us ate all we wanted and we loaded up their car and left.

I dropped Phyllis at the apartment of my pal Donnie Clark's girlfriend to change for the dance that night and went to Berry Dorm to do the same. Thankfully, the dance was better attended. We danced until midnight and then headed home to Albemarle.

Here was a choice I made that changed my life. First, I decided to give up my Dickson scholarship after my sophomore year. I wasn't making the academic progress I needed to, and I realized that I was not going to change the textile world. I was relieved, but NOW what do I do?

Since I had rescinded the financial aide, I had to find funds to continue. I decided take a year off to get a job and save enough to return to school in another curriculum. I thought it would be better to transfer to Pfeiffer College in Misenheimer, just 10 miles from my house. I would be a day student and save some more money.

I decided to change my major to English and teach in high school. I also thought I might have a chance to coach baseball. Mrs. Fry had given me a love of reading and English in high school and this would give me the opportunity to possibly make a difference in kids' lives.Now my path was set for the future, or was it? I didn't know just how wrong I was.

CHAPTER FOUR
Marriage and the Real World

I was sure that that the right decision was to leave N.C. State and go to work for a year, then head back to college and look at a new career. First things first. I had to find a job. Pfeiffer was a small, private college that was very good academically, but expensive, even for a day student. I knew that I could go back to the mill, but the pay wasn't that good, and I had lost interest in textiles. Some of the retail stores downtown were always looking for workers, so I might find a job there. Again, money wasn't that plentiful as a sales or delivery person. But, retail seemed like the better road to take. I found a job with Lowder Hardware where I hoped to work in their sporting goods department. Wrong!! I was assigned to the warehouse, delivering building supplies. Sometimes the appliance deliverymen needed help to install a washer or refrigerator or put a TV antenna on a roof. Thankfully, I was in great physical shape. Unloading railroad boxcars of roofing, cement and appliances is backbreaking. That job lasted ten months.

Millingport High School's graduation was on May 30, 1962 and the next week Phyllis enrolled in business school in Charlotte. We were getting more serious, and my 1952 Plymouth was getting in serious trouble. I can remember keeping a hammer in the car for those occasions when it 'got ornery' and wouldn't go into gear. This happened on several dates and I had to get out of the car with the hammer and crawl underneath it and bang on the transmission while Phyllis worked the gearshift into first gear. After that it would shift fine.

December 16th was a big day in our lives. I was attending Canton Baptist with her, and at the conclusion of service that morning, two of our friends, Edward Huneycutt and Linda Speight were married. I ate Sunday dinner with Phyllis' family, and afterward asked her dad, Paul, to walk outside with me. We talked about the weather for a few minutes, and then I asked for Phyllis' hand in marriage. I think he knew it was coming for quite a while. He said he thought I'd make a good son-in-law. What a relief!!! Phyllis and I went into her living room and I got down on my knee and I asked her, again, to marry me. This time she said yes, and we set the date for June 2nd.

Paul Shoe was born in 1901, three years before Daddy. Wilma was 15 years younger. She, at 5'11" tall, was a pretty good basketball player at Endy High School where she graduated in 1934. She had a scholarship offer to play for a business college, but the stipend only covered tuition and she didn't have the money for room and board and books, so she headed for a life in the Efird Manufacturing Company. They were married in 1939.

Paul made furniture for Lentz' Shop in Mt. Pleasant for a number of years. He also worked in cotton mills in Concord and Albemarle. He was employed by the North Carolina Highway Department when Phyllis and I got married. Later in that summer of 1963, he was diagnosed with lung cancer and passed away on December 10th, just six months and eight days after walking his only daughter down the aisle. I wish I could have had more time to really get to know him. He was a colorful character who decided to take off and join a carnival for one summer when he was a younger man. That must have been the reason he always told his family to "watch out for carnival people 'cause they'll crook ya." Like mine, Phyllis' great-grandfather fought in the Civil War, known in Stanly County as 'The War of Northern Aggression."

I left Lowder Hardware because a new shoe store was coming to town. Since I had sold shoes at J.C. Penney for the three Christmases I was in high school and State, I felt eminently qualified for the sales position at the new Albemarle Shoe Center. I don't know if it was my 'extensive' experience, or they were just desperate for someone to measure feet, but I began work there on April 1st, 1963, for the grand salary of $50.00 a week BEFORE taxes!!

After two months and one day of fitting shoes, Phyllis and I were married on Sunday, June 2, 1963 in a packed Canton Baptist Church. "HOW SWEET IT IS!!!" After the ceremony, we drove to Virginia Beach for our week-long honeymoon and stayed at the Holiday Sands Motel right on the ocean. Remember, I'm taking home less than $50.00 a week!! I went down to the motel office on Monday morning to get some milk for our breakfast cereal (which we had taken with us) and they had no cartons of milk to sell, but they said I could buy two 12-ounce cups of milk, for $1.00. I could have bought a whole gallon at a store for 49 cents. We came home through Raleigh that Saturday, and went to Gino's Italian Restaurant on Fayetteville Street in downtown. It was one of my favorites from my days at State. After the meal, I asked Mr. Gino if he had any Chianti-bottle candles that he might part with for my new wife. He had given me one during my college days, but Phyllis needed "her" candle. He gave us another with all the different colored wax droppings from the candles it had held. My bride was pleased. We still have the candles, but 47 years of carrying them everywhere we moved destroyed most of the candle drippings.

BOB & PHYLLIS HONEYMOON AT VIRGINIA BEACH

When we got married, Phyllis was not a cook. It took her years to learn the 'tricks of the trade' so we have had a few experiences that cannot be forgotten. It was our second week of marriage and Phyllis wanted to make a peach cobbler for me. She didn't know how to do it, but she planned it out and worked all day on that cobbler. She peeled those fresh peaches, sliced them and added just the right amount of sugar. She made the dough and rolled it out and floured it and kneaded it and rolled it some more and floured it some more and worked so hard to make it look good. She put that cobbler into that oven to bake and it looked so pretty. When it was baked, she let it set in the oven for about 5 hours to keep it warm. She didn't know that the longer it was in the oven, the harder the crust became. When she put it on the table that night, I tried to spoon out a serving and couldn't get the spoon into the crust. Then I tried a kitchen knife to cut a piece, and that knife would not go through the crust. Next I used a steak knife and managed to 'saw' a little through that tough crust. I found raw peaches inside that cobbler and we couldn't eat it...but that crust sure was pretty.

We also discovered something in those first couple of years. Both of us had saved all of the 'love letters' we had received from the other while we were dating. Neither of us knew the other was keeping them

On our 16th wedding anniversary, Phyllis and I were eating at a special restaurant, and out of the clear blue, she said, "Did I ever tell you about that chocolate pie I made for you?" Well, I was shocked because in all those years, she had never made a chocolate pie for me, so I had to hear more.

Phyllis told me that when we had been married about two months, she had decided to buy chocolate pie mix in a box. She wanted to surprise me with my favorite pie so she got up after I went to work and began working on it. But let her tell it. She does it so well.

I read all the directions on the box and followed them ever so carefully and soon the house began to smell so wonderful. Of course, I had not eaten breakfast so that aroma was enhanced and it was now close to lunchtime. Well, that pie was ready around noon and it was beautiful. I decided to cut a slice and try it so I would be sure it was good. I didn't want it to be like the peach cobbler, so I had to taste it. I ate that piece of pie with gusto and loved every bite. I thought about it for a few minutes, and since it was lunchtime, I decided to cut another slice and have that for my lunch. Then I thought again how great that pie was and rationalized that I would eat a piece with Bob when he got home that night, so I cut another slice and ate that one. I did NOT cut timid slices...they were healthy slices. After finishing off that one, I looked down at that pie and saw that there was only one piece left and I thought how awful it would be if Bob thought I had eaten that much of the pie so I ate that piece too.... and never told Bob.

Well, not until she confessed during our 16th year of marriage. You know, Phyllis has never baked another one in all our years together. She said she couldn't be trusted with a chocolate pie. But the best part is when she tells that story to our friends, someone will always bake me a chocolate pie because they feel so sorry for me. I've had a lot of great pies since she started telling that story, and a lot of laughs.

Phyllis had finished business school and was working as a Remington Rand keypunch operator for Johnson Motor Lines in Charlotte until I proposed in December of 1962. In January, she went to work as a PBX switchboard and Teletype operator at the Collins & Aikman plant in Albemarle. She was bringing in a whopping $35.00 a week, BEFORE taxes. The Rockefellers, we weren't!

I went back to work at Albemarle Shoe Center on Monday after the honeymoon, and learned that the owner, Herbert Humphries, had given me a surprise wedding present. He raised my salary from $50.00 to $55.00 per week!! A married man has to have more.

One Tuesday afternoon, I was helping a customer decide on just which pair of Florsheim shoes he was going to purchase, and chit-chatting with him while he was making up his mind. While trying on one pair for the second time, he leaned down and asked me, in a whisper, if I was looking for another job. This got my attention, and I asked what kind of job it was. Bob Medlin was looking for a commission salesman at his Goodyear Service Store right around the corner. I met him at the store the next afternoon and he told me all about this position.

Goodyear Service Stores always had a great national reputation for their quality tires, as well as GE appliances, televisions, and stereos. They had just over twenty stores in North Carolina and nearly thirty in South Carolina. It seemed like a great opportunity. I really liked what I heard and asked if I could think it over for a day or so and talk with Phyllis about it. He agreed.

Speaking of stores closing on Wednesday afternoons, this was not unusual around the South. In fact, it was pretty commonplace. The main reason retailers worked only a half-day midweek was that things just move a little slower in the smaller towns than in big cities. Charlotte stores didn't close. Most of Albemarle's stores stayed open until 9:00 on Friday night and all day on Saturday, so employees got that half day off do their yard or household work, or get ready for Wednesday night prayer meeting and choir practice.

In today's world, store owners wouldn't think of locking their doors at noon Wednesday, and giving employees the afternoon off. Back then it was as normal as a holiday, and just as welcome. Things were really good for us. In February 1964, I was promoted to Credit Sales Manager in Albemarle. Phyllis and I had our first daughter, Paula, who was born August 26, 1964. This is one of those ' HOW SWEET IT IS!' moments. In September, Goodyear sold our store and I commuted to the Monroe store for six weeks. My transfer to Charleston Heights, S.C. as Credit Sales Manager was approved in October.

My first priority was to find the best mobile home park in Charleston.I did, and we headed south to begin a life in Hawthorne City. Most of the residents there were in our age bracket, and a large contingent was military. Our next-door neighbors, Don and Joyce Blackledge were our best friends there. They were Michigan natives and he was in the Navy, attached

'THE 5 STEPS TO A TIRE SALE' BOB IN CHARLESTON 1965

to a nuclear submarine based at nearby Goose Creek. He would be home for six months and then go to sea for six.

In Charleston, we went through another time in our lives that helped define who we are today. Being on our own for the first time was the best thing that could have happened for our marriage. We learned to depend on each other, make our own decisions AND mistakes, but we learned how to cope with the problems that all newly married couples encounter. You might say that we 'grew up' together during those two years in Charleston. With Phyllis staying home to care for Paula, we depended solely on my salary. I will say that it was a lot more than the two of us brought home two years before, but we STILL were not living in the lap of luxury.

We were looking for a church there and our store secretary invited us to hers, Charleston Heights Baptist. It was about two miles from our home. We loved it even though it was about five times the size, area and members, of Canton Baptist. That took some getting used to. But the Young Marrieds Sunday School Class really helped with that. When we visited in the fall of 1964 there were 16 members. I was elected president of the class in June of '65, and in June of '66, on the second anniversary of its formation, I looked out over a crowd of 124 members. Dr. John Huss, our pastor, taught the class and it was like a big family.

In January of 1966, General Electric, the appliance supplier for Goodyear, held a special promotion for employees ONLY. We could purchase their latest model color televisions for $10.00 over store cost. Our little black and white portable was on its last legs and we looked at our budget and finally figured a way to own a brand-new, 25" CONSOLE color TV. We financed it for six months at $50.00 a month. We just knew we could afford that payment. We took some of it from our grocery money. It sounded like a good idea. All we had to do was cut a few corners. No new clothes for six months. No problem. No eating out for six months. No problem. Really watch all other expenditures. Again, NO PROBLEM.

Well, it did turn into a problem about the fifth month. My commission check from Goodyear was late and we were running low on groceries. Baby food and milk for Paula were priority one. No problem. Dosher's

Red & White had Gerber's for SIX cents a jar. We also had very little money for bologna either.

I came home for lunch one day and all we had in the house were two cans of beans. Phyllis fixed both (and over salted one of them) and that was lunch, with our usual glass of Kool-Aid. We drank so much of that stuff during that period of time that we both swore we'd never drink it again. Our kids grew up WITHOUT Kool-Aid at home. They would get it at friends' houses occasionally and think it was something special. I haven't had a glass of it since 1966.

Yes, we had hit that plateau. I didn't know what we would do for supper that night. I drove back to work and walked across the street to the post office to get the mail. HOT DOG!!! The commission check had arrived. I rushed back to the store, called Phyllis and told her to make out a grocery list. The eagle has landed!!! We went to the Red & White store and filled TWO grocery carts. We spent nearly $65.00 on groceries and there was no meat in the carts. We went to a meat market the next afternoon and bought about half a cart full of meats only. That ran us $12.00 and change. We ate 'high on the hog' and the cow for a good while after that. We learned a valuable lesson from this; never buy something without knowing that you can pay for it.

G.E. held a sales contest early in 1966. The prize was a three-day, two-night trip to New Orleans. Each Goodyear store was given a quota for TV and stereo sales for January and February. Those store managers who made quota won the trips. My Store Manager, Ray Lee, said that he couldn't go because wives couldn't go along. I asked if I could take the trip if we made quota. He checked with GE and they OK'd my using it. Now the plan was to sell the required number of TVs and console stereos to earn it.

After-Christmas sales of those items usually hit the bottom in January and February. That's why they ran the contest at that time. Our store went 116% to quota and I was off to 'The Big Easy' on my very FIRST airplane trip. We flew one of Delta's big jets from Charleston to Augusta to New Orleans. Just as we hit cruising altitude, I finally looked out the window and saw the wing kinda flapping up and down in the wind. It scared the liver out of me. I asked my seatmate what was wrong. He informed me that if they weren't flapping like that we would be in trouble.

New Orleans in the mid-60s was a bustling city. There were so many things I had never seen. Bourbon Street, Rev. Bob Harrington in his red suit, preaching from his red Bible on the corner, music coming from all the doors in that section, women who weren't women, and some who made sure you knew they were by what they didn't have on. This WAS 'sin city.' I was sure of it. We stayed at the famous Roosevelt Hotel. G.E. had reservations for the entire group at Arnaud's the first night, and the Court of Two Sisters on the second night. We also had 'Breakfast at Brennan's.' All three were "must-do's" in the mid-60s. I was so intrigued with the glass candles on the tables at Court of Two Sisters. They were different colors with the restaurant logo on the side. I asked if I could buy one, but was told they weren't for sale. Just before we left, one member of our party handed me something wrapped in a cloth napkin from the table. He told me to put it under my coat and he'd explain when we got out. I put it between my arm and body under my sport coat, and by the time we were outside, no explanation was necessary. It was one of those candles and the flame hadn't been out for long before I put it under my coat. My ribs were nearly blistered, but we still have that candle.

We went back to the Roosevelt and freshened up and then went to the Blue Room. I had heard radio broadcasts from there because we could pick up WWL Radio in Albemarle at night. It was a 50,000-watt, clear channel signal that covered 30 states at 870 on the A.M. dial. They always had top-flight entertainers on the shows. That night, Frankie Laine was the star. After his performance he was in the lobby selling albums and meeting fans. I parted with $2.00 and got his latest album, which he autographed to me. Another first.

I had the opportunity to go back to New Orleans in December of 1980 with the Duke basketball team for the Sugar Bowl Basketball Tournament. We stayed in the Hyatt Regency at the Superdome since that's where we would be playing. When I got to my room, I opened the drapes to get a view of the city. The first thing I saw was a billboard on top of a nearby building. "APPEARING NIGHTLY IN THE BLUE ROOM OF THE FAIRMONT HOTEL----THE FOUR LADS." I didn't see anything else. Leo Hart, a record setting Duke quarterback from the early 70s, was the group sales director for the Fairmont and had told me to call him when we arrived. I quickly dialed his number and as he said hello, I blurted out, "Can I come to see The Lads?"

"Hey Bob. When did you get in to town?"

"Just now and I hope you can get me into see them."

"No problem. What night and which show."

"Tonight, and the later show. We have to go to a Tournament function at 6."

"How many with you?"

"Just Danny Highsmith and me."

"I'll have a table for you for the 9pm show. Just tell them you're my guests. I'll see you when you get here."

Hot dog! I'm going to see The Four Lads. Danny and I got a cab as soon as we finished the Tournament party and headed to the Fairmont. We were early. The first show was just clearing out and the hostess said it would be a few minutes. She asked if we had our tickets and I told her that we were Leo's guests.

"Mr. Hart is having dinner and will see you inside." We were ushered into the Blue Room and seated at the first table at the corner of the stage. And then, it's show time! The Four Lads sang every song they'd ever recorded. A favorite part of my record collection just came to life. When they finished their forty-five minutes, another group hit the stage. My gosh, it's The Ink Spots! We stayed on. The table beside us had been vacant for the first part of the show, but now four men were seated there. It was The Four Lads! I whispered to "Bernie" Toorish, the tenor, that I thoroughly enjoyed the show and that I was softly singing along on all of them, especially "Moments To Remember." He asked which part I was singing and I told him tenor and he said, "I wished you had come up and helped me. I have a throat problem and was struggling." Oh, how I wish I had known THAT!! That night would have been perfect.

At the end of the Ink Spots set, The Four Lads asked if we wanted to go with them to another club for some 'real' New Orleans music. Highsmith went back to the hotel, I jumped into a cab with The Lads and we stayed at that club until about three in the morning, but it was worth it.

After twenty-one months at the Charleston Heights store I got a big promotion. I was made Store Manager in Dillon, S.C., just east of Florence. In July 1966, Phyllis, Paula, and I tied everything down, and moved our mobile home again. Phyllis was almost ready to give birth to our second child, Bobbi. She was born on August 14th, about a month after we arrived in Dillon. Another 'HOW SWEET IT IS!!' moment. I was almost twenty-four years old and was the youngest Store Manager in the Southeast Region. I didn't like moving every couple of years, but that was the Goodyear progression. I was doing well enough that I put all my thoughts of a college degree on permanent hold.

As the new Store Manager, my first duty was a physical inventory of the major appliances, TVs and stereos. That completed, I matched my count with the inventory book. I almost fainted!! It was as bad as you could imagine. The previous manager was a good ol' boy who just liked helping the customers. Keeping accurate books was not a major emphasis. I took three physical counts of those items and every time I got more scared. I called the regional auditor in Atlanta. I explained the situation and asked him to come to Dillon as soon as possible to make sure that my audit was correct, and to tell me what to do. He said he would be there at 8:00am and that I should be also. I got to the store just after 7:30 the next morning, and M.B. Paden was already waiting for me at the front door. "This trip better be worth it," he muttered as I opened the door.

I didn't open for business at the usual time. After taking his own count, he checked the books like they were the U.S. Constitution. When he finished, he looked up, and said, "I don't think that this is anyway to run a railroad." His numbers agreed with mine. The best explanation we could come up with was that my predecessor would send a customer's ailing TV or stereo to our outside repair vendor and just give the customer a new one off the shelf. This certainly satisfied the customers, but he didn't keep any records of it in the inventory book. We found all of the mess at the repair shop, and wrote-off over $2,700.00. That came directly off the bottom line of MY profit and loss statement right then. Since my year-end bonus was based on the profit the store made I took the big hit.

Inventories had not been taken for over six months in other categories.

The Assistant District Manager, who was my immediate boss, was livid. His tirade would have made even the most veteran sailor ashamed. I'll bet that blue cloud of profanity he rolled out that day is still hovering somewhere over Dillon County. Unfortunately, all of his cussing was aimed at me, not the man who caused all the mess

I politely told him that I was the person who found the problems on my first day, and I was the person who brought the problem to the auditor and asked him to come up and sort it out.I wanted to get things back in order. He finally apologized and told me all would be forgotten and we would start over. Guess what? After I found several other irregularities in the truck tire inventory and showed him that tires were 'going out the back door' with no record, he called me to the Charlotte office and told me that he was "going to take me out of Dillon before it covered me up." I was sent to the Florence store as a salesman, again with a 'clean slate.'

I began to look at my future as a Goodyear employee. On January 19th, he showed in Florence store and ran the Store Manager out of his own office, and brought up everything that had happened in Dillon. I told him point-blank that I would not take another 'cussin' from him. It was all I could do hold back as he railed. I reached my limit. I stood up, looked him straight in the eye and said, "Mr. Owens, before either you or I end up on the floor, you have my resignation, effective immediately." I packed up my belongings, got in my car, and drove up Highway 301 to Dillon. Anything would be better than all the abuse that I had been given the past seven months. As I drove home, I hoped that Phyllis wouldn't be mad. She wasn't, and within a week, we headed back to Stanly County, with no job and a family to support.

One really nice thing happened for me while we lived in Dillon. Another businessman in town asked me about joining the Junior Chamber of Commerce. He invited me to one of their meetings and as a 'hook,' he said they were having a nationally known speaker. When I walked into the meeting that night I quickly recognized the Stetson hat and southern drawl of Hall of Fame pitcher Jay Hanna "Dizzy" Dean of the fabled 'Gashouse Gang' of the St. Louis Cardinals. Ol' Diz was a holdin' court, entertaining everyone with his baseball stories. He was in town on a promotional tour for Busch Brewery. After his stint as a sportscaster, he stayed in St. Louis and went to work for the Busch family. The local distributor was Alan Schaeffer, and Alan was a member of the Jaycees. Ever the opportunist, I got a handshake and an autograph from Diz.

CHAPTER FIVE
Me, On Radio?

I needed to find a job fairly quickly. With a family depending on just my income, I was in a hurry to find good employment. For as long as I can remember, my family was insured with Western and Southern Life Insurance Company. J.C. Hinson was our agent and he had worked his way to staff manager, and he tried to hire me after Phyllis and I were married, but I declined. I phoned him the day before we moved from Dillon to ask about openings on the staff. He told me that one position was coming open in April. I needed income immediately and went to see Mr. Humphries at the Albemarle Shoe Center again. I told him about my entire situation, and he gave me a job, even knowing that it was only for a few months. He knew that I needed a job and he, like a lot of people in my hometown, helped me.

We scrimped and saved every penny we could, but several times we were down to our last nickels, REALLY. I still have the checkbook that shows a balance of FIVE CENTS!!! It was September 12, 1967. We had the money for our household expenses, food and our tithe to Canton Baptist Church, but that was it.

I learned one thing several months after I entered the insurance business; it wasn't my 'cup of tea' as they say. I know a number of people who have made a great living selling insurance, and the reason they did is because they love the insurance business. It didn't take long for me to see that my Western and Southern Life Insurance career would be short lived, but I was dead set on giving it my best effort. At the time I thought, "Maybe I'll like this." Uh, no, I didn't like it. "Sometimes, you have to back up the hearse and let them smell the flowers." That was a piece of advice I got from one of the veteran agents on our staff. I didn't like the thought of hearses and I just couldn't browbeat anyone into buying life insurance even though I knew it was a good product. I have and always will be a proponent of life insurance.

BOB, PHYLLIS, PAULA & BOBBI 1966

I learned something else in the insurance business. I learned that when you're collecting a debit route, you encounter many things. The most prominent and worrisome thing is a dog, especially one that doesn't want you to come up on the front porch to knock on the door. J.C. showed me just how to get around that obstacle the first week I was on the job. I had noticed that all of the agents in the office wore a hat. The hat was not worn for looks or weather, necessarily. Just as much as a friendly dog will try to get away if you blow in his face, the angriest dog will back up if you try to put anything on his nose. Follow me closely here. You walk up to the steps to collect the policy premium; the dog comes from under a chair barking his head off; you reach up and grab the crown (top) of your fedora; and in one motion, pull it off and turn the bottom (part that fits over your head) straight toward the oncoming barker and try to put it on his nose. I have backed quite a few unhappy canines into a corner and kept them there until the policyholder I was there to see came to the door and took control of his dog.

I had only been selling insurance for about three months when a chance meeting changed my life completely. I was downtown one day and happened to bump into an long-time friend Ralph Gardner. He had been a customer at both the shoe store and Goodyear. Both stores had advertised on WZKY, and Ralph was the contact. We talked about a lot of community things and the subject of high school football came up. Ralph said that WZKY could not broadcast the local games in the fall because he didn't have anyone to broadcast them. Off- handedly, I said, "I'll do them for you." Hey, just like my marriage proposal on my first date with Phyllis, my life changed. That night I told Phyllis about it. And she was as excited as I was. Now to figure out if I could broadcast the games, and handle my full-time job.

Gardner must have been really, really desperate. He wanted to air West Stanly High football in September, and put together a package for local sponsors. He wanted me to go to several businesses in Oakboro and Locust with him, to try and get sponsors for the games. I was excited to go, thinking that I was going to learn some of Ralph's selling techniques and meet some of his sponsors too.

That did happen, but so did several other things. We went to see Larry Williams at Williams Oil Company and as Ralph ended his sponsorship pitch, he said, "I want you to meet Bob Harris. He is our new play-by-play man." "WOW," I thought. "That sounds great." In a nutshell, that is how my broadcast career began. Youngsters wanting to become sportscasters ask me, "How did you get your start in broadcasting?" It began in the office of Williams Oil Company, in Oakboro, North Carolina, and that's a long way from Cameron Indoor Stadium and the NCAA Championships.

When that first Friday of football season rolled around, I went to WZKY to get the broadcast equipment. Ralph gave me this big reel-to-reel tape recorder in a case that looked like a Samsonite suitcase. He handed me a microphone and two tapes that would record for an hour each and told me to turn off the recorder when there was a time out to save tape. He asked me if I had any questions, and I said, "Yes, how do I set it up?" He went pale. He showed me where everything went and we left for Oakboro. The 'we' was Phyllis, Paula and Bobbi, and the two high school kids who worked weekend shifts and would be my spotters. Phyllis and the girls went along to get out of the house, and each one carried a piece of equipment so they could get in free. I couldn't afford to buy their tickets.

That equipment might seem ancient to today's broadcasters, but in 1967, it was fairly up-to-date, at least for our needs. Transporting that gear around was a job in itself. If the weight was not a big enough problem, at every stadium I had to haul it all up to the press box or roof. There was usually a wobbly wooden ladder to climb that looked like we would be taking our lives in our own hands just trying to climb up it. But we also had to lug this suitcase-sized recorder plus the other gear.

As my spotters, it was the duty of the two teenagers to make sure I called the right players who were involved in the plays. They stood on either side me and watched the game through binoculars and pointed out the players' names from the game program.

WZKY was a low-power station. The license allowed us to broadcast from sunrise to sunset only. During the summer months, the earliest sign-on time was 5:30 am and the latest sign-off was 8:45 pm. In the winter, broadcast days were much shorter. December had the shortest days, so sign-on was 7:30 am and sign-off was 5:15 pm. This meant that the football games were not broadcast live. We taped them on Friday nights and then aired them on Saturday mornings at 11 am. Why do it like that? The fans that went to the game got chance to hear the ball game; the players and coaches could to listen to the plays that were made the night before. It was a win-win situation for fans, players, advertisers and the station.

Phyllis and the girls sat with me that first Saturday morning and listened to every word of my broadcast. I cringed a bunch of times. I didn't like hearing my own voice.

THE YOUNG FAMILY - BOB, PHYLLIS, PAULA & BOBBI 1967

As soon as the game broadcast was over my phone rang, and it was Ralph. The first words I heard were, "If there's anything I hate, it's a liar. You told me you'd been in South Carolina selling tires, when you'd really been broadcasting sports." I didn't know what to say. He laughed and said, "I'm kidding. I thought you did a great job for your first game. Can you come by the station the first of the week and talk about the next game?" "Sure. Whatever you need." I 'm not sure if I was happier with his words or just relived that I did a decent job. Either way, I thought that I had finally found a career. I would no longer be selling shoes or tires if I could help it. However, there was one thing I still had to resolve, and that was meshing insurance and sportscasting. This is how my radio career began. Without very much warning and absolutely no experience, I became the play-by-play announcer for WKZY. This was a "HOW SWEET IT IS!!" moment.

The more games I broadcast, the more I knew that this would be my future. At the end of the final football game of the season, I almost cried because I thought it was my last broadcast. I had been told during the season that I shouldn't be doing the games because of my contract with the insurance company.

BOB & 1st HIGH SCHOOL SPOTTER
MIKE LOFLIN 1967

I had found a job that was fun as well as rewarding, and I asked Ralph if he might be able to use me full-time. He told me that there was a better chance for that in May or June. The advertising sales picked up again after Christmas. I passed the Federal Communications Commission test in Winston-Salem and earned my third-class radio license in January of 1968. This enabled me to be on the air live and not be just a part-time play-by-play man.

With this license, an engineer wouldn't need to be in the station when I was on the air in the studio because I was qualified technically. I didn't know my opportunity would come so soon.

We had a staff meeting at the insurance office on February 1st, and the District Manager came in from Concord. In the course of the meeting he stopped his talk and looked at me and said, "I want to see you when we're through here."

You've heard about the proverbial 'long car ride?' I had one that morning. I sat in the back seat and they were up front. After a few minutes the manager looked around at me and said, "Bob, you have a decision to make. You need to get IN the insurance business, or get OUT."

Without hesitation, I said, " I have made up my mind."

"Good," he said. "I am glad to hear you're staying."

"No, I'm getting out." I said. "I'm going to work at WZKY."

I had to give a 30-day notice. This was another positive career choice.

I hadn't much more than gotten those words out of my mouth and he blew up.He began raving about 'everyone associated with music and the radio business all being 'dope-heads' and that I was crazy for this decision. He told me that I would never get anywhere by working for some small time radio station.

I told him that Phyllis and I had talked it over before and decided that would be the best avenue for us. End of conversation! Things were VERY quiet on the trip back to the office. I quickly drove out to WZKY and told Ralph all about the 'ride' and about my decision to give them a one-month notice. I had no idea how he would react. His face lit up and a big smile came across his face. Then came the words that I can still hear today, "Bob, this is great news and it came at a perfect time. I have been elected President of the Merchants Association and I need someone to take a bit of a load off me and sell advertising and work my 10-noon air shift. Are you interested?"

Did he REALLY think I'd turn him down? "Interested, you bet I am." Goodbye insurance business, hello radio! Now I could focus on a career that would enable me to do something full-time that I really enjoyed in that three month 'taste' with West Stanly football.

WZKY was exactly like hundreds of small town, community-oriented radio stations around the country. Our music format was known as 'block programming.' WZKY played three different genres of music. The country music featured artists like Buck Owens, Loretta Lynn, The

Statler Brothers and Charlie Pride; we played the rock and roll of The Beatles, Olivia Newton-John and other stars of the late 60s and early 70s, and, my favorite, easy listening that everyone could enjoy. The station had four announcers, including Ralph.

A high school friend, Roger Smith worked the sign-on shift until 10 am. Ralph had hosted the next shift that ended at 12:15. Engineer, John Ingold, (air name 'Hillbilly John') had the slot from 12:15 until three. He and his wife Honey (Helen) had been in radio in the Carolinas since the 40s. David Loflin handled the rock show from 3pm until sign off. Now, I was a staff member, taking the 10-12:15 shift for Ralph.

The hardest worker on the staff was our receptionist/traffic manager/ bookkeeper, Foy Barrier. I had known Foy almost all my life. We lived beside her sister and father when I was a kid. One of her daughters was a year ahead of me in school and the other was one-year after me. Foy was a sweet lady who handled all three facets of her job with professionalism and still took time to be a second 'Mom' to us. She loved Perry Como and his music. After I moved to WDNC and became involved with the Duke Children's Classic Golf Tournament, I became friends with "Mr. C". I had him autograph his picture on the Classic program cover and took it to her. It was one of her prized possessions.

My schedule on the air was as varied as our listening audience. From 10 to 11am I played easy listening music. My opening theme song was Ray Conniff's "Rhapsody in Blue." I played Patti Page, Johnny Mathis, Perry Como, and 'easy' chart songs. At 11 o'clock we went into our 'Grocery Boy Program.' I asked our listeners to send in their grocery receipts for the previous week. I pulled two entries from the box each day, and then pulled one envelope from the ten at the end of the Friday show. We paid that listener's weekly grocery bill. By the way, the lucky contestants had three minutes to call in to verify that they were listening, otherwise, the envelope was put back in the box and another was drawn. At 11:30, I changed to a Southern Gospel Quartet format and played about six Gospel songs until 11:45. At that point I played a pre-recorded program called 'Be Still and Know' which was a five-minute inspirational thought. This gave me a break at the mike, and the listeners got uplifting messages just before lunch. Also during this time period, believe it or not, I read the local obituaries on the air. Of course the obits were be sponsored by one of our local funeral homes and I announced them in my most solemn voice with recorded organ music playing in the background. There always seemed to be at least a few to read each day, but on the days there were none to report, I would announce our sponsor, cue up the organ music and say "There are no obituaries for today," and let the organ play until noon when we connected to the Capital News Network for North Carolina news. I then read local news and did my sportscast. At 12:15 Hillbilly John took the air with country music.

John was late several times because he couldn't get away from a sales client, and I started his theme song and maybe even his first tune. One day his theme song ran out and two more songs as well, and still no sight of his '54 Chevrolet coming down the road. In a smart-alec mood, I opened the mic and announced, "Hillbilly John will be a little bit late today because of an accident. He was washing the boss's car, and his tongue went dry." I thought it was funny. By the time his shift was over at 3, people were calling the station wanting to know how badly he was hurt in the wreck, and one lady even asked when the funeral would be. Never again!!!!

At 3:00 pm, when school let out, we switched to Rock 'n Roll, and David Loflin played it until 6:00 pm. We ended the day with easy listening until sign-off at sundown.

I had two favorite phrases that I used throughout my eight-year career at WZKY. I always reminded my listeners to vote on Election Day by saying, "Please remember to exercise your right and responsibility and vote. And if you don't vote...don't gripe, you don't have a leg to stand on." I always signed off my last show on Friday or Saturday with this advice, "Please attend the church of your choice this Sunday/tomorrow, and take someone with you, won't you? You'll both be glad you did." In larger markets this may not have been allowed or appreciated, but it was more than welcome here at home.

There is basically no job description when you work for a small radio station. You do anything and everything that needs to be done for the station to succeed. For example, I had that two-hour and fifteen-minute air shift, plus a five-minute sportscast at 5:10pm. The rest of my day was taken up with sales calls, writing and recording commercials, AND whatever sporting events we were airing. Ralph handled the vast majority of the sales in addition to taking care of the station's business. He was the master of the 'low-pressure' sales technique.

In 1968, the weekly broadcasts of the West Stanly football games were one of the staples of WKZY, and their fans were just beginning to appreciate the game. Here's a bit of background. The Stanly County school system had 10 'all-white' high schools and three 'colored' high schools until consolidation in the fall of 1962. Albemarle City Schools had only Albemarle High and Kingville High. They became one as well.

West Stanly was made up of Endy, Oakboro, South Oakboro, Ridgecrest and Stanfield schools, but none of them ever played football. West had to play 'catch up' with its program. North Stanly incorporated Richfield, New London, Millingport, Badin and West Badin. West Badin was the 'colored' school for that section of Stanly County, just like South Oakboro, Norwood Colored School and Kingville. I differentiate these schools for no other reason than to explain the county system prior to integration. West Badin was the only 'colored school' that had a rich history of athletic success. Badin High played '8-man football' for a long time, so they gave North Stanly some football experience. South Stanly pulled together the former Norwood, Norwood Colored and Aquadale High Schools. They drew on the experience of Norwood, which fielded a team for a good number of years. The reason WZKY had made the choice to broadcast West Stanly was that WABZ, our competition in town, had always broadcast Albemarle, North and South games because they had been more successful on the field, and had larger business communities for advertising support. West Stanly was our niche.

The North Carolina Association of Sportscasters was formed in June of 1968 in Greensboro, N.C. I was fortunate to be at the first meeting and workshop. I say fortunate because it had a great impact on my life and career. First of all, it helped me meet so many of the sportscasters that I had listened to for a large portion of my life to that point, and be able to learn my craft from them.

Legends like the man who started the Duke Radio Network in

1938, Add Penfield; WGHP-TV's Charlie Harville; the first 'Voice of the Tar Heels," Bill Curry; Salisbury's Marty Brennaman, who became the play- by-play man for the Cincinnati Reds; Leo Morris; WBTV's Jim Thacker; Gene Overby of the Wake Forest Network; WRAL-TV's Nick Pond and WPTF Radio's Wally Ausley were among the founding fathers of the Association. Other 'local veterans' who had broadcast local sports for their communities were invaluable. There were four men from Fayetteville Jim Pritchett, Danny Highsmith, Lloyd Foster, and Bill Hennessee, Larry Dunlap from Greensboro, Glen Walls of Shelby, Bill Huff from Burlington and the Elon Network, Ebb Gantt of Belmont and Chuck Moseley of Valdese. Ebb and Chuck both worked for Suburban Radio Group, which owned WZKY.

And there were the 'young pups' like myself who were just getting into the business and wanted to learn from the men who had made North Carolina a hotbed of sportscasting. Ron Bennett of Asheboro; Bob Rathbun, who got his start in Belmont; Tom McKimmey from Wanchese, Dave Lingafelt from Newton-Conover, Lincolnton's Larry Seagle, and Ken Smith of High Point were relatively new to radio.

It was these workshops, provided by NCASB that gave me the background and new ideas with which I could improve what I was doing in Albemarle. One of the best ideas I ever 'stole' was the All-County Team. The four high schools in Stanly County were aligned with three different conferences. Albemarle was in the South Piedmont, North Stanly was a member of the North Piedmont and South and West Stanly were in the Rocky River Conference. I brought the All-County idea to Ralph Gardner, and he urged me to implement it. I gave printed certificates and trophies to the selectees. My childhood neighbor, Lawrence Smith and his brother owned a jewelry store and agreed to furnish the trophies, and Mallie did the engraving, in exchange for advertising on WZKY. It was a win-win situation for all of us. I presented the trophies and certificates at each school's athletic banquet in the spring. I had a wonderful ally in all this, the Sports Editor of the Stanly News & Press, Sam Andrew. Sam was a local legend in his own right, being a member of the 1940 American Legion Junior baseball team that won the Little World Series. Sam would come to a central location and make pictures of the teams for the paper as the selections were announced at the end of the respective seasons.

I only picked the football teams for the first three years and then added boys and girls' basketball and baseball for the last five years I was at the station. The sports section of the newspaper would have pictures of the All-County offensive and defensive teams, Players-of-the-Year and Coach-of-the-Year at the end of football season along with an article about the players and their accomplishments. For basketball, I picked the ten best boys and ten best girls, along with Coaches and Players-of-the-Year for both. At the end of the baseball season, I chose nine starters and three utility players as well as the Coach-of-the-Year. All of the recipients showed up for the pictures in full uniform. This project brought lots of recognition to the student-athletes, many of whom didn't make All-Conference. It also drew attention to WZKY's sports coverage as well.

To this day, I still have some of those players tell me that they still have the trophy and certificate framed in their home, and it was one of their most treasured memories of high school days. It WAS worth it all!!

Ralph had a very simple sports programming philosophy and I had only two rules to adhere to; it had to be in good taste and it had to be totally sponsored before it went on the air.

WZKY always had a very good audience for the mixed music format, but after I went to the there full-time, sports broadcasts became our moneymaker. We added to the West Stanly football broadcasts with boys' and girls' basketball and baseball games for Albemarle High. After three years, we broadcast games for all four schools in those sports. We augmented those high school games by broadcasting Optimist Little League baseball games on summer afternoons.

I'm sure some of you might look at this as being "small-time" sports broadcasting. Believe me, to the youngsters and their families, plus the fans of the schools, it was pretty important. I have told these stories to some groups and I could almost hear them, in their minds, asking where were Andy, Barney, and Goober. This was an integral part of the culture and lives of small towns, especially throughout the South and Mid-West. In broadcasting these events, we were having a great time and it brought a lot of enjoyment to a bunch of hard working people who loved their high school sports every bit as much as Duke or Carolina fans love theirs.

I firmly believe that broadcasting those games prepared me to call some of the greatest college games in history.

Several fans in Albemarle told me that I called those Little League games like it was the 7th game of the World Series. Teams sponsored by the Optimist, Civitan and Rotary clubs, American & Efird, Federal Pacific Electric, Collins & Aikman, Stanly Hardware and E.J. Snyder battled each other just like it WAS their World Series. Hey, several alums of that program DID play in the majors. Why not call it that way?

City League men's slow pitch softball became very popular and we got advertising support from businesses, including our station, and broadcast their games on Mondays and Thursdays in the summer.

In the eight years I broadcast sporting events at WZKY, we originated more local sports than any other radio station in the state. During that whole period we remained a daytime-only station. Sometimes we couldn't finish a broadcast because of the 'sundown' rule. If the games had not reached completion, I had to sign-off. Listeners were aware of this and listened for a recap on my sportscast the next day.

Some days we had sports marathons when we broadcast slow-pitch softball tournaments. The 'big' tournament of the softball season, locally, was the Jack Fesperman/Memorial Day Tournament. The games were very fast-paced. And since each game took about an hour, they would cram as many into the weekend as they could. The schedule usually had five games on Friday, beginning at 5pm and eight on Saturday starting at 10 am. Four more games on Sunday afternoon finished up the tournament.

Since the games were so fast, the commercial breaks had to be altered. In other games we broadcast, the normal commercial break was 60-seconds long; not that way with slow–pitch softball. I learned this in my first softball broadcast. We finished the top half of the first inning and I took the 60-second break. There were two outs in the bottom of the inning and two men were on base when the commercial finished and I got the mic back. The next day I shortened the commercials to 30 seconds so they would fit the format.

Even this timing wasn't always reliable. Sometimes 30-second commercials were TOO LONG, but I got help with this dilemma from an unusual source, the umpires. They started looking up at the press box, and would fidget with their equipment or whisk-off the plate again until I gave them the "high-sign." They then yelled, "play ball." Maybe it was a little bit Mayberryish after all. I am glad that it was.

Sometimes I pulled double duty. Since WZKY sponsored a team, I broadcast the early games with my uniform on, and was in the lineup if we were playing a late game. A couple of my teammates tried to think up a system whereby I could be rigged with a microphone and could play and broadcast at the same time. 1970s technology had not advanced to that point, but if there had been a way, I would have darn sure tried it.

Passionate fans are not limited to colleges, pro franchises or even high school teams. I found that out the hard way. Little League rivalries could be as intense as, say, an ACC Tournament game. My problem was with parents in the bleachers.

I was broadcasting a game at Optimist Park and things began to unravel as the game progressed. A couple of the families of the two teams were beginning to get a shade rowdy. Their uncivil tirades were directed at each other, and not the kids on the field. I was in a press box that was not enclosed, so I could get the 'flavor' of the game. The language was awful, and I was very concerned that our listeners could hear all of this vulgarity.

Because the FCC broadcast rules were a lot different in the 60s and 70s, I was afraid we might lose our license if it had been reported. Almost anything can be said in today's radio and TV, but in 1970, just one of the 'seven prohibited curse words,' would possibly have gotten me fired and our station fined. The FCC was a lot more conservative then than now.

During a between-innings commercial break, I got the attention of Joe Kelly, the league director, and told to him what I was hearing and asked if he could stop those families from cussin' at each other. I explained that I would have no choice but to quit broadcasting if they kept at it.

I never did ask Joe what he said to each group, but it worked. I saw several of the fans look up toward my booth and they became quite civil. There were no more problems the rest of the season. You know, the power of radio is quite beautiful.

Broadcasting sporting events and handling my air shift wasn't all I did for WZKY. All four of our full-time guys had to contact every business or industry in the county and offer them the opportunity to see just HOW beautiful the 'power of radio' really was. I had some faithful merchants like Phillips' Clothing Store, Gables, Phillips Drug and First National Bank. Others included Alcoa, Yadkin Brick, Stanly Fixtures, Williams Oil, Young Manufacturing, E.J. Snyder & Company, and Rocky River Fish House, one of the most popular restaurants in the county.

As you probably surmise, we didn't sell advertising just because it was a part of our duties. We all got fifteen percent of the revenue for each spot we sold. That said, you know that sales was for my family's welfare too. It is still a lucrative part of a radio career today.

I remember my first sale at WZKY like it was yesterday. It was in March of 1968, my first full-time month, and was to Stanly Refrigeration. The contract was for fifty-five spots, and the total sale was $55.00. My commission was all of $8.25; life was good!! We referred to that rate as 'a dollar a holler.' You can't get that rate today .... anywhere! In my years there, spots were never more than $2.50.

Small town radio had a few perks too. The Suburban Radio Group owned WZKY, and the home office was in Belmont. The company owned nine other stations in Belmont, Concord, Greensboro and Valdese in North Carolina, along with Blacksburg, Christiansburg, and Hillsville, Virginia. Concord and Blacksburg had both AM and FM stations so, even though we were located in eight cities, we had ten stations. The company had trade-outs with various vacation locations. The trade would be our airtime for a discount on their hotel rooms. All of us could use trade-outs by paying just the 15% sales commission on the price of the vacation package. Phyllis and I could get a week in Florida for less than $50, or a weekend at Myrtle Beach or Six Flags for less than $20 if we economized.

One summer we took the kids to Florida for a week and stayed in one of the motels on the trade package. We saw a sign advertising Alligator Alley. The kids wanted to see the 'gators, so I pulled in and asked the lady in the ticket booth if I could speak to the owner. She was it. I offered to talk about the park on WZKY if she let us in for free, and promised to send her the tape of what was said. She agreed. My family had a great time and Alligator Alley got several days of free advertising in Stanly County.

BOB 1972

PHYLLIS 1972

We loved to go to Atlanta to see the Braves each summer. I found a hotel in the city that would trade. I called and made the reservations for the room and we asked John and Eula Cranford, our next-door neighbors, to go with us. They were like another set of parents since their oldest daughter was two years behind me in school. I drove our 1968 Ford Country Squire station wagon; this was in the pre-minivan and SUV days. We packed enough food for the two-day trip and put it on the picnic table on our patio with the clothes and other things to put in the car. John and Eula brought their things over as well, and we put everything in the car and headed for Atlanta.

Near Harrisburg, about 25 miles from Albemarle, we had a flat tire. We had to unload the back of the station wagon to get to the jack and spare tire. I was not a member of AAA. As we loaded everything back in after changing the tire, I noticed there was something missing... the food. In 1972 it was cheaper to drive back and get the food than it was to buy food on the trip. The boxes of groceries were on the picnic table, right where I left them, and no critters had bothered any of it.

We checked in at the Georgia Hotel and the desk clerk said we still owed the state tax. It came to 74 cents. John magnanimously said, "I'll take care of that." We took the elevator up to our room on the 18th floor. It was your basic railroad hotel room; two double beds, a dresser, a closet and bath. No frills like air conditioning. We kept the window open all night and the constant blare of car horns kept us awake most of the night. Several times when a horn would blow, Eula would holler out, "I'll be right down." We did have a lot of fun. We didn't have a lot of money to spare, but we used what we did have frugally. Thank Heavens for trade-outs and complimentary tickets. Had it not been for comps, we would have never seen the sights and events that we did.

It was because of these things and a good friend that we were able to purchase our first home. We had been renting a five-room duplex since we moved back to Albemarle from Dillon in 1967. Two years later we moved our church membership from Canton Baptist to Second Street Presbyterian Church. The reason for this move was simply Ruby Still. 'Miss Ruby' owned the Little Red Schoolhouse. We enrolled Paula and Bobbi there when they were four and two because Phyllis had gone to work at Wiscassett Hosiery Mill, and then to Federal Pacific Electric.

'Miss Ruby' invited them to come to Second Street for Vacation Bible School that summer and they had a wonderful time and learned so much, because she was their teacher there too. We visited several Sundays and decided this was the church for us. Not only was 'Miss Ruby' the kids' kindergarten and Sunday School teacher, she was a family friend. She began the Little Red Schoolhouse in the late forties, and influenced several generations of children. That influence continues today under the direction of her daughter, Starr.

I knew a lot of the members there, one being a sales account of mine from the radio station. A.I. 'Ike' Napier was the owner of Shoe Town. His wife ran the store most of the time because 'Ike' was a rural mail carrier. He told me on one particular sales call that they were moving just outside the city limits and wanted to sell their house on West Park Avenue. He said, "Why don't you and Phyllis buy it?" When he told me the price, I knew it was reasonable. Phyllis and I went to see it and we both loved it. It was a quite neighborhood on a dead-end street a half block from West Albemarle Elementary School. That's where the girls would eventually go, and Phyllis would eventually become a teacher's assistant and bus driver. She had driven a school bus route during her junior and senior years at Millingport.

'Ike' said that he would need a $1,000 down payment. We didn't have it. He suggested borrowing it from our parents. We nixed that idea. As long as they lived, we NEVER borrowed or asked for money from either of them. 'Ike' offered 'Plan B' for us to consider. He would have a note drawn up and would finance the amount for four years and we could pay him $250 a year, plus interest. That's friendship. We signed the papers with him and with the bank for the mortgage and moved in.

The thing that I loved the most about radio was all of the sports broadcasting. The sport didn't matter. Sometimes I had to love it in spite of the situations. The best example of that was Forest Hills High School in Union County. The press box was the second level above the concession stand in the CORNER of the football field. To do the broadcast, I stood, straddling a hole in the floor. When I looked down, I saw the top of the popcorn popper. In all truth, I didn't do a football broadcast sitting down until I got to Duke. Most high school press boxes had nowhere to sit because they were small and there wouldn't have been any good sight lines to the field if you could.

It was a different story with baseball. All those games were played in the afternoon, and we broadcast them live. I carried a card table and folding chair, plus a mic and a small mixing board. My first baseball game was Albemarle at Asheboro. I was really excited to do a live broadcast and I had everything I needed, at least I thought I did. I found the radio location at McCrary Park and set up my gear. My broadcast that afternoon was surely worthy of the Baseball Hall of Fame. After the game I headed back to Albemarle. I called the station on my two-way radio in the car to find out how it sounded.

"Where have you been?" Hillbilly John yelled from the studio.

I came back with, "What do you mean? I was here in Asheboro. Didn't you hear my broadcast?"

"Bob, no one heard your broadcast. There was nothing on the line from the telephone company. Did you order a line from the phone company?"

"What phone line? Nobody told me about any phone line."

Boy, did I mess up big time!! I really hated that my inexperience had cost the station revenue. My lack of technical knowledge had robbed our listeners of a chance to hear a fantastic piece of broadcast journalism.

Basketball was just as challenging from a press facility perspective.

BOB CALLS ALBEMARLE HIGH BASKETBALL 1/72

'BEARDED' BOB @ AHS STATESVILLE HIGH BASKETBALL 1973

Station promotions, especially in smaller markets, were always popular with everyone concerned. They brought additional revenue to the stations, they heightened interest for the listeners, and they gave the sponsors a new way to promote their businesses and hopefully get new customers into their establishments. Some were geared to auto dealers or mobile home dealers. At WZKY, we had a promotion that really got all of us fired up and involved in all aspects of it.

Probably every radio station in the country has used a 'bumper sticker' promotion at some time. Ours was just a slight variation of it. We sold sponsorships to businesses that had walk-in traffic. They bought a package of commercials to use at their discretion, and we listed them as a sticker distributor throughout the day on the air. These stickers had our call letters on them and the listeners had to put them on their car's back bumper. When one of us saw a sticker during a prescribed time period, we called the station on our two-way radio and the DJ put us on the air live.

Our announcement was something like, "I'm behind a red Chevy heading west on East Main Street. If the driver is listening, please pull over.I have a WZKY Prize Package for you." The package had all sorts of products from the sponsors. This was always our most popular promotion. There were hundreds of WZKY bumper stickers and it seemed like every car in Stanly County was advertising for us. Some people recognized our cars and would actually blow their horns at us to try and persuade us to select their car. We gave away only four or five packages a day for the promotion period.

Automobiles were not the only modes of transportation we saw the bumper stickers affixed to. I didn't fully realize how much fun the listeners were having with it until one afternoon at Optimist Park. During one commercial break during a game, I heard someone yelling to me down near the field. I looked down there, and saw a guy on a HORSE. On that horse's rear-end, big as life, was one of our bumper stickers. I could barely control my laughter as we came back to the game broadcast. Before the inning started, I announced" If the rider of a brown horse that is heading down the right field line at Optimist Park is listening, please pull over to receive your WZKY Prize Package." He was listening to a transistor radio and jumped off his horse, tied it to the fence, and ran to the booth to pick up his package. Again, the power of radio! We tweaked the bumper sticker promotion and brought it back every few years and it was always successful.

Things like these made towns like Albemarle memorable. They made working for a community radio station worth all the things we might not have had. But soon those days would be far behind.

I thought I would be leaving for a 'big' job in the spring of 1974. Wally Ausley of the N.C. State Radio Network called me just after the Wolfpack won the NCAA basketball title. He had taken over the play-by-play duties after the illness, and subsequent untimely death of the long-time 'Voice of the Wolfpack' Bill Jackson. Wally needed a 'color man' for football and knew that I had attended State. He asked if I would be interested, and I almost went through the phone line to tell him in person that I definitely would.

The procedure worked through their system and he called in early June to let me know that I was one of two finalists for the job. I knew that this was my big break. I was going to Raleigh. I was so confident that I purchased a red blazer to wear to the games. BAD DECISION. Ausley called again two weeks later and told me that the other candidate had been doing some part-time work at WPTF, and they wanted to give him a one-year trial. "If he doesn't work out, you'll get it next fall." I asked who the other candidate was and Wally told me his name was Garry Dornburg. Anyone who follows ACC sports knows the rest of that story. Garry was the color man for the State Network until his death in February, 1998.

Not getting the State job was a big disappointment to me. I then resigned myself to the fact that I wasn't going to get any more chances to move up in the radio industry. I was SO sure that Phyllis and I had a nice den with a fireplace built onto our home in Albemarle the next spring. Yes, 1975...the summer I got the job offer from WDNC.

For years, Wally and I would reminisce about that situation, and he would always tell me that he did me a big favor by not hiring me in '74. I had the play-by-play job at Duke nineteen months after he turned me down. Good decision...by Wally.

I had other duties at WZKY that kept my job anything BUT boring. I helped cover news at the station and by doing that I was exposed to all sorts of new experiences. Take the date April 6, 1968. Two days earlier in Memphis, James Earl Ray assassinated Dr. Martin Luther King, Jr. The nation was in mourning, and there were reports of anticipated violence throughout the country. The Stanly County Chapter of the NAACP announced that there would be a march in downtown Albemarle on Saturday afternoon to commemorate King's life.

I was to help news director Roger Smith with live coverage of the march. He was positioned at one end of the route and I was at the other. The county Sheriff was near my post and I sought him out to see if his department was expecting any problems. He said they were not, but would take care of anything that might arise. I asked if he had enough manpower in his department, combined with the local police force, to do it. He said there were 'back-ups' in place. I gave him a puzzled look and he pointed to several cars parked along the street. There were three to five men in each one. He didn't have to tell me what organization they belonged to. I recognized several of them, and knew of their association with a very old group. They didn't move a muscle the entire afternoon. The march went off just like it was supposed to.

We were close enough to Atlanta that we could drive down to see baseball and football games, and I could get interviews for my sportscasts. It was on one of these ventures in 1970, that I 'stumbled' upon a great interview.

I was in the Los Angeles Rams' locker room in Atlanta-Fulton County Stadium waiting to get an interview with QB Roman Gabriel. I hadn't seen Gabe since our days in West Raleigh. There was a huge crowd of writers, so I just waited on the periphery until they had finished. One writer moved back to let another one out, and kinda pushed me back. As I stepped back, I felt someone's foot under my heel. I turned to apologize and was face to face with Jim Nabors, aka Gomer Pyle.

I said, almost in one word, "Oh, excuse me, may I interview you?" He agreed, and I rolled tape, and started out with, "We're talking with Gomer Pyle, sometimes known as Jim Nabors." He chuckled at my nervousness, and did a great interview. Nabors was a huge Rams fan, and had traveled to Atlanta with the team and sang the National Anthem before the game.

When I finished the Gomer interview, the writers had finished with Roman, and we re-acquainted ourselves, and did the interview. He also recorded a promo for my sportscasts.

I had never really understood the attraction to NASCAR, but during my early years at WZKY, I learned how to appreciate it. All it took was my first visit to the pits. I was at Charlotte Motor Speedway covering time trials for the World 600 and interviewing the drivers. I interviewed the Allison Brothers, Wendell Scott, Richard Petty, David Pearson, Buddy Baker, Benny Parsons and actor and country singer Marty Robbins. While I was interviewing one of the drivers, someone started the engine of one of the racecars right beside me. When they cranked that engine, I thought it would jar the fillings right out of my teeth. I have loved NASCAR since that day.

BOB & NASCAR's BENNY PARSONS KIBBITZ IN 1996

NASCAR BUILDER LEONARD WOOD & BOB IN THE PITS @ CHARLOTTE MOTOR SPEEDWAY

I was NOT a hot-rodder in the late 50s and 60s after I got my first car. Shucks, a 1952 'Maypop' (Plymouth Mayflower Belvedere) wouldn't go fast enough to get a speeding ticket, much less win a drag race. I was not mechanically inclined, so I couldn't do anything to the engine to make it run faster. And, to top it off, I didn't WANT to go any faster. I always wondered what it was like to be strapped into one of those driver's seats and go around the track at speeds approaching 200mph. I never had THAT experience, but in 1977, the Atlantic Coast Conference football tour bus made a stop at the Speedway and I had the opportunity of riding with a youngster named Ricky Rudd or a wily veteran, Tim Flock. I made several laps with each at about 125 or 130mph. I told Flock that I had always wondered what it would be like to ride at 150. He kicked it up a notch on the next lap and the back straightaway was a blur. The posts in front of the stands looked like a picket fence. As he let off the gas going into Turn 3, Flock said, "well, you can tell your buddies that you've been over 150. We hit 153 just before I let off." I have a certificate signed by him to that effect.

In 1992, I was named North Carolina Sportscaster of the Year and received the plaque at the National Sportscasters and Sportswriters Association banquet in Salisbury. On Sunday night, Phyllis and I, along with all of the other winners and their spouses, were taken to a dinner at the Speedway Club at CMS, between Salisbury and Charlotte. A special guest was NASCAR driver Kyle Petty, Richard's son. He had wrecked at Martinsville earlier that afternoon, but flew down for the dinner because Coca-Cola was his sponsor and for the banquet as well.

It was announced that there would be 5 pace cars available for anyone who wanted to ride around the racetrack. Kyle would be driving one of them. Phyllis' eyes lit up. SHE was going to ride with Kyle and no one else! As luck, or persistence, would have it, we were the first to get in with Kyle. Phyllis was in the front seat with Petty and I climbed into the back with my video camera rolling. We started down pit road and Phyllis was talking to him all the way. Just as we got out onto the banking at the first turn, she asked Kyle if he knew who I was. He said that he just knew that I was a state winner. When she told him, Kyle turned all the way around and began telling me that he'd always been a Duke fan and had come to Youth Day at Duke football games almost his entire life. I thought Phyllis was going to have a stroke. She 'encouraged' him to watch the road because she didn't like the idea of taking out a guardrail at the top of the banking. He turned his body and eyes back to the front, but continued talking about Duke. The pace cars wouldn't do 150, but Kyle got all he could out of it to give Phyllis a thrilling ride.

That night Phyllis and I had dinner at the same table as two NSSA and Baseball Hall of Fame broadcasters, Ernie Harwell and Jack Brickhouse. I told Phyllis that I wished I had brought my tape recorder and just laid it on the table to record their stories. I didn't say a dozen words during the meal, as I was too enthralled with their adventures. Little did I know that fourteen years later I would get the opportunity to work with Ernie on his "Audio Scrapbook."

This time it WAS recorded. My long time friend, advertiser and mortgage guru, Gordon Miller, had an idea. He envisioned audio books with sports legends. He enlisted my help and our first target was Roxboro legend Enos "Country" Slaughter. I broached the subject with Enos and he loved it. He LOVED to talk about baseball. Unfortunately, Enos was diagnosed with cancer, and passed away before we could do the project.

Gordon grew up in Detroit and was a huge sports fan. In addition to his very successful mortgage business in Cary, he wanted to live his dream of being a sportscaster. He got that opportunity with a Raleigh station and one of his first guests was Ernie Harwell, the "Voice of the Tigers" for 42 years. He had grown up listening to Harwell on his transistor radio. From that interview came the idea of an audio book with Harwell. Miller called me one afternoon and announced, "you're doing an audio book with Ernie Harwell." It caught me a bit off guard, but I agreed and started reading as much as I could about the legend, since I would be the host of the book.

I flew to Detroit for the first recording session. We went to the studio around noon and I was 're-introduced' to Ernie. We had decided that it would not be a 'Bob interviews Ernie' CD. It would be a 'two guys, sitting on a couch, talking baseball' CD. Ernie and I sat down in the recording studio for what we thought would be a get-acquainted session. They rolled tape and we began talking. I know there was a concern about our two personalities meshing for this project.

After about a half hour, I sneaked a peek through the glass at Gordon, Ernie's agent and the two engineers to see what their reaction might be. I was VERY pleased to see smiles and nods at what they were hearing. An hour later, we took a break and everyone was gushing over how at ease we were with each other. More importantly, Ernie was happy. He was so easy to work with. No ego, no feelings of remorse over agreeing to the project. It was a very easy three weeks. We worked a half day for five days over the three week span and I went to a radio studio in Raleigh the following week for a couple of 'clean-ups' on my part. The book was a hit and Ernie was featured on numerous talk shows, game broadcasts, and newspaper and magazine articles. I even got in on a few.

We kept in touch by phone several times a year until he passed away May 4, 2010, at age 91. Ernie Harwell was a class act, a perfect gentleman, great baseball resource, a Baseball Hall of Famer, and...... a friend.

I was totally fascinated by the way the field for NASCAR races was set. In the 60s and 70s there were three days of qualifying starting on Thursday with the first twenty cars qualifying on lap times. Friday the next twenty qualified, and then on Saturday, there was a 25-lap race for those who didn't make the field through the time trials, and the top four finishers would be the last four in the field of 44. The 600 was run on Sunday. I was amazed at all that went in to putting on the event; the hundreds of hours and multitudes of people it took to get everyone to the starting line.

I even have NASCAR play-by-play experience, if you want to call it that. Ray Cook was Sports Director at our station in Concord, WPEG. He was covering time trials too, and we decided to join forcesand supply live reports on qualifying to our ten stations. We did two reports every hour on Thursday and Friday, and decided to broadcast the entire qualifying race for the final four spots on Saturday. The radio coverage in those days was nothing like it is today and there was no national network. I interviewed all the great names in NASCAR at that time from Richard Petty to David Pearson to Bobby Allison to 'Chargin' Charlie Glotzback.

BOB INTERVIEWS CHARLIE GLOTZBACK 1973 CHARLOTTE

We set up our equipment in the press box and went at it. I found out quickly that you needed more than two days of qualifying reports to be ready to broadcast a race, even with only 10 or 12 cars in it. The only thing I remember from that race is a first-lap wreck.

When speaking at civic and sports clubs, I always say, "To steal a phrase from the great Lou Gehrig, today, I am the luckiest man on the face of the earth. One of the reasons is because I get to work with, meet and learn from some of the most brilliant coaching minds in the history of sports." I met one of the greatest in the early 70s in Buies Creek, N.C. Camels coach Fred McCall and Wake Forest coach 'Bones' McKinney started the Campbell Basketball Camp in 1956. It was such a success that word rapidly spread, and when big names like Bob Cousy and John Wooden began coming in as counselors and speakers, the number jumped to 1,500 during the two one-week sessions.

McKinney said, "People were hungry for basketball then, and we were the first camp – all of the others came after us. And hey, we were cheap." For $25, young stars could learn basketball from the best.

In the early 70s, I heard about their media day that invited all writers and broadcasters to come in and interview the coaches and players who were there. I sent in my form and prepared questions for the coaches and players that I wanted to interview on note cards. I was as nervous as a 'long-tailed cat in a room full of rocking chairs' when it came my time to interview the 'Wizard of Westwood.'

After asking a couple of my 'prepared' questions, Coach Wooden said, "Do you mind if I offer you a little advice?"

I gulped. Had I said something wrong? I said, "No, I'd appreciate anything."

He gave me a piece of advice that I have used for nearly 40 years.

"Always have an idea of what you want to ask your interviewee, but don't be so concerned with your note cards. Listen to what the person is saying. They might say something that will lead you to more information than you were anticipating. You might uncover something big."

BOB AND LEGENDARY UCLA COACH JOHN WOODEN

The most successful basketball coach in the country was offering his help to a young sportscaster from a 250-watt radio station in a town of 12,500 people! WOW!

I interviewed Coach Wooden several years at the Campbell Camp. When the Wooden Award was established in 1977, I was already broadcasting Duke games, and was asked to be a voter in the selection of the men's National Player-of-the-Year, and a ten-man All-America team. The picture on the previous page of Coach and me was taken in the late 70s.

At the 1986 Final Four in Dallas, Coach K introduced me to another legendary coach, Henry Iba. Many young coaches sat at Iba's feet, learning his methodical, ball-controlling philosophy. Coach Iba was known as 'the Iron Duke of Defense,' and he always wanted things done perfectly. He drew a large crowd at the practice day in Dallas, and I was honored to just listen and observe.

In December 2000, Duke traveled to Oakland to play Stanford in the Newell Classic. The event is named for the great instructional coach, Pete Newell, and I had a chance to talk with him for several minutes after the game. He is one of only three coaches to win NCAA, NIT and Olympic titles. Coach Newell ran the premier 'big-man' summer camp in the country until his death in 2008.

It was at WZKY that my golf interest bloomed. The Kemper Open was one of the nation's top PGA tournaments during its run. Arnold Palmer won the first championship at the Pleasant Valley Country Club in Sutton, Mass. in 1968. The next year, and for ten straight years, the Quail Hollow Country Club in south Charlotte hosted the event, and I covered it all ten years. It afforded me the opportunity to meet and interview the greats, the near-greats, and the 'rabbits' of professional golf. Arnold Palmer, Jack Nicklaus, Gary Player, and Raymond Floyd were among the luminaries I had on my twice-hourly five-minute reports each Thursday through Sunday afternoon.

The first few years I did the reports for just WZKY. Later, I added other Suburban-owned stations in Concord, Belmont, and Valdese. The sports director at WPEG, Ray Cook, had a friend, who had played Armed Forces baseball with Joe DiMaggio. Joe was a celebrity in the Kemper Pro-Am in 1970, and was kind enough to pose for a picture with us. When he came to the Duke Children's Classic in the mid-eighties, I carried the picture with me one day and he autographed it for me.

Probably the best thing about covering the Kemper Open was, all of my reporting could be done from the comfort of the media tent. There, out of the weather, I would prepare twelve different reports a day. They ran at the top and bottom of the hour from noon until 6pm. The leaders would come to the tent for their interviews and I pulled 20-30 second bites to use on air.

BOB, RAY COOK, JOE DIMAGGIO
1970 KEMPER OPEN CHARLOTTE

I don't remember any incidents of golfers not being cordial and willing to give me an interview, no matter how they had played. Gary Player was the best whether he played well or not. Larry Hinson, Chi Chi Rodriguez and Tom Weiskopf were my favorites too. Weiskopf could be "Temperamental Tom" on the course, but he was always very courteous and funny in our interviews.

CHAPTER SIX

The 'Best Of WZKY'

In 1972, I had the opportunity to free-lance some college basketball games for WBT radio in Charlotte. They had decided to augment their regular schedule of UNC broadcasts with Davidson and UNC-Charlotte. I had the opportunity of broadcasting one game for the Wildcats and two games for the 49ers. The first trip was to Huntington, West Virginia for the UNCC - Marshall contest. I met the team at Douglas Airport in Charlotte and had an evening flight through Pittsburgh to Huntington on Alleghany Airlines. This flight was just over 15 months after the tragic crash of the charter flight that claimed the lives of the entire Marshall football team, but that event was still on the minds of a lot of those passengers that night.

The Thundering Herd had played in Greenville, NC on a November 14th Saturday night in 1970, and were headed home. The Huntington airport is situated on the only flat spot in the area. Builders just cut off the top of a mountain and put in a runway. The Marshall charter flight came in too low, in a driving rainstorm, and hit the side of the mountain. Even though it had been more than a year, there were still remembrances of that event as we headed toward Huntington. It had begun to rain just after we took off and it grew worse as we neared the airport. As we made our descent through a full-blown thunderstorm, the plane was bouncing around quite a lot. There wasn't a single sound except the roar of the engines and the rain slapping against our windows. I found out that night the true meaning of the term, "white-knuckle time." When the wheels touched the runway there was a loud cheer from every passenger. A lot of prayers had been answered.

My other UNC-C game was in the Charlotte Coliseum. I did the color with the late Jim Thacker as the 49ers played the "Golden Flashes" of Kent State.

The Davidson broadcast was a road game in Greenville, N.C. against East Carolina. If you've never flown in a DC-3, you've never lived. We flew Southern Airways down on the afternoon of the game, and back that same night. The head coach for Davidson was a former player, Terry Holland. Little did either of us know that we would interact many, many times before our careers would be over. Terry went to Virginia as head coach 17 months before I came to Durham. He won 326 games in Charlottesville before his Alma Mater called him to be Director of Athletics in 1990. Five years later, he was back in Charlottesville as Athletic Director for the Cavaliers, a post he held until 2004. I don't think he flew a Southern DC-3 down there, but he is at East Carolina, at this writing, as the Pirates' Athletic Director. In 2002, I had the pleasure of inducting the Clinton native into the North Carolina Sports Hall of Fame.

While I was at WZKY, professional basketball came to North Carolina. The Houston Mavericks moved from Texas and became the Carolina Cougars, a regional franchise. They played half of their games in the Greensboro Coliseum, a third in the Charlotte Coliseum and the other eight in Dorton Arena in Raleigh. In the five years they were in Charlotte, I only missed three games because of conflicts with high school games.

I had a seat on press row to watch the game, interviewed the coaches and players afterward and played parts of the interviews in my sportscasts the next day. I always got three comps, in addition to my press pass, and Phyllis and the girls went with me. If they couldn't go during the week, I would take Daddy and John Cranford. It was an exciting time for all of us.

'Bones' McKinney was their first coach after relocation. He led the team from 1969 through 1971. It was here that I first met "Bones." I had watched his Wake Forest teams play in Reynolds Coliseum when I was a student at State. He was a great high school, college and professional basketball player, a successful college and pro coach, and a television analyst. He was a public relations representative for a state wide business and a widely acclaimed after-dinner speaker, not to mention, an ordained Baptist minister. If you look at the first letters of his three names, you get the word HAM. That was perfect for him. He was FUNNY!

Early in his life, he earned the nickname "Bones." Why? He was eventually 6'6" tall and rather gangly; a 'sack of bones.' His family moved to Durham and he was the star of the famed Durham High School teams that won state championships and even beat the Duke freshman team. He played basketball at N.C. State for two years before entering the military in World War II. When he came back from service, he enrolled at UNC, where he earned his degree.

After his retirement from coaching, we saw each other much more because he moved to Willow Springs, just south of Raleigh. We played in a lot of charity golf tournaments. He invited me to play in his tournament at Keith Hills at Campbell University, and he played in my tournament its' entire five-year run. The last year I had mine was 1997, and it was in mid-April, right after basketball season. About a week before the event, "Bones" called me and said that he didn't think he could make the

BOB, BONES McKINNEY & ENOS SLAUGHTER 4/97

tournament. His cancer was taking its toll and he felt he didn't have the strength to play 18 holes. He said he would really miss getting to see his friends. I had an idea. I asked him to be the 'Celebrity Putter' and just be on the 18th hole and putt with every group and he loved that idea.

"Bones" had a ball, reminiscing with old friends, and telling stories to all. It was his last public appearance. He went into the hospital later that week, and died May 16th. "Bones" gave me some great advice for later life. He said, "Bob, if you drop something, when you bend down to pick it up, look around and see if there's anything else you can do while you're there." That was Horace Albert McKinney. He always looked around to see if there was anything else he could do while he was down here.

The Cougars were full of promotions. One that I was invited to participate in was a 'Bastravaganzaballathon." Simply put, a triple-header. In the 4:30 game two Charlotte high school teams played. About 6:45, there was a 'game' between a group of NASCAR drivers and a group of area media who covered the Cougars. The Cougars played the 8pm game with the Miami Floridians. Being only 40 miles from Charlotte and given my loyalty to promoting the team, I was asked to play for the media team. We practiced a couple of times in the weeks prior to the game and I played about a third of the game.

My two most memorable happenings were a breakaway for a lay- up attempt and guarding Buddy Baker. I was 'streaking' down the court, about to make a basket and all of a sudden David Pearson caught me, and fouled me. He had caught me so fast, I looked around to see where his #21 Wood Brothers Mercury was. I made the free throws for my only two points of the game.

BOB'S FREE THROWS

I was defending the 6'4" Baker and he decided to bring the ball up the floor instead of posting me down low. I backed off as he stopped behind the three-point line and just stood there. He faked and I said, "Go ahead and shoot." He did. And he made it!!! Those were the only points he had while I guarded him.

Covering the Cougars also almost got me thrown out of a game. In 1970, their first year in North Carolina, they qualified for the playoffs and lost the first two games to the Pacers in Indianapolis. The series moved to North Carolina and I drove to Raleigh to cover a game. Roger Brown was a great player for the Pacers, but I was of the opinion that he shuffled his feet a lot before shooting. I was fuming at my press row seat and at one point fumed a little to loud. It was something like, "Come on Earl, he's walking every time he touches the ball." Veteran referee Earl Strom started back peddling up the floor and pointed at me and yelled, "One more word outta you and I'll throw you outta here." I believed him.

When I was at N.C. State in the early sixties, the ACC had a crew of characters refereeing basketball games. Dr. Phil Fox, Charlie Eckman, Lou Eisenstein, Red Mihalik, Lenny Wirtz, Steve Honzo, Otis Almond, and the Mills twins, Jim and Joe.

Probably THE most colorful was Lou Bello. He began officiating when he was a student at Duke, and worked the ACC and other conferences from 1946 until 1971. 'Footsie' Knight booked him to work YMCA games in Durham while Looooo was at Duke.

Did I say colorful? I'm talking about getting tangled up in a UNC cheerleader's feet along the baseline, tripping, and falling into her lap, leaning over and kissing her cheek, jumping up and following the action to the other end of the floor, colorful.

He was officiating the State-Carolina freshman game played in Fayetteville one night, and was the lead official on a fast break. The shooter was fouled and Lou, racing at full speed to stay in front of the play, blew his whistle. He had forgotten that at that end of the court was a stage, about three feet off the floor, where the scorer's table was. When Lou realized he couldn't stop, he leaped up to the stage, grabbed the PA mic and said, "Ladies and gentlemen, that foul was on #23 in the white. #14 in the blue will shoot TWOOOOOOOOOO."

He officiated in the SEC quite a bit as well. Every time he worked an LSU game when 'Pistol' Pete Maravich was playing, Lou would see Pete in warm-ups and put his arm around Maravich's shoulder and say,

"Pete, every time you shoot with a player near you, I'm gonna blow my whistle. If you make the basket, you'll get a free throw. If you miss the basket, you'll get two free throws." Lou always said that's why Pete led the nation in scoring.

"Pistol Pete" Maravich changed college basketball. He learned at a very young age that he could do things with a basketball that other players were not capable of doing in the 1960s and 70s. Maravich starred at LSU, and for three NBA teams. He is STILL the all-time leading scorer in NCAA Division I with 3,667 points. He averaged 44.2 points per game without the benefit of the three-point shot. At the time Pete played at LSU, NCAA rules prohibited players from playing on the varsity team as freshmen. He was one of the greatest players in college basketball history who never played in the NCAA tournament.

During the 1977-78 season, an injury started Pete on a downward spiral into alcoholism and that began the decline of his career. After he left basketball in 1980, Maravich became a recluse for two years. He said he was searching "for life."

Pete was inducted into the Basketball Hall of Fame in 1987. At 39, he was one of the youngest players ever to be inducted. I had the opportunity to spend some time with Pete in the late 80s, when he came to Duke to speak at Youth Day prior to a football game. I introduced him that day and his testimony kept the crowd of nearly 17,000 spellbound. He told of the booze, drugs, women and all of his problems. The statement I'll always remember him making was, "I want to be remembered as a Christian, a person that serves Him to the utmost. Not as a basketball player."

On January 5, 1988, Pete collapsed and died, at age 40, of a heart attack while playing in a pickup basketball game in a church gym in Pasadena, CA. According to Focus on the Family head James Dobson, Maravich's last words were, "I feel great."

Youth day at Duke is very special. Athletic Director Carl James began the annual event in the fall of 1974 in Duke Chapel. Several years later it was moved to Wallace Wade Stadium. It happens on a fall Saturday afternoon before a home football game, and each year, the promotions department secures a great speaker who has an inspirational message. Youth groups and church groups from all over the state are invited to come for the program and the game on one special ticket. Crowds have numbered into the thousands and I had the honor of emceeing the program from 1980 until 2006.

Speakers have run the gamut, but have been mostly sports figures. The likes of Maravich and Julius 'Dr. J' Erving from basketball, football's Roger Staubach, Tom Landry, Joe Theismann, and Darrell Green, NASCAR's Ernie Irvan and Bobby Hillin, Jr., baseball's Brett Butler and "The Rookie' Jim Morris, and Vietnam Silver and Bronze Star honoree Clebe McClary.

Back to Lou Bello. His banter with coaches was legendary, especially with 'Bones' McKinney. One night when Lou was working a Wake game, 'Bones' got so upset that he kicked one of his loafers onto the floor and went out to retrieve it. Lou turned and saw him in the court and blew his whistle. Lou told him, "Coach. for every step it takes you to get off this floor, it's a technical foul." 'Bones' called two of his biggest players out onto the court. They picked up 'Bones' and carried him off the floor. Lou couldn't do anything but grin at him.

Lou not only refereed basketball but football, and baseball too. In his very first high school game as a referee, the home team was losing, 7-0, but scored in the final seconds to make the score 7-6. The kicker came on and sent the extra point kick up for the apparent tie, but Lou waived it 'no good.' After the final gun, the losing coach walked off the field near Lou, and said to him, "Sir, I never question an official's call in a game, but I have to say that, from where I was standing, the ball went right between the uprights."

"Yes sir, it did," replied Lou.

"But why did you call it no good?" "Coach, it was too high. Too high."

Legendary also described the long-time football coach and athletic director at Clemson, Frank Howard. Bello was working one of his earlier games as the Referee in a Clemson-Presbyterian game in Tigertown. The Pale Hose had the Tigers 6-0 with time running out in the game.

Clemson called timeout. And Lou walked over to Coach Howard to ask what he should do with the game ball at the end of the game. Howard wheeled around and said, "You dumb #%@**%, you can stick it up your butt."Lou said, "Coach, is it okay if I let the air out of it first?"

I first met Lou in 1971 when the Carolina Cougars came to the area. Former Pfeiffer basketball coach Francis Essic brought Lou to WZKY on a promotional visit. Lou was working with the team in the Raleigh office and he did a thirty-minute interview for the station.

When I came to WDNC, Lou was Sports Director at Channel 28 in Durham. Actually it was a two-man news operation with Lou running camera while Tony Riggsbee did the newscast and weather. When Lou did his sportscast, Tony ran camera. It was a 'shoe-string' operation, but Lou kept it lively, blowing his referee's whistle when there was a big story coming up. In the final year of Lou's career there, the owner cancelled the Associated Press News service, leaving Lou with no way to get the day's sports news. He asked for my help and for about a year, he would call me at WDNC and I would read the AP sports headlines and any other bits of local information I had, and Lou would re-write it for his sportscast.

Lou became a good friend of our entire family. When Bobbi was married at Duke Chapel, we had a boutonnière for Lou and seated him with our family. He cried. When Bobbi was expecting Tripp, Lou kept saying that he wanted to know when she went to the hospital. Phyllis had told him, and others, that we were going to order pizza to the waiting room and have a party. On the night that she went to the hospital I called Lou, but he was out, so I left a message on his answering machine. About 11pm, the elevator door opened and out popped Lou.

"Am I late? Did she have the baby?"

"No Lou, you are on time."

He stayed with us until about 2am, and then called me off to the side and told me that his medications were wearing off and he needed to go home. He told me to call him as soon as the baby came, no matter what time it was. He then did something unusual. He reached out to shake my hand. Usually he hugged me, and everyone else, for that matter.

I felt something in my palm, and looked down to find a $100 bill. He said, "Use this to start a college fund for the baby." Lou would be so proud of Tripp today. He enrolled at Campbell University in August of 2009 on a Presidential Scholarship. He made Dean's List both semesters his freshman year. His mom earned that same scholarship in 1998.

Lou was diagnosed with cancer and died in 1991. I cried. I visited him in the Veteran's Administration Hospital here in Durham three or four times a week until he passed away. Lou had fought in World War II and was captured and spent about eighteen months in a German prison camp. He lived in mortal fear that the Germans would find out that, even though his last name was Italian, his mother was Jewish.

The January after Lou's death, I saw his son Tommy at the Raleigh Hot Stove League banquet. He asked me not to leave until he could give me something after the program. When it was over and most of the people had left, Tommy handed me a box. I opened it and found a couple of pictures of Lou and me at the 1985 Rose Bowl Game. He had accompanied the Iron Dukes to Los Angeles for a basketball tournament at Southern Cal. Also, there was one of Lou's striped shirts, and one of his whistles. They hang in a special place in our home.

Ralph Gardner wasn't the station manager for the full eight years I was at WZKY. Things had gotten a bit rocky at the station and it all came to a head one Friday afternoon. The owner of Suburban Radio Group, Bob Hilker, and Vice President Bill Rollins came to the station and had a long meeting with Ralph. The full staff was sitting in the lobby, nervously waiting to find out what was going to happen. After a while, Mr. Hilker came out and told us that Ralph was being relieved of his duties. That was a shock to us. We fully believed that Ralph was doing a good job. When Mr. Hilker said Ralph would be leaving immediately, Hillbilly John said, "Well, I'm leaving too." Bill Rollins made a statement that I thought was not true, and I laughed out loud.

"Harris, you're fired!" he roared. That was the only time I've EVER been fired in my life.

Foy then quit too. Roger Smith looked around, and said, "Well, if you're all going, I am not staying by myself."

With that, we all started gathering up our personal possessions and putting them in our cars. Ralph had already finished loading his and had left.

We were all without a job at this point but Mr. Hilker asked all of us to come into the manager's office. He showed us letters and explained the situation from the company's perspective. Then he looked at me and said, "How do you feel now?"

"I think I'm going to be sick," I replied.

He looked at all of us and said, "I wish I had the loyalty of my staff in Belmont that you have to Ralph, mislaid as it might be. I want to talk with each one of you individually before you leave." He was going to try to keep us as employees.

When it was my turn, Bob asked if I thought I could continue under a new manager. I told him I thought I had been fired. He then chastised Rollins in front of me for 'flying off the handle' and firing me in anger. Bill apologized, and I said I would stay.

Hillbilly John said he wanted to think about it over the weekend. That left no one to pull the sign-on shift for the next morning. I volunteered. Foy and Roger both agreed to stay. I left my things in the car and headed home. I knew Phyllis would be worried because I was never THIS late coming home.

John recanted his resignation and we were back to some semblance of normalcy on Monday. Richard Norwood moved down from Concord to be the new manager. We all knew and liked him and had a great relationship. Bob Hilker was relieved that we all stayed. As he sat in the office that Friday evening, he chuckled and told us he was wondering how he was going to keep the station on the air with two weekend part-timers as his ONLY employees!

Where does loyalty come from? My guess is that it could be inborn, or it could be acquired from early experiences. I'm not sure where mine came from. Maybe it was a combination of the two. Given the time period of my youth, loyalty was a good thing. Loyalty to your family. Loyalty to your church. Loyalty to your neighbors. Loyalty to your employer. Loyalty to your country.

Daddy exhibited one of my earliest examples of loyalty. We had recently moved into our 'mill house' on Wilson Street in 1950, when a movement to unionize the employees started in the Efird Manufacturing Company. The longer it went on, the worse things got. The attempt divided departments within the mill, and divided families outside it. I remember two brothers who didn't speak to each other for years after the issue was settled. Daddy was adamantly against the entire union concept. He felt that it had been a necessary thing when unions began, but had long outlived its usefulness. He was very appreciative to the company for his job and showed it by working against unionization.

On the evening of the vote, the entire town was concerned that there might be violence, no matter what the results of the vote. Daddy was selected to be an observer of the count, so he was at the mill until everything was official. The counting continued after sundown. All of a sudden, we heard a sound most of us had never heard. It was a loud horn blaring continuously for about five minutes. It scared so many because they thought it was a call for help. It was once used to signal the beginning and ending of the workers' shifts, and to signal twelve-noon, but it had been silent for years. We saw Daddy running toward the house, shouting to all the neighbors, "We won, we won, we won." The union had been handily defeated and the company was celebrating with the horn.

Daddy never wavered in his support for management, even after this event. He had a job as long as he wanted it. Loyalty has taken a backseat to so many other things today. Some employers have no loyalty to their employees and many employees have no loyalty to their jobs. Loyalty (read that 'patriotism') to our country has slipped tremendously, but not in THIS house.

For a couple of years before I joined the Blue Devils on the air, I did the play-by-play for Pfeiffer College in Misenheimer, N.C. I called a few of their basketball and baseball games as an addition to our schedule of the local high schools' games. It may not have been Division 1, but it was great competition. I learned a lot of baseball strategy from the veteran coach of the Falcons, Joe Ferebee. He not only coached at Pfeiffer, but in the summers, he guided the Rowan County American Legion baseball team to great accomplishments. In 2002, I had the honor of inducting Coach Ferebee into the North Carolina Sports Hall of Fame.

I also learned more basketball from Francis Essic and Tom Childress. I had a Saturday morning interview show with each of them during their tenures in Misenheimer.

During one particular ten-day stretch in the early 70s, I broadcast a combined 14 baseball games for Pfeiffer and the high schools. That included four double headers. I also had the opportunity to broadcast a game involving my alma mater when the Wolfpack came to Pfeiffer in 1974 with a team that included newly crowned NCAA Basketball Championship team members Monte Towe and Tim Stoddard.

Covering a baseball game at South Stanly High School was a unique experience at their home field in the early 70s. It was different because there was no fence in the outfield. If a ball was hit between two outfielders, it would roll until one of them got to it, and the batter would have 'all he could get.' This field gave me one of my most memorable, albeit, embarrassing calls of my entire career.

Late one March afternoon, I was broadcasting an extremely close game there, when a South Stanly player rocketed one into the gap between left and centerfield. With no fence, the ball just kept on bouncing. The center fielder finally ran it down near the school building. I knew when it was hit, that it was probably a home run. As the player took off for first, I took a deep breath, so I could bring him around the bases in grand style for our listeners. Given the time of year, flying bugs were quite common. You're getting ahead of me here. I swallowed the most vile-tasting bug you could imagine. By the time I finished gagging and coughing and trying to save what little dignity I had left, the player was seated in the dugout. It wasn't funny at all at the time. I have been known as the 'voice' of the Christian Laettner shot, since 1992. But, in some Stanly County circles, I'm still known as the guy who swallowed a bug on the radio at South Stanly.

Rivalries come at all levels of all sports. One of the bitterest rivalries is in Cabarrus County between the Concord High School Spiders and the Little Wonders of A. L. Brown High School in Kannapolis. During the 1958 football season, some Concord fans sneaked into the brand new stadium at Kannapolis, and poured rock salt on the field to spell-out 'CHS' Any agronomist will tell you that rock salt will kill grass in a few days. The evidence of the rock salt was not noticed immediately, but by the time the two played each other a week later, it was VERY evident. This incident sparked even more animosity, and during the game a fight broke out that emptied both stands. It took a lot of law enforcement a quite while to quell the skirmishes that kept breaking out.

In 1973, I worked a brief stint at our stations in Concord, WEGO-AM and WPEG-FM. I broadcast one of the most bizarre basketball games ever, and it was a result of that rivalry. The two had played in Kannapolis a month before I got there and several fights broke out on and off the floor. Instead of canceling the re-match, it was played at 4:00 in the afternoon instead of 7:30 in the evening. The School Superintendent would not allow any fans, parents, or anyone else to attend the game. The only people allowed to be at the game in the Concord gym were the teams, coaches, two scorekeepers, a clock operator, two referees, and me.

Also while working for WPEG-FM, I was required to run the board (man the controls) on Saturday afternoon. My main responsibility was to make sure that the Metropolitan Opera broadcast was on the air PERFECTLY. Yes, in the middle of an all country format, we carried the Met. A group of opera lovers from Charlotte paid a considerable sum to have the weekly show on the air live. If you think country music fans are fanatical, or Duke fans are obsessed, or Dale Jr fans are loyal, you ain't seen nothin' until you see an opera lover. I had a 'fuzzy' signal on my first day with this program and I tried to correct it, but nothing helped. On Monday morning, the station manager called me into his office and read me the 'riot act'. He showed me the stack of phone calls he had gotten in 36 hours and the comments that were made about the terrible quality of the broadcast. It was my fault! Let's just say I never let that happen again.

CHAPTER SEVEN
It's Time To Spread My Wings

WZKY was the quintessential small town radio station. It pounded out 250 watts of power and could be heard throughout Stanly County, but not much more. I really loved working and living in my hometown, but I wanted to spread my wings and see what I could do in a larger market. I suppose that almost every person who has tried radio and liked it, wanted, at one time or another, to 'test the waters in a deeper pond' and see what it is like to work at a larger radio station. We all knew that the financial rewards were greater.

On four or five occasions, I heard about opportunities in larger cities that I thought might be a fit for us. Every time I tried, I was rejected, then dejected. None of this kept me from trying again once a new avenue opened up. I knew deep down that I had the ability and desire necessary to be a success.

The old TV show, 'Candid Camera' always began with the line, "Just when you least expect it…." I joined the N. C. Association of Sports Broadcasters at its inception in the spring of 1968. This organization of radio and TV sportscasters helped stations to improve sports programming as a whole. Twice-a-year clinics were held to find ways to make our broadcasts better, and to raise sports sales and profits. NCASB began working with the North Carolina High School Athletics Association to bring down, and in some cases eliminate, broadcast rights fees for game broadcasts. We acted as a body for all stations and negotiated with telephone companies to set standard regulations and fees for phone lines which every station had to use to broadcast a live event.

As the secretary and treasurer of the Association, I drove to our board meeting in Raleigh in July of 1975. Howard Wilcox was there as the liaison from the N. C. Association of Broadcasters. We talked about sports possibilities at his station over lunch. He had recently moved to WDNC in Durham and told me that he couldn't afford a sportscaster at that time, but hoped to have one within twelve months. He told me to send him a tape of my work and a resume so when revenues increased sufficiently, he would have them.

I wasn't as diligent in my efforts to get that done after I got back to WZKY. I didn't think he would need my information so soon. I sent it to him on a Friday about a month later, but Howard called me on Monday before he received it. He told me he needed a salesperson right away, and had always hired salespeople from smaller markets because of their work ethic. The next day Howard and I met in Durham and his salary offer was $5,000 a year more than I was making. I told him I always talked things over about family matters with Phyllis. She agreed that it looked like a good situation. We never know where things will lead, but I had a great feeling about this one. HOW SWEET IT IS!!

On Labor Day, September 1, 1975, I began my Durham career at WDNC. Wilcox and I began talking about what my sales goals and station policies and such, when I got a bad case of nerves and quickly went to the men's room. Howard still hasn't let me forget it.

I made my temporary home in the Downtowner Motor Inn. Phyllis stayed in Albemarle and the kids continued at West Albemarle Elementary. I had to find a house that we could afford, and I did. She came up, looked at it, liked it, and we put the wheels in motion. I probably should have taken more time and looked at it more closely.

The house we found was in a nice neighborhood in northwest Durham. It was a split-level, just like were hoping to build in Albemarle. The owner was an insurance agent with the same company I had worked for in Albemarle. He had an option on another house and wanted to sell this one. He said we could move in and close at a later date. BAD choice.

On our first night in Durham we all slept on the floor because the furniture would not be there until the next day. We brought the necessary sheets, quilts, and pillows in the car and bedded down. I told Phyllis that night, "I don't know where this job is going, but please don't ever let me forget that I am just a cotton mill boy."

We were to close the house after twelve days. The night before the closing we found a problem that changed everything. Phyllis was washing clothes on the lower level and called me down there to help her move the washer. She thought a towel had fallen down behind it. I leaned the washer forward and she reached behind it, and screamed. It was definitely not a white towel. She pulled up a mushroom with a cap about eight inches across. The stalk was about two inches thick. I knew that if there was enough moisture to grow a mushroom that big, that quickly, we had a major problem that we wanted no part of.

So, under the house I went. This night started off badly and it quickly got worse. That whole area was cold and wet. A large part of the insulation had drooped and some was falling down. I saw where some of the floor had been replaced but the pile of old wood had been left there and had started to rot. I crawled out of that mess as fast as I could. I told Phyllis what I had found and she was very upset. I got the owner on the phone and told him about the problem, and that we were moving ASAP. Lady Luck shined down on us. One of my fellow salesmen at the station was had just moved and his house was for sale. We did a deal, closed on the loan and moved to Robbins Road in the eastern part of Durham County within two days.

It was shortly after we moved there that we decided to plant a garden, Phyllis and I thought it would help the expenditures for groceries if we had one to grow our own vegetables. She had grown up in the country and had gardens every year, and cows as well. Even though I grew up in the 'city' we always had a garden too. We knew the routine, but had never done it all ourselves. Oh, there were times after we were married when we'd plant a few tomato plants around the house, but never the serious undertaking of an entire garden.

We had a large lot on Robbins Road. It was 110' wide and 300' deep. The back yard was LARGE. We decided that the back half of the backyard would be perfect for our first garden. We had a neighbor bring his tractor over and 'break up' the 60'x60' plot. When I say 'break up' the plot, he ran over the ground several times with a turning plow that left some pretty big clods. He then changed to a disc and that cut those clods into manageable dirt. That condition then had to be worked into rows for planting. We didn't have a tiller. Daddy had given me his push plow after he quit 'farming.' For the uninformed, a push plow is two wooden handles that extend, in a 'vee', from the large metal wheel back and up to the person who will use it. Right behind the wheel is a plow blade. There are various sizes of blades, depending on what you need to do to the dirt.

The 'operator' must bear down on the handles while pushing forward to make the rows for planting the seeds. I was sweating bullets trying to get the blade to stay in the ground and make forward progress at the same time. Phyllis tried her hand at it, too. We had about the same success. She came up with a brilliant idea. Tie a rope on both sides of the wheel at the axle and have enough of a loop out front that 'one of us' could get inside the rope and pull while the other concentrated on bearing down on the handlebars to keep the blade in the ground. Naturally, I took the first turn in the rope, but she didn't have enough weight to keep the blade down. We switched places. That arrangement worked SO much better, as evidenced by the picture below.

We used that method until J.C. Penney's at South Square put four $179.00 tillers on sale for $99.00 one Friday evening. Phyllis and I went early and stood at two different entrances. When they opened the doors, we both RAN to the display. I ran up the escalator and Phyllis took the stairs and we managed to get one of the four tillers. We still have that tiller today and it still runs. Now we work a little flower garden with it and loan it to Bobbi and her children when they need to do little jobs around their house. It was the best $99.00 we ever spent. We still laid off those 13 rows with our push plow each year and kept the weeds down by that old plow. We still have that old plow too.... now hanging in a place of honor in our garage.

By the way, we had fresh corn, green beans, lima beans, potatoes, okra, squash, tomatoes, and every now and then, cantaloupes all through the summer until we stopped 'farming' about 10 years later. Our family picked the crops, shelled the peas and pealed the tomatoes together. Not only did we have fresh vegetables all summer, we shared our excess with our neighbors and we even canned vegetables and stocked our freezer with our 'garden' each year, which helped carry us through the winter months.

PHYLLIS PULLS THE PLOW 1980s

Phyllis has always jokingly told our neighbors and friends that "this picture is going to be the measuring stick to gauge any possible interest from any potential future wife, if or when the time arose. Bob should show them that picture and ask them if they were interested in pulling a plow and if they weren't, then he could move on to another lady." We have had many laughs about this small, but really positive and down-to-EARTH, activity in our family for years. Neighbors came over to watch her pull that plow every day or two and to watch how well we did it. Several of the men even wanted to implement this with their wives, but not one would accept their offer. We sure had a lot of fun and made a lot of great memories in those lean years.

When Bobbi was a seventh-grader at Neal Junior High, a teacher gave her class a project that called for them to find a pen pal somewhere in the world and write to them regularly. Bobbi chose another 13 year old who lived near Paris, France. They began corresponding in 1979, and continue to this day. Nathalie Sellier, like Bobbi, married and had two children. Her girls are both younger than Tripp and Meredith. In the summer of 2005, our five family members spent three weeks in Europe. One of the highlights of the vacation was the three days and two nights we spent in the Sellier home. Nathalie baked croissants each morning for our breakfasts. She and Laurent wanted to give us a Parisian tour of the 'City of Lights' and it wasn't the typical 'tourist' view. They knew the best sidewalk cafes and all the shops and unusual stores for us to enjoy. The best thing about that visit was that we found that the average French family is much like Americans. Nathalie said that they didn't think all Americans were just like a particular President and hoped we didn't think all French people were like Jacques Chirac. We agreed!!

BOBBI & NATHALIE SELLIER ON THE SEINE 6/05

OUR FAMILY & NATHALIE'S AT NOTRE DAME CATHEDRAL IN PARIS 6/05

Our sales manager at WDNC was a veteran of the sales game, Terry Bane. He not only was a fine salesman, but he knew how to transfer that knowledge to others. He molded us into a pretty good staff.

Terry went with me on my first sales call to Alexander Motors, the local Ford dealer. Bill Clough bought 100 spots at $4.80 each. $480.00 was certainly more impressive than my first sale in Albemarle.

That sale was just the beginning. On Wednesday I was informed that I would host a sports talk show that Sunday night. I would have help for the first couple of months from the Sports Editor of the Durham Herald, Art Chansky. 'Sports Comments' was a one-hour call-in show that covered all facets of sports. We got local sports celebrities and players from the Duke football and basketball teams as our guests. Mike Gminski and Jim Spanarkel were regulars during the basketball season. The first thing I noticed about the Duke players was how poised they were answering questions on the air.

The show was not just a Duke University show. We talked about all sports. I am really proud that the show had a hand in bringing minor league baseball, and the Bulls, back to the Durham. The Bulls hit it big in 1988 with the movie "Bull Durham." It was filmed at Durham Athletic Park where the Bulls actually played.

Even before the movie became a hit and showcased the team, the Bulls had a very colorful history. Sometime during the spring of 1978, 'Sports Comments' listeners began talking about minor league baseball in Durham, and many thought there would be enough interest to support a team again. Miles Wolfe, a local entrepreneur and baseball fan himself, came on the show several times and informed our listeners that he was trying to get an MLB affiliation agreement with the Atlanta Braves with the idea to bring the Bulls back to Durham. He asked for their support to get the Bulls playing again in the "Bull City." Homerun champ Hank Aaron began serious negotiations as the Braves' Director of Minor League affiliates, to help Miles and his group get a team here. He was in studio with me twice .

BOB INTERVIEWS HANK AARON IN ATLANTA 8/72

Our audience continued to grow and so did 'Sports Comments.' It then became a nightly call-in show and was not limited to sports. We brought in guests from all facets of the community. We were fortunate to have a great charity golf tournament, the Duke Children's Classic, in Durham and the event brought in sports and entertainment celebrities. I had comedian Buddy Hackett and pro golfer Bob Lunn in the studio for shows.

Probably, the most challenging interviews I did on that show were not sports related. One was with the widow of one of the 'Greensboro Four.' The four African-American college students at North Carolina

A&T in Greensboro were killed in riots around the desegregation of the Woolworth's lunch counter in 1960. This interviewee didn't want to focus on the importance of that event, she turned the one-hour interview into an anti-government tirade, and berated the United States for everything else. She obviously had an agenda and tried to dominate the show. Finally I had had enough. I told her that what she was spewing was nothing more than Communist propaganda. I asked her point-blank, "Are you now or have you ever been a member of the Communist Party?" I was not going to allow her to mouth this garbage without my objections. She refused to answer that question, even though I put it to her three different ways.

The Madelyn Murray O'Hare interview/debate was almost as caustic. O'Hare was the person who pushed so hard for removing prayer from our schools. It started out as an interview, but a few minutes in, she made fun of me because of my beliefs and it turned into a debate about the existence of God. That day, I saw the devil in person. I really believe that she was the worst person I have ever come in contact with. I hope that before she met God face-to-face, she changed her life and begged His forgiveness.

Things like that were not the norm. My usual guests were community and regional leaders. I interviewed parapsychology proponents, politicians, sports figures and entertainers that appeared at various Triangle venues. Singers Margaret Whiting and Julius La Rosa, along with The Addams Family's John Astin dropped by to promote their appearances.

In early '76, I was fortunate to meet Ronald Reagan at a news conference at the Raleigh-Durham Airport. He was hoping for the Republican nomination for President, and was on a series of meetings with media and supporters all over the country. After his opening comments Reagan answered questions and then greeted any people who wanted to talk with him. I might have been in the back of the line, but I got 4 or 5 minutes with him after all the others had moved on. Reagan won the N.C. primary and then the General Election that November. I met three other future, sitting or former Presidents of the United States. Several years later I got a quick handshake from Jimmy Carter in Winston-Salem.

WDNC was the flagship station for the Duke Radio Network, and I was hoping to get involved with the Duke athletic program and the Network. The thought of not broadcasting football games that fall was really eating at me. I missed it. I knew I didn't have a chance to broadcast the Duke games, but I was glad to be so close to the program.

The first week I was in Durham, I went to the Duke football press conference at Cameron Indoor Stadium. I also started going to their Monday night practices since I had nothing else to do, being alone in town. As is common practice, the University had an outside agency run their network for them. G.H. Johnston Company in New York City was Duke's rights holder. They paid Duke a rights fee to originate the football and basketball game broadcasts but the on air personnel were still hired by Duke. That first week, I gave Richard Giannini, the sports information director, a visit. I wanted him to know that I would help out in any way he needed me to that season. I volunteered to be a spotter or statistician, anything to stay close to the broadcasts.

The network was trying a novel idea that fall, a different guest color commentator for each game. It was a good thought, but it wasn't practical. There must be a relationship between the color man and the play-by-play man. Under this setup, there couldn't be any. The "Voice of the Blue Devils," Add Penfield, could never get comfortable with a different person each week. Richard said he could possibly get me a game later in the season. That's all I wanted to hear.

I had grown up listening to Addison Pierce Penfield, and he could paint a 'word picture' with the greatest. His brush was his descriptive delivery and his canvas was the airwaves. The way he wove those images still comes to mind when someone mentions his name. Before I ever saw it, I knew how Wallace Wade Stadium looked. Unfortunately, I'll never hear his eloquence again. I talked with Add on a Monday, April 26, 2010 about his upcoming golf tournament, and he passed away four nights later.

Penfield told me that it was Coach Wallace Wade that "set my life pattern" by asking, no, telling, him right before the season started that he wanted the Blue Devils football game against Virginia Tech at Greensboro

Memorial Stadium to be on the radio. That was 1938, and Wade had seen Penfield in several Duke plays and figured he'd be perfect for the job. Add had come to Durham from Meriden, Connecticut because of a high school teacher, and the fact that the tuition was $200 per year. The Duke Radio Network was born.

Add's broadcasting abilities were not limited to sports. He talked to me in later life about reporting on the Nuremberg War Trials on the Armed Forces Radio Network right after World War II. Add had enlisted and the Army picked up on his radio talents.

> *I was with the US Army Radio stationed in Frankfurt, Germany, and reported there just before the trials started. One of the first assignments I had was to go to Nuremberg with the commanding officer of that particular division of the network, the radio division. We went down for the opening of the trials. I believe it was November 29 or 30 of 1945. I was there and sat fifty or sixty feet from Herman Goehring on the first day of that trial. I remember the job I did that first day was to interview an American captain who was assigned to command the detail that took care of guarding Goehring all the time. And how Goehring ever got away with what he did to cheat the hangman, I don't know, because this guy, I thought, was pretty efficient. You know Goehring concealed a tablet of cyanide on him and took it right before they were scheduled to hang him, and they never got the pleasure of doing that. We wanted to do a broadcast of that, Bob. It's come up a couple of times lately, I think—should the executions be broadcast or televised. Tommy Phipps, who was a captain in my same office, and I actually sat down and wrote a script about the hanging of Herman Goehring. I never will forget the ending. Tommy wrote movie scripts later on when he came back to the States and had several of them on TV. Phipps had the whole thing ending with the sound of the trap door going "Blam!" and then complete silence. Then, "This is US Army Radio in Nuremberg, Germany. That was the end of it. It was very dramatic.*
>
> ***Reprinted from a Blue Devil Weekly interview I did with Add***

He came back to the Duke Network in 1952 after several jobs in Atlanta and New York. It was there that he broadcast Rochester Royals NBA games. All in all, Add had four stints with Duke until health issues forced him to retire in 1976. That 1975-76 season was an honor for me to work with him.

NC SPORTS HALL OF FAMERS, GEORGE WHITFIELD, ADD PENFIELD, CLYDE KING & BOB 5/06

Penfield did make a brief return to the air in 2000 in Asheboro, when Ron Bennett offered the mic to Add to broadcast part of an American Legion Baseball game. He became one of the few broadcasters to be on the air in EIGHT different decades. I listened to him on radio as a kid. I learned from him by observing as a 'young pup' broadcaster. I learned even more as his color man at Duke. He has been an inspiration, a source of knowledge, my mentor, and my FRIEND. I can't give any higher compliment. One of my finest career moments was inducting Add into the North Carolina Sports Hall of Fame in 2005. Add will always be the original "Voice of the Blue Devils."

I welcome the opportunity to express my appreciation and that of Regional Consolidated Services to Bob for his long-standing support of the agency's annual golf fundraiser, now known as the Add Penfield/ RCS Classic. He was here for the first one in 1993. He has appeared in and loaned his name to the event with generosity and enthusiasm that would be hard for anyone to duplicate.

JANICE SCARBOROUGH
Executive Director - Regional Consolidated Services

Here is another "HOW SWEET IT IS!!" moment. Richard Giannini offered me the guest color opportunity for the Duke-Clemson game, October 18th, in Wallace Wade Stadium. I was extremely excited, and busily prepared myself with all of the stats I could find and I went to all of the practices that week.

I was sitting next to a legend!! Even though I was very nervous, I knew I was where I wanted to be. Add helped me tremendously that afternoon. When the game broadcast was over my appetite was whetted. I did color on the ACC road game at Wake Forest, and the final two home games against N.C. State and UNC. When football season ended I didn't lose a beat, I swapped the ovate spheroid for a round ball and the green grass of the field for a hardwood court.

Duke Athletic Director Carl James asked me if I wanted continue on the Network as the 'color-man' for basketball that winter. It took me all of about three seconds to accept his offer. I didn't want him to have time to reconsider his offer and look for someone else. The job didn't pay all that much, but Carl did include three season tickets in the deal, and we've had those same three every year since 1976. Section 1, Row 0, seats 6, 8 and 10.

Duke's first basketball game of the 1975-1976 season was a home game and the Blue Devils defeated John Hopkins 103-72. I was really happy with that first broadcast. I got my feet wet and didn't embarrass myself. I did five home games, plus two games in the Big Four Tournament in Greensboro and the Holiday Doubleheaders in Raleigh before the team went on the road for three straight games. My job at WDNC kept me from traveling with the team.

Ah, the good ol' days of the ACC in the mid-seventies. The Big Four Tournament replaced the extremely popular Dixie Classic that had been held every year in Reynolds Coliseum in Raleigh. Duke, Carolina, Wake Forest, and N.C. State played a two-night tournament in Greensboro from 1971-81. It was stopped because one coach didn't like it due to the possibility of playing the other three schools four times in one season.

The Network broadcast all four games of the Big Four event. At the 1975 Tournament, Add was going to do the play-by-play and I was to do the color for the Duke games, and in the other two games, I would handle the play-by-play and Add would add color.

I got my BIG break at the microphone at Duke in that Big Four. In the mid-seventies, our setup was much, much less than today. Our broadcast equipment consisted of a small mixing board and two headset microphones. Our pre-game show was only 15-minutes long, so I could get to the arena an hour before airtime and I was OK, even if there was a problem. The gear was connected and working properly that night and I had all my things ready. The only thing not in place was Add.

With game time approaching, I was beginning to worry when Add's son, Cameron, came up to the front of the broadcast booth.

"Where's your Dad?" I asked.

"Bob, didn't anyone at the station tell you?"

"Tell me what?'

"Dad came down with the flu, and there is no way he can make it"

I didn't panic. I was a bit shaky because I had only prepared to do the play-by-play in the games that Duke didn't play in each night. I just had to quickly make some adjustments, which I did.

The game action wouldn't be a problem. It moved pretty quickly and I had been doing that for eight years. The 15-minute pre-game and ten minute post game were not that involved either. It was the halftime that I had to get lined up. Guests on the air during halftime were easy to find. Usually, there were newspaper writers who loved to be on the air, so I asked a couple of them to come over at intermission.

I was now the play-by-play announcer for all four games in those two nights, and Donnie Tuck, our student engineer was ready to add in some commentary when I needed to catch my breath. Donnie didn't have all that much to do during the game except give me countdowns at the end of timeouts so we wouldn't have 'dead air' surrounding them.The telephone company wherever we were rented us a 'dry pair' dedicated phone line that plugged in to the mixer. We used that method to send the broadcast directly to WDNC, where a board operator inserted the sponsors' commercials. The complete feed would then be sent via trunk line to AT&T in Durham and they processed the signal for distribution to the other stations on the Duke Radio Network.

Several others traveled with the football and basketball teams. One was the University photographer who filmed the games for the coaches. Thad Sparks filmed all Duke football and basketball games at that time. Thad was an outstanding videographer.

I distinctly remember a game that the football team played in City Stadium in Richmond, Va. The University of Richmond hosted Duke in the 'Tobacco Bowl' on October 13, 1979. It was "Red" Wilson's first season at Duke. This wasn't really a Bowl game, but a number of mid-season games held that designation around the country. It was pouring rain when we got to town Friday afternoon and it didn't let up. There was plastic draped around the back and sides of the 'press box' to keep the rain from pouring in. Thad's spot was beside me. It wasn't much of a game, and the number of fans was diminishing with every raindrop. The 3rd quarter ended, and I took a commercial break. I looked over at Thad and he was stuffing the equipment into the cases.

I said, "Thad, where are you going?"

"Shoot, the game's over. I'm getting wet."

"No it's not. That's the end of the 3rd."

"Heck, I'm not taking all this stuff back out and settin' it up again. I'm soaked. Nothing's gonna happen any how."

He was lucky. The only thing that did happen was the rain. Jimmy Wallace was Sparks' successor and we became good friends because he liked to 'hang out' with the radio crew on the road. All of us ate together the night before a game, or went looking for model trains for my

BOB 'DRIVES' SUGAR CANE TRAIN ON MAUI 11/97

layout and even rode Maui's "Sugar Cane Train" from the whaling town of Lahaina to the resorts of Kaanapali.

Jimmy loved eating with the broadcasting crew because he knew I'd find some good food.

We played in Indianapolis in the Wooden Classic, and, as usual, ate at St. Elmo Steakhouse because of their Prime Rib Theirs is among the best I've ever eaten. John Brockwell, our engineer, Jim and I headed to St. Elmo for the 'Prime' and a shrimp cocktail.

The waiter brought out the shrimp first, and because we were starved, I forgot that it was Jim's first time at St. Elmo. I didn't sound the fire alarm for the horse-radish in the cocktail sauce. He dipped his first shrimp in the sauce and took a big bite. He didn't chew. His eyes got really big and started watering. I could have sworn that smoke was coming out of his nose and ears. John saw it the same time I did and said, "Bob, you forgot to tell the Governor how hot the cocktail is!" John gave Wallace the nickname of 'Governor' referring to the former Alabama governor of the same last name.

BOB & JIM WALLACE @ LEWIS & CLARK'S FORT 12/01

Jim gulped down a whole glass of ice water and put out the fire. He loved his horseradish, but he used very little for the rest of the meal. Henceforth, and forever more, he always asks me if there are any surprises he needs to know about when eating at a new restaurant.

I believe that Mike Krzyzewski was the last coach in the NCAA to stop filming his games and practices. 'The Governor' is sorely missed on road trips. Jim snapped many of the photographs that are spread out on the pages of his book. Like Add Penfield, Jim Wallace is an artist. He has a knack for getting just the right angle on a candid shot, and just the right 'tilt of the head' on the posed ones. We finally got him on the other side of the lens on a December, 2001 visit to Portland, Oregon.

January of 1976 found me in the play-by-play chair again at the

Wake Forest game in Winston-Salem. Add was at the Raleigh Hot Stove League banquet receiving the Broadcaster of the Year Award from that organization. I just tried to do the broadcast like Add would, and I felt like I was getting more and more confidence and perfecting my craft with, but Add was still the 'Voice of the Blue Devils.' and I was just filling in for him on those special occasions.

February 7th brought forth another opportunity to do the play-by-play on the road. Duke had flown to Maryland for a Saturday afternoon ACC game and about 4pm on Friday I got a call from Duke Assistant Sports Information Director, Tom Mickle. Donnie Tuck, and I had planned to drive up after he got out of class that afternoon. Mick told me to find Donnie and get to College Park as quickly as we could. Add had missed the team plane earlier in the day and I probably would have to do the play-by-play.

Tom also gave me the weather report, and that was the reason for his urgency. A huge snowstorm was headed for College Park and they expected eight inches by morning. I hustled over to campus and found Donnie. He skipped his late class and we headed to College Park, about a four and a half hour trip.

We made REALLY good time and the next morning, we found that it HAD snowed a lot but not eight inches. Even though we didn't have time to do much prep before we left Durham, I was ready. I had prepared two pre-games, one for play-by-play and one for color. I kept the 'color' sheet on top until I was certain that Add wasn't coming. That broadcast was my best up to that point.

My career as the 'Voice of the Blue Devils' had begun. Carl James was waiting in the tunnel at Cole Fieldhouse after the game and told me that he appreciated what I had done for the University under some unusual circumstances. He told me the next Tuesday morning that Add was having some health issues and he wanted me to finish the season.

This was not the way I had envisioned this playing out. I owe a tremendous debt of gratitude to Richard Giannini, Tom Mickle and Carl James. I could have never repaid Add for his guiding hand and his kindness and encouragement. I hope fans hear some of Add's qualities in my work.

CHAPTER EIGHT

Duke University and the Classic

Duke University is one of the most prestigious institutions of higher learning in the world. Duke Medical School is known throughout the world. The Law and Divinity schools are on par. The Fuqua School Of Business, Nicholas School of Environment and Earth Sciences, and Pratt School of Engineering draw students from every continent. Duke graduates continuously show up in politics, research, the media, and entertainment.

The national media, electronic as well as printed, is dotted with Duke alumni. Included are NBC's White House correspondent, Judy Woodruff, and talk show host Charlie Rose. Add to those ESPN basketball analyst, Jay Bilas, Mike Gminski, Jim Spanarkel, Jason Williams, CBS studio reporter Seth Davis and sportswriter/author John Feinstein.

Not only are there stars from the ranks of Duke alumni. But lots of other stars from various fields come to the Duke campus on many occasions. One of those was the Duke Childrens' Classic. It was one of the premier celebrity tournaments in the country, and throughout its 35 years, drew celebrities from all facets of the sports and entertainment world.

The Duke Children's Classic began in the fall of 1973 as the brain-child of Drs. John Griffith and Sam Katz. Katz was head of the Department of Pediatrics and Griffith was a ranking staff pediatrician. They saw that the Crosby and St. Jude's charities raised money with Celebrity Golf tournaments, and felt it was a great idea for Duke. They approached Vice-Chancellor for Health Affairs, Bucky Waters for his opinion. Waters played 'Devils advocate', explaining all the pitfalls that could arise. He was wary of this idea. Three days later, the two went back to Waters with the blessing of Chancellor Dr. Bill Anlyan who loved the idea. It began. Dr. Jay Arena was a long-time friend of Perry Como and they approached 'Mr. C' about being a part of the event. Como had a long-standing relationship with Duke and Durham through the Liggett & Myers Tobacco Company. Chesterfield cigarettes sponsored his radio shows and many of the "Chesterfield Supper Club" shows were broadcast live from Durham and Duke. He did a number of his Christmas Specials on national radio from Duke Chapel. He was a natural to have his name associated with the tournament.

PERRY COMO & BOB AT CROASDAILE CC

Bucky was given the responsibility of recruiting celebrities for the first tournament. He traveled to various tournaments around the country to entice sports and entertainment stars to come to the Classic. A lot of the responses were, "where's Durham," or "where's Duke." After the first tournament, the listed profits were $5,000. It was more like a wash. Como also had one request. The impromptu 'celebrity show' was too long. "I can't close the show after midnight and play golf at 9 the next morning," said Perry.

The founders tried to persuade Como to let them call it "The Perry Como Classic." He refused, saying that he would always come and do everything he could, but, "don't put my name or anyone's name on it." Perry recorded "Wind Beneath My Wings" and closed many of the celebrity shows with it. He usually dedicated it to his lovely wife, Roselle. He also told another group it was for them. As with every event like this, the volunteers are key. They can give it star status, or a bad reputation.

Duke's volunteers gave it star status. Celebrities and sponsors always raved about the treatment from the entire brigade of folks who devoted their time and energy to the 'Classic Weekend.' Many of them worked the same holes as a marshal every year, or distributed food on the course, or drove cars for the celebrities or a myriad of other things that HAD to be done for 'The Duke' to succeed. The volunteers were the "Wind Beneath My Wings" that allowed the Classic to soar above most of the other tournaments of its kind.

In 1977, the Classic hired Jerry Neville as the Executive Director of the event. It was under his leadership that the event took off to another level. Jerry was a people-person and was great with sponsors, paying patrons and celebrities alike. Dr. Katz said that one of Neville's greatest assets was that he was "a committed child advocate," so it was easy for him to convince sponsors to join in and celebrities to come to Durham. Jerry was so fortunate to have a tireless assistant in Wanda Edwards as his 'right arm.' Wanda handled all of the day-to-day things and made sure that little glitches didn't grow into large problems. She also had the ominous task of co-coordinating over 400 volunteers for the Classic. Neville said Wanda "had a special ability to interact warmly and professionally with celebrities, sponsors and volunteers."

A tennis tournament was added in 1980 and a Running Festival in '85. Wimbledon Champ Stan Smith was the tennis Honorary Chairman and Dr. Leroy Walker was Chairman for the Running Festival. The tennis enabled the Classic to draw another sector of celebrities to Durham. The Running Festival wasn't so much for celebrities, but for the community to come together.

The Classic enabled me to meet and interact with hundreds of celebrities over the 32 years I was associated with it. My involvement started very simply. Phyllis and I had taken our girls to Duke for the 3rd year of the tournament. It was the spring of 1976, about seven months after we moved to Durham. We were sitting on the grass bank around the 18th (now the 9th) green. Someone from the committee came over to me and said, "Are you Bob Harris from WDNC?" I said that I was. They asked if I would come over to the tent where there was a microphone and just identify the celebrities and players in each group so the gallery would know who they were watching. Yes, there were huge galleries for the majority of the Classics. Only in the last 8-10 years did that part of the event dwindle.

I was an announcing fixture both Saturdays and Sundays for about six or seven years, until committee member Betty Jarboe convinced the committee that I should be allowed to play as a celebrity one day and announce the other. I had subbed for a celebrity who didn't show up in my second year at the Classic. The celeb was baseball Hall of Famer, Willie Mays. I always brag that I once subbed for Mays, but I don't tell people it was on the golf course, not in a baseball game. In 2006, at the request of Honorary Chairman Jeff Foxworthy, I was moved to 'full' celebrity status, meaning I played both days.

Some times there were more celebrities than teams, so two celebs played with three or four paying players. One of the greatest days I EVER had on a golf course was the year I played with Grand Ole Opry comedian, Archie Campbell. I had met him several years before at the Classic, and was excited when I saw that pairing. As luck would have it, the celeb in the group right behind us was George Lindsey, "Goober" from the Andy Griffith Show. With such a large field of teams, we were always getting backed up and having to wait to tee off. Archie and Goober were 'on' all the time. We were howling at their antics as they joked with each other, our playing partners and the gallery.

A couple of years later I became the announcer at the first tee. Archie asked me on Friday night at the pairings party if I wanted to have a little fun if things got backed up on Saturday. I agreed to help him. Sure enough, when his group got around to #1, things were backed up. As we sat under the announcing tent, he said, "are you ready?"

I said, "ready for what?"

"We're gonna sang."

"OK, what are we gonna sang?"

"Let's do 'Where, oh where, are you tonight.' You know it don't you?"

"Yep"

"Alright, you introduce it."

Because I played musical intros for most of the celebrities before I introduced them, I had my cassette recorder there and punched record, grabbed my mic and we walked out from under the tent.

I said, "Ladies and Gentlemen, you are now going to have a surprise serenade. Me and Archie are gonna sang."

BOB & 'HEE HAW'S
ARCHIE CAMPBELL 5/82

With that, we took off on the afore-mentioned "Hee Haw" standard. When we got to the part where Archie turns and does the "and PTTTTT you were gone," I ducked. Everyone in the crowd roared, and Archie grabbed the mike and said, "Nobody likes a smart-alec. I think he's seen that before." Archie was a jewel.

Singers were always big favorites, and "The Duke" always had some great ones. Of course Perry Como was always the headliner; he was the Honorary Chairman from day one. I had a little fun with him once on the 18th green. His team always teed off on #1 so they would finish with the huge gallery around 18 where the awards ceremony took place. Perry had about a six-foot putt for a team birdie. He was known to take his time over a putt. Just as he was lining it up, I opened the mic and sang, "It's Impossible." It got a big laugh from the crowd AND Perry. Several other times in the same situation I would make a snoring sound as he stood over the putt. He was so laid back.

Como always liked to help the up-and-coming entertainers by giving them some exposure in the celebrity show in Cameron Indoor Stadium. One year, he brought in a young comic named Leno, and finally made a name for himself. Como also could draw the superstars from the entertainment world like Bob Hope, Barbara Mandrell, Rosemary Clooney, Lorne Greene, Jamie Farr, Mickey Rooney, Roy Clark, Buddy Hackett, and his pal, comedian Woody Woodbury, the 'Mayor of Ft. Likkerdale, Florida.' Woody was always the emcee for the celebrity shows. When the Saturday night shows moved to Cameron, they became an event all to themselves. The sponsors, players and celebs had dinner on the court level of the Indoor Stadium and the general public and all volunteers were seated in the upper stands. That place was packed most years. The Durham community came out to see a show that they would have had to pay hundreds of dollars to see in Las Vegas, if anyone could have gathered that many stars together even there.

How's this for a sample lineup? Comedian Foster Brooks doing his drunk routine, Donald O'Connor dancing, Chet Atkins playing guitar, Archie Campbell doing his "Pee Rittle Thigs", Don Cornell belting out "It Isn't Fair", Buddy Hackett keeping the audience in stitches, and closing out with Perry Como singing 5 or 6 of his greatest hits. Throw in a surprise visit from the "Chairman of the Board" Frank Sinatra, and THAT'S ENTERTAINMENT!!!

DINAH SHORE & BOB

One Saturday night, the 'West Virginia Bunch' stood on stage in Cameron and donated $1,000,000 to the Perry and Roselle Como Children's Endowment for the Pavilion of the Duke Pediatric wing at DUMC. These men had been with the Classic almost since its inception. Sam Snead brought them down and they had a lot of fun while they were here. Lawson Hamilton, Vic Green, George Aide, Joe Holland, Dr. Tom Dotson, Chris Walkup and Jim Justice and their friends loved the Classic.

Other regulars on the golf course included Fred MacMurray, Pat Boone, Robert Newman, Kim Zimmer, "Spanky" McFarland, Kathryn Crosby, Don Cornell, Dinah Shore and Dennis Franz. One of my favorite years was 1987, the one year The McGuire Sisters came. I met them at the pairings party and had some pictures made with them. I told them I had most all of their singles and the majority of their albums. Dottie asked me which song was my favorite, and I quickly told her it was "May You Always." I asked if they would sing it on the show on Saturday night. She said they would try. The next night I sang, very softly, all the words as the girls sang all their hits. They left the stage to a thunderous ovation, but I was so disappointed. They didn't sing my request. Guess what? They came back for an encore and said, "This is by special request for a special fan." I sat there and cried all the way through "May You Always." I'm glad the house lights were off!!

BOB, MONROE MAULDIN & THE McGUIRE SISTERS

"Spanky" McFarland and I developed a great friendship that lasted until he passed away in 1993. The first year he appeared at the Classic, Phyllis and I were leaving the Celebrity Show at Cameron Indoor Stadium. I noticed "Spanky" and his wife, Doris, waiting out front. I went over and introduced Phyllis to them. I had met him on the course that afternoon. I asked if there was a problem, and he said that their driver might have left for the hotel without them.

BOB & 'LITTLE RASCALS' SPANKY McFARLAND -WDNC/ SPINA BIFIDA 4/92

I offered to take them to the Governor's Inn. It was only a couple of miles from our house. They were very appreciative of the gesture and we talked all the way to RTP where their hotel was located. Phyllis offered to pick up Doris the next day and they would go to the flea market at the State Fairgrounds in Raleigh. That was right up Doris' alley. They had a wonderful time there while "Spanky" and I played golf.

I invited him to be my 'star' celebrity for a small, one-day tournament that I ran in Durham the next summer. We held the tournament for five years. Our funds benefited the Eastern North Carolina Spinabifida Association, the Durham Rescue Mission, and the Durham Community Kitchen. We flew "Spanky" to Durham from Ft. Worth the day before the event. He and I had a wonderful dinner at the Angus Barn that night and we played the next day.

Phyllis and I had the opportunity to have dinner with them on a trip to Dallas several years later and talked by phone several times a year until he died. Phyllis still calls to check up on Doris about once a month and she still lives in Ft. Worth.

BOB & REDS HALL OF FAMER JOHNNY BENCH

BOB & YANKEES' HALL OF FAMER YOGI BERRA 5/94

PHYLLIS & HALL OF FAMER ENOS SLAUGHTER 5/92

BOB, WHITEY FORD & TOMMY BYRNE

BOB & PACKERS' HALL OF FAMER JIM TAYLOR 5/94

DOLPHINS HALL OF FAMER DAN MARINO SIGNS FOR BOB

APPOLLO 13 JACK SWIGERT & BOB

Sports figures were always hits. Yankees greats Enos Slaughter, Bill Skowron, Hank Bauer, Roger Maris, Mickey Mantle, Yogi Berra, Whitey Ford, the legendary Joe DiMaggio and Bobby Richardson came. The Dodgers countered with Carl Erskine, Clem Labine and Roger Craig. Hall of Famers Hank Aaron, Stan Musial, Harmon Killebrew, Brooks Robinson, Johnny Bench and Al Kaline also represented baseball. I even had dinner one year with Bobby Thomson, the old New York Giants slugger who crushed me with his 1951 "Shot Heard 'Round the World" that beat my Dodgers. He was a nice man after all.

From football came Johnny Unitas, Gale Sayers, Joe Theismann, Paul Hornung, Jim Taylor, "Night Train" Lane, Garo Yepremian, Jan Stenerud, Don Maynard, Franco Harris, Chuck Bednarik, Terry Bradshaw, Dick Butkus, Dan Marino, Bob Griese and Roger Staubach.

Astronauts Jack Swigert of Apollo 13, and Alan Shepard, the first US man in space, came several times, as did golfer Sam Snead and champion billiards player Willie Mosconi.

Basketball stars Sam Jones, Bob Cousy and Michael Jordan made appearances. I had some fun at MJ's expense one year. I was working the first tee at Croasdaile and again, we were backed up. Michael was sitting under the tent with me and was hearing how I was picking on the celebs before him. Just before his team headed to the tee box, he told me, "Don't get on me about the Duke-Carolina thing, OK?" I said, "I won't even mention UNC." When it was time for the intros, I named the four in his group, and then said, "Ladies and Gentlemen, your celebrity in this group played high school basketball at Laney High in Wilmington. He was NBA Rookie of the Year with the Chicago Bulls and averaged ??? points this past season. He played at East Carrboro Tech." As the crowd laughed, he turned toward me and swung his driver like he was going to drive his ball straight at me.I said on the mic, "I didn't mention Caro... OOPS!!"

The broadcast industry brought in NBC's Bryant Gumble and ABC's Jim McKay. Jim's son, Sean McManus was a new Duke grad. He is now president Of CBS News and CBS Sports.

Former President Gerald Ford played in many charity tournaments and was more famous for hitting SPECTATORS than GOLF BALLS. A large part of the gallery that came to Croasdaile Country Club probably

ABC'S JIM McKAY & BOB

NBC's BRYANT GUMBLE & PHYLLIS 5/82

LOUD PANTS LATE-80s

came to see if one of his drives would hit someone here.

Spectators being hit at events like this are not all that uncommon. The non-golfers who come just to see the celebrities have only seen professionals on TV and they hit the ball straight. Sometimes the celebs and those who pay to play with them are not that good. A shank here, a duck-hook there, and an accident can happen, especially if the spectators are not watching when the golfers are hitting. I know from personal experience that it can happen. Several years before President Ford came to the Classic, I hit a terrific slice from a blind view to the green on #10 at Croasdaile. There was a large gallery around the 10th green and 9th tee box, because they were only 50 feet apart. My ball headed to the area between the two. As the scorer and I rode up the fairway toward the green, I saw a large commotion in that area. I tried to see where my ball had landed, when a friend of mine, Dr. Jim Morris of Duke Cardiology, came running down the fairway toward us. He told me not to go any closer, that my ball had hit a lady who was walking from the green over to the other tee. I lost it. He calmed me down and said that it looked a lot worse than it was. The ball had hit her about an inch above the right

PERRY COMO HOLDING TRIPP AND MERE

temple and 'caught a bleeder.' There isn't a lot of padding on the head and it is full of veins. There was a lot of blood. Jim told me she would go to the hospital to get stitched up and would be fine.

I rode on with my foursome but I couldn't even pick up a club for four holes. Finally a marshal came over to my cart and said that the hospital had just called and the lady was fine and was coming back to the course. I was SO relieved!! After I finished the round, I found the lady and we both started apologizing at the same time. She said it was her fault for not knowing a group was approaching the green. She wasn't looking. Turned out that she worked near Phyllis at Nortel and knew her.

President Ford was luckier than I. He didn't hit anyone and had a lot of fun interacting with the huge gallery that followed him all day long. Every golfer who played in the Classic got a bag tag for his golf bag each year. The tags usually had a picture of Perry Como holding a small child. Many years it was a patient at Duke Medical. Other years it was Perry holding a child that he just picked up on the course the previous year and pictures were taken. In 1992 the youngster was our grandson, Tripp. Granddaughter Meredith was accorded the honor two years later.

After 23 years as Chairman, Perry retired. Jeff Foxworthy was asked to come on board, and was Honorary Chairman until the last year, 2008. There was a press conference when Jeff was introduced, at Bullock's Barbeque. I got there after it started and asked a member of the board to introduce me to him. "Mr. You-Might-Be-A-Redneck" didn't wait on an introduction. "Aw heck. I've known who Bob is for years. We used to come up here to Duke to see my brother, Jay, play football and we'd listen to Bob on our radio in the stands." That was a switch!! We developed a great friendship, and he used his 'power' to make me a full celeb in 2006.

BOB & JEFF FOXWORTHY 5/97

Jeff's connections brought Faith Hill and Tim McGraw, Branford Marsalis, John Michael Montgomery, Rudy Gatlin, Gary Mule Deer, Will Shriner, the Friday Night Comedy Club and the famous Blue Collar Comedy Tour to Duke.

Some bad decisions by people who succeeded Jerry Neville may have led to the beginning of the demise of the Classic. Against the better advice of the 'older heads', a decision to bring in the Celebrity Players Tour for two years was implemented. Duke had to pay the CPT's Tournament purse of over $200,000 plus other demands of the Tour. These were former athletes and entertainers, who were pretty fair golfers, but instead of the galleries being able to pose for pictures with, and get autographs of these celebrities, it was run just like a PGA event and they couldn't be approached until they'd signed their scorecard after the rounds. This was a big turnoff to the thousands who had enjoyed the freedom of the other years of the tournament. The 'Classic' portion was played at Governor's Club south of Chapel Hill (a gated community) and no galleries were there. On top of that, the sponsors and paying players had to play on Thursday and Friday.

There was an effort to 'resurrect' the Classic after the two year CPT debacle, but the damage was done. They lost a lot of great volunteers and sponsors. They lost the galleries, and they never came back.

I am not the only one who hated to see the Duke Children's Classic end. Many wonderful memories are now shared about the days at the Duke and Croasdaile golf courses, and nights watching the Celebrity Shows in Cameron Indoor Stadium, the Carolina Theater, Page Auditorium, as well as the Governors Inn and Royal Villa where the shows really began.

The Classic is just like "Mr. C", gone, but never forgotten.

Charity-Celebrity golf tournaments get a lot of my attention each spring and summer. I love playing in them, not because of my great golf game, but because I'm a part of something bigger, and certainly, more important than I am. There was some jealousy toward me for that when I worked at WDNC. Some of the guys couldn't understand why I got invited. "Your game's not that good." "Is your ego that big, that you want people to see you all the time?" "You just want to get out of work." I finally decided to answer the barbs by saying, "I wish I could write a check to each one of these charities for $10,000, but I can't. So, I give my time. If the charity raises $1.00 more because I'm there, then it's worth the travel and time." I got no more remarks.

> *If God painted one square inch of Heaven Duke blue every time Bob Harris showed an act of love and kindness, then all of Heaven would be Duke blue. This probably is not a book quote but it is the truth about Bob Harris.*
>
> *CHIP CHESSON*
> *Developer & Family Health Ministries Board of Directors*

I get so much satisfaction out of being able to help people less fortunate, especially children. As you might guess, a large portion of the monies raised from the events benefit children. I also love meeting new people and making new friends. A lot of those people have been friends for 20 or more years. A case in point is Doug Flynn. He played Major League Baseball with the Cincinnati Reds, Montreal Expos, New York Mets and Texas Rangers from 1975 through 1985. The second baseman has World Series rings from 1975 and '76.

Doug is a very giving person. He volunteers for numerous charity functions. His main charity is the Children's Charities of the Bluegrass in Lexington, Ky. Doug helps get celebrities for the event each June along with his 'celebrity partners,' Hall of Famer Johnny Bench and former UK star Kyle Macy.

At the Coastal Classic tournament in Wilmington in May 1999, Doug asked me what plans I had for Fathers' Day weekend. I told him that it all depended on which fast food place my family took me. He said he wanted me to come to their shindig in Lexington and I said, "no." With a hurt look on his face, he asked why. Doug and I had been friends for about ten years through the Duke event. I said that my golf game "broke down a lot, and there weren't any spare parts for it." He then asked what the REAL reason was. I explained that it had been only six years since Christian Laettner had broken the hearts of thousands and thousands of Kentucky Wildcats fans. He promised that I would never have a problem.

Phyllis and I flew out on Wednesday afternoon. On Thursday I played a practice round at the Greenbrier Country Club. I was teamed with Artis Gilmore, the 7'2" center for the Kentucky Colonels of the ABA. I had covered several games when they played the Cougars in Charlotte. On his first swing, "the A-Train" hit the highest, biggest fade I've ever witnessed. For all I know, that ball may STILL be in the air. Seventeen holes later, he had almost all of the pot in our little 'Skins' game. I still think he set us up.

That night there was a big party for sponsors and celebrities as well. It was in Rupp Arena, of all places. Doug would read a short bio on each celeb and they would parade across the stage and say a few words to the crowd and move along. He hadn't gotten half way through mine until I began to hear some whistles and catcalls. As I made my way to the microphone, from the crowd came, "Where's Christian Laettner?" I looked out and replied, "He's backstage, waiting to see if ya'll kill me." The place broke up!! Doug was right. I have NEVER heard one derisive word about it. There has been some good-natured teasing, but I quickly get even with, "I was in St. Louis in '78 when 'Goose' Givens put 41 on us in the NCAA Championship." 'Nuf said.

In 2006, Doug arranged for all of the celebrities that year to be made 'Kentucky Colonels' by the governor of the Commonwealth.

One of the first celebrities I met there was actor Burton 'Bubba' Gilliam. He has starred in Blazing Saddles, Evening Shade, Honeymoon In Vegas, Back To The Future Part III, and the first series of Pace Picante Sauce commercials. His line, "New York City?" is a classic. Bubba and Susan have become very good friends.

In 2003, another friendship was made. Jim Hampton and Mary came to Lexington. I recognized him immediately as the character 'Caretaker' in the movie The Longest Yard. He also portrayed Hannibal Dobbs in F Troop, and was in the Doris Day Show, Sling Blade, and Teen Wolf casts, along with about 80 other movies and TV shows. Mary's grandfather ran a clock shop on Main Street in Salisbury, and that was the icebreaker.

Bubba, Jim and I always play our practice rounds in Lexington with

BOB & DOUG FLYNN AT HIS KENTUCKY SPORTS HALL OF FAME INDUCTION

BUBBA GILLIAM & SUSAN W/ PHYLLIS & BOB 6/04

BOB & 'THE LONGEST YARD'S JIM HAMPTON

tournament photographer extraordinaire, Bill Straus. On Christmas and Thanksgiving mornings, there is always a race to see who can call the others first. Seeing as how we live on the East coast, and they live in Texas, we have a one-hour advantage

In 1999, I was invited to the Coastal Classic Golf Tournament in Wilmington, to benefit the New Hanover Medical Center. They have raised over $7,000,000.00 in the first 16 years of this event.

I was pretty nervous when I had to tee-off in that first practice round, but the butterflies were there because I was playing with three sports legends. Vida Blue pitched for 15 years for the Oakland A's and San Francisco Giants. Durham's own Roger Craig broke into baseball with my Brooklyn Dodgers and played with them for seven seasons. The third iconic member of our foursome was Garo Yepremian, the man often referred to in his early career as 'the little Cypriot tie-maker' when he played for the Miami Dolphins.

The only other thing I remember about that day was, I finished 4th on the scorecard.

BOB AUCTIONING AUTOGRAPHED BKB

One of the things I enjoy in charity events is occasionally 'playing' auctioneer for their live auctions. This is another way for charities to add funds to the cause. I did one in Asheville, and word spread, thanks to Phyllis, that I could help raise extra dollars for the charities with the live auctions and more charities began asking. What began as selling a few sports items has grown to include other types of memorabilia and services. Yes, services. Talk about unusual items!! At an event for March of Dimes in Fayetteville, I auctioned off Lasix eye surgery, a root canal, and a vasectomy. Yes, a V A S E C Y O M Y!!! A lady bought it for her HUSBAND!!! He didn't put up any resistance either. He DID blush when I pointed out his wife as the winning bidder.

You can find celebrities in other places too. Charlton Heston came to a book signing in Raleigh, and Phyllis took our five year-old grandson,

TRIPP MEETS 'MOSES' (CHARLTON HESTON) 7/79

Tripp, with her. Several years earlier, Bobbi was pregnant with Meredith, and nearly every day, she would watch 'The Ten Commandments' with Tripp. He would act-out Moses parting the Red Sea as Heston so dynamically did in the movie. Phyllis told him on the trip to Raleigh that Mr. Heston would not look like Moses did in the movie. They arrived two hours early, and were number ten in line. They were instructed to refrain from conversations or asking for pictures with the great actor.

As Phyllis and Tripp got to the front of the line for him to sign her books, Heston looked at Tripp and said, "My grandson, Jack, is just about your age. How old are you?" Tripp told him that he was five, and Heston reached across the small table and shook hands with Tripp and Phyllis. He then asked him, "What's your name?" He asked Tripp how he was doing. Tripp answered him with awe in his face. During all of this, several pictures were taken of Tripp talking to Heston. When the books were signed, and they were walking away, Tripp looked up at 'Mommaw' and said, "He didn't look like Moses, but he sounded like Moses."

CHAPTER NINE
WDNC, THE BEGINNING

WDNC and WZKY were quite different in many respects. After four months in the sales department, I was transferred to the news department so that I might have more freedom to travel with the Blue Devils basketball team.

I was excited to move into the news department, until my first news assignment came along. It was a murder case. A female census-taker had been found beaten to death, in the northern part of the city, and the suspect was on the run. I knew I was definitely NOT in Stanly County.

Soon after, workers at the Liggett & Myers Tobacco Plant downtown went on strike. I had seen these strikes on TV, but now I was seeing one up close, and personal. Tempers boiled over, as management kept the plant running by working the machines themselves. A large number of employees sided with management and kept working. To keep them safe, the company had them park at the fenced-in warehouse about three miles away and be bussed in and out. They had to leave the area through a gauntlet of union members.

The strikers hurled rocks and bricks at the busses and cars, sending their message and trying to persuade those non-striking employees to back the union. I was out at the warehouse one evening, and was standing beside a newspaper photographer I knew. I noticed that he was wearing a coat even though it wasn't cold. I thought that was kind of odd, so I asked him why.

He looked around and said, "You have to be prepared for anything."

He had on a bulletproof vest. "This is great, this guy is ready for gunfire and all I've got is a doggone tape recorder." I didn't get hurt.

Jim Boyd was the News Director and the only other full-time newsperson. That meant I covered courtroom action and City Council and County Commissioners' meetings and most anything else that happened at night because he had the morning news shift.

At the first murder trial I covered, I had the worst experience that I have ever had. A meat cutter at a small downtown grocery store had been robbed and murdered. The murderer hung him up on a meat hook. In the process of the D.A. showing the gruesome pictures to the jury, the man's widow caught a glimpse of them, and became hysterical.

I covered a house fire that looked, to investigators, like it was set by the owner to collect insurance. I stayed close to the fire marshal as he looked through the house and around the yard. The back door was blown off its hinges during the explosion and we were using it as a walkway to get from the steps into the house. The authorities discovered that the man who was hired to set the fire was under the door, DEAD. The explosion that blew the door off apparently killed him before he could run.

I had heard news reporters often refer to being 'in the field.' I did that once, literally. One afternoon our family was eating supper and watching TV in the kitchen. There was a short bulletin about a small plane crashing on approach to RDU Airport. I grabbed my cassette recorder and headed off to the airport that was about ten minutes away. This was WAY before cell phones.

I followed emergency vehicles to the area of the crash. I found out from my neighbor, who was in the Civil Air Patrol, that a small Cessna went down in a wooded area. I asked if I could tag along and they agreed. We criss-crossed the woods for about an hour with no luck. TV crews had joined the search and had to use their battery powered camera lights to enable us to see where we were going. A short time later, word came over the walkie-talkies that the wreckage had been found about a hundred yards from where we were. News crews were not allowed too close to the plane for fear of an explosion of the gas tanks.

My neighbor, Wayne Fowler, was in the group that found the plane and he came over to where I was and told me that another reason we couldn't go any closer was that there were drugs and money all in the wreckage. Two drug-dealers were bringing the stuff into the Triangle. We didn't learn whether they had flown somewhere to buy the drugs and were bringing them back, or whether the men were just delivering the stuff to potential buyers here. No matter which story was true, two drug-dealers were dead, and their drugs would never hit the streets.

John McNabb was selected to be my color analyst for Duke football in 1976.

John was a former Duke player from 1963-65. He lettered three years as an offensive lineman and received the Jacobs Blocking Trophy his senior year.

The Atlantic Coast Conference gave this award to the best blocker in the league each year. John was on the football staff for two years and then moved into the Development Office.

BOB & ANALYST JOHN McNABB 1976

John had a player/coach mentality and added greatly to the broadcast. Bristol Maginnes was a friend of John's and became our statistician. Bristol worked for the University as the union negotiator and he handled all matters between Duke and its various unions. I'm sure he had dual personalities. He was a gregarious, fun-loving teddy bear around the broadcasts, but I just couldn't see him taking that tact with a union representative as they haggled over pay raises and matters like that.

Bristol had a sister named Nancy. She had a husband named Henry. Their last name was Kissinger. Yes THAT Henry. He was Secretary of State at that time. They had been married just three years before. Bristol began telling the broadcast crew that he would take us to 'Henry and Nancy's house" when Duke played at Maryland on October 22, 1977.

We checked into our hotel on Friday afternoon and preparations were underway for the trip over to Georgetown to have dinner at the Kissinger's house. As we left the hotel, Maginnes said he needed to stop at a grocery store to pick up some things. He came out of the store with several bags of food and told us that he was supposed to bring the steaks and fixings. As we arrived at the house, Bristol let himself into the kitchen. I thought that was a little unusual; no knock or doorbell. Any way, we went in and Bris began fixing the meal. I asked him when we would meet the Secretary and his wife.

"Oh, they're in Europe. They just let us use the house for the evening," came his reply.

Great! I was all set to meet the Secretary of State and now the bubble was burst. After the steaks, Bristol gave us a full tour of the home, right down to the basement area where a Secret Service surveillance and security unit was set up. They were monitoring every move we had made with security cameras trained on every inch of the property. The officer was very nice and explained how it all worked. He didn't say a word about the matchbook I had picked up from the kitchen. Hey, I asked Bristol if I could have it and he said I could!!

To this day, I have never met either Dr. Kissinger or Nancy. Bristol died suddenly a couple of years later, much too early in his life.

Let me give you a bit of insight into the duties of the broadcast crew members and how we interact. My job is, basically, to describe what is happening on the field/floor. It is the job of the color analyst to watch the action, analyze it, and explain what the teams were attempting to do. He must do this quickly and not too technically, so every fan can understand the explanation. The reason he has to do this quickly is because, unlike TV, I have to begin the next play description as the offensive team is breaking its huddle. Our sideline reporter is near the Duke bench and has a different view of the game. He can interject things he picks up from coaches, players, the medical staff in the event of an injury, and he can help with officials rulings too.

We had a statistician for about 15 years, but the computer replaced him. Since I started in the business in 1967, I relied on two spotters. In 2002, I began using only one. The engineer has to be a 'multi-tasker.' He is responsible for all of the equipment. He must maintain it and make sure it is operational on game day. This includes not only the gear in the booth but getting feeds of the referee's mic to get the penalty calls, and wiring the Duke locker room for our post-game players' and coach's interviews.

This is just for football broadcasts. Our basketball staff is only three now, and the play-by-play, analyst and engineering tasks are the same. We do not have a mic on the officials. In 1991, we were the first network in the NCAA to have a sideline reporter who listened in on the timeout talks, and synopsized what Coach K said. Our basketball post-game show is different than football. I anchor the football shows from the press box, and our sideline reporter handles interviews with the coach and various players in the locker room. In basketball, John Roth, our analyst, anchors, and I go to the locker room.

The most important thing in sports broadcasting is the preparation you do before you go on the air. You can't just grab a microphone and start talking and making things up on the spur of the moment. I guess you could, but you wouldn't have many listeners or keep your job for long. You not only have to know your subject, but you have to do plenty of research on the players, their backgrounds, key moments in their careers, and anything else that would make, not only the game, but the pre- and post-game interviews something that your listeners want to tune in to hear.

Danny Highsmith replaced McNabb for the 1978 season. We had been friends through the NCASB for10 years. He was General Manager of our Fayetteville affiliate, WFAI. In 1980 we added former Duke wide receiver and punter Wes Chesson as an analyst in the booth. When Wes graduated in 1971, he held almost all of the Duke pass-catching records. He spent five years in the NFL with the Philadelphia Eagles and Atlanta Falcons. We had no idea that Chesson's addition would be the start of the longest running duo of play-by-play and analyst in ANY sport in ACC history. The 2009 season marked our 30th year together.

In 1980, Bob Harris allowed an ex-Duke football player, with no radio or announcing experience, to become his partner in the Duke football radio broadcast booth. I knew something about football, but nothing about radio broadcasting. Because of Bob's experience, expertise, patience, and ability to carry the broadcast as I learned from him, I was able to participate in one of the most enjoyable and rewarding experiences of my life.

Bob is a pro who sets the stage for the broadcast and brings out the best in everyone who works with him. Over the past thirty years, I have always been amazed by Bob's knowledge of the game (unlike many play-by-play announcers, he understand the strategy and fundamentals of the game) and how vividly and accurately Bob is able to communicate to listeners what is happening on the field. Not only does Bob describe the action on the field, but also just as importantly, he communicates a sense of feeling and emotion for what is happening.

Studying Bob - what he cares about regarding the broadcast of the football game - has allowed me to more effectively add analysis to the action Bob is describing. Duke football over the past thirty years has not always been the best product from a win/loss standpoint, but from Bob, I quickly learned, and have grown increasingly to understand and appreciate, that the focus of our broadcast is not the wins and losses. The focus of our broadcasts, and Bob's announcing, is the Duke players. Bob knows and loves the Duke players and through his broadcasts, he wants the Duke fans to better know and appreciate them. To understand Bob Harris as the "Voice of the Blue Devils," to appreciate Bob's long time success, and to enjoy as I have the thirty years working with Bob, one needs only to know one thing – it's all about the players.

Wes Chesson - July 2009

He and I are like family. Their daughter Meredith was little when he began with us, and their son Mark was born in '82. Meredith finished at Duke, and is a mom with two children and Mark joined Wes' staff after graduating from TCU. Bobbi named her daughter after Meredith.

'Our' Meredith is a now young lady of many talents. She played violin for two years at Easley Elementary, and then at Carrington Middle. She also became interested in choral music and was a chorus member for two years at Carrington and at Riverside High. Meredith was inducted into the National Junior Honor Society at Carrington, and continues to excel. She writes poetry and paints as well.

Athletically, she played volleyball at Carrington for two years, and was student manager for the Riverside team as a freshman. She picked up a lacrosse stick for the first time in January of '09 and made the varsity team.

You know how, in some marriages, one can start a sentence and the other can finish it? Wes and I are that way, and that helps our 'on-air' cohesion.

DUKE RADIO NETWORK CREW 1979-
WES CHESSON, DANNY HIGHSMITH, BOB, PAUL MATTHEWS,
JOEL STUTTS & CLYDE CUPPLES

The Network added Anthony Dilweg in 1999 handle the sidelines. He was ACC Player of the Year in 1988, as a record-setting QB. His Duke records in passing yards for a season and TD passes for a season still stand. Steve Spurrier made QBs do things like that.

I love Bob. He is a sincere, loyal and accomplished gentleman.

He is fiercely passionate about his profession and is unwavering in his commitment to broadcast excellence. I've known Bob for over 15 years as a player and sideline radio analyst for the Duke Radio Network, and have always found him to be gracious and supportive.

I'll never forget the joy he brought to my father's heart on November 19th, 1988 when I told Bob that I would like for him to surprise my father during the Duke/UNC football radio broadcast, and I asked Bob to wish him a Happy Birthday during the game. Without hesitating a second and with a warm and robust smile Bob said, 'You bet!' My father was avid listener to Bob's play by play and I knew he would be listening to the radio broadcast that day. After my touchdown pass to wide receiver Keith Ewell in the first half, Bob wished my father Happy Birthday. Although it may seem like a simple gesture from an unrelated third party, it was one of the most meaningful gifts my father received that day and he still talks about it. My gift to my father that day was to win the game, and thanks to a clutch reception by my fullback, Rymo (John Rymiszewski), and some nifty running by Roger Boone on our final drive, we came from behind in fourth quarter to defeat UNC. Now that was fun!

Anthony quarterbacked the Green Bay Packers for two seasons, 1989 and '90, and replaced "Mr. Versatility,", Tony Haynes.

When I moved from color to play-by-play in late January of 1976, the University did not have provision for a replacement for me. Assistant Sports Information Director Johnny Moore filled the role several times. Even the Business Manager for the Athletic Department, Paul Detomo, filled in for the West Virginia and Duquesne games on a road trip my second year.

For the ACC Tournament in 1976, Athletic Director Carl James added a color man. We were to broadcast all six games in Landover, Maryland, and he knew I couldn't do it by myself. Glen Smiley was a fund-raiser for the University in the Development Office. Smiley had played for the Blue Devils from 1968-70. His Dad owned a station in Montana and Glen had a good radio background and a great voice. He had also done color on several ACC televised games. Glen and I had a good mesh and he was retained for the 1977 season.

Following that year, Glen accepted a fund-raising position with Baylor Medical School in Texas, and was replaced by Danny Highsmith.

BOB & GLEN SMILEY @ CLEMSON 2/77
REFEREE JIM BURCH

Tony Haynes roamed the sidelines, did color, was our engineer and called play-by-play for us. His play-by-play was in 1989 and 1994 when Duke went to Bowl games.

I opted for the Bowl sites each year and Tony flew to Honolulu for the Rainbow Classic each year. In '94, when the Rainbow Classic wrapped up, he flew all night to Tampa, and was on the sideline that afternoon. D-E-D-I-C-A-T-I-O-N. He started with us as a football sideline reporter in 1987 and was the engineer/color analyst on the basketball network from 1993-98. Tony's wit meshed perfectly with the rest of the crew.

Tony can do a tremendous sportscast in studio. He can engineer a game broadcast flawlessly. He can handle the sidelines with the best. He is an astute observer of the intricacies of the game. He is an outstanding analyst. And, he is a very competent play-by-play announcer. Most of us are lucky to do a respectable job at ONE of those things. Some are talented enough to do two, but I've never seen one person who was so talented that he could handle all with the professionalism of Haynes. In 1997, Tony not only handled the engineering duties for basketball, but the color job as well. The confirmed bachelor is truly amazing.

I could write several chapters about Tony. Not only were we co-workers for twelve years, we have been best friends for twenty-two years, and counting.

Between Tony singing Sinatra tunes and 'debating' Bilas on anything, the road trips with those two were never dull. 'Lawyer Jay' would take the opposite view on everything Tony would say. If Tony said that the sun was shinning, Jay would find a point to prove that it wasn't.

In the summer of 1997, the working relationship came to an end. Tony's everyday job was as Sports Director for Capitol Radio Network, which was owned by Capitol Broadcasting Company. Capitol Broadcasting also had owned the broadcast rights to the Duke Network since 1981. The contract ran-out at the end of the 1996-97 academic year. Capitol had plans to negotiate a more involved contract for the next three years and add in stadium signage and game program advertising. Duke wasn't ready to give up those things.

BOB, JAY BILAS & TONY HAYNES
1994 FINAL FOUR

Capitol's network manager called me to let me know what they were proposing and said that it was an all-or-nothing proposal. If Duke didn't agree, Capitol would not renew the agreement. My exact words to him were, "I saw this movie in 1980. You won't like the ending." Capitol's proposal was not the exact same scenario as the one in which Duke switched the local rights from WDNC to WDBS, but they were close enough to warrant the analogy. The Capitol manager was convinced that he could talk Tom Butters into doing it. I knew better. When their meeting began, George started his spiel and handed the written proposal to Tom. When he said it was all-or-nothing, Butters pushed the proposal back across the desk and said, "This meeting is over."

Moore Productions bid on the Duke rights and began to administer the Network that fall, and Tony was on the horns of a dilemma. He knew he couldn't continue to travel with Duke and work at Capitol at the same time. Haynes really loved being a part of the Duke family, but he loved his Capitol employment too.

Phyllis and I were out of the country when this came about. Among our phone messages when we returned was an urgent one from Tony. I hurriedly called him to see what was wrong, and we talked for 45 minutes. For about half of that call, someone was in tears. Haynes told me that he had tried to work every angle he knew of to continue in both capacities. It wouldn't work. He had written all the advantages of staying with Duke in one column of a legal pad, and the advantages of staying with Capitol on the other. When he had finished, there was a page and a half for Duke and only one item for Capitol. That one was more overriding than all the reasons to stay with Duke ---- his security and retirement. Capitol Broadcasting is one of the best broadcast entities to work for in the country. I know, I worked for them when they owned the Lease Management Agreement for WDNC from 1992-97.

Tony was like son, age-wise and we had a bond. Tony wanted my advice. He wanted me to 'sell' him on one or the other. I had to put my selfish feelings aside and try to advise him on his best interests. It was difficult for me. I would be losing a valued partner if I told him to leave the Duke Network. I would be losing a great friend if I didn't tell him the truth. I have always told people who worked with me that I would always try to help them with their careers and would never stand in their way to move up in their quest. Now, I had to put up or shut up.

As much as I hated to hear the words come out of my mouth, I told Tony that he had no choice. He had to stay with Capitol for his future security. There was relief in his voice. Our loss was N.C. State's gain. Capitol owned the rights for all of the Wolfpack's sports broadcasts and wanted Tony to become the sideline reporter for football and the analyst for basketball. He's doing the same wonderful job for them as he did for us. We still miss him, and we're still best friends.

Tony was in his element when he and Jay Bilas matched wits because each knew how to get the other one started. That scenario made basketball road trips so much fun.

Jay Bilas was recruited to Duke in 1983 from Rolling Hills, California. He graduated in 1986 with a degree in political science, and was selected in the 1986 NBA Draft by the Dallas Mavericks. He played professionally in the Italian Professional League from 1987-88, and the Spanish Professional League from 1988-89. He averaged over 20 points and 10 rebounds per game for his career.

His first appearance on the Duke Network came in 1988. His European season finished during the NCAA Tournament and he returned to Durham. We used him as a third voice through the Final Four in Kansas City.

I had interviewed Jay numerous times during his Duke playing days and he was so articulate. Inevitably, he would comment at the end of those interviews, "Some day I want your job." My retort would always be, "Don't sell yourself that short." I knew he could do whatever he wanted to do. He was that talented.

I first met Bob Harris in 1982 when I was a freshman in college. I knew very little of what I was getting myself into playing at Duke and in the ACC, but Bob was always a friendly face whether he was interviewing us after a win or a loss. And, whenever we traveled together, Bob had a smile on his face. I have never forgotten that.

I used to joke with Bob that someday, I wanted his job. Of course, I was only kidding, but if I were serious, I had no idea that I would have to wait until I was in my sixties to even have a sniff at his job! In 1988, I worked with Bob as his color analyst on the ACC Tournament after I had returned from my second season playing professionally in Europe. Bob was kind enough to show me the ropes of radio, and it was really fun listening to him and watching him work. Then in 1993, I began working with Bob on as his color analyst on every Duke game. It was then that I really gained an appreciation for the professional that Bob is.

Bob prepared for every game the same way, and treated every game like it was the NCAA Championship game. And, every minute of the game was important to Bob, even what some would consider "garbage time". It was in those situations that I could see what a pro he is. Anyone can give you the lowdown on the All-Americans, but Bob would give you a nugget of information on the last player on the bench.

The only thing I can take credit for in Bob's career is his attire on game day. In Cameron Indoor Stadium, the broadcast position is up in the catwalk at the top of the building. And, it can get really hot up there, especially before air conditioning. When doing a home game, I started to wear a golf shirt and jeans to the games so I wouldn't sweat through a coat and tie and burn all of my money on dry cleaning. Well, Bob was not pleased with my unilateral clothing choice. He told me that we were a professional operation, and that we were to dress as professionals. Of course, today, Bob can be seen in his Cameron broadcast position in a Duke golf shirt. But, he's still a pro.

Bilas has been a member of the Screen Actors' Guild since 1987 and appeared in national television commercials and the feature-length movie "I Come in Peace" (also known as Dark Angel). In 1990, Jay also appeared in an episode of the TV series 'The White Shadow.'

Following his playing days, Bilas came back to Duke and served as a graduate-assistant coach under Mike Krzyzewski for three seasons from 1990-1992. During that time he also attended Duke University School of Law and received his law degree in 1992.

No, he didn't invent the internet, climb Mt. Everest, or fly the space shuttle, but I'll bet that he could have, if he had wanted to.

After graduation from Law School, Jay moved to Charlotte and is currently Of Counsel to the office of Moore & Van Allen, where he maintains a litigation practice. We persuaded him to re-join us in the booth, and he did. From 1993 through 1996, Jay climbed the ladder to the Crows Nest and was our analyst on the Duke Radio Network. There he honed his broadcast skills and landed a slot with ESPN.

In 2007, Bilas was nominated for an Emmy Award as Outstanding Studio Analyst. He is equally adept in the studio or on the sideline adding expert commentary to the ESPN telecasts.

In 1997, we had a new analyst in the basketball booth. Johnny Dawkins, Duke's all-time leading scorer at the time, retired from the NBA after 9 years, where he averaged 11.1 points per game. At Duke he was a two-time All-American. He returned to his alma mater and worked as an administrative intern in the athletic department for a year in addition to working with us on the Network.

Johnny was Duke's all-time leading scorer with 2,556 points. That mark stood until 2006 when J.J. Redick surpassed it. In Dawkins' last year at Duke, the '86 season, the Blue Devils amassed a record of 37-3, which was an NCAA record for both games played and games won in a single season. That year Dawkins averaged 20.2 points a game and won the Naismith College Player of the Year Award. He also was an alternate on the 1984 United States Olympic basketball team. He graduated with a degree in political science.

His jersey number 24 was retired at the end of that season. Dawkins was named one of the 50 greatest players in Atlantic Coast Conference history and the 78th greatest player in college basketball history by The Sporting News's Legends of College Basketball book in 2002. In the 1986 NBA Draft, Dawkins was selected by the San Antonio Spurs as the 10th pick overall. He also played for the Philadelphia 76ers and the Detroit Pistons.

He joined the Duke coaching staff in 1998, working alongside head coach Mike Krzyzewski, and he was promoted to associate head coach in charge of player development in 1999. In April 2008, he was named head coach at Stanford University, succeeding Trent Johnson.

Several other former Duke basketball players have worked on the broadcasts. Bob Bender and Steve Wojciechowski both came back to Duke and went through the same Athletic Department internship as Johnny Dawkins. Like Dawkins, Bob and Steve worked as analysts for one season. Both went from the booth to the bench along side Mike Krzyzewski.

We revamped the basketball and football networks in 1999 and added John Brockwell as our engineer for both sports. We added John Roth as analyst for basketball and Anthony Dilweg as sideline reporter for football.

Brockwell and I had worked together briefly at WTIK Radio in Durham in 1983 and he had been the engineer for the Wake Forest Network for a number of years, so we had developed a friendship through those two avenues. Not only is John a gifted technician, but also he has a great radio voice and handled our scoreboards during both football and basketball broadcasts.

Matthew Laurance joined the radio team at the beginning of the 1999 season as the sideline reporter I referred to earlier. He reported, on air, on what was said in that huddle, and the listeners got a hint of things that might happen before they actually did. Duke was the first network in the nation to use this arrangement, mainly because Mike Krzyzewski is one of the very few coaches in the country that is so secure in his position that he will allow that kind of access. As a matter of fact, the idea WAS Mike's. It worked very successfully

JOHN BROCKWELL, BOB, JOHN ROTH & MATTHEW LAURANCE - MAUI 11/01

In August 2009, Matthew left the 'blue of Duke' for the 'blue of Kentucky.' He went to work with LM Communications and their six radio stations in Lexington. He is doing a bit of everything, including co-hosting a sports call- in show on their ESPN outlet. For Matthew, it's a great opportunity with a big upside. He will be missed.

I have been so fortunate to have had great people around me every year since 1976. I always let the new guys know that we can have fun AND do a great job on the air. A good sense of humor is a prerequisite for working on the Duke Radio Network.

The addition of John Roth was a stroke of genius on the part of Moore Productions President Johnny Moore. Moore hired Roth to work in the Sports Information office at Duke when the later was a student. When Moore left Duke in 1991 to form his own company, Roth came with him. The two published Devilirium, a fan's news letter that focused on all Duke athletics. Shortly afterwards, they changed the name to Blue Devil Weekly and it became a newspaper. It is now 'GoDuke the Magazine' and John is the editor and Johnny continues to write for it as well as running the Radio network, the coaches' TV shows, and selling advertising for all three. He finds a little bit of time to improve his golf game. He currently has a 4 handicap.

John Roth graduated from Duke in 1980. He was a sportswriter for the Danville Bee and Durham Sun newspapers before heading back to Duke as an assistant, then Director of the Sports Information department. He probably knows more about Duke athletics and its history than any man alive today. He has written millions of words about Duke, the successes and failures, the athletes, coaches and administrators. His book, 'The Encyclopedia Of Duke Basketball,' is the most comprehensive book of its kind anywhere. In addition to the magazine, John helps produce the TV shows, hosts the football pregame and halftime shows on radio, and is the analyst on the basketball network. His basketball duties also include the pre, halftime and postgame shows. I never argue with John about a Duke fact. He's that good.

One other young man was a staff member for six years. Tripp Winkler began work on the Network carrying the parabolic crowd microphone on the sidelines when he was in sixth grade. After two years on the field, we moved him up to the booth to keep drive charts for me and help the engineer and anyone else who needed it. He was also a batboy for the Duke baseball team for his three middle school years, until he became a 'recruitable student-athlete.' The NCAA, because of the pre-existing relationship, cleared Tripp to continue to work for us. He was a three-year starter on the Riverside High School JV football team, and in the North Carolina 4-AA Championship at Wallace Wade Stadium. To say that I was proud to watch him run out of that Duke tunnel at the start of the game is an under-statement! He was recruited by several schools for football, including the U.S. Naval Academy, and was presented a Triangle Chapter National Football Foundation Scholarship, which is also based on ability, academics and citizenship.

Really competent remote-broadcast engineers are very hard to come by. I have had only one that was not, and he only lasted three football games before I had to replace him. He was a terrific studio engineer, but had never worked a remote broadcast.

Donnie Tuck was my first game engineer in 1976. He had worked with the Network in 1975 and I got to know him when I did the color for four games. Donnie was a senior at Duke and loved working the football games. After he graduated, I had to find a new man. Our station engineer at WDNC, Barry Hayes, used young engineers to help with various projects he did and told me of a talented student who would be a great addition. There was one problem. He was a student at UNC. I agreed, after some 'selling' by Barry, to interview him. Paul Matthews was a 6'4" youngster who was very confident in his abilities. I hired him. By the time the Duke-UNC football game rolled around in November, Paul was pulling AGAINST his school. I had succeeded in brain-washing him.

We formed a great relationship right away. He knew what he was doing and was a lot of fun to be around. He was very confident that he could do ANYTHING that involved engineering. He could make equipment that we might need and repair anything that might break in the course of a broadcast.

PAUL MATTHEWS KEEPS US ON THE AIR

His confidence was questioned two times. The first was on a football trip to Clemson. We stayed in Greenville, SC, and drove down to Death Valley on Saturday morning. I knew a back way to Clemson that I felt would keep us out of traffic. WRONG!!! We were creeping along in HEAVY traffic and were getting antsier all the time. Evidently a LOT more people knew that 'short-cut' than I anticipated. We arrived at the press box 15 minutes before we were supposed to go on the air. We all carried cases of equipment to our booth and I asked Paul what we could do to help. His answer was very succinct. "Put down the cases and get the hell out of my way." We did. In 13 minutes, he yelled down the hall for us to get down there. As we walked in the booth, everything was set up and Matthews started his two-minute count-down to airtime. We hit the 11:00 airtime right on cue. I forgot to tell you that the set up USUALLY took an hour to complete. No one but the crew knew the difference. The broadcast went off without a hitch.

The second time Paul was put to the test was actually two times in one. We were to play a basketball game at the Brendan Byrne Arena in the Meadowlands complex near East Rutherford, New Jersey. Johnny Moore needed to go into the city early that Saturday morning to shoot some 'stand-ups' with me at various Gotham City landmarks for the TV show. We did one with me sitting in the seat with the driver of one of the Central Park hansom cabs. Another was shot with the World Trade Towers behind me for a feature about Mike Gminski who was playing for the New Jersey Nets at that time. Another was shot in Times Square. We all loaded into our rental car, a Lincoln Towncar, and headed back through the Lincoln Tunnel toward Secaucus and the Brendan Byrne arena.

We were pushing the time and Paul was getting antsy again. You guessed it, traffic tie-ups. The maintenance crews had closed down all but one tube of the tunnel coming out of the city. Six roads were trying to feed into that one lane. I was playing bumper cars with other drivers. I made a lot of folks mad that morning because I was cutting them off and forcing my way in front of them. We got to the media lot at the Arena and grabbed all of the equipment and headed to the nearest entrance.

As we headed up the outside steps a security policewoman told us we couldn't use that entrance. We had to go a fourth of the way around the building to the media entrance. Paul was adamant. We were late and he WAS going in that entrance. The policewoman was a little firmer with the second refusal. When the 6'4" Matthews tried to walk around her, the 6'1" policewoman raised her left hand with the 'Halt"' sign and placed her right hand on her service revolver. I INSISTED that we go around to the media door. Paul agreed. That was the ONLY time his will didn't win out. But that was just the beginning.

We were already closer to airtime than at the Clemson football game. As we got to our broadcast location, Paul pulled the telephone out of the case and hooked it to our outlet and dialed the Capitol Radio Network studio and handed the receiver to me. He said, get your opening out and when I give you the signal, start talking. When you finish your written part, keep talking until I signal you, and then throw it to a commercial."I only had to adlib a few seconds and took the commercial break. He had hooked up the board and was sending a signal down the line to Capitol. When the commercial was over we went on with our regular pregame show. Again, no one knew except the four of us. I've NEVER let Paul forget about his challenge of the lady cop.

Our current engineer also came to us from UNC. He is a Carolina graduate, and worked for the Tar Heel Network for several years. When John Brockwell's station duties forced him to give up the Duke Network, we asked the network engineer at Capitol Radio Network, Rusty Helser, for his assistance. He didn't hesitate in his recommendation of John Rose.

John has been in radio most of his life. His late father owned and ran WIZS in Henderson. He has performed every duty at a radio station. As with those already mentioned, John is a talented technician. He handles problems that arise without anyone, including me, knowing there IS a problem. That is professionalism at its best.

Sports events and game broadcasts are a major part of my life. As a radio engineer and announcer, there are many opportunities to travel and see things and do things, but the relationships are what matter most.

The things I appreciate most about working with Bob Harris and our Duke Radio Network crew are the atmosphere and the working conditions. It is a pleasure to go to work and to work hard for people that you not only consider friends, but also think of as family. Consider that a radio engineer is often the first to arrive and the last to leave. The highest mark of performance as a radio engineer is to be invisible. You are there and ready, so the talent can do his or her job. Not one time at Duke has there been a broadcast when Bob and others haven't said thank you.

It's good to be in an environment where what's meant is what's said. Bob arrived particularly early to a home basketball game in my first season at Duke. Feeling poorly that all the equipment was not yet set, I said, "Bob you're here early." Bob said, "I would rather be an hour early than a minute late." Not bad advice for anybody. I quote that often. Please understand. What's awesome is, Bob wasn't saying

I was late or holding him up, he was just saying, in his personal way, that he had chosen to arrive even earlier than usual.

Bob's enthusiasm for Duke Football and Men's Basketball is well documented. He combines preparation, reporting and wit to announce the games. He is a great radio personality. And that great personality remains true when the microphone is turned off. I appreciate who Bob is, how he talks and how he treats me off the air even more.

Our broadcast crew often acts much like the members of a family would. We eat together, travel together, laugh together and make tough decisions through conversation, consideration and planned action.

I love good food. Bob, John Roth, Wes Chesson, Anthony Dilweg, Matthew Lawrence and I have enjoyed many fabulous meals. I have to be honest when I say that I've had the chance to follow the Duke Men's Basketball and Football teams to some places I would have never been in on my own.

Bob picks great restaurants too. Gallagher's and Alfredo's in New York, plus Dailey's in Atlanta, are a few at the top of our list. Nearly as often as we eat out, we find ourselves in the hotel restaurant. The conversation is just as good. We have a good time. That's what's important to me.

And, breakfast is as interesting as dinner. We often talk more seriously in the morning; the news, what's going on at home, what the outcome of the game might be. My first season at Duke, Assistant Athletic Director for Marketing Mike Sobb got up a delegation to go to City Lobster in New York. I had eaten lobster tail before but never the whole thing. Excuse the crude nature of my somewhat rural upbringing. Sobb was intent on showing me how a lobster was eaten, which he did. To this day, I'm not sure which Sobb enjoyed more, his meal or watching be devour a two-pound lobster. I think the result was that I showed Sobb how to eat a lobster.

It's a special gift to translate something as visual as sports in a way that listeners get the picture. Bob paints those images well.I tell you this now. My first day on the job at the Duke Radio Network, Bob said, "We will work hard, and we will play hard." We do. Something told me right then it would be fun. My own father taught me to work hard. He too, knew how to have a good time. My dad said, "Radio is suppose to be fun." It is fun on the air and while not on the air at Duke.

And what more could you ask of my friend Bob Harris? He has offered me a world of fatherly advice, none more appreciated than those key moments since my own father's death.

What makes Bob so good? He knows what love is. Love of God and love of family."

John Rose, July 2009

Rose has a vast knowledge of things other than technical. He loves cars, especially Corvairs. He loves trains. I owned a Corvair in the 70s, and I love trains. Shall we say that we have a lot of common ground? He now loves Duke, but I haven't brainwashed him about UNC. I haven't tried. He is happy for Duke when they win, but isn't unhappy if the Tar Heels win.

It seems as if I've had a run of UNC grads handle our engineering. We picked up David Modlin for one season. He had worked for WCHL and the Tar Heel Radio Network while a student. I first met David at the weekly UNC football press conferences. WCHL carried them live and he was an engineer for those. The reason he left after such a short time was a full time opportunity with Capitol Radio and he picked up the N.C. State Network engineering job along with it.

Since 'Mod-Squad' still works at Capitol, we're always working on some facet of networking. He's even filled in for us when we've had a football and a basketball broadcast near the same time on the same day. He's still a quasi-member of our crew.

The Capitol Radio Network attracts great talent. Quite a few years ago, they made a great hire in Rusty Helser. Rusty is a studio engineer without equal. He is the most conscientious man I've ever worked with. We never worried about getting on the air correctly, or commercials not being run properly. He handled all of the production for our network commercials and made sure they were current and what the advertiser wanted. That can be a headache at times.

Not only did he do all of this for the Duke Network, but he did the same things for the N.C. State Network, the Capitol News Network, WRAL-FM and 99.9-FM. He handled distribution of the Carolina Hurricanes, East Carolina and the Tennessee Titans broadcasts as well as the coaches' radio shows for all of them. Does he need to be cloned? YES, several times. I still don't understand how he did it all. He did have help. His wife Norma helped him do many of the things he had to be responsible for when there were multiple feeds going out of Capitol.

Rusty is more than a valued co-worker. He is a treasured friend. We have developed a bond that allows us to be complimentary of each other, and at the same time, be totally honest with each other as well. Rusty and I have laughed together, cried together, brainstormed together, and confided in each other.

The Duke Radio Network owes a deep debt of gratitude for the talents and hard work of Rusty Helser. He retired in the fall of 2009.

Through all of this, there have been two constants, Bob Harris and Clyde Cupples. Clyde and I became friends when I was teaching the Couples Sunday School Class at Second Street Presbyterian Church in Albemarle in 1970. Keystone Steel & Wire had transferred him as a regional sales manager, and made Albemarle his headquarters since it was centrally located in his territory. That fall I needed a spotter for my high school broadcasts and he agreed to do it. With the exceptions of the 1975 and 1980 seasons, we've been together since 1970. 1975 was the year I did color for four games here at Duke, and in 1980 Clyde 's company transferred him to Peoria, Illinois. That move only lasted a short time and he was back in Albemarle, and back on the Network as my 'extra eyes.' Actually, he worked one game with me in that '80 season. We played Indiana in Bloomington and he drove over from Peoria to spot for me.

Clyde and Sharon still come to 80-100% of the games each fall. Depending on where Duke is playing, they won't miss over 2 games in a season. Both have retired and love to travel. They have driven from Albemarle to Navy, Knoxville, Atlanta and Chicago to continue to help a friend.

In my 35 years (as of this writing) of association with the Duke football and men's basketball teams, I have had the pleasure of working with some of the most brilliant coaching and administrative minds ever. Carl James was Athletics Director when I started in 1975. He gave me my break with a college network. Tom Butters succeeded him in 1977. Butters was a national leader in athletic administration in his tenure that closed when he retired in 1998. Tom was followed by Joe Alleva who held the post until he left to run the athletic department at LSU in the summer of 2008. The latest Director, Dr. Kevin White began his tenure on June 16, 2008, and started an immediate transformation of the athletic department.

Four Athletics Directors in 34 years isn't bad. The football situation has been a bit different. Outland Trophy winner Mike McGee was coaching at his alma mater when I began broadcasting Duke football games. He became head coach in 1971 and continued through the 1978 season. His successor was Shirley S. "Red" Wilson. Red was a tremendously successful high school coach in North Carolina for a number of years before taking Elon College to national prominence. He brought an exciting passing game to Durham and, in 1980, hired a young assistant with a 'gun-slinger' mentality, Steve Spurrier. Former Alabama quarterback Steve Sloan came in for four years from 1983-86. He left to become Athletic Director in Tuscaloosa and was succeeded by the afore-mentioned Spurrier. He took the Blue Devils to the All-American Bowl in 1989. Spurrier's three seasons produced 5-6, 7-3-1 and 8-4 records.

When Ben Hill Griffin's money lured Spurrier back to the campus where he won the 1966 Heisman Trophy, Assistant Coach Barry Wilson was elevated to the big office. In his four years, Duke was 13-30-1. Fred Goldsmith was summoned from Rice in 1994 and he promptly gave the Duke fans something that hadn't enjoyed in a while, national ranking. His 1994 Blue Devils ran off seven straight wins to open the season and were ranked 16th in the country when they rolled into Tallahassee for game 8. It wasn't pretty. 59-20, Seminoles. Duke earned another bowl bid and lost to Wisconsin in the Hall of Fame Bowl in Tampa. 34-20. Unfortunately, that 8-4 mark would not be equaled again and former

Duke tight end and assistant coach Carl Franks was given his first head coaching position. The Duke alum was given the axe midway through the 2003 season. One of his assistants, Ted Roof, was elevated by virtue of his finish that saw Duke beat Roof's alma mater, Georgia Tech, 41-17 and UNC 30-22 in Chapel Hill. As with Goldsmith, that was the high-water mark and Roof was fired after the 2007 season.

The David Cutcliffe era began with a new emphasis on Duke football. His resume started it off and the administration's commitment to upgrade facilities and put an all-out effort to bring winning football back to the "Methodist Flats."

Coach Cut's first season saw the beginning of the restoration of Duke football. The Blue Devils went 4-8, and could have won eight if five plays had gone Duke's way. Those four wins equaled the win total of the previous four years, COMBINED. In Cutcliffe's second season, the Blue Devils won five and lost seven. Again, the record could have been better but for a couple of plays.

Basketball has been an entirely different animal. Bill Foster led Duke to the 1978 Final Four, and Mike Krzyzewski has taken the program to dizzying heights with 11 Final Fours in 30 years. He guided Duke to four NCAA Championships in that time frame.

Duke's main athletic facilities are named for former coaches. The baseball stadium is named for Coach Jack Coombs. Dedicated on October 5, 1929, Duke Stadium changed to Wallace Wade Stadium on September 30, 1967 to honor the legendary Hall of Fame coach. The basketball arena was officially opened on January 6, 1940, and the Duke trustees changed Duke Indoor Stadium to Cameron Indoor Stadium on January 22, 1972. On that night, a heavy underdog Duke team upset No. 3 North Carolina 76-74, as Robby West drove the length of the court and pumped in a jump shot for the victory.

Wallace Wade came from Alabama (without a banjo on his knee – I just couldn't resist that) in 1931. Eddie Cameron had come to Duke as basketball coach in 1928. Cameron took over the football job from 1942-1945 while Coach Wade served his country in World War II.

I got to know Coach Cameron a little better than Coach Wade, probably because Coach Cameron was around the athletic offices more after 1975. In 1981, I was invited to the 50th reunion of Coach Wade's first Duke team. It was held at Kidd Brewer's home that overlooked Cameron Village Shopping Center in Raleigh. Kidd was captain of that first Wade- coached team, and yes, the players DID call him Captain Kidd. The two coaching legends were seated side-by-side for pictures with individual players, and after all of them had been 'snapped,' I asked the photographer if I could get one with them. It is one of my most prized pieces of memorabilia. I was lamenting the fact that I didn't get the legendary duo to autograph that picture while showing it to our grandchildren one night and Bobbi said, "Dad, you didn't need it signed. You are in the picture with them." I do have a video of a feature that I did with Coach Cameron for our Duke Basketball TV show.

BOB & DUKE ICONS EDDIE CAMERON (L) AND WALLACE WADE AT 50TH REUNION OF WADE'S FIRST DUKE TEAM 1981

CHAPTER TEN

FOREVER'STEAM, THE BACKGROUND

They were given the title "Forever's Team" by Duke grad John Feinstein in his book by the same name. This team went from one game over .500 the previous year, to a team that had to win the ACC Tournament to make the NCAAs, to a team that captured the hearts of college basketball fans nationwide

When the 1978 basketball season began, Duke wasn't predicted to be in the upper echelon of the ACC. The Blue Devils had struggled since Vic Bubas retired. There were not all that many wins to cheer about for the Duke diehards. Duke Indoor Stadium became Cameron Indoor Stadium in 1972 but the results of the teams were still the same. Like other 'Cinderella' stories, this one had a great ending. Duke fans got a glimpse of what might be in November, but in late February, it just didn't seem feasible. Duke? Win an ACC Championship? Are you crazy? Yes, on all three counts.

Bill Foster was well known in Division 1 circles because of the job he had done at Rutgers and Utah. Foster had turned those two programs from also-rans into tournament teams. Could he work the same transformation at 'Buck' Duke's school? If he did, he would have to go, in Bill's own words, "from the outhouse to the penthouse.'

Some people STILL want to know what happened that caused that team to make such a dramatic about-face in such a short period of time?

I am sure everyone has their own opinion about it, but I had the pleasure of witnessing a great reclamation story.

Foster knew that he had to rebuild from the inside out. That begins with the staff of assistant coaches, and Bill brought Lou Goetz and Bob Wenzel with him from Utah. He also retained Jim Lewis, who had been an assistant under McGeachy. Bill also changed the playing style of the team just like he did at Rutgers and Utah. He excelled at coaching a "run and gun" style of play. Fans loved it too, and more would come to see the exciting style in action. At Rutgers his teams were called the "Running Knights." At Utah he had the "Running Utes", so guess what? The "Running Dukes" became the catch phrase in Cameron.

In my first season sitting in the Crows' Nest, 1975-76, they didn't set the woods on fire, but they did find matches and the gasoline to start it. They finished 13-14 and beat Virginia, Wake Forest and Maryland in the league. 13-14 was an improvement over the 10-16 record two years previous.

The '76-77 season saw Duke finally break through with their first winning season since 1972. To many ardent Blue Devils' fans, it seemed like an eternity. The five-year drought was over as they ended the year 14-13. Even though there were only two conference wins, Bill could see that his team was beginning to play with more confidence. That feeling was starting to take hold of the Duke fans as well. There wasn't one noticeable point in the year where the program just took off. It evolved over time, and with a great deal of effort. I do think there was one thing that changed the make up of that team and was the prelude for one of the most amazing sports stories of that decade.

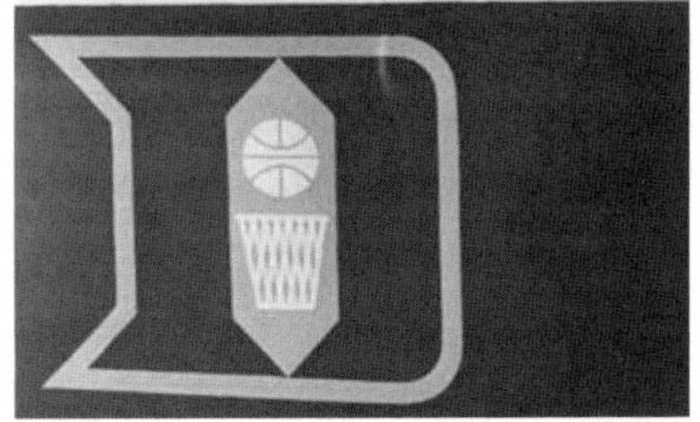

BOB TAPES PREGAME INTERVIEW WITH BILL FOSTER 1977

Senior point guard Tate Armstrong broke his wrist in the

game at Virginia January 17th. He was through for the season. Tate was a terrific shooter, but had a rash of injuries his first two years and didn't get much playing time. He became a starter at the beginning of his junior year and went on to be a key player for the Blue Devils. If the three-point shot had been in the game at that time, there's no telling how many points he would have scored. In 1976 he averaged over 24 points a game.

In 1977, the Blue Devils were 10-3 and riding as high as they had been in a long time when they traveled to Virginia, and then it happened. In the first five minutes, Tate was knocked down and fell on his wrist. He never came out of the game. He scored 33 points, and all but two of them were after his fall. There was another break that night. Duke broke a 41-game ACC road losing streak, 82-74 in overtime.

Duke won the game, but lost Armstrong for the remainder of his senior season. We found out the next day that he had broken the navicular bone in his wrist. The leading scorer in the ACC would not play for Duke again. I am still amazed at Tate's unselfishness and courage. With this news, the Blue Devils were facing more difficult times. Foster found a new court leader who would become the 'face' of Duke basketball for two and a half years.

James Gerard Spanarkel was the first player Bill recruited to Duke. He played at Hudson Catholic High in Jersey City and was almost as good at baseball as he was basketball. After two years of baseball he concentrated on basketball. It was fun to watch Jim grow into the player and leader he did over his last two years. The season had started at 10-1, but ended 14-13.

They lost ten of the last thirteen games and finished 14-13. It was but not quite what fans had hoped for in the first weeks. One of those 3 season-ending wins was an 85-73 victory over St. Joseph's in the Palestra in Philadelphia. I got my first look at the Liberty Bell.

BOB AT THE LIBERTY BELL 2/76

Talk about an 'bell-ringing' effort, Spanarkel played 519 out of the 520 minutes after he became the starter.

The 1977 season also brought about one of the more noteworthy basketball trips of my career. The Duke team left Durham on the afternoon of January 27 to fly to Morgantown, W.Va. for a game the next night. We had to change planes in Washington, D.C. for a flight to Pittsburgh. During the lay-over, we learned that the Pittsburgh airport had been closed because of snow. Coach Bill Foster and trainer Max Crowder changed the travel plans. They chartered a bus and we headed for Morgantown. About the time we hit the western Maryland mountains we hit snow. By the time we reached the West Virginia Turnpike, they were preparing to close it. Coach pleaded his case with the authorities and we were allowed to continue. As we rolled into the edge of Morgantown it was getting late, and because of the urgency in getting there, we had not eaten since lunch. I forgot, we had a snack on the plane. Yes, they served food in those days, FREE. Still, the players were getting hungry, and began asking to stop somewhere, anywhere, to get food. On we went. Finally, someone spotted a house beside the road, and the interior lights were on. Mike Gminski, a growing boy of 6-11 and 235 pounds, yelled up to the coaches in the front of the bus, "stop and lets go eat with those folks. They're in the dining room and I can see the table and they're having chicken!" Of course, he couldn't see any of that, but it was worth a try. We finally made it to the Holiday Inn in Morgantown and Max persuaded the manager to arrange food for us.

With the snow and ice on the ground at the motel, the footing was treacherous. Sports Information Director Tom Mickle was the first to find out just HOW treacherous it was. As he stepped off the bus, he slipped and fell. Undaunted, he gathered his luggage and headed for his room. Keep in mind that the old Holiday Inns were all 'outside access' rooms. I was walking to my room, which was on the second floor, when I heard a 'whomp' behind me. I looked around, and there was 'the Mick' with a suitcase on one side and his briefcase on the other, lying flat on his back. His glasses were about to fall off his nose. I REALLY didn't want to laugh because he might have been hurt. But the sight was hilarious. Mick was one of a kind.

"THE MICK"

When most people hear that nickname, they automatically think of Mickey Mantle. Not me. I think of Thomas P. Mickle. He was the Assistant Sports Information Director when I came to Duke in 1975. Tom came to Duke fresh out of Penncrest High in Media, Pennsylvania. He graduated from Duke in 1972 with a degree in Engineering. Following his graduation, Athletic Director Carl James hired Mickle as an assistant to SID Richard Gianinni. "Mick" had a rather high-pitched voice, for which he took some good-natured kidding, and was VERY laid-back. So at ease was he that Coach Foster called him 'Eddie Sominex.' Tom would just grin and go on about his business of taking excellent care of the media. A prime example of his thoughtfulness for the writers and broadcasters, took place one August morning in the early 80's. The ACC Football Tour had made its Duke stop the day before, and as all of us came out of our rooms at the Carolina Duke Motel in Durham to board the bus we had a surprise.. We always had breakfast on our own at all the other schools, but not this morning. There were several card tables with tablecloths set up for us. The 'M&M Boys' had sausage and ham biscuits and juices for all of us. I heard they even had Bloody Marys for any members of the 'fourth estate' who might be so inclined.

Tom served the Duke athletic department for 17 years in a variety of positions, including Sports Information Director from 1976 until 1986. He was promoted to Director of Sports Services and Director of the Varsity Club, the school's fund-raising arm for former student-athletes, and held those positions until he left for the Atlantic Coast Conference office in 1989.

In Greensboro, Mickle took on many duties for the conference. He managed the conference finances, supervised the marketing, public relations and video service divisions and was in charge of implementation of the conference's major public events. He also played a key role in reshaping the bowl landscape of major college football over the last 20 years. This took place over dinner in a Greensboro steakhouse as Tom laid out his ideas to the Commissioner, for a 'Bowl Coalition.' There was no multi-media presentation, just Mickle's notes on a mustard-stained napkin. The original Bowl Coalition eventually evolved into the current

Bowl Championship Series. Post-season football conference revenues increased from a pre-Coalition $1.2-million to nearly $15-million as a result of Mickle's forward-thinking efforts. Tom also played a significant role in procuring ACC bowl slots in the Toyota Gator, Chick-fil-A Peach and Tangerine Bowls. He was also instrumental in bringing Florida State into the league, realizing that a football program of that caliber would greatly increase revenues.

"Mick" was an integral part of the negotiations of the ACC's football and basketball television agreements that increased revenues and exposure, and produced the most lucrative college basketball television package in history. Mickle also changed the conference's football scheduling philosophy to a yearly process enabling the ACC to put its best games in the most advantageous positions for maximum television ratings and exposure.

From Greensboro, Tom moved to Orlando, Florida as Florida Citrus Sports Executive Director. Mickle's vision throughout his four plus years at FCSports was to make Orlando the nation's 'Capital of College Football.' During the summer of 2005, Mickle led a series of contract negotiations with the Atlantic Coast Conference, Big Ten and Southeastern Conference, as well as ABC Sports and ESPN.

The Mick" left us on April 17, 2006 at the age of 55. As I write this I realize that it was four years ago today.

Mickle is Scottish for 'a great quantity or amount.' Thomas P. Mickle was just that.

CHAPTER ELEVEN
1978 REGULAR SEASON

The start of the 1978 season was a little like most of the previous seasons. The exhibition game against St. Francis of Canada was what got the excitement started. The Blue Devils won by a score of 122-79 before a packed Cameron Indoor Stadium. Foster's squad walloped Johns Hopkins and Washington College by a combined NINETY points. That's right, 90. It certainly looked like there was a new and improved Duke product on the floor. From those first glimpses, fans got a taste of what was to come from Bill's fourth team, and they liked the flavor of the 'tid bits' that they were sampling.

After losing to UNC and beating Wake Forest the Big Four Tournament in Greensboro, we headed west. Phyllis got to join me on a big trip, as flew to Dallas to play SMU. While in Dallas, we visited the Dallas Cowboys' complex. Johnny Moore, was a good friend of Gil Brandt, the Director of Player Personnel for the Cowboys. Gil OK'd the visit, and I went to get a couple of interviews to use on the SMU broadcast that night. The players couldn't be at the game the arena because they were getting ready to play the 49ers in San Francisco.

I caught Tom Landry and Tony Dorsett between meetings and had hoped to interview Roger Staubach. His quarterbacks' meeting was running long, so we waited. Charlie Waters, their All-Pro safety stopped and questioned me about the Duke logo on my shirt. Since Charlie was a former Clemson player, I taped some comments with him. We were running short on time and were walking to the car when someone called my name. It was Staubach.

BOB & COWBOYS QB ROGER STAUBACH 12/8/77

He was so apologetic for making us wait, but I was impressed that someone of his stature would try to find ME to do an interview. Everybody at the car would just have to wait on me. Staubach gave me a great interview. Phyllis even got a chance to make my picture with the All-Pro. Several years later our paths would cross again. His son got a baseball scholarship to Duke and I got to see him on several of his visits to Duke. One of those was the Youth Day service in Wallace Wade Stadium. He was the speaker and I got to introduce him.

We handled the Mustangs that night, and flew to Los Angeles the next morning. The team hotel was the Sheraton Universal Studios where Evel Knievel was living while under house arrest. We saw him getting into his wild sports car one morning. As for the game, Southern Cal played tough and physical just like the scouting report read. Former Duke All-American Jeff Mullins was the Assistant Director of Athletics during this time period, and I asked him to be the analyst on the broadcast.

With the clock winding down in regulation, Mike Gminski went to the basket for the potential game-winner. He got fouled, not once, but twice. One Trojan player blocked him with his body and the other fouled him on the arm while Mike was shooting. There was no call by the referee and we went to overtime. The mild-mannered Mr. Mullins was incensed and I agreed. PAC-8 referee Booker Turner swallowed his whistle on that one.

I don't know if the team didn't get over the call, but we lost, 87-81. Even though I say that an official's call shouldn't decide a game, they can. I know almost all of the ACC officials well enough to say that the vast majority of the calls these guys make are right on the money. They very seldom receive praise for their work. That game in Los Angeles wasn't called very well, and it probably did cost Duke a CHANCE to win the game. The reason I say this is not because I am the announcer for the Blue Devils. I am just letting you know that the Commissioner of the Pac-8 sent a letter of apology to Duke about the officiating. It was a nice gesture, but the score remained the same.

One of the biggest wins of the regular season came in a two game road trip to Roanoke to play Virginia Tech, and to College Park to face No. 12 Maryland. Tech was undefeated, and Duke won by seven. The Blue Devils were developing a number of offensive weapons, something that would be very beneficial down the stretch. They showed the same tenacity two nights later when they beat the Terps, 88-78.

Fans listening to the 107-85 win at Clemson heard Duke assistant SID Johnny Moore adding color to the broadcast.

BOB & JOHNNY @ CLEMSON 1/78

Senior Night was the last home game for the only senior, former walk-on Bruce Bell. Clemson came to Cameron and Duke finished up the home schedule with a sixteen-point win.

Almost every college coach will tell you that he places no more value on one game than any other. Wins are the same way. You don't get extra credit for a conference win or one over a nationally ranked opponent. The margin of victory is of no consequence. A win over your closest rival, however, is just a bit sweeter.

Until 1975, a team had to win the ACC Tournament to get the league's ONLY bid to the NCAA Tournament. The NCAA expanded its field to 32 teams that season, most felt the second-place team would get into the field.

This Duke team was as colorful and different as anyone could imagine.

Take a couple of Jersey guys; add a kid from Connecticut; toss in a Philly phenom, a small town North Carolina jokester, a preacher-to-be from Georgia, a transfer from Indiana and another one from Durham, and you have the makings of a Final Four team.

Jim Spanarkel was the first Duke player to score 2,000 points in a career. Jim had some very special qualities about him. He had a quiet charisma that drew the respect of teammates and fans alike. I always kidded about him being pigeon-toed, slow and couldn't jump. The only thing he did on the court was beat you. Jimmy had as much court savvy as any player to play at Duke. He was so cool under pressure. I don't remember him ever getting rattled on the floor. Everybody called him Captain, because he was that for two years. Jim was drafted by the Philadelphia 76'ers, traded to Dallas, and played five years in the NBA. He is a Vice-President and financial planner for Merrill Lynch and is a basketball analyst for CBS and the NBA telecasts.

The center may the youngest player ever to suit up for the Blue Devils. Mike Gminski was 16 when he enrolled at Duke after graduating from Masuk High School in Monroe, Ct. a year early. His 17th birthday was after practice started.

My road to Duke was unconventional, to say the least. As a 15 year-old sophomore in high school, I made the precocious decision that a freshman year in college would benefit me more than a senior year in high school, so I decided to graduate early. Already being heavily recruited, I decided to let only 6 schools know of my decision - UNC, Maryland, South Carolina, Davidson, William and Mary and Notre Dame. You'll notice Duke is not on that list. Here's where things got interesting.

My first unofficial visit to a school on the list was to Maryland's basketball camp. Lefty Driesell was a gracious host and a heck of a recruiter. While there, I befriended a counselor who was working the camp - Duke center Terry Chili. Chili noticed how well I was playing and started to chat me up about Duke. I told him of my plan to leave high school early and he asked if he could contact his coaching staff. I agreed to let Duke into the process.

Duke was my first official visit and it was love at first sight. I immediately hit it off with Coach Foster and his staff, saw they had a critical piece in place with freshman Jim Spanarkel, and had a great time on campus, squired around by, of course, Terry Chili. I got on the plane for the trip back home knowing I had found my home for the next four years. I called the other schools and told them of my decision. It turned out to be one of the best decisions of my life! As a side bar, Lefty never had another counselor at his camp from the ACC!

Mike Gminski – May 7, 2009

Very few players had nicknames in the late 70s, but ABC's colorful color analyst, Al McGuire gave him the moniker "The Aircraft Carrier." At six feet-eleven inches tall and 245 pounds, he was the biggest 'ship' in Duke's harbor. He started from day 1 and was named ACC Co-Rookie of the Year. His first ACC experience in a Duke game was a daunting one.

Bob Harris played a huge role in my introduction to ACC basketball. We were about to play the Big Four Tournament in Greensboro, and it would be my first game against league competition. As we approached the arena for practice, I saw a large number of people strung along the roadside, offering to buy tickets. Once inside, I remember taking a look around the empty arena. Keep in mind my hometown had a population of around 6,000 people. The Coliseum held close to 18,000. I remember turning to Bob and asking, "Do they fill this place?" He smiled broadly and in his paternalistic style, tried to prepare me for what I was about to face. I was so overwhelmed by my first game experience, a four point, two rebound effort vs. Wake, I was pining for home and wondering if I had made a terrible mistake leaving early. But things got better for me and that started a long and wonderful relationship with Bob.

Gminski earned All-ACC three times, ACC Player of the Year as a junior, and 1st team All-American as a senior. He was an Academic All-American his sophomore, junior, and senior years. Mike was drafted by Philadelphia and played 14 years in the NBA. After he retired, Mike looked to broadcasting. Again quoting:

I started my broadcasting career on radio, working for the then-Charlotte Hornets. One of the allures of radio for me is that nothing happens for the listener unless the announcers say so. They are dependent on us for all of the game action. Well it is fair to say that nothing happens for Duke fans listening to basketball or football unless Bob Harris says so. You have to have many qualities to become the voice of a program - great pipes, a great work ethic, a love of the sport and a love of the institution you're working for. Bob has all of these. While being the voice of one of the great basketball programs in college sports, Bob has witnessed many incredible moments in his three plus decades behind the mic.

Yet he has remained humble throughout it all, never believing himself to be bigger than the program or the sport. He is an iconic voice with an incredible sense of himself. I am proud to call him a mentor and now a colleague. Most of all, I am proud to call him a friend of over thirty years. I will never tire of the big smile and the extended handshake when I see him. Who knew such a friendship would develop from such an innocent question!

He came from Pennsylvania where he played for the "Speedboys" of West Philadelphia High. He was, arguably, one of the most athletic players to ever play at Duke. That high school nickname alone should have told Duke fans what to look for when Eugene Lavon "Tinkerbell" Banks stepped onto the Duke campus. Gene was the most sought-after high school player in the country his senior year, and according to Tink; Foster put on the full-court press in his recruitment.

Being from Philadelphia, all the Big 5 schools (Penn, Villanova, St. Josephs, LaSalle, and Temple) were telling me that I should stay home and help revive their programs, but I wanted to get out and see what was in the outside world. Coach Joseph Goldenberg prepared us for all the attention we were getting as a team and as individuals. We were 30-0 and No. 1 in the country. The recruiting process was wild and crazy at times. The attention I was getting was great at first, but then it got overbearing. UCLA, N.C. State, Notre Dame and a bunch of others were after me.

There were two things that influenced me to come to Duke. Harold Morrison and William H. Detwiler, who was my English teacher. I didn't know much about Duke. I didn't even know where Duke was. Coach Bill Foster left me a book about the Duke campus, no basketball. Dr. Detwiler was tutoring me after school and he suggested that I at least visit Duke. He talked to me about academics only, no basketball. The visit was wonderful; it was a comfortable setting.

When I announced that I was coming to Duke, the Philly people thought I had lost my mind. My mom told me she couldn't go to school for me, and that I should pray about it.

Notre Dame continued to pursue me, saying that comparing Duke and Notre Dame was like comparing a Volkswagen to a Cadillac. They brought in several big-name former players, but it didn't sway me at all. When we played in the Knights of Columbus event, Duke assistant Bob Wenzel was there, and the Notre Dame guys cornered me and were really putting pressure on me. Coach Wenzel was steaming, and when I finally got away, I walked by him and winked, and told him not to worry about it. Everything would be okay.

Gene was ACC Rookie of the Year. He was very image conscious. He was a hair over 6'5" but always told people he was 6'7." His 'Speedboys' teammates hung the "Tinkerbell" tag on him because Gene moved around the court like the character in Peter Pan. I don't think he really liked 'Tinkerbell' because he asked me early on to refer to him as 'Magnum Force.' He always had something unique for his interviews. Gene had a six-year career in the NBA with San Antonio and Chicago. He now lives in Greensboro.

A freshman from the hamlet of King, North Carolina, just outside of Winston-Salem, was the power forward. Kenny Dennard's standard description of King was, "We don't have a stoplight yet, but we have picked out the colors."

I knew from the summer of 1977 when Tinker Bell and I played pick up games against each other on rubber floors in the intramural building that something special was going to happen for us at Duke. And all I know now, some 30 plus years later, is that my life was forever changed because of that special feeling. I remember saying on many occasions during the 1978 season that, "I hope I never forget these times" ... and I have kept my word. My hope for everyone is that they can have a year like that to remember for themselves, a year where lifetime relationships are forged from common goals turned into extraordinary accomplishment.

As eloquent as Kenny was, he was also considered the "class clown." Kenny was always pulling pranks on teammates, coaches and broadcasters alike. But when he hit the court, 'Dennis the Menace' turned into a junkyard dog. He was tenacious on defense and always attacking on offense. His quick release jumper would put his defender on his heels. At 6'7" and 210 pounds, he could take his man into the paint. Kenny was the first college player to make a reverse dunk on national television. There is a long story behind this. Well, it's long with Kenny telling it.

THE TRUE AND COMPLETE STORY OF THE FIRST BACKWARDS DUNK IN NCAA HISTORY By Kenny Dennard, April 19, 2009

The opening tip, seconds away. The best and only set play from the tip-off that I had ever seen or been a part of is about to be successfully run again for probably the 20th time of the season. G-Man readies himself to tip the ball to Tinker Bell who's straight in front of him towards our end of the floor. Spanarkel and I are mid-court extended nearly to the out of bounds line opposite each other. The ref enters the circle, tosses the ball up in the air, and then BAM, the game begins, Tinker Bell gets the tip, turns, dribbles to the top of the key, Sparky and I are racing down the wings for a three on two fast break. Gene head fakes left to Sparky and then drops me a little bounce pass to the right side. I catch, go up for a slam-dunk and then it happens, the defender hits me on the attempt, knocks me off center and then time slows down. In super slow motion, I am rotated and reverse dunk the ball completely out of necessity, and then hear the whistle from the ref for the foul. I land and time comes back to normal, but I can't feel anything and now hear a phone ringing. I line up for the foul shot and still hear a phone ringing. I hit the foul shot and phone ringing gets louder. The biggest game in my life has started: Duke 3, Villanova 0. The ringing is maddening.

SNAP! I jump up and out of bed then realize I am alone in a hotel room somewhere in Rhode Island, and the phone is shaking off the hook like in a movie. I pick up the handle and it's my wake up call. It's Sunday morning, March 19, 1978. We play Villanova this very afternoon for the Eastern Regional title and a ticket to the Final Four. I immediately realize that which just took place was not real, it was just a dream. It had to be a dream, I made the foul shot. But man, what a great freaking dream.

I didn't want to forget this dream.

So I immediately called my brother, Tommy, and told him my dream in rapid bursts, the way you tell dreams as you try to remember the exact events again for the first time. And as I was telling it to him I was getting as excited as I had gotten when I was dreaming it. He listened patiently to me to the end and then calmly told me to come down out of the clouds, get my head out of my a## and get real. This was the biggest day of my life, my team's life, and I shouldn't be having dreams or illusions of grandeur. It could be counterproductive.

He was right, I thought. Gene and I had grown up with the dunk shot outlawed and illegal. Most coaches did not support any form of dunking, even goofing around before practice. "You play the way you practice" was a common saying by coaches. It was almost as meaningful at the time as, "You don't marry who you don't date." I heard that phrase from my mother time and time again when she commented on my relationship with my future wife. Maybe they were right? But let's not get ahead of ourselves.

We practiced all kinds of crazy dunks that year away from prying coaches' eyes, the kind I guess all players our age and ability were working on in the secret labs of practice courts across the country. The early results of our lab work paid immediate dividends for Duke Fans primarily by watching Gene Banks' tomahawk one-handed and rock-the-baby dunks that, for their time, can easily be compared to anything LaBron James is doing today. G-Man was two-hand slamming everything he could. Even Spanarkel would get the crowd all pumped up when he would jam a breakaway lefthander. But all that is fine, unless you missed a dunk, then you would be in deep do-do with your coaches. Rule of thumb - you never went out in a game and tried something that you might possibly miss and watch bounce back to half court and start the opponents' fast break. That's the quickest way to serious bench time.

Back, Back, Back, Back, Back, Back!

Back to the '78 Eastern Regional finals. Back to the first half where the dream I had earlier that morning had been shelved for the "reality of the moment." Back to the first half where I badly twisted my ankle and had to go into the dressing room for the doctors to examine. Back to when I told our trainer, Max Crowder, that I was going back into this game. Back to when I asked him to re-tape over the tape he had layered on prior to the game, and to re-tape it very tight. He did and I went back onto the court, back into the game.

In the second half, we extended our lead over Whitey Rigsby and his Wildcats to nearly 20 points with about 10 minutes to play. They were pressing full court and desperately trying to cut into our lead. Then the funniest thing happened. Keith Herron missed an uncontested dunk on a fast break (remember, coaches hate missed dunks) but was then fouled when he grabbed the rebound and tried to lay it in. He made both foul shots and Villanova set up for their anticipated full court press defense.

Newton's third law is: "For every action, there is an equal and opposite reaction."

We also had a full court offensive play from a foul shot and after Herron made his second foul shot, we all began moving to our designated places on the court. My assignment was to block out the foul shooter and then run to center court on the right side and be ready to come back to the middle to receive a pass. However, when running to mid-court, I noticed no one was behind me and I kept running at full speed down the right side of the court.

That's when it hit me.

That's when time slowed down, just like in my dream. That's when I turned to look back at the play and the basketball was floating perfectly towards me like an orange pillow. That's when, as I caught the ball, I felt this huge grin pop up on my face. That's when I took one dribble and executed the first backwards dunk on national TV in NCAA history – and it was in super slow motion in my mind. Gene had thrown the perfect pass and I had made the perfect backwards dunk. That's when life as I knew it was forever changed.

The crowd went crazy.

But my coach, Bill Foster, was ticked and cussing up and down the bench. Billy Packer told the national audience to "get out the mustard, what a hotdog move by Dennard." In fact, NBC only showed the replay one time. Seriously, only one replay ever. We went to the Final Four the next week and it was never shown or used to promote the weekend. It was so unexpected and so radical at the time; the "powers that were" did not see this behavior as behavior they would like to promote. But over the next few days, I heard from everyone I knew and many that I didn't know about how much fun it was to see my grin and then see that dunk.

I spoke with Tommy after the game. He said he, too, had a big grin pop up on his face at the same second I did because he knew that only we knew this dunk was going to happen before it happened.

It's funny, I didn't tell anyone the complete story for many years.

It was special. It was Tommy's and my secret moment. Obviously years later, I have verbally told friends and reporters this story ad nauseam, especially since I am now old and deformed. However, and only for Bob Harris, this is the first time I have ever written the true and complete story of the dunk for publication. I may reprint this when I write my own book one day. Oh that's right, I am being paid handsomely by friends and associates to never write the true and complete story of my life. And remember, I will never be a suicide, call Colombo!

After Kenny graduated from Duke he had a five year career in the NBA, playing for Denver and Kansas City. He is a very successful businessman and part owner of a public relations firm in Houston. His greatest win? Beating cancer.

John Harrell was a two-sport star at Hillside High School in Durham. He played two years at North Carolina Central where his father was the head of the math department. John transferred to Duke in the summer and didn't have to red-shirt because Central was not Division I. 'Johnny Gunn' was an exciting player. He was lightening quick running and shooting. That's where the nickname 'Gunn' came from. He fell right in to the 'Runnin' Devils' style.

John suffered a heart attack at his home in Fairfax, Va. and died in July 2008. Rest in peace, my friend.

Duke had another transfer who became eligible in '78. Bob Bender began his collegiate career Indiana and was a member of the undefeated 1976 National Championship team. Duke recruited Bobby but he wanted to play for Bobby Knight. After just one year there, Bob wasn't happy and decided to look for a better opportunity. He was a back-up point guard at IU, and felt that his chances for extended playing time were not all that good with the talent coming back. He also found it difficult to put up with Knight's coaching style. He called Duke. Foster was glad to have him. Bender had to sit out the 1977 season because of the NCAA transfer rule, but was a tremendous help to the Blue Devils in practice that year. He is the only individual to play on two different teams in an NCAA Championship game. After graduation Bob came back to Duke as an intern in the athletic department, and was my analyst on the network for the 1983 season. In 1984 he was added to Krzyzewski's staff as an assistant. He was Head Coach at Illinois State and Washington, and is now an assistant with the Atlanta Hawks.

If you have never had an opportunity to visit Cameron Indoor Stadium, the Crow's Nest is in the rafters at center court.. To get up there, we have to use the Section 7 portal from the concourse into the seating area. Then, you trudge up to the last row of seats, turn to face the court, and climb an eight-step ladder. When you get to the top of the ladder, you have to step over a metal crossbeam that helps support the booths. Hey, I've been doing this at least three times each home game for 35 years!! The problem isn't getting UP there. It is the coming down part that darn nearly killed me in 1978.

With all of my going up and coming down that ladder, you'd think that I would know how to do it. Not so, as evidenced on January 28 in our game against ECU. Jim Woods, the 'Voice of the Pirates" asked me to be his half-time interview. I needed to visit the Gentlemen's 'powder room' before the interview. In trying to hurry down, I failed to make sure the ladder was securely blocked against the concrete step. I put my left foot on the second step of the ladder and was bringing my right leg over that beam when the ladder shot out from under me.

"Grab hold of something, ANYTHING.' I got my right arm around a vertical support but my upper left arm caught on the top of a short piece of 'angle-iron.' OUCH!!! My right leg shot out on top of the 'chicken-wire' shelf that keeps things from on the spectators. That night, it prevented ME from falling on them. OK, that's three of the four limbs accounted for. My left leg was dangling below me about five feet from the concrete steps.

Several men in the seats jumped up to help. They grabbed my leg and told me to stiffen it and they could push me back up.WHEW!! What about the ladder? It grazed the right side of the head and shoulder of a lady who was sitting on an aisle seat. She had no injuries, but you KNOW what would happen in today's 'suit-happy' society.

After I collected my wits about me, I went on the air with Jim. The 'powder room' had to wait. At the next home game there was a new ladder with metal hooks at the top to keep it from falling. There is a better ladder there now that is all aluminum with a slip-resistant covering on all steps.

CHAPTER TWELVE

IT WILL SNOW IN GREENSBORO BEFORE...

The 1978 ACC Tournament was played in Greensboro and the Blue Devils actually beat Clemson in the opening round game. They hadn't done that since 1966. After the game, Coach Foster told the media that he normally packed just a handkerchief for the ACC trip, because the Blue Devils were only there for one day. He also confided to them that he brought along enough clothes to stay the whole tournament. Duke beat Maryland in the Semi-Finals, the Tar Heels lost to Wake Forest.

UNC's loss really put the monkey on Duke's back. The Demon Deacons had the NCAAs as their goal, just like Duke did. Duke now had to win. The last time Wake won, Bones McKinney was the coach of a Chappell-Packer led team. Mike Lewis, Bob Verga, Steve Vacendak and company propelled one of Vic Bubas' best teams to Duke's last one. Think there might have been a little emotion in those dressing rooms?

When the tournament began on March 1st, the temperature in Greensboro was a balmy 71 degrees. On Friday, the 3rd, the Triad got six inches of snow!! Talk about putting a different spin on everything? At the Friday morning press conference, Foster quipped, "They always said that it would be a snowy day in Greensboro when Duke made the finals. I guess they were right."

Saturday, March 4, 1978 was a red-letter day for the Atlantic Coast Conference. The Tournament finals were on national television for the very first time. In the past, maybe a dozen college basketball games were nationally televised. This game was being shown on ABC AND CBS. Prior to the game, I had the five starters introduce themselves for our pre-game show. You can hear THAT on the accompanying CD.

Duke broke that twelve-year drought with an 85-77 win. The ACC Tournament Championship and the automatic berth in the NCAA Tournament belonged to Duke.

Since there was snow everywhere, we all stayed at the team hotel in Greensboro that night. Phyllis and I were sitting beside the pool, playing cards while the players were horsing around in the water. I got worried when I heard Kenny Dennard say, "are you guys ready?" There was a commotion behind me and the next thing I knew, I was picked up by Gminski, Banks and Scott Goetsch. They were going to throw me into the pool, clothes and all. Over Kenny's objections, they let me take my watch off, and my wallet and keys out of my pockets, and take my shoes off. Do you know what it feels like to be 'hurled' into a pool?? I do, and I loved it. I felt like I was a special part of 'Forever's Team' and I still do.

Dennard has been a special friend since his undergraduate days in Durham.

Bob Harris and I shared many meals and many stories during my four years at Duke. Bob's ability to patiently listen to the ravings of a hormonally oversexed kid from King, North Carolina 'back in the day' is only exceeded by his ability to make you feel like you're the most interesting person in the world. Bob is loved and respected by all because he has the innate ability to make celebrities feel like they are normal people and normal people feel like they are celebrities. I have admired that quality since I met him and have tried, always in my own humble way, to make it one of my own.

I get from one to ten emails from Kenny almost every day. A lot of it concerns his public relations firm, but there is always something to make me laugh. He keeps the '78 team informed on everything, and I'm included. He's one-of-a-kind.

The 'first' season was done, and season number two was about to begin. We were going to the East Region, and play Rhode Island in the Charlotte Coliseum just over two hours down I-85. The trip was about 130 miles, less than a trip to Clemson, but this was the NCAAs. From this point forward, the basketball world was looking on and Bill Foster's team had to make a statement. They just had to take care of business.

The Rhode Island-Duke game came down to the final seconds. The Rams' star, Sly Williams, put up a shot with just seconds remaining. G-man blocked it. Williams threw up another one. SWAT!! The "Aircraft Carrier" blocked two shots to save the 63-62 win.

Duke was one of only16 teams that still had a shot at the title. The Blue Devils advanced to Providence, Rhode Island, for the next round. Pennsylvania, Indiana, and Villanova, completed that quartet for Friday night.

Forgot to tell you, there was snow in Charlotte. Are you superstitious??

Duke + snow = WIN.

Bill Foster + blue blazer + plaid pants = WIN

Heck yes, I'm superstitious! The Duke fans just KNEW we'd win if one flake of snow hit the ground, and Bill just knew we'd win if he wore the same outfit. After each win, he would send it to the cleaners immediately to make sure it was clean for the next game. Some of us had other superstitions or rituals we went through for every game. I STILL have three trimmed pencils, and a red pencil, beside my score sheets for every basketball game. The red pencil is used for three-point field goals made. This superstition is about thirty years running!

Duke was housed in South Attleboro, Massachusetts, just over the state line from Providence, for the Regionals. We played Penn, the Ivy League Champion, on Friday night. Gminski blocked three consecutive shots in the late stages of the game and Duke won 84-80. Bill Foster's team was now among the elite eight teams in the country. The college basketball world was probably surprised because a bunch of kids wearing Duke Blue was just one game away from going to St. Louis for the Final Four.

In the first game on this St. Patrick's Day Friday, Villanova pulled off another shocker by beating favored Indiana 61-60. After our Penn game was over, Coach Bob Weinhauer told the media that the Blue Devils were 'as slow as a herd of elephants' and that Villanova would run all over us.

Sunday afternoon, Duke ran all over Villanova. It was a laugher, 90-72. This was one of Duke's best games of the season, and they were having fun doing it. Not bad for a 'herd of elephants.'

SNOW? Oh, yes. It was there when we arrived on Thursday, and more came while we were there.

The Duke fans were on cloud nine. The East Regional Championship would have been enough, but to get back to our hotel and see a UNC graduate dancing on a table was over the top!! Wade Cavin was the Mayor of Durham and he was having a wonderful time.

After a busy week of interviews and press conferences in Durham, the Blue Devils headed off to The Final Four to the strains of 'Meet Me In St. Louis.' The Checkerdome was the site for my first trip to the Final Four on Easter weekend. Duke, Notre Dame, Kentucky, and Arkansas were the last standing. Duke would play the Fighting Irish in the opener on Saturday with the winner taking on the winner of the later game between the Wildcats and the Razorbacks, on Monday night. We needed snow since it was now our good luck charm, but there was no snow when we arrived in St. Louis. Cold, damp, and rainy would have to do for now.

The NCAA held open practices on Friday, and I as I was walking into the Checkerdome, I kept thinking how crazy it was for the officials at the Checkerdome to schedule another event the weekend of the Final Four and at the same time of our practice. This WAS my first Final Four. I just thought that was the way they did things in St. Louis. By the time I made my way through the crowd into the arena, I realized that the only thing going on was the Blue Devils practice. Everyone was there to watch Duke run drills. There were more people at our practice that day than had been at most of our games the season before. We all were in shock, but enjoying every second of it.

Notre Dame was No. 6 in the polls, and had some big bodies, led by Bill Laimbeer, Dave Batten, and Kelly Tripucka. From that roster, eight players went on to careers in the NBA. Some thought Duke was a fluke and didn't deserve to be in the Final Four with the three 'powers.' Duke was only a preliminary in the minds of the Irish. A 'tiptoe through the tulips' with Duke, and then, bring on Kentucky.

The Checkerdome held 20,000 fans for basketball and kind of dwarfed most of the other arenas we had played in that season. Duke had a little extra motivation for this game. Notre Dame coach, Digger Phelps, didn't respect the ACC a whole lot, and during the preceding summer, chose to ignore Banks' National Letter of Intent that he signed with Duke. Notre Dame did not recognize Letters of Intent in any sport, and kept recruiting him very hard. It was almost like telling Gene and everyone else that his commitment to Duke didn't matter. He didn't know Gene as well as he thought he did. It DID matter to Gene and the whole program.

Duke led by two, 88-86, with twenty seconds left. Eleven seconds later, Spanarkel knocked the ball away from Laimbeer and a scrum ensued. John Harrell got his hands on the ball and was fouled. He had played a great floor game but had only four points. Duke led the nation in free throw percentage, and 'Gunn' was one of our best at 83%. John had a one and one, and if he made the first, the game was over. There wasn't a three-point shot in 1978. A miss coupled with a Notre Dame rebound and basket, and we would go to overtime. The crowd went eerily silent.

The quiet didn't last long. John swished the first one, and that put the game on ice for Duke. He made the second one too, and as the horn sounded, pandemonium broke loose. Duke won it 90 to 86.

In the second game, Kentucky got more than they wanted from Arkansas, but won a great game, 65-61.

Some of our listeners have asked why we do not broadcast the other games that are being played at our venue. For the NCAA Tournament, the radio stations on each participating university's network are the only ones who are permitted to air their games.By the same token, the rights holders of those networks are allowed to broadcast only games that their school is involved in. Other radio stations throughout the country may carry any tournament games, but they must be purchased through the NCAA's own network. This has been the policy every year that I have been privileged to work the tournament. As of the 2010 season, I have had the opportunity to broadcast at least one game in twenty-nine of my 35 basketball seasons.

The only other season that the Blue Devils had been to the NCAA title game was 1964 when UCLA won, 98-83, for their first NCAA title.

Every Division 1 college basketball team begins each season with hopes of hoisting up the championship trophy at mid-court on the last night of the season. For some it is ONLY hope, for the elite, it is expectation. Kentucky had begun this 1978 season with the bull's eye squarely on their collective chests.The Wildcats' fans would accept nothing less. On this Monday night, they were going to face a Duke team that had started the season just thinking about the Final Four.

For the Blue Devils, the first thing they wanted to accomplish was extricating themselves from the cold, dark recesses of the cellar of the Atlantic Coast Conference. When that was accomplished in Greensboro, Coach Foster and his young team may have allowed themselves to think about loftier goals, but realizing that it would take a wild series of happenings for it to become reality.

For Kentucky, it was totally opposite. They were anointed champions-in-waiting by the media in the preseason.The two top collegiate sports in Kentucky are Wildcats basketball and Wildcats basketball recruiting. They eat, sleep, live and die with UK basketball. A religion? Some have intimated as much. Kentucky lost just twice that season, and rabid Wildcats fans said that was two too many. The trophy was theirs. It was their destiny, their birthright. Nothing else mattered. Duke had no pressure, UK had pressure, and it was as big as the entire Commonwealth of Kentucky. The whole sports world was watching. They would be embarrassed if they lost to, not just Duke, but anyone.

Let me bring it a little more into focus. Joe B. Hall was the coach of Kentucky. He had played basketball at Kentucky. When he cut himself shaving, he saw Kentucky blue blood, not red. He said, " The only way

I will consider this season a success is if we win the national title." A loss to Duke in this championship game would mean "that our entire season was a waste." Some writers reported that he had been told by some of the top Wildcat supporters that if he didn't win the title, he 'shouldn't bother getting on the team plane for the trip home.' His coaching career at UK was full of pressure. After all, he replaced Adolph Rupp. Joe B. was in the championship game in 1975, but lost to UCLA. He had to win this one or live in shame forever.

At the hotel as we were getting ready to go to the game, I told Phyllis "I can't believe that just three years ago I was broadcasting the high school 2A Regionals in Stanly County, and in a few hours, I will be broadcasting the NCAA National Championship game." If I had thought, I would have said, "HOW SWEET IT IS!!!"

The basketball game paled in comparison to something that unfolded earlier that day. In the afternoon before the game, Jay Randolph, the sports director of KMOX-TV in St. Louis, received a phone call. The man told him, "If Banks plays tonight, he will be killed." Shortly after the first call, another one came in. I ran into Jay outside the media area and he told me about the calls and asked me who he needed to talk to. I had known Jay for a number of years, so I knew he was very serious about this. We found Tom Mickle, Duke's Sports Information Director in the hallway outside the locker room and the three of us went to the dressing room and located Coach Foster, and President Terry Stanford. After weighing all the possibilities, they decided not to tell Gene. They all suspected that it was a hoax. The team wasn't told until after the game. Police security was more than usual around the Duke bench but Coach told the team this was the NCAA. Banks wasn't aware that anything was going on.

I found out about the threat after the game. I was told that they didn't want to tell me before the game so that I would be focused. They put policemen around my parents during the game, and had extras around the court as well. I was oblivious to all of that. Once I heard about it, I kinda shrugged it off, because, coming up in Philly, there was a time that I elbowed a guy, and he ran and got a gun and chased me home, just for playing basketball. Crazier things than that threat had happened to me before. After the game, I wasn't as concerned about the threat, as I was disappointed over the loss. I was just thankful that all of the game personnel took the necessary steps to insure my safety.

I rode the Iron Dukes bus to the Checkerdome and carried my equipment with me. We got there about 6:00pm and I set up the mixer and head-phones at our assigned broadcast position on the first press row behind the Kentucky bench. I tested the signal back to Durham, and at 7:45, we hit the air with our 15-minute pre-game show. Duke President Terry Sanford and North Carolina Governor Jim Hunt were my pre-game interviews.

There was a sea of royal blue in the St. Louis Checkerdome. Fans of the Wildcats of Kentucky and the Blue Devils of Duke all wore their blue and white. The 'Cats were supposed to be here. The Devils were just happy to be here.

BOB INTERVIEWS DUKE PRESIDENT TERRY SANFORD & GOVERNOR JIM HUNT BEFORE 1978 NCAA TITLE GAME.

The Blue Devils had a great following for the Final Four, including Dr. Sanford and the Governor.

Tip-off came just little after 8:00 pm CST, and both teams were alittle nervous at first, but they settled down.

Duke trudged to their locker room at the half behind 45 to 38. Bill Foster and the staff had to get them refocused in that locker room. Duke roared out of the gate, and in very short order, the deficit had been cut to only three. For the rest of the game, the deficit was manageable. It was three to five points. Duke was trailing 51-46, when the momentum

'DON'T LET ME MESS THIS UP'
1st NATIONAL CHAMPIONSHIP
GAME BROADCAST 3/27/78

turned to Kentucky and the Devils never got it back.

The game turned for a final time on a terrible call from one of the officials. On a play that looked like a travel to BOTH fan bases, Referee Jim Bain, only a couple of feet from the action, didn't do anything. Close calls, judgment calls and no calls are a part of basketball. Here's where things got bizarre. Coach Foster stood up in front of the bench signaled a play to Harrell and Spanarkel, and yelled the instructions to them. Bain was headed away from Duke's basket on the other side of the court. He looked over at the Duke bench and mistook Coach's actions as unwarranted protest over the no call. He hit Bill with a technical foul. If the travel call had been made, the Blue Devils could have cut the disadvantage back to three and possibly gotten the momentum back. 'If ifs and buts were candy and nuts, we'd all have a Merry Christmas.' With the two made free throws off the technical and a jump shot basket, Kentucky rolled out to its biggest margin of the night, 55-46.

The irrepressible Jack 'Goose' Givens had the audacity to bank in a jumper from the corner across the floor from my vantage point. BANKED IT IN!! I doubt if you'll ever see too many NBA players do that. Right there I just shook my head and thought, "this just isn't our night." To Duke's credit, they never quit. This bunch fought tooth and nail until 0:00 popped up on the scoreboard. Final, 94-88, but the Duke players had so much to be proud of.

The comments from the national media were, "these Duke players don't know when to quit." And, "this is a gusty group from Durham." It wasn't that Duke didn't know WHEN to quit, they just didn't know HOW. That's a good thing.

When it was over, the Duke team headed to their locker room. I witnessed a lot of tears and hugs in there. This was a tremendously close-knit group of kids, and they were not losers, regardless of what numbers were on the scoreboard. They were summoned back to the court for the trophy presentations. In my forty-plus years in broadcasting, this sight remains as one of the most amazing I have ever witnessed. The Blue Devils linked arms and walked to the court as one. They would never allow that final score to measure them as men. It was about what they had accomplished in thirty-four basketball games in 1978.

As the players went on the court accepted their trophy, someone in the Duke crowd started chanting, "We'll be back, we'll be back." It began in the corner to my left and swelled until it almost filled the Checkerdome. The Duke team had been crowned champions by their own fans.

Twenty years later, I happened to see Jim Bain in Madison Square Garden before a Duke game. When I saw him I had a flashback to that Duke-Kentucky game. It would anger me every time someone brought up that game. An official's call does not win or lose a game. They sometimes influence the way a particular game is played.

I went across the court and introduced myself to him. After a few pleasantries, I said, "Jim, I broadcast the Duke-Kentucky National Championship game in 1978, and there's ..." He didn't let me finish. His comment floored me. "Bob, I blew that technical call. It is the only call in my career that I wish I could take back. I saw Bill standing and I thought he was trying to show me up. I made a terrible mistake. I talked with Bill several years ago and apologized to him. We're OK now"

I was so relieved to hear that. I shook his hand and thanked him. I told him I wasn't concerned any more. After he retired from active officiating, Jim spent about twenty years as an NCAA observer, watching games and critiquing officials. He hasn't missed a call.

I was standing in the back of the media room later with a writer from the Los Angeles Times. He wanted to know if this was my first Final Four. I asked if it showed that much. It really showed with my follow up comment, "Yes, but we'll be back next year because we have 12 of the 13 players on the roster coming back." He grinned at me and gave me a lesson I've never forgotten, "It's a lot harder to get back than it was to get here the first time, nothing is guaranteed." A portend of things to come!

CHAPTER THIRTEEN

DUKE FOOTBALL, MY EARLY YEARS

My Duke responsibilities mainly center around the football and men's basketball programs. I have helped out with broadcasts of women's basketball, and even done guest shots on the student station's baseball broadcasts. I am involved with the coaches TV shows and assist the Athletic Department in any way I can.

I began broadcasting Blue Devils football games in 1976. For about twenty-five years I hosted the weekly coaches' TV shows, but in 2007 the format changed and I began doing special segments of the shows. I have also hosted a five-minute daily radio show with the coaches during the seasons for about 20 years. I really love being a part of both programs. Some of my most favorite memories are from the football field.

I got my first taste of Division 1 college football at Duke. The very first college football game I broadcast was the opening game of the 1976 season. Simply because I had broadcast high school football games for 8 years, I felt that I was definitely prepared to handle the Duke play-by-play duties. The things I experienced on that trip to Knoxville to play Tennessee let me know that this was major college sports.

I flew with the team, and as we were deplaning in Knoxville, I heard the Duke Fight Song. Had the Duke Marching Band gone out before the team to welcome us there? Not at all. Dr. John Yarborough, a Duke graduate, and the team physician for the Alcoa High School athletic teams, paid for their band to come and play for us. He and his wife Marshall were Duke through and through. After the 'welcome' our three busses headed for downtown and the team hotel. Eight Tennessee Highway Patrolmen on their motor-cycles escorted the caravan. I had never witnessed anything like this in the South or North Piedmont or Rocky River Conferences. This WAS the big time.

On Friday night, the UT Sports Information Director, Haywood Harris, took all of us to eat at Ye Old Steakhouse. What a meal. The next night, 80,250 Tennessee fans, all clad in orange, jammed the 'giant Erector set' on the banks of the Tennessee River. I was starting my Duke career in a setting like this? The Volunteers were solid favorites to thrash the Blue Devils that night. I think Coach Mike McGee and his players might have known that.

Upon arrival to the press box, I could not believe the massiveness of Neyland Stadium. The atmosphere was something I had never experienced either. 'Smokey,' the Tennessee mascot was cavorting around the field and the Tennessee Marching Band played "Rocky Top" about 143 times during the evening. This was truly big time football.

In the press box, I had the opportunity to meet two of the true broadcasting legends that night. John Ward was doing the play-by-play for UT, and Lindsey Nelson, the first play-by-play announcer for the Vol Network, were both introduced to me. Nelson did the play-by-play of the Cotton Bowl for 25 seasons on CBS television.

Tennessee featured future All-Pro Stanley Morgan, and All-America wide receiver Larry Sievers. It was a close game with Duke winning, 21-18, as the UT kicker missed three extra points. Duke made three HUGE defensive plays in the last two minutes of the game. With just minutes to play, and QB Randy Wallace driving the Vols down the field, Duke defensive back Bob Grupp deflected passes on successive downs to force a fourth down for the Vols. The defense stopped a fourth down play one yard short of the first down and with 1:13 left in the game, the Duke offense took over at their own 32 yard line. With :50 remaining, I made the statement, "Somebody put that clock in fast-forward and let's get this one over with." Fans thought I was wishing the clock would run out before Tennessee could score. Not at all. In my excitement over my first

Duke broadcast, I forgot to visit the restroom. It was a physical thing!!!

About that time, fullback Tony Benjamin ran right through the Volunteer defense for 15 yards and the Blue Devils ran out the final few seconds for the upset win. It was a memorable way to start my career with Duke football and a great start for the 1976 season. By the way, you can hear bits of that first broadcast on the CD in the back of this book.

The ACC has not been, by most standards, a major football conference. There have been occasional blips on the radar. Maryland laid claim to the 1953 AP and UPI National Championship honors. Clemson won it in 1981, Georgia Tech in 1990, and Florida State in 1993 & 1999. The 1976 ACC preseason poll had Duke in the middle of the league. The schedule showed all seven ACC teams plus four non-conference games at Tennessee, South Carolina and Miami, and a home game with Pittsburgh.

After that win at Tennessee, we lost at South Carolina and won at Virginia. In the season's first home game, Pittsburgh and future NFL Hall of Fame running back Tony Dorsett (pronounced DOR sett) won 44-31. Duke's defense held him under 100 yards rushing for the only time in his final two seasons. Tony was not much of a factor, but QB Matt Cavanaugh was. He earned National Player of the Week honors for his performance. Cavanaugh later played for New England.

On October 9th Duke traveled to Miami to play the Hurricanes. As was the norm, we arrived on Friday to let the guys settle in. I had read that Muhammad Ali was in town to finish shooting the movie, "The Greatest". I told Phyllis, my color man John McNabb, his wife and Tom Mickle that we needed find him and see if he wanted to come to the game. They told me I had gone goofy. Mickle cracked, "There's no way we can find him, and if we do, there is no way that we can talk to him. Even if we do, why would he want to come a Duke game?"

I'm thinking, "Why WOULDN'T Ali want to come to the game and be on our broadcast?" They finally agreed to give it a try. I got the address of the Fifth Street Gym. That's where Ali always trained, and was supposed to be filming this weekend. We got our rental car and lit out to find one of the most famous people on the planet.

Since I didn't know how to get there, it took a while to get across town. When we got to the gym I walked in and told the manager who we were, and that we would like to see the "Champ" if at all possible. Without batting an eye, he said that Ali had finished shooting there and had relocated to the Miami Beach Auditorium to film another portion of the movie.

Off we drove to Miami Beach. We parked the car at the front door and went to the first open door we saw. We started to walk in, but a huge guy stopped us. He wanted to know what our business was, so I told him we were the Duke Radio crew and wanted to offer some tickets to Ali for the football game. After a couple of seconds, he said, "Stay right here." He left us standing there, and was off to the interior of the Auditorium.

After about twenty minutes, Phyllis said, "He's not coming back. He just said that to get rid of us." Shortly, he reappeared and said, "Come with me." I finally remembered who this man was. Drew Bundini Brown, Ali's assistant trainer and corner man. He was also one of Ali's speechwriters. He wrote Ali's famous: "Float like a butterfly, sting like a bee. Your hands can't hit what your eyes can't see."

The five of us followed Brown down the hall without being too conspicuous or nervous, but we were. We went through the room where they were shooting one of the locker room scenes. Ernest Borgnine, who was playing Ali's manager Angelo Dundee, was in there as well as Angelo himself. With Brown leading the way, no one tried to stop us. He ushered us into a small cubicle and there, on a small bench, was Ali. He wasn't imposing figure I was expecting. He had on a white long-sleeved shirt with the sleeves rolled up. I quickly told him who we were and why we had come to see him. I shook his hand, then handed him a 3x5 card that had the five-second promo I had written for him to record. I asked if he would give me permission to play it in the broadcast opening the next night.

Ali read over the four-line poem that I had tried to write in 'Ali' style. After a moment or two, he flashed that famous Ali grin and asked, "Who wrote this?" I didn't know whether to own up to it or not. I wasn't sure he approved. I said, "I did." He grinned again and said, "Sounds just like me.

Are you ready to go?" My recorder had been running the whole time.

With all of the people outside the cubicle there was some noise. They were working even though Ali wasn't there. "Y'all be quiet," he yelled. "We're gonna tape something." They got quiet. He read it twice while I recorded him, but because of some slight noise from outside, he wanted to go to another location. As we walked back through the cast and crew, I could see their quizzical looks at us. I introduced him to Phyllis, John and Suzie, and Tom, and the five of us stood out in this dimly lit hallway with 'The Greatest.' He did another 'take' and put the 'Ali touch' in it. "From the Orange Bowl in Miami, down by the sea. It's Duke versus Miami, this is Muhammad Ali." He frowned and said, "Can we do this again?" "No problem, Champ."

We did 13 more takes and he ad-libbed several, and messed up a couple. We all could not believe how much time he took just to get a five second promo right. Even after 16 takes, I used the second one and we played it five times in the game. You can hear all 16 takes on the CD. We Asked if he'd like to come to the game, and he said, "How many tickets can I get?" Mickle stepped up with, "How many do you want?" He only wanted six.

We thanked him and headed back to our hotel. The next morning we took the six tickets to the Fontainebleau Hotel on Miami Beach. The seats were occupied, but not by Ali.

Several years later, Ali spoke to a convocation at Durham College, and I covered the speech for the station and interview him. I was surprised and happy that he remembered that meeting in Miami and the promo. It is so sad to see this former great physical specimen of a man broken by the effects of Parkinson's Disease that he has battled since 1984.

I think Ali's poem brought Duke good luck because the Blue Devils defeated Miami, 20-7, in front of only14,000 fans.

Another highlight of that season was the following Saturday afternoon, when we spoiled the Clemson Tigers homecoming weekend. It was one of the most exciting finishes of the season. The Blue Devils were trailing 18-15 when Vince Fusco, who had already kicked five field goals in the game, kicked an ACC record 57-yard field goal to tie the game 18-18 as time expired. The Blue Devils ended the season with a 38-37 loss to UNC, but it was one of the most exciting games of that 5-5-1 season

On my very first ACC Football Tour in August 1976, I became involved in the 'longest, continuous bridge game' you could imagine. First off, 'The Tour' was a bus trip that the ACC sponsored for many, many years. It served the sports media from the conference footprint and enabled them to get interviews from players and coaches of all the ACC schools prior to the season. The Tour spent a day at each school and we attended practices in the morning, ate lunch with the players at the training table, did the interviews in the afternoon and filed our written, audio or video stories before dinner that evening with athletic department staffs.

What began as an eight-day trek in 1953, decreased to seven when South Carolina pulled out of the league after the 1971 academic year. With the admission of Georgia Tech in 1980, it went back to eight days, and then to nine in 1992, when Florida State came in. With the advent of the computer age, the Tour became less and less attractive to the media outlets. The schools began putting audio and video clips from players and coaches on satellite, so radio and TV didn't need to see them in person. The ACC was the last conference to abandon 'The Tour.'

At the beginning that 1976 trip I heard someone near the back of the bus ask if anyone played bridge. I had played a bunch in college (that might have been one of my problems), but none since 1962. I said that I had, and was summoned to the rear two rows as the 'fourth' for the game. Some guys read, some slept, some just looked out the window and talked to pass away the hours between schools. Not the guys on the back two rows.

Bill Brill, the sports editor of the Roanoke Times and World News, was the man who had asked for assistance. His partner for a number of years wasn't making the tour any more, and he needed a new partner. I became it. We were always paired against Caulton Tudor of the Raleigh Times (later the N&O) and either Larry Keech of the Greensboro News-Record, or a 'player to be named later.'

The game ran for the entirety of the Tour each August, and Brill and I only lost TWICE in 22 years!!! It had nothing to do with my prowess as a player. Brill was terrific. He could make a '3 no-trump' bid with 10 points in his hand. No, LK, he didn't cheat!

The ACC also held another summer event that was well attended at Linville and Grandfather Mountain. All members of the media were invited along with all of the football Head Coaches. Our host was Hugh Morton.

When I think of Grandfather, I think about the Highland Games and Gathering of Scottish Clans, gorgeous vistas, the animal habitat and beautiful fall colors. I also think of the man who made my family more aware of that beautiful and serene spot in the mountains of North Carolina near Linville.

Hugh MacRae Morton was born in 1921 in Wilmington, NC. His great-grandfather, Donald MacRae, had bought the development rights for the area around Grandfather Mountain in 1885. Hugh inherited this property from Hugh MacRae, his grandfather, in 1952. He foresaw the mountain as a possible tourist venue, and proceeded to build a road to the top of Grandfather. The Mile High Swinging Bridge was his creation as well.

Photography was Hugh's passion. He snapped every UNC athlete and dignitary from the time he returned from service, until his health failed in 2005. I have heard the story that people at UNC basketball games were warned not to block the view of "Mr. Morton's seat" which was on the baseline at Woolen Gym, Carmichael Auditorium and the Dean Smith Center.

I remember one particular photo that he took, and asked my assistance in obtaining permission from one of the subjects so he could use it in 'Hugh Morton: North Carolina Photographer,' which was published in 2006. The picture was a very candid one of the late Jim Valvano and Mike Krzyzewski before a basketball game that Mike was coaching in and Jimmy was broadcasting. I talked with Mike and he called Hugh and gave his permission. 'Mr. Morton' was a TRUE fan of Carolina sports and a friend of many influential North Carolinians.

His realm was not confined to UNC. His first photo collection book was 'Hugh Morton's North Carolina.' He relished sports figures, North Carolinians at work and play, and nature. He had the perfect setting for his nature pictures, his backyard, Grandfather Mountain.

In 1968, he bought two black bears; one male and one female, to release back into the wild. The female bear that he named Mildred, had to be recaptured and put into an enclosed habitat. Mildred became the 'face' of Grandfather. He took thousands of pictures of Mildred alone. I have two of them and this is the best. Mr. Morton gave me verbal permission to use it in this book in 2005. After Hugh died in 2006, the Morton family sold Grandfather Mountain and surrounding land to the state. It is now North Carolina's 34th state park. Hugh's entire photographic collection has been donated to North Carolina Collection Photographic Archives at UNC. I thank them for agreeing to my usage of two of his pictures in this book.

"C'MON MILDRED, IT'S MY SHOT." BOB & MILDRED THE BEAR AT GRANDFATHER MTN

I want to talk a bit about the man who was the head coach of the Blue Devils when I went to Duke. Mike McGee grew up in Elizabeth City. He was a guard at Duke and won the Outland Trophy (Duke's only winner) in 1959. Also in 1959, Mike made the Time Magazine All-America team, was voted Athlete of the Year in the ACC, and elected captain of the annual Chicago Tribune College All-Star Game. He had a brief career in the NFL with the St. Louis Cardinals before a neck injury sent him to coaching.

After serving as an assistant at Duke, Wisconsin, and Minnesota, he was picked to succeed the legendary Clarence Stasavich at East Carolina in

1970. After one year there, Mike became Head Coach at his alma mater.

About the middle of the 1977 season things began to 'go south' for McGee. Disgruntled fans were calling into my Sunday night Sports Comments show and blasting his coaching ability. I was defending Mike as best as I could. At a Monday press conference, he started his usual opening comments, and after just a few minutes, he stopped and looked straight at me. "I want to see you after we're through." I couldn't tell you one thing he said for the rest of the press conference. I tried to replay every word I had said on the talk show and even on the game broadcast Saturday. Mike is an imposing physical presence. I was concerned. The press conference ended. I followed him to his office. He closed the door behind us, took off his sport coat, and told me to sit down on the couch. He sat down beside me, not at his desk like the other times I had talked to him in the office. He began, "I heard your show last night." Gulp. "I thought you handled things well. May I assume that, judging from your comments, you are on my side?" "Absolutely," I said, relieved that I wasn't in trouble. "Good. If you're going to fight my battle for me, you need some ammunition."

We sat there for a half hour and he told me many things that I had no idea were factors in the situation. Mike made it through '77 and '78, but was fired after losing in Chapel Hill on the final day of the season.

Ironically, Mike earned his master's and doctorate degrees in sports administration at UNC in 1979, and served as Athletics Director at the Universities of Cincinnati, Southern Cal and South Carolina. Mike gave everything he had to everything he did. He remains a good friend to this day.

Over the next 11 seasons, Duke had three more head coaches. Red Wilson coached for four seasons after McGee, Steve Sloan had the next four, and Steve Spurrier put in three very successful years, taking the Blue Devils to the All-American Bowl in 1989 before taking the Florida job.

Wilson had been an ultra-successful high school coach in Fayetteville and Winston-Salem, and his teams won two state championships. He then coached at Elon College from 1967 to 1976, where he compiled a 71-35-2 record. The 71 wins are tops in school history. In three out of his final four seasons at Elon, his teams won 10 or more games and took the 'Fighting Christians' to the NAIA title game. At Duke, his teams were 16-26-1. 'Red' is an extremely intelligent man, having graduated from Davidson College. Perhaps the greatest thing he did for Duke football was hiring a young quarterback coach, Steve Spurrier, and turning the offense over to him.

BOB INTERVIEWS DUKE FOOTBALL COACH 'RED' WILSON '79

One story that I have the most fun telling took place in Steve Sloan's first season in 1983. Steve came to Duke after coaching the University of Mississippi. He had a great career at Alabama, succeeding Joe Namath at quarterback. He had success in stints with Vanderbilt and Texas Tech.

Clemson came to Durham on October 15th. The biggest and most visible Tigers player that year was William Perry. "The Refrigerator" gained national notoriety later on with the Chicago Bears. He played defensive nose guard in front of Duke guard Mark Miller. Because of his aggressiveness, Duke's offense had a field day drawing Perry offside. In fact, four of the six offside calls were on the 'Fridge.'

One of the funniest things I have ever heard about on a football field happened near the end of the game. Duke had the ball on offense and when they broke the huddle and came to the line of scrimmage, Miller asked center Philip Ebinger out loud, "What is the snap count. I can't remember?" Ebinger said loudly, "It's on 'one.' The snap is on one."

You know that every Clemson lineman heard it and when QB Ben Bennett started his cadence, "down, set, one," BOOM!! Perry roared across the line of scrimmage and here came another yellow flag for offside. Stay with me here. The Duke offense knew the count was never on 'one.' It was actually on 'two,' if he didn't jump. They knew they could get a free five yards and have some fun at William's expense. "Fridge' jumped up and argued with the umpire that there was no way he was offside because he heard Ebinger tell Miller that the count was on one. Duke may have lost that afternoon, 38-31, but we've had a great story to tell for years.

BOB & RED

From May 1, 1982, until October 31, 1982, Knoxville, Tn. hosted the World's Fair. It was the only one I ever attended, and the reason that I got to see this particular one was the fact that Duke opened the 1982 football season against Tennessee in Neyland Stadium.

As always, our headquarters hotel was the Hyatt, which was within walking distance of the stadium. Not only were we staying there, but various notables who were working at the Fair were too. I rode in an elevator with actress Patricia Neal that weekend. She grew up in Knoxville, and Fort Sanders Regional Medical Center in Knoxville dedicated the Patricia Neal Rehabilitation Center in her honor in 1978.

On Friday afternoon, I was wandering around the lobby of the hotel, and saw a gentleman go into one of the shops to buy a paper. I wandered closer to see if it really was who I thought it was. About that time, he turned a bit, and sure enough, it WAS Red Skelton. The autograph seeker in me took over. I boldly walked up to him and introduced myself and told him why I was in town. We chatted for a few minutes about the game, and about him. I told him of the nights our family sat around the radio in the late forties and listened to 'The Red Skelton Show.' Of course we followed him to television in the fifties and for the rest of his career. I asked if I might trouble him for an autograph for Phyllis and me.

He got a small gift card from the shop attendant and drew a small clown face on it and signed it, 'To Phyllis and Bob, Red Skelton.' We said our goodbyes and I went out to eat with the network crew that night at Ye Olde Steakhouse. It is one of my 'Bob's Top 25 Restaurants On The Road' which I formulated for my 25th year with Duke.

The next morning, we were finishing breakfast when Stan and Blossom Schneider, two long-time Iron Dukes, came over to our table. They had eaten in another part of the restaurant and Blossom said to the crew, "You'll never guess who was eating at the table next to ours back there."

Stan said, "Bob would. He talked a lot about meeting you yesterday." After they left, I made a 'beeline' for the other room. Red was finishing his meal and I again approached the greatest comedian in history, in my opinion. I asked him if he would like to be our guest in the broadcast booth for the game that night. I wanted to interview him on the air at halftime. He said that he appreciated the offer, but he had a 'sound and lights check' at the auditorium where he would be doing his one-man concert starting the next night.

I know I had a dejected look on my face because he said, "Is there any way we could tape something this morning?" "Absolutely, I have my recorder in my room, if you wouldn't mind." He explained that he only had about 15 minutes to spare. I asked if he'd like to come to my room to save some time and he agreed.

We started across the lobby and he stopped to talk to nearly everyone between the restaurant and the elevator. He even spotted a group of our football players and wanted to meet them. I introduced him to the guys and he chatted with each one of them for a second. My 15 minutes were almost spent, and we hadn't even gotten on the elevator.

Finally in the room, we proceeded to tape a six-minute piece for the game. Fortunately, I saved it, and it is on the CD in its entirety. As I was wrapping up the equipment, I told him that I wished Phyllis had made the trip so she could have met him. Out of the blue, he asked if she was at home. I said that she probably was, and he said, call her and I'll talk to her for a minute or so. The phone rang, and rang, and rang with no answer. He said, "let's wait a few minutes and try again. She might be in the yard. Several minutes later I dialed the number again, but got the same results. During the wait, he drew a larger clown on a piece of hotel stationary, and that one is framed. It's an original. He said he probably should be getting along and take care of some things. We again said goodbye.

Later that afternoon, we were getting ready to go to the stadium. Paul Matthews and I were waiting on the others in the lobby, when his eyes got as big as saucers and he started stammering. I asked him what was wrong, and he managed, "Red Skelton is right over there." I looked behind me and asked if he'd like me to introduce him to Red. He couldn't figure out how I knew him well enough to call him 'Red.'

We walked over and Paul talked to him for a few moments. We were standing in front of a small boutique, and Red looked me and asked what color parasol Phyllis would like. There was a container of frilly parasols of every color. He told me to pick out one. I said that he didn't need to do that, but he insisted. "If you don't pick the color, I will. I'm just sorry I couldn't talk with her this morning, and I want her to have this from me." Naturally, I picked a Duke blue one, and he had the lady to paint Phyllis' name on it with some flowery decorations. I told him I'd be more than willing to pay for it, but he wouldn't hear of it. I gave him my business card and took the gift to my room and we departed for the game.

Three years later Red came to Memorial Auditorium in Raleigh to do his concert and Phyllis and I got tickets. There was a media conference the afternoon before the concert. I was sitting on the front row in the last chair from the door. He came in and proceeded to go down the row introducing himself, as if anyone didn't know him. When he got to the last chair, he looked at me and said, "I'm really glad to see you. I was hoping you'd be here. Are you and your wife coming to the show tonight?" I told him we were, and he told me to bring her backstage after the performance so he could meet her. I forgot to mention that we had exchanged Christmas cards every year since the World's Fair.

After the show, we went backstage and Red made pictures and talked to Phyllis for a long time. It made her year.

We didn't see each other anymore, but the Christmas cards continued until his death on Phyllis' birthday in 1997. Good night Red, and may God Bless.

CHAPTER FOURTEEN

PROMOTIONS, DOUBLE DUTY AND MAX

Jim Sackett was our program director and morning personality on WDNC. He was a former actor and 'voice-over' announcer for a number of years. In his dual role, he began repositioning the station into the community station it was in its heyday. We became more aware of area functions and tied our station into various programs and promotions. We did remote broadcasts from the 'Festival for the Eno' over the 4th of July holiday, and Hillsborough's 'Hog Days' weekend. The Durham Arts Council was always a source of community pride and we tied into many of their functions. Advertisers loved to be a part of our promotions. For the 'Old-Fashioned Days' at a Durham mall, Jim and I were attired in 'roaring twenties' bathing attire. Check out the picture of 'Smilin'Jack and Buster Keaton' before being a part of the dunking booth.

BOB & JIM SACKETT ON WDNC REMOTE

Funny looking pictures were not just for station promotions. Halloween 1979 brought out the 'alter egos' of Phyllis and I.

The last year that WDNC and G-105 were under the same ownership, 1992, saw

'GUNSLINGER' PHYLLIS & 'MRS' BOB

my LAST venture into 'competitive' team sports. G-105 was sponsoring a Michael Bolton concert at the Walnut Creek Amphitheater. Bolton also had a softball team comprised of his 'roadies' and other staffers. "The Bolton Bombers" were a very good team, with many having played more softball than worked with a recording star. They didn't lose. They would play teams made up of station personnel in venues where they played.

There were not enough guys on the G-105 staff to field a full team with the necessary subs, so they enlisted the help of the guys from WDNC. Knowing that I had played baseball and softball most of my life, I was 'set upon' by the guys to play. My 50 year-old ego said, "Why not?" The 50 year-old body said, "You've gotta be nuts! You'll break something or pull something or embarrass yourself."

Old ego won that battle, of course, and I agreed to play only if they would let me catch. There was a lot less running at that position, and that was my natural spot.

In the top of the first, Bolton came to the plate and shook hands with me and wanted to know what I did at the station, and a bit of small talk. In the bottom of the 3rd, I came up and hit, arguably, the hardest line drive I ever hit. It caught the third-baseman squarely on the kneecap before he could get his glove down. Down he went, writhing in pain. I thought I had broken

MICHAEL BOLTON BATTING, BOB CATCHING 8/92

MICHAEL BOLTON'S leg!!!

He left the game for an inning or two, and his next time at bat, I got NO chatter from him. At the end of the regular seven innings, the score was tied. Our captain asked Michael what he wanted to do. He wanted to play until a winner (presumably the Bombers) was decided.

We held them scoreless in the top of the eighth, and in our half, we got a runner to second base. I came up and lined one right over second. The runner had taken off with the hit and rounded third before the center-fielder could get to the ball. He slid in to the plate with the winning run, and I stood on second with a broad grin on my face. There were no grins in the Bombers' dugout. The driver brought their bus ONTO the field and they loaded up and left for their hotel. No handshakes, no autographs, no pictures with the fans. Yes, there were several hundred fans that came out to watch. They were not happy either.

One of my teammates that day, was still with G-105 when Bolton came for another concert a year or so after I left the station in 1999. He told me in early 2009 that the first words uttered by Michael when he got off the bus with the Bombers was, "Where's that #%@^*% that nearly broke my leg last time we were here?"

I said to him, "Well, Bolton didn't remember my correct name, but he still remembers me."

Duke was so close to winning the NCAA Championship in 1978 and only Bruce Bell was missing from that team. Bill Foster had also recruited Vince Taylor out of Louisville, Ky. The players' goal from the 'git-go' was the national title.

The Blue Devils were ranked No. 1 in nearly every preseason poll, and were in almost the same spot that Kentucky had been in the year before. Why even bother with playing? Duke was a lock. Not only were they ranked No. 1 in the NATION; they were also ranked No. 1 in the WORLD. Sports Illustrated ranked all the amateur basketball teams in the world and Duke was in the top spot, with the Russian National Team second, and they hadn't stepped foot on the court for a single practice. This was insane, but I have one of the S.I. plaques.

Since I got the Duke job in 1976, I had always wanted to broadcast a game for two different sports in one day. Well, I got my wish with the first basketball game in '79. The season-ending football game was played in Chapel Hill on November 25th. The basketball team opened the season against Western Kentucky in Bowling Green, 570 miles away, that night.

Duke was ahead of UNC 15 to 2, but the Heels were driving into Duke territory as time was running low. The Tar Heels ran a draw play with Amos Lawrence carrying the ball four straight plays and scored. UNC only needed touchdown to win. Duke fumbled on the ensuing drive, and Carolina recovered. They went right back to that draw play that Duke obviously could not stop. "Famous Amos" ran it in again, this time for the game-winner TD as time expired. 16 - 15. After we got to Kentucky I found out that Mike McGee had been fired.

I closed my already-packed brief case as Lawrence scored. I did the shortest post-game wrap up on record and signed off by saying, "So long from Chapel Hill, and stay tuned, we'll have Duke basketball from Bowling Green, Kentucky at 7pm."

Football is finished, basketball is starting. Now the trick was to get from Chapel Hill to Bowling Green in time for the tip off. We had to have a private plane to pull this off. A great supporter of Duke athletics, Dr. Bill Claypool, made it happen.

We arranged for a Highway Patrol car to take us from Kenan Stadium to the airport in Chapel Hill. Dr. Claypool had a four-passenger plane and his son, Durham Sun sports writer Frank Dascenzo and I filled out the quartet. About an hour before scheduled arrival, Bill said his radar was showing some bad weather and it was pouring buckets in Bowling Green. I don't like turbulence and we were all over that northwestern Tennessee sky. I rethought my decision to do this, but Bill touched down on the runway like a puppy with sore feet.

We had made arrangements for someone from Duke to be waiting for us when we landed to get us to the arena. When we walked into the terminal and looked around for our driver, a man told me that my rental car was in space 'so-and-so.' I told him I had no idea where the arena was, but I would gladly pay the day's rental if he would drive us to Diddle Arena bring the car back to the airport. He agreed.

The game clock hanging over center court was near the 5:00 mark when I got to my seat on press row. Danny Highsmith, our color analyst, flew out with the team on Friday, and was already on the air. He always handled the pre-game show so it was nothing new. Danny took a commercial break just about the time I reached my seat. "Hey, Bob," he said, as the worry slowly seeped away. He could have done play-by-play if there had been a travel problem, but he wouldn't have to now. "Catch your breath, we've got two minutes for this break."

We were right on schedule. The football game ended about 3:30 and we were airborne by 4:00. The flight was just less than 600 miles. Bill did a masterful job piloting us through the storms AND Bowling Green is in the Central Time Zone. That gave us an extra hour. If the town were on Eastern Standard Time, we would not have even attempted this doubleheader for me. We would have let Danny do it. Commercial over. "Good evening everybody, and welcome to Bowling Green, Kentucky. Tonight the Duke Blue Devils take on Western Kentucky in the opening game of the 1979 basketball season."

The Blue Devils hit the court running, and a total team effort led to a 78-53 win. It looked like the Blue Devils had not skipped a beat. Maybe that is what everybody was thinking.

The results of that game may have given some false sense of security. Five more wins and Duke was 6-0, and still the nation's number one team. The Blue Devils took pride in that, but remember this, 'Pride goeth before a fall.' There were no games for sixteen days.

Most teams take some time off in December. First of all, the players had to concentrate on final exams. They ARE student-athletes. When finals were over, the players headed home for Christmas. They got back to campus in time to practice a couple of days before flying to New York.

Duke faced Ohio State in the ECAC Holiday Festival first round in Madison Square Garden and they took Duke apart, 90-84. Less than 24 hours later, the Blue Devils got hit in the mouth again. Unranked St. Johns played giant-killer this time, and Duke had a second straight loss, 69-66. When the polls came out on Monday, Duke had fallen to No. 5. All of this brought on questions about what was going on inside the Duke basketball program. Bill took the brunt of the criticism. Some said he didn't recruit well off the Final Four year. He brought in a freshman class of one, Vince Taylor.

"What's wrong with Duke?" That question was circulating throughout the community, and in the media as well. There were rumors of dissention on the team. Coach Foster had changed the lineup a bit, but I don't know if any of this was the problem.

The team that grabbed the national spotlight the year before wasn't about to let two losses and the questioning of some fans and sportswriters affect their approach. They went back to work and tried to put all that other stuff out of their minds.

Duke lost at Maryland on February 16th and the next game was one to be remembered for two reasons, peripheral things that day and what resulted three years later. We flew from Dulles back to RDU, let several folks off, and went on to Charlotte. We were to play Louisville on national television on Sunday afternoon. This wasn't an unusual venue. Duke played Davidson, UCLA and several other teams at the Coliseum on Independence Boulevard. The Cardinals played a nationally televised game with UCLA in Los Angeles on Saturday and flew all night to get to Charlotte to play in less than 24 hours. Bad scheduling

Guess what? It started snowing heavily about midnight Saturday and there were 18 inches of snow on the ground Sunday morning. Charlotte wasn't used to that and traffic was almost non-existent. The team stayed at the Holiday Inn right across the street from the Coliseum. Great planning. The driver couldn't move the team bus, so the coaches said that we would just hike across the street rather than trying to dig the bus out of the snow. No problem, NO traffic.

Here's a Kodak moment. Oops, no Kodak. Picture this, the No. 3 team in the country, trudging across the street, knee-deep in snow. We knew that the game, if Louisville made it, would be played before a 'less than capacity' crowd.

I don't think they even announced the official attendance, but by the end of the game, I don't think there were more than 100 fans in the Coliseum. We beat the road-weary Cardinals 88-72, and Foster took it easy on them.

That measure of revenge? Denny Crum got it on January 2nd, 1982 in Freedom Hall in Louisville. Second-year coach Mike Krzyzewski took an under-manned Duke team up there and were 'run out of the gym.' They faced the McCray brothers and the 'Doctors of Dunk' and Crum DID run up the score, 99-61.

I got back to Durham Sunday evening, and Phyllis and the kids got home a couple of hours later. They had been visiting her Mom in Stanly County. I was hurting. Phyllis drove me to Duke Medical Center's ER. I had convinced my self that I was having a heart attack, but after extensive tests, the doctor said I was NOT.

My triglyceride and cholesterol levels had gone berserk. I remembered what caused it... me. Saturday night after the game, I took on the inimitable Max Crowder in a frog-leg eating duel at the New Orleans East restaurant. First of all, they had an all-you-can-eat seafood buffet and the radio crew and Duke trainer Max Crowder wanted to get our money's worth. Waiters brought the frog-legs around to the table as often as we wanted more. Max had no challengers around Duke, for his eating challenges, and for his love and dedication to Duke and all of the athletes he had ever come in contact with since 1961.

Max was everyone's friend. He was as voracious at Gin Rummy as for food. He and I played some when we were waiting in an airport. I never won. I came close one afternoon in Roanoke while we were waiting for the plane to take us to College Park. I was beating Max, and was close to winning. About that time Max cocked his head like he was listening for something and said, "Game's over." I said, "What do you mean." "Bob, our plane is here." I was a few points from beating him when he laughed," Too bad, Bob. Nobody got to 500, so I guess nobody wins this time." How could you get mad at Max?

Crowder was a very unique person with a colorful personality. He had his quirks, but don't we all? In 1960, the native of Cherryville, N.C came to Duke from Gardner-Webb Junior College to finish his degree. He became a student trainer for the legendary 'Doc' Chambers while still a student. He eventually became head trainer for basketball, and then for the entire athletic department. Max stayed at Duke and worked 899 straight basketball games.

For someone who never wore a Duke uniform or coached a game, he was one of the most popular people in Duke history. In 1989, he retired as Head Athletic Trainer, but continued as the basketball trainer.

Every athlete who has ever played at Duke knows card Gym. Max was like that too. As a matter of fact, Max's living quarters were in the Card Gym tower from his student days until his death in 1992. Max had worked in an asbestos plant in Cherryville while in high school and on breaks from Gardner-Webb and Duke. He was diagnosed with mesothelioma in 1991 and died the next spring at the age of 62. The loves of his life were Duke and the players and coaches he served for 30 years.

About a month before he died in 1992, Max was appropriately inducted into the Duke Sports Hall of Fame. Nothing could keep him away from Cameron for this last time. Medical personnel brought him by ambulance, and he stayed behind a curtain until it was his time to be inducted. Max walked to the podium by himself, straight and erect. He accepted his honor and made the proper thank you's. At the end, he reminded the audience of his love for Duke and for all of us. He left the stage and went back to the hospital.

Max had a wonderful heart and a soft spot for the less fortunate. Every Christmas, Max "adopted" several families in Durham county. He couldn't stand to see children without gifts and he made sure that they

PHYLLIS & MAX CROWDER 1979

had a Christmas to remember. Several times, I saw Max in the mall, buying gifts and he always told me, "Keep this to yourself." I promised that I would, and I kept my promise to Max, until now. This is too nice for me not to share. Sorry, Max, I couldn't keep the secret any longer. I know you will understand.

Duke played the Tar Heels in the last game of the regular season. I guess they are the most appropriate opponent for that game since they are just 10.68 miles away, according to MapQuest. It is a prelude to 'March Madness.'

Carolina was the No. 4 team in the country and Duke was No. 6 when they met in Cameron. This game is still being discussed and cussed more than thirty years after it was played. Is it because two of the top six teams in the polls played such a spellbinding game? No. Is it because the game was such a monumental defensive struggle? No. It is because it was one of the most boring games in the history of collegiate sports and brought on the shot clock.

Dean Smith was THE master of holding the ball with his 'four corners' offense, if you can call it offense. It certainly was offensive to opposing fans. Normally, the 'four corners' was used late in games when Carolina was leading, to limit possessions by the opponents.

Duke got the opening tip and scored. The Tar Heels immediately went 'four corners' and stayed in it for more than ten minutes. Foster wouldn't change from his patented 2-3 match-up zone defense. This was a very boring chess match.

Dean's plan turned the best rivalry in all of college basketball into 'stall-ball.' Very few in college basketball had supported a shot clock, at least not until this 'four corners' nonsense began to get on the nerves of coaches and fans alike. Rich Yonakor was so wide open in the left corner that he had to take a shot. It missed everything but the hands of a Duke player. It was so bad that the Cameron Crazies began chanting, "Air-Ball, Air-Ball." I believe that was the first time that the phrase was ever heard.

A Carolina player fouled a Duke shooter and he made one free throw to make it 3-0 Duke with just over three minutes left in the half. Then the tempo picked up. Dave Colescott missed UNC's second field goal of the half. Spanarkel made it 5-0, and then 7-0 as they went to halftime.

Now you understand why some scores in the 1960s and '70s were 12-10, or 16-8?There is nothing worse for me than a fiasco like this. We try to paint a word picture of what is happening for our listeners. Trying to paint a word picture for that first half was like painting a mud fence with motor oil. U-G-L-Y!!!

Tom Mickle and Johnny Moore got their reward for all of their hard work on the media guide that night. Sports Information staffs probably think we don't use them, but rest assured that we do. We used every page of the game notes and some of the media guide too. We were talking about the players' parents, majors in college, high school careers, favorite songs, color of their eyes and even what they got for their last birthday. My final comment of the first half was, "If Dean is going to hold the ball the second half, I'm gonna sing." There was nothing else to do.

Possibly, someone told Coach Smith what I said, because the second half was the game we all wanted. UNC didn't hold the ball. Each team scored 40 points. Duke won, 47-40. Poetic justice?? I like to think so. The Tar Heels lost by the margin that Duke had at halftime. And I didn't have to sing!!

Duke was seeded second for the ACC Tournament in Greensboro.

Anyone who has ever listened to a game on the Duke Radio Network since 1976 knows that I MIGHT get just a TAD excited. I really do try to adhere to the best advice I ever received. It came from "Ted" Mann, Duke's Sports Information Director emeritus. Ted retired about ten years before I got to Duke. He always came to the football press conferences, and we had become friends. One Monday afternoon he said, "Harris, I've been listening to your call of our games, and I like your style. You love Duke and it shows. I like your excitement, but let me give you a bit if advice, if you don't mind. Don't ever get so excited that you don't have something extra, so if Jesus Christ comes back to earth while you're talking, you can get up to another level to describe it."

I didn't have to worry about too much reigning-in my excitement that night against Carolina.

After the win over UNC, I went into their locker room to get some comments from Smith for my ACC Tournament Preview Show on WDNC. I happened to over-hear two of the players talking about Coach Smith's decision to hold the ball. "We could have won if Coach Smith had let us play the full 40 minutes," was the exact words. That's the only time I ever heard a UNC player say anything bad about him or his decisions.

In Greensboro the Blue Devils took care of Wake and State. We went into the championship game with Carolina shorthanded because Bob Bender didn't play. He had an appendicitis attack, and they took him back to Duke Medical Center.

UNC won, 80 to 78, but the loss didn't keep them out of the NCAA Tournament. The Blue Devils and Tar Heels both got byes to the second round of the Eastern Regional.We both played in Reynolds Coliseum in Raleigh.

Tournament parings were different in this era. With only 40 teams in the bracket, teams from the east stayed in the East Regional and so on. Also, the NCAA only seeded the teams in their regions. They did not seed the entire field from 1 through 40. Neither Duke nor UNC had to play in that first round. They had two extra days to prepare for their first NCAA opponents in the second round double header on Sunday in Reynolds

The No. 1 seed in the East Region, UNC, played ninth seeded Penn. The Tar Heels were eliminated by the Quakers, 72-71. Upset # 1.

The Blue Devils were at a distinct disadvantage against St. John's. Bender still wasn't there, and Kenny Dennard was out of uniform, too. He got in a pick-up game with several football players LATE Wednesday night and sprained his ankle. Mike Gminski was as sick as a dog. Given his seemingly insatiable appetite, Mike ordered a pizza to his room, on top of the team meal. Mike gave it his best. He would be in for five minutes, sub out, throw up behind the bench, and go right back in the game. He did it the whole game. As I used to say on my record show, "The hits just keep on coming." John Harrell got poked in the in the eye early in the second half and missed nearly ten minutes. Duke still came close, 80-78.

March 11, 1979 is still known as “Black Sunday.” Duke and Carolina would both love to forget that day.

When I think of St. Johns, I think of ‘Little Looie’ Carnesecca, and Al McGuire. Al and his brother, Dick, played there, and Al became a successful coach in his own right before getting into TV.

Dick Enberg and Al McGuire brought college basketball to viewers all over the country in a fashion not seen before. Dick and Al made up an unusual tandem in that, Dick has the wonderful baritone ‘pipes’ with a Midwestern style, and Al was the New Yorker; a fast-talking former coach who was well known for his colorful personality. They were made for each other.

Dick began his career as an assistant professor and baseball coach at California State - Northridge from 1961 until1965. From 1975 until 1981, he was the face of NCAA Basketball on NBC. CBS signed him in 2000, and he is back home. His resume covers the entire spectrum of sporting events, including the Olympics, Wimbledon, Major League baseball, NFL and the Rose Bowl.

AL McGUIRE, BOB, DICK ENBERG & DANNY HIGHSMITH 2/85

McGuire coached basketball at Marquette from 1964 to 1977. He was the son of an Irish immigrant saloonkeeper, and played at St. John's from 1947 through 1951. After four years in the NBA, Al found his calling, coaching at Belmont Abbey College, just outside of Charlotte. People in Gaston County couldn't understand a word Al said for the first two years, according to Ebb Gantt, sports director at WCGC in Belmont. Ebb and I both worked for Suburban Radio Group, and he told me 'Al stories' on more than one occasion.

Dick and Al worked a good number of nationally televised games in Cameron Indoor Stadium. On one occasion, Al, donned in a safari pith helmet and brandishing a lion tamer's whip, ventured into the Duke student section to 'attempt to tame the animals' that ringed Cameron. He immediately became a crowd favorite.

Whether it was a home game or away, if Dick and Al were the talent, I knew to look for Al about an hour and a half before the game. He would seek me out to 'pick my brain' about the players and the game itself. He always had a pencil and a folded piece of paper. That would do for his 'scouting report' for the game. "Tell me something, just one little thing that you're not going to use today about Jimmy Spanarkel. He's smooth," Al would say. He would do this for each starter and those I thought would even get into the game. McGuire gave Mike Gminski the nickname 'the aircraft carrier' because he took up so much space in the paint.

AL McGUIRE EXPLAINS THINGS TO BOB 1986

McGuire was inducted into the Basketball Hall of Fame in 1992. In 2000, he was diagnosed with leukemia, and passed away January 26, 2001 in Milwaukee, Wisconsin. I called Al before Christmas and we had a nice chat. He was getting weaker and knew that he wouldn't last long. He wouldn't say that death was imminent; he told me that there was a 'big gray elephant' in his room. We said our goodbyes that morning. College basketball lost a great ambassador.

Dick and I see each other from time to time during basketball season. He is still one of the best in the business.

The football pressbox that overlooked Wallace Wade Stadium in 1975 when I first laid my eyes on the green grass of the venerable horseshoe, was the one that had seated the members of the media for the first game ever played there October 5, 1929. The 'press corps' that day watched Duke play host to Pittsburgh. Coach Jock Sutherland's Panthers routed the Blue Devils 52-7 before 25,000 fans. Pitt went on to win the National Championship.

Duke Stadium was home to many monumental battles with the likes of Tennessee, Auburn, Bobby Dodd's Georgia Tech teams, No. 4 Navy in 1960, Michigan, West Virginia, Stanford, Washington, and Purdue coming to Durham.

On September 30, 1967, the stadium was re-named Wallace Wade Stadium to honor the legendary coach who put Duke football on the national map.

In 1979, the press box came down. The Duke Sports Information Department, read that Mickle and Moore, invited members of the media who had covered Blue Devils football games in the building to a Champagne Brunch and Destruction. They provided a sledge hammer for all who wanted to take a whack at it. I took my turn. We didn't make many large dents in the job. Even after all of us hammered it, the demolition crew still

DEMOLITION OF PRESS BOX @ WADE STADIUM 1979

had almost as much work to do as they would have. But, let's face it; it's hard to get any power behind a swing wearing a coat and tie. For the one season before the new Finch-Yeager Building was completed, the radio crews worked out of a small wooden 'shelter' at the five-yard-line on the home side of the field. It was the five nearest the scoreboard at the open end of the horseshoe.

Thankfully, we didn't have any bad weather that fall. The first game of the '79 season was a home game with East Carolina. They played Duke, N.C. State, U.N.C. and Wake Forest that season, ALL on the road. Senior QB Leander Green brought his wishbone offense to town, and it seemed like the Pirates had the ball at the opposite end of the field from our vantage point all afternoon. It would have been hard for me to find the ball if I had been right across the line of scrimmage from them, but with Green's fakes and deception, I had no idea which player had the ball for most of the game. Both of my spotters were as 'bumfuzzled' as I was.

When the 1980 football season began, the Duke Radio Network, along with the entire media contingent, occupied the third floor of the Finch-Yeager Building on football Saturdays. Finch-Yeager is a multi-functional facility. For 358—360 days a year, it is home to Duke Sports Medicine, one of the finest facilities of its kind anywhere. The other five or six days, depending on the number of home football games, the top floor is converted to press areas, radio booths, PA and replay booths and coaching boxes. There is a nice section on the second floor for a portion of the Iron Dukes to escape any uncomfortable weather.

The 1980 basketball season brought several surprises. Duke was ranked No. 3 at the beginning of the year. Jim Spanarkel graduated in May, but Gminski, Banks, Dennard and Bender returned. Taylor moved into the lineup. The biggest surprise came in the post season when Bill Foster announced that he would leave Duke for South Carolina. Something else surprised a lot of fans; Duke won its first twelve games, and jumped to No. 1 in the polls.

This was almost a Jekyll and Hyde team. Would they play like the unit that began the season 12-0, or the group that won only two of its last seven games of the regular season?

To win the ACC Tournament, the Blue Devils had to beat the top three seeds in three days. That had only been accomplished by UVa in 1976. It was the only way Duke could get an NCAA bid. The Devils rolled through the three games and won the Tournament, and the automatic NCAA bid.

Rumors about Coach Foster leaving Duke to coach at South Carolina had been whispered around the Duke community for several weeks. Some were really upset that Bill would even consider leaving Durham for Columbia, but it became a reality at the end of the season.

In Duke's opening ACC Tournament game against No. 3 N.C. State, the Blue Devils eliminated Coach Norm Sloan's team, 68-62. That was his last ACC game. Norm said earlier in the season that was leaving West Raleigh for the Florida Gators. In the semi-finals on Leap Day, Duke leaped on the Tar Heels, 75-61. This was the second meeting in a seven-day span. Bill Foster beat Dean Smith in their last head-to-head confrontation.

Duke now faced top seeded Maryland for the championship. The Terps won big in College Park, but the Blue Devils took the Durham game by five. Two things were on Duke's side, momentum and snow. Hey, snow makes Duke play great. Early Saturday, Greensboro was shut down by a blizzard. Just over 10,000 brave fans managed to get to the Coliseum, and they saw a great game as Duke came from behind to beat Maryland by a point. King, North Carolina's Kenny Dennard taught Rocky Mount's Buck Williams a lesson in the Laws of Physics. Here is Professor Dennard's brief synopsis of those Laws.

I did not undercut Buck Williams. I hope people will take the time to understand the laws of physics. Two strong men, six feet eight, pushing each other, pushing back and forth, a chess game, a physical chess game. And then, of course, Buck jumped backwards into the air, where was I to go, except to go under him, which made it look like I undercut him. But I didn't. And that's why there was no foul called. Because I think one of those referees was a physics major in college and understood the principals. Now, it was great news and great pub that Kenny Dennard undercut Buck Williams to win the 1980 ACC Championship, but that's just not the truth and I am glad I get to set the record straight."

Buck still disagrees.

On Sunday, Coach Foster made it official; he was going to leave Durham for Columbia at the completion of the season. In his press conference, he told the reporters that there was some unfinished business to attend to. He wanted to coach the Blue Devils to the NCAA title.

Duke was the No. 4 seed in the Mideast and received a first round bye, and Foster's kids beat Penn by ten in their first game.

Next on the path to the Final Four was RUPP ARENA, and the Kentucky Wildcats in the Regional Semi-Finals. This was the second meeting of the season. The Blue Devils beat them 82-76 in overtime, in the Hall of Fame Game in Springfield, Ma. The Wildcats were ranked second in the polls, one spot ahead of Duke. As you might suspect, the Wildcats were favored, but Duke defied the odds and won, 55-54. That was the biggest upset of the tournament that year. My friend, Kyle Macy, missed a jumper at the buzzer that would have won it for the 'Cats. The NCAA Selection Committee had positioned Kentucky and Indiana for a Regional Championship showdown, but it never materialized. Purdue took out the Hoosiers in the other Semi-Final, 76-69.

The Blue Devils were on a roll as they prepared for the Mideast Regional finals. Just one win and Bill Foster, Mike Gminski, Bob Bender, Gene Banks and Kenny Dennard would be their second Final Four. Lee Rose's Purdue Boilermakers stood in the way. That was enough. Joe Barry Carroll had a great game and ended Duke's season, and Coach Foster's career at Duke.

Opinions are like noses. Everybody has one. Why did Bill Foster leave Duke after doing such a great job of bringing the Blue Devils' program back to respectability? Some felt sure it was over an unpaved parking lot behind Cameron. Maybe it was. The gravel parking area on the north end of the arena was muddy when it rained for many years. Some said that he and the administration had disagreements about a a lot of things. ALL coaches have that situation from time to time. To this day, I think he was just ready to move on to another building job. That was his strength. He proved it at Rutgers, Utah and Duke. He loved the challenge of starting at the ground floor and building. He liked to maintain them for a while and find another project. In 1980, South Carolina was looking for a coach, and Bill was looking for a new challenge.

CHAPTER FIFTEEN
LOOKING FOR COACH WHO?????

Now Athletic Director Tom Butters had something else on his plate. He had to find a replacement for Bill Foster. Every North Carolina news outlet and others around the country were beginning to formulate their own lists as to who the next coach of the Duke Blue Devils would be. Tom was way ahead of them. He had started his search a lot earlier than the reporters had. That is the way great administrators do things. If Tom Butters had not become the Duke Athletic Director, he might have been the head of the USGA, or had a successful career in the CIA or FBI. This former Pittsburgh Pirates relief pitcher did not interview his early candidates for the soon-to-be-vacant job in Durham.

All of the sportswriters tried to get some inside info. They couldn't risk a competitor scooping them on this. Tom's process kept all of them in the dark. Speculation was running rampant, so the Durham Morning Herald ran a story on the morning of the scheduled announcement that boldly declared that the next head coach of the Duke Blue Devils would be a Coach "W."

Supposedly, Butters' short list included Bob Weinhauer of Penn, Bob Weltlich of Mississippi, Paul Webb of Old Dominion, and Bob Wenzel. Bobby was an assistant coach for Foster at Duke, and made it known that he wanted the job. The writers said they had inside sources. Don't they all?

Remember the old Coasters' song, Along Came Jones? Well, along came Vacendak. Steve was ACC Player of the Year in 1966 at Duke.

Let's go back a few years. Vacendak was working for the Converse Shoe Co. in Annapolis, Md. His high school coach in Pennsylvania was Jack Gallagher, who was a close friend and east coast scout for Bobby Knight. Gallagher arranged for Steve to meet Mike Krzyzewski. Jack told him that he should go over to the Naval Academy and watch Mike coach his U.S. Military Academy Cadets team against Navy. He even arranged for Vacendak to sit in with Coach K, Pete Gaudet and the staff as they put the final preparations together for Navy. Steve listened to Krzyzewski in that meeting and watched the game, and came away very impressed with Mike. The game was a 'coach's game' in that both would get the maximum from their teams. Mike got more from his that night.

In 1980, after Steve came back to Duke, Gallagher called him and asked if he might be interested in Krzyzewski for the open job. Steve told Gallagher that 'K' was already on the list. Mike was a 33 year-old and his 1980 Army team 9-17. Tom badgered Vacendak to see why he thought Krzyzewski should be the Duke coach. Steve explained to Butters that it wouldn't be the easiest thing to do. He knew that Tom didn't back away from a challenge, and often did something BECAUSE it wasn't the easy way. He knew that Tom believed that defense was not only the way to win ball games, but also the way to build the program. And if he held to that belief, Krzyzewski was the man they needed.

Now, let's end all of the speculation and part-truth newspaper stories and other 'urban legends' about this period, and let Tom Butters, himself, tell us EXACTLY how Mike Krzyzewski came to be the Duke basketball coach. This is the FIRST time this has ever been in print. It was told to me, in the presence of Vacendak, and recorded at Treyburn Country Club on October 30, 2009.

I would have never hired Mike Krzyzewski if it were not for Steve Vacendak. The interesting thing is, I had hired Steve to become my Associate Athletic Director and he was not on the payroll when all of this took place. He was to begin in May. He was my choice for my right-hand man, but he was not yet on the payroll, and yet I was listening to every word he said because he wouldn't let me 'not listen.'

I was fascinated by, and I don't think it's ever been reported, a man from Kansas State, Jack Hartman. I was very intrigued by him, and when I called Bob Knight, which I did after Steve told me about this young, defensive, brilliant mind, Mike Krzyzewski. When I got hold of Knight I said, "You know Bill Foster left, do you want the job, tonight?" And he laughed, and he called our local sports-writers by name and said, "You don't want me, because I wouldn't get along with them."

Bob was so bright. He had a photographic memory. And then he started talking about his protégés, in particular, Dave Bliss, who was at Oklahoma. That was his first and foremost. And then he mentioned Bob Weltlich of Mississippi and Don DeVoe of Tennessee. And I said, "What about Jack Hartman?" He said, "He's a great basketball coach. And he's gonna be absolutely thrilled and flattered that you called him. He's gonna come and visit three or four times, and five weeks from now, he's gonna say, 'Tom, I'm flattered, but I'm going to stay in Manhattan, Kansas.'"

I said, "Well, what about a guy named Krzyzewski?"

He said, "You've always liked the way I coach. Mike Krzyzewski has all of my good qualities, and none of my bad ones." And that rang a bell with me.

Steve and I had met numerous times, maybe a dozen, and every time we would talk about Bob Weinhauer at Penn, Weltlich, Bliss, DeVoe and Jack Hartman, but before the meeting was over Steve would always say, "You need to think about Krzyzewski." After that conversation with Bobby, I said that I was going to interview him.

I believe the first time we interviewed Mike was in West Lafayette, Indiana. We played Penn there in the NCAAs. We had a nice four-hour interview, and I really liked him. But, there was no way I was going to hire a 9-17 coach from Army. So, I sent him home. The next weekend I called Willis Casey, the A.D. at N.C. State. Willis was one of the toughest Athletic Directors that's ever lived. He was on the Basketball Committee. I told him, "I don't know what that committee is all about, and the fact that you're a part of it really disturbs me, because you're making Duke go to Kentucky to PLAY Kentucky in the East Regionals. That's unconscionable." And he chewed my butt OUT, as only Willis could do. I didn't back down. I let him have it from both barrels.

So we went to Kentucky. Prior to leaving Durham, I called Krzyzewski, because I couldn't get him out of my mind. I just could not get him out of my mind. I asked him if he could get to Lexington. We were playing in the Sweet 16 there. He said, "We've had thirteen inches of snow here, but I'll find a way to get there." He came and we interviewed him for four-and-a-half or five hours. Chancellor Ken Pye was in the interview as well as Vacendak, and I believe that if the decision had been up to Ken, he would have hired Dr. Tom Davis from Boston College, who was also on my list. He was a damn fine basketball coach, and I had brought him in for an interview.

I was even more intrigued after that second interview than I was after the first, but I couldn't get 9-17 out of my mind. And, quite frankly, I couldn't get Army, or the Military Academy out of my mind, because that's not exactly ACC basketball.

We came home after that interview, and the loss to Purdue to end our season, and we cut the list to four people. Weltlich was there. Paul Webb, a really fine basketball coach at Old Dominion, was on that list, but he had more age on him than I was looking for. I told Steve, "If we are going to build a program of national caliber, all we have to do is beat the team eight miles down the road. If we can be successful against them, we're going to be a national power." We had to find someone that could defend them and play that kind of defensive basketball in order to achieve it.

We got it down to Bob Weltlich, Paul Webb, Bob Wenzel and Mike Krzyzewski, and I asked them to bring their wives in, because I've never thought that you just hired just a coach, you hired a family. It was important for me to understand that family, and for them to understand us. So we interviewed the four in front of a committee, and Mike was last to be interviewed. Steve took Mike and Mickie to the airport, and I sat down with the committee, and they said,

"Look, these are all quality people. It's your decision."

This interview was conducted at the home of Duke Vice-President Chuck Huestis along with university counsel, Gene McDonald.

I went out to the kitchen table with Gene and Chuck, and we discussed it, talked about it, and I asked them to give me just a few minutes. I picked up the telephone and called the airport and had them page Steve. I got Steve on the phone and told him, "Don't let Krzyzewski get on the plane." Steve said to me, and I do remember this, "My gosh, you're not going to interview him again." I said, "No, I'm not, I'm going to hire him."

Steve said, "WHAT?"

He had been pounding and pounding and pounding and then when I told him my decision, now he's going to take the other side and question it, which is fairly typical of Steve Vacendak, which is why that was the greatest five or six years of my time at Duke, because I didn't have a 'yes' man. He has NEVER been a 'yes' man.

Steve took Mike to the Angus Barn for dinner and on to see Butters again.

It wasn't that I was afraid of getting turned down. I wanted to phrase it that way to see what his reaction was. Shoot, I've been turned down a hundred times. I can give you a list of people who've turned me down over the years. He said he'd like to talk to Mickie, and I agreed that it would be the smart thing to do. He accepted the position, and the rest, as they say, is history.

Did Bob Knight have a lot to do with it? Yes, he did. He made a couple of comments that just got me intrigued with this guy. Vacendak was just relentless. I kept telling Steve that it wasn't his butt that was on the line for making this kind of decision. Steve didn't have a job to lose. He WASN'T employed at Duke yet!!! It was one of the best pieces of advice that I received while I was at Duke.

An unemployed man had my ear for several weeks and kept pounding it and everywhere I went, whether it was Bobby Knight or others, because I checked him out with a lot of people. Steve Vacendak had my ear to the fact that I didn't have a choice but to put my butt on the line. There are some times in one's career when you have to put your butt on the line, even when it's uncomfortable. This was one of those times. But, I think it's going to work out.

This is absolutely, according to my recollection, the true story."

Michael William Krzyzewski was born and raised in Chicago. William and Emily were both second generation Polish-Americans, a heritage he is very proud of. It was this working class background that made him the man he is today, hard working, diligent, loyal and a master of time management. That latter trait was probably due more to his education at the United States Military Academy. His brother, Bill, retired as a Captain from the Chicago Fire Department, where he NEVER missed a workday. The 'Duke Captain's Award' honors Bill's work ethic and devotion to the team.

Mike once told me the story about his adjustment to Knight's coaching. Mike was un-nerved by Knight's constant screaming, swearing, and threatening the players. Sometimes he would be singled out and Knight would use expletives and refer to his Polish heritage. He hated that, and on a phone call to his mother, he mentioned the nasty verbal abuse. 'Miss Emily' took it all in, and said, "Well Mike, at least he is talking to you."

Mike graduated from West Point and served his five-year obligation in the Army. He then went to Indiana to work as a graduate assistant under Knight for a year.

The evening press conference to introduce the new Duke coach was held on Tuesday, March 18, 1980, in the Duke News Bureau Building. The place was overflowing. As Butters introduced the 19th head coach of the Blue Devils, Mike walked into the room. Surprise was evident all around the room. Who is this man? Without the benefit of cable TV and the internet, there was no inkling. Tom never turns down an opportunity to mess with the minds of the writers. "I know you all," Tom said, "You will all go back and write that you were right with your prediction. It is going to be Coach 'W,' as in 'Coach Who?' And with that he said 'Here's our new coach.'

As Mike came forward, it dawned on me that I had seen him in the lobby of the Holiday Inn in Lexington. I thought, "That's who that guy was."

"The last name is spelled K-R-Z-Y-Z-E-W-S-K-I and if you think that is bad, you should have seen what it was before I changed it. I have been called a lot of things, but Mike or Coach K is fine with me." Mike had cracked his first funny.

After Mike's remarks and the conference was about to wrap up, several writers continued to question Butters on why he had picked Mike. Tom steeled and unequivocally defended Mike and the bold decision he made. "He has a brilliant basketball mind. This job was not offered to anyone else. He is my first choice and will remain my first choice." Tom told them, 'He may not be a household name now, but he will be."

The Duke Chronicle, the student newspaper, may have had the funniest headline the next day, "THIS IS NOT A TYPO." The A-1 headline in the Durham Morning Herald (Wednesday, March 19, 1980) read: "Duke Names Krzyzewski Basketball Coach." An Art Chansky column on page B1 had the headline "Coach Who? 'Brightest Young Talent In America' " In the Durham Sun that afternoon, the coverage was on B1. "Bobby Knight Disciple Inherits Blue Devils" was Frank Dascenzo's column headline, while the main news story by Al Featherston had a hammerhead:

"K-r-z-y-z-e-w-s-k-i

Duke's Butters elects to hire 'big name' coach."

(Thanks to Sports Editor Jimmy DuPree for his research of the Herald-Sun archives to make sure these headlines were accurate)

More changes came in 1980. My WDNC tenure temporarily ended because of a disagreement over the local rights to Duke football and basketball broadcasts. The snag in renewal negotiations was between the manager at WDNC and Tom Butters. The manager felt he was dealing from a position of power, but he found out the hard way that WDNC was no longer the network's flagship station. I was privy to the situation on both sides, and in full agreement with Butters' position. I wasn't bound to anyone. Remember, I've NEVER had a written contract in all the years I've done the Duke broadcasts. My agreement has always been sealed with a handshake,

WDBS was a 3,000-watt FM station and was owned by the Duke Board of Trustees because it had been the student station. WDBS had been replaced by the 25,000-watt WXDU. WDBS was made a not-for-profit, education-owned station. Butters persuaded the trustees to agree to move the Duke games to WDBS in April of '80. There was a stipulation. I would become an employee of WDBS and continue as the 'Voice.' My position was Sports Director and I sold advertising on the station with an emphasis on the Duke game sales.

Two and a half years later, the trustees sold WDBS, and I moved to WTIK, a country station with its sights on the Duke games. I was there for 90 days. During this time, WDNC changed managers and Jim Sackett headed up the operations. His first priority was to put Duke back on 620. The agreement was worked out, and Duke and WDNC got 'remarried.'

CHAPTER SIXTEEN
THE BUILDING OF A DYNASTY

Just how does Mike Krzyzewski motivate his teams like he does? Mike always tries to teach his team that it's not about just the winning or the losing of a basketball game. He has a bronze fist on his desk. This is symbolic of his teams. If you look at your own hand, you see four individual fingers and a thumb. While the digits are different sizes and shapes they are a part of the hand. They are minimally effective when spread out, but make them into a fist, and collectively, they become much more effective. He applies that principle to his five players on the floor. Individually, they are good. Collectively, they are great and can accomplish far more. He always tells them to put the losses and the wins behind them. Learn from them. Next play!!

Followers of the Duke basketball program during the Krzyzewski years have had the privilege of watching some of the greatest teams and players to have ever played the game. With eleven Final Four appearances and four NCAA championships, you might think that from that Tuesday in March of 1980 when Mike became Duke's coach, that Duke had a bull's eye on its back. It seems like they have always been in the top twenty of all the polls. Let me take you back.

A 73-59 record at your previous job doesn't usually get you a ride into town on a white horse. Butters was still getting questioned about his choice three years later. Given the atmosphere of college basketball in the 21st century, Mike's record at Army wouldn't even get him considered for most major programs. The first three seasons of his Duke career seemed to prove, to the casual observer, that he was NOT the man for Duke. Coach still says that in his first three years, he turned the 'Iron Dukes' into the 'Concerned Iron Dukes'.

On November 29, 1980, the Stetson Hatters came to Cameron to ring in the Krzyzewski Era. Duke prevailed, 67-49. The team went down to Tampa and beat South Florida, 83-73. I remember spending several hours at Busch Gardens with the players, coaches and families the day before the game. Duke had its own tournament for three years, the Iron Duke Classic, which brought in three non-ACC teams.

We went into the 1980 Classic with a 3-3 record and won it by beating Brown by 31 and Detroit by 40. No, Dickie V was not coaching Detroit-Mercy at that time. He had left for the Pistons three years before that game. See Dick, I told you I'd get you into my book!!! In 2001, Dick had a poll and asked folks to vote for their favorite play-by-play announcer from his 'All-Cawood Ledford' Team. There were 16 of us listed on the 'Team' with six coming from the ACC. I finished first with 46.5% of the vote. The second place finisher had 10.5%. My buddy, Johnny Holliday, the 'Voice of the Terps' teased me a lot about the 'ballot-stuffing by my family and the Duke fans.

VITALE, TRIPP & BOB 1/02

Bob and I have been friends for over 30 years, ever since I started broadcasting Maryland athletics, and he welcomed me as the new kid on the block in the ACC. There is no one in the country that has the total package like Bob. His play-by-play work and interview style is unlike any other broadcaster that comes to mind. Be it Duke football or basketball, Bob's love for the game comes across loud, clear, and concise! For Blue Devil fans.... Bob Harris is Duke. It's a gimmee that Bob is a terrific play-by-play guy, but to me, he's more than that. He's a friend, a dear friend, who has never let the athletic competition between Duke and Maryland affect our friendship. We often kid each other that if we lived closer, our wives Mary Clare and Phyllis would see less of us, because Bob and I would be doing so many things together. You will never meet a better person than Bob Harris. The Duke fans are the luckiest fans in the world to have Bob as their 'Voice' on radio.

JOHNNY HOLLIDAY
"Voice of the Maryland Terrapins"

The last ACC game of the season was in Cameron. North Carolina came up U.S. 15-501 on Senior Day and the home crowd was going to say 'goodbye' to the seniors, Gene Banks, Kenny Dennard, Jim Suddath and Larry Linney. Before every Senior Game, the graduating players have a special introduction before the starting lineups are introduced. 'Tinkerbell' Banks had something special in mind.

On the Friday night before the Carolina game I went over to Duke Chapel, and it was open, and I went in and sat down to think. It hit me that the game would be my last in Cameron. I wouldn't play at Duke anymore or before the students. I cried a little bit, and then thought about this being Carolina and not wanting to lose to them. For once it hit me that my career was winding down.

I had decided to do something at the Senior Salute that I had done before my last home game at West Philadelphia. I brought six red roses to pass out. There were four to say 'thank you' to the students (one for each section), one for my mom, and one for my girl friend Isabelle. She later became my wife. I couldn't have written a better script. The game was back and forth and it came down to the wire. Carolina went up two and we passed the ball to mid-court and called timeout. The shot was supposed to be taken by freshman Chip Engelland off the in-bound pass. I broke the play and got open near the top of the key. Dennard and I never looked at each other, but he got the ball to me and I turned to my left and went up for the shot. I didn't see Sam Perkins coming at me. The only thing I saw when I turned was his hand, and I think that made me adjust my shot just a bit. By him, with his long arms, being there I had to put just a little more arch on the ball, and that's probably why it went in.

People pray and dream about things like that, and to have that happen for me in my last game of the season to cap off my career here at Duke was magical. The students put me on their shoulders and carried me around the floor. I was in the clouds. I felt like I was in Heaven.

Duke won the game in overtime, 66-65, and finished 6-8 in the ACC, and tied for fifth going into the ACC Tournament. We lost in the first round to Maryland in Landover 56-53. Duke did get an invite the NIT, and won two games at home against NC A&T and Alabama. Banks took a hard fall in the Alabama game and broke his wrist. He was lost for the rest of the season. Unfortunately, the 'rest' of the season was one game. That third game was at Purdue where the Devils lost by 12. I always go to the locker room after the last game of the season and talk with each player. I finished talking with Suddath and hugged him. As I turned, a Durham sportswriter said sarcastically, "What was all that about?" "It was something you will never get to experience," I replied. I am most proud of the relationships I still have with every player who put on a Duke uniform. Duke ended with a 17-13 record, but things were about to take a turn for the worse.

CHIP ENGELLAND, BOB & TOMMY EMMA AT UCLA 3/1/92

In 1982 and 1983, fans became more and more frustrated with

records of 10-17 and 11-17. The one thing the fans overlooked was the fact that Bill Foster loved the 2-3 match-up zone defense. These were mostly his players, recruited to play that style. Coach K didn't even acknowledge the word 'zone' at that time, except to talk about opponents' defenses. He was strictly man-to-man.

Tom Butters stayed the course about his decision even with K's record of 38 wins and 47 losses in those first three seasons.

> *In the fourth year of his contract, we had to renew it or let him go. We had won about eight in a row with a rather weak schedule and went to the Rainbow Classic in Hawaii. We got beat in the first round by SMU. We beat Pacific and Navy with a young David Robinson to go to 10-1. We came back and won four in a row, and promptly lost three league games in a row. I used to meet with coaches all the time in THEIR offices, because I always felt that they were more comfortable there.*
>
> *I stopped in the basketball office about eight o'clock one morning and asked his secretary if he was in and she said he hadn't come in yet. I said, "When he gets in, have him come down to my office, I want to talk to him.*
>
> *She said, "Your office?"*
>
> *I said, "My office."*
>
> *He came down to my office a short time later and said, "You wanted to talk to me?"*
>
> *I said, "I've got a problem." I could just see him tense up.*
>
> *"Let me tell you the problem, Mike. I've got a public that doesn't know how good you are. I've got a press that is too dumb to tell the public how good you are. And right now, my biggest concern is that I've got a coach that may not know how good he is." And with that, I took out a new five-year contract. I'll never forget it as long as I live and I slid it across the desk. He looked at it and tears started coming down his face.*
>
> *He said, "Coach, you don't have to do this."*
>
> *I said, "I not only have to do it, I have to do it right now."*

He signed the contract and we went on to win 24 games. We lost in Pullman, Washington to Detlef Schrempf and Washington. Two years later we won 37 games and played for the NCAA Championship. It was the right time. He stuck to his guns with his defense when everybody was yelling, "ZONE." We weren't going to build the kind of program we needed by playing zone.

In the last game of the 1983 season, the Blue Devils were blown out by Carolina, 105-81. That put them at 3-11 in the ACC, and Duke was matched up with UVa and Ralph Sampson in the first round of the Tournament in Atlanta, and the final score wasn't pretty, 109 - 66. After I finished broadcasting all four games, I went to our hotel, the Ritz Carlton in Buckhead. I walked into the lobby and was met by a well-known Iron Duke. He grabbed me by my coat lapels with the look of a deranged soul. He was shaking, his face was beet-red, and the veins in his neck were about to pop. He screamed, "When are we going to get rid of that stupid *#%# Pollock and that dumb SOB that hired him?" I finally got him to turn me loose and fired back, "Why are you asking me? Give the man the time he needs to build this thing the way it should be." I knew why he was venting his frustrations at me. He couldn't get to Mike or Tom, and I guess I was next on the food chain.

Nine years and 17 days later, on the day Laettner became famous, I saw this man and his wife having lunch with Bill and Pat Krzyzewski in the team hotel. He was all giddy over Mike, and saying how he had never doubted Mike at all. I'm sure Coach doesn't remember the man's feelings being EXACTLY like that.

Before Mike got Butters' new contract, I remember talking with him in the locker room after a home game. He looked at me with misty eyes, and his lip quivering a bit, and said, "Bob, if they will just leave me alone and give me time, we'll win. I know what I am doing. I am not coaching a team for just one season. I'm building a program. We could have won several more games if we had played some zone, but that would have defeated my whole approach. Man-to-man teaches discipline. And I have to have that to win."

After winning the 1991 NCAA championship in Indianapolis, Mike and I were the only two left in the small coach's room in the locker room after taping our daily radio shows. As I finished putting my gear away, I looked at him and said. "Mike, I'm so glad that they gave you time." He looked at me quizzically and said, "You remembered that, huh?" I told him that I would never forget it.

Mike continued to build for the future, and his first recruit for the 1982-83 season was Bill Jackman from Grant, Nebraska. Bill only played one season at Duke and transferred to Nebraska to be near his mom. His dad passed away right before his senior year in high school.

Krzyzewski plucked Weldon Williams from Park Forest, IL. Weldon wanted a strong academic school and he fit right in. He graduated with a degree in Biomedical Engineering and became an engineer with General Electric. He answered his call to the ministry in the late 1980s. After graduating from Westminster Theological Seminary near Philadelphia, he was an ordained a Presbyterian minister. Williams is now pastor of the Triumph Community Church in Bolingbrook, Illinois, and is Quality Manager for Diageo in Plainview.

Mike then went after the top-ranked player in California, Jay Bilas. Jay was also recruited by USC, UCLA and Iowa, but on his official visit to Iowa City, the Southern Californian found it cold and snowing. Jay made his decision to come to Duke in January, and here's why.

> *I was really fortunate to play for Mike Krzyzewski at Duke. I grew up in Los Angeles, and never dreamed I would play far away from home. I decided early on in the recruiting process that I wanted to play for a coach that I trusted, and that the coach I played for would be the most important factor in my decision. When Coach K first recruited me in 1981, I had never heard of him. But, after getting to know him, I was unconcerned about his record or perceived lack of experience or accomplishment relative to the other coaches recruiting me. He had something special, and I trusted him.*
>
> *My decision to play for Coach K was the most important and impactful decision of my life, and the best one. Through that one*

decision, I played for arguably the game's finest coach, attended one of the nation's finest institutions, and spent every day with many of the best people in their fields. If the quality of one's experience is measured by the quality of people with whom one associates, I could not have had a better experience at Duke.

I learned so many valuable lessons from Coach K, but none more important than making everything I do important. In 1982, before playing an opponent we were expected to beat rather easily, Coach K walked into the locker room and told us that this was the most important game on our schedule. As young players, we were taken aback. How could it be the most important game when we had North Carolina, Maryland and Virginia coming up? Coach K told us that it was the most important game because it was our next game, and because we were playing it. And, he said, everything we do is important because we are doing it. In practice, it should be the most important two hours of your life. That is, until it is over and you move immediately on to the next thing. Whether you are devoting your time to class work, yard work or leisure time, if you are doing it, you should make it important. I carry that lesson with me in everything that I do.

The next commitment came from Scottsdale, Arizona's Mark Alarie. Mark's final three were Duke, Stanford, and Notre Dame.

Johnny Dawkins was one of the most coveted players in the country. He wanted to help Krzyzewski in building the Duke program back to previous heights. Maryland Coach Lefty Driesell asked Dawkins why he picked the Blue Devils. Johnny D said, "Coach, I admire you so much I wanted to go to college where you went." The 'Left-hander' was at a loss for words.

The final recruit had grown up wanting to play for UNC. David Henderson, from the community of Drewry, NC, near the Virginia border, was offered by all three Triangle schools. Coach K made a home visit and that clinched it. I did a phone interview with David the day after he signed, and I could feel the emotion in his voice. David was the first member of his family to ever go to college.

FROM PEARL HARBOR TO HIROSHIMA

There have been several events that have changed the course of United States history. July 4, 1776 was the first, and three others come to mind quickly, Sunday, December 7, 1941, Monday, August 6, 1945, and Tuesday, September 11, 2001.

I wasn't born when the Japanese attacked Pearl Harbor, and not quite 4 when the crew of the American B-29 bomber Enola Gay dropped the nuclear weapon 'Little Boy' on Hiroshima. That event basically ended what the air raids on Ford Island, Hickam Field, Wheeler Field, Barber's Point, and Kaneohe did to start the U.S. involvement in World War II.

In December 1983, Duke participated in the Rainbow Classic. Phyllis and I joined several other Duke fans on the 'City Tour' to get a good look at our surroundings with a native guide. Included in the package was a motor launch trip from the Honolulu port along the coastline and into Pearl Harbor. We circled Ford Island and saw the other points as our guide told of the havoc wreaked upon the U.S. military forces and equipment early that fateful Sunday morning. The final stop was at the USS Arizona Memorial. The captain killed the engines right beside the hull of the sunken ship. He pointed out the oil that is still, to this day, leaking from the ship.

He tossed a lei into the water. He then asked for a moment of silence for the men and women who had lost their lives in service to their country. As we opened our eyes, we realized that there was a group of Japanese on our tour. There was not a dry eye on that boat.

It is one thing to read the accounts of that event, or to see movies, even with military footage. But it is awe-inspiring to stand where it all took place.

Four years later the team was back in Honolulu for a different tournament, the BYU-Hawaii Thanksgiving Classic in Laie, on the north side of Oahu. This time we took the 'Navy Tour' and drove to Pearl and walked over the pedestrian bridge to the USS Arizona Memorial and got another perspective of everything.

That '83 trip also marked a new opportunity for my career. WRAL-

TV's Tom Suiter had hosted the Duke football and basketball coaches' TV shows for a number of years. His duties at the station would not permit him to be away for an entire week and the show had to be taped in Honolulu because of airdate. I was asked to host the show. We hired a cameraman in Hawaii and set about shooting video of the team at various locales, as well as game footage. There was even some footage of Max Crowder wearing a grass skirt and doing the Hula. I did several 'stand-ups' at these venues to setup the feature. A 'stand-up' is just that; an announcer standing in front of some recognizable scene and talking about what the audience was about to see or had just seen.

I did several of these at the Ilikai Hotel, our team hotel on Waikiki Beach. We involved the entire Duke fan entourage in the closing. We had them say, in unison," Mele Kalikimaka" which is the Hawaiian way to say, "Merry Christmas."

The next fall, beginning with new Duke football coach Steve Sloan's first game, I was the regular host of the shows, a job I still love doing. I look back at the tapes of those first shows and cringe. Thankfully, someone didn't feel quite as bad about my performance as I did.

In 1991, Duke was invited to give up a home football game with Clemson to play the Tigers in Tokyo, Japan in the Coca-Cola Japan Bowl. We left Durham on Sunday, November 24th, the day after losing badly at North Carolina. This was a fourteen-hour trip, and I don't think I EVER got on the right time schedule. Since we didn't play until the 30th (late Saturday night in Durham, but midday Sunday in Tokyo), Phyllis and I bought Japan-Rail passes so we could travel around the country easier. We could ride any train or bus in Japan. The wonderful thing about this was, I finally got to ride the Shinkansen, the Japanese Bullet Train. This was the world's first high speed train with speeds of 200 km/h.

We left Tokyo about 6:30 on Wednesday morning and got a seat in the Vistadome Dining car. We were eating our breakfast salad as we passed Mt. Fuji with its snow-capped peak and the sun shining brightly. We arrived in Hiroshima a little after 10:30 after a stop in Kyoto. That's 423 miles in four hours with 15-20 minutes for the stop in Kyoto.

We first visited the Peace Memorial. The 1945 nuclear explosion occurred almost directly above the building (490 feet up). It was the closest building to withstand the explosion. The building has been preserved in the state that it was in immediately after the detonation. We stood at that building and looked straight up and could not fathom what took place there just over 45 years before. The Hiroshima Peace Memorial Museum has remnants and artifacts from the bombing. When we saw a child's twisted bike, it sent the same shivers through me as when I stood in the museum at Auschwitz and saw children's toys that had been taken from them by the Germans just before they were taken to the gas chambers. Phyllis and I stood in one of those death chambers and looked up at the pipe in the roof where the poison gas was dropped in on the unsuspecting Jews.

From the site of the beginning of World War II for Americans in the Pacific, to the site of the event that began the end, these were several trips of historical importance that I had only read about before.

TERRORISM STRIKES HOME

The third event that changed U.S. history was the terrorist attacks on the World Trade Center, the Pentagon, and another attempt that failed on a western Pennsylvania farm. We all remember where we were and what we were doing on that Tuesday morning. Little did I realize that three months and sixteen days later I would be peering down into that crater in Manhattan that had once been a symbol of the economy of the free world.

On Tuesday, September 11, 2001 between 8:46 am and 10:28 am, the world changed forever. 9/11 is not a day that only Americans remember in horror. It's a day that the entire world remembers.

On September 11, 2002, almost every community in the United States held services commemorating the people who lost their lives. That morning, I participated in the Durham service, and then drove to Albemarle to be the featured speaker in the 'Stanly County Remembers' service. It was held on the front grounds of the YMCA. The city closed off North First Street as the crowd numbered close to 5,000. Not only was there seating in front of the YMCA and First Street, but Cannon Park across the street was packed. It was a coming-together like that county had not seen in many decades.

I was honored to be asked to speak at the service. I had several ties to the New York City destruction. Two former Duke athletes were killed in the WTC collapses. Former Duke basketball star Tommy Amaker's sister narrowly missed injury or death.

BOB SPEAKS @ 'STANLY COUNTY REMEMBERS' 9/11 SERVICE '05

One of my best friends from Albemarle High, Harry Whitley, was on his way to work and watched in horror as the second plane went into the South Tower. The Staten Island Ferry he was on turned back. Harry was to have picked up new glasses at a shop in the Center that morning. They were ready two days early, and he got them on Sunday afternoon on his way home from church.

I recounted all of this and my own emotions as we watched TV that entire day at the office. It became more and more bizarre as time went on.

Stanly County held the service for five straight years, and I was a part of it for four, twice as speaker, and twice as emcee. The only year I couldn't, Duke played football at UConn on September 11, 2004.

The Duke basketball team flew from Durham to the airport at Teterboro, NJ on the afternoon of December 17. We boarded the team bus and headed for one of Coach Mike Krzyzewski's favorite restaurants, Capri Mia, in the heart of Hackensack, NJ. After a wonderful Italian dinner, we boarded the bus again but instead of going to our hotel, we headed for the Lincoln Tunnel, and Manhattan. As the bus cleared the eastern end of the tube, we were met by three NYPD squad cars. We were escorted down the West Side Highway and into the backside of the World Trade Center area. As we got off the bus, it was already dark and a misty rain had begun to fall. We were ushered onto the VIP viewing platform that looked right down into that pit. This was the day after the crews had extricated a whole fire truck that had been buried under the rubble.

There were representatives from NYPD, Port Authority Police and NYFD. They answered any and all questions any of us had. Some of them had cameras and made pictures of the Duke players and coaches. I asked one of the NYPD Lieutenants about the design on the north wall. It looked like several strata of rock formations. He told me that the division lines were floors and ceilings. They were once nine feet apart. Now they were SIX INCHES apart. That's the result of 110 stories collapsing and 'pan-caking' on top of each other. Each floor was a 4-inch thick lightweight concrete slab that laid on a fluted steel deck. When the towers fell, they came straight down.

After a few minutes on that viewing platform, it was obvious that it was not rain on the cheeks of the entire group. It was a very emotional night.

Several weeks later, that Lieutenant emailed me at the office and asked if I might be able to get the pictures that he had taken to those players and coaches. I assured him that I would. A couple of days later, I had the pleasure of handing them out in the Duke locker room. Lt. Charlie McEvoy was a Duke fan before that December night, but what happened over the next couple of months cemented his feelings.

I told Coach K about Charlie and how he felt about the Blue Devils. I asked if we might find a couple of tickets for he and a fellow policeman to come down for a game. NO PROBLEM!! Coach insisted that the two officers AND their wives come down for the season finale against North Carolina. He put them in four seats right behind the Duke bench. Charlie and Patty were ecstatic. The game was on Sunday. The four got into Durham on Friday evening. Phyllis and I gave them the grand tour of campus and Durham. They loved the Chapel, but when we walked into Cameron Indoor Stadium they were swept away. We all had dinner together that night, and they were ready for Senior Day at Duke the next day. Duke made their trip complete with a 93-68 blowout of the Tar Heels. As a bit of icing on the cake, I took them into the Duke locker room after the game and Coach introduced them to the team. They got autographs and the coaches gave them some Duke memorabilia to take home.

Charlie and I continue to correspond by email. He is now CAPTAIN McEvoy. Every game we play in New York, Charlie and his son are there and always come by the broadcast location to spend some time. He is TRUE BLUE forever.

Out of tragedy ....

CHAPTER SEVENTEEN
THE NIGHT I ALMOST GOT SHOT

The 1984 Duke team was beginning to show some of the progress that Mike had envisioned when he took the job. The foundations were laid for a program that would soon be compared to the greatest in college history.

The feelings were not limited to the inner circle of players and coaches. The students, fans, and finally the media were all beginning to see it. I am often asked what the turning point might have been, I always say there wasn't just one or two things. There was one incident that probably turned a lot of question marks into positive reinforcement. It was a moment in a Duke-UNC game on January 21, 1984. Duke lost that game but something happened that let fans and media know that Mike would not be pushed around by Dean Smith, the Tar Heels, or anyone else.

With about four minutes to play in Cameron, Duke was ahead 67-64, and UNC's Sam Perkins had gotten his third foul. Coach Smith, according to those AT the scorer's table, stood up to ask the officials who the foul was on. He wanted to get Perkins out, if it was on him.

The officials obviously didn't see him, because they put the ball in play. Smith went to the scorer's table and began slapping it, to try and get the officials attention. They ignored him and that sent him off. He yelled at the scorekeeper to hit the buzzer. The scoreboard operator (a University of North Carolina graduate, by the way) refused to stop the game because rules forbade it. Smith then reached over to push the buzzer himself, and hit the button that controlled the score instead. That action put 20 extra points on UNC's side. Hey, it gets better!!!

Cameron Indoor Stadium went nuts. Coach K was yelling to the officials to stop Coach Smith and his antics. They ignored BOTH coaches and didn't even 'tee-up' Dean. I never witnessed anything even close to that. But, this thing was not over.

Coach K blew into the media room and jumped on the issue before any one could ask a question. This was a benchmark in ACC history. It certainly let everyone know that this was a new era for Duke Basketball.

He took issue with the writers in their reporting about his team and the University, and basically told them, as a group, that they had no class. He then told them that they had never witnessed any of HIS team pointing or yelling at the officials during the game, or slamming the scorer's table. His next statement was most telling. "You can't allow behavior like that without consequences, and you cannot allow a coach to act like that and the officials not even call a technical on him." He said they 'should get things straight and stop the obvious double standard that was going on in the ACC.'

There was a 'new sheriff' in town.

Duke made the NCAA's, but lost their first game to Washington, IN SPOKANE, by two. Guess what? Several problems at the scorer's table didn't result in histrionics. The 'hometown' clock operator had problems with the clock in the waning moments.

In 1985, the Blue Devils played what was supposed to be the final game in Carmichael Auditorium. Construction problems with the Smith Center later kept that from being fact. Duke did beat Carolina that day, 93-77. They won the first and last games they played on that floor, but none in between. It was the only Duke victory I ever broadcast in that building, and as we were leaving, Phyllis and I ducked back into one of the entrance portals and I blew the facility a 'goodbye kiss.' I walked out happy.

The Blue Devils were seeded 3rd in the NCAA Midwest Regional and gave Coach K his first NCAA victory, Pepperdine went down 75-

62 in Houston, Texas. Two nights later unranked Boston College upset Duke, 74-73.

I had a rental car for the network personnel and the four of us left the arena that Sunday night way before the team. I returned the car at the airport, and asked an attendant to take us to the general aviation terminal. I had forgotten which terminal the plane was at. I finally saw the charter's tail fin sticking up over a building. We pulled in and began unloading equipment and luggage. For some reason, I looked back at the plane and saw it pulling away. I panicked and ran to the office and beat on the window to get the attention of those inside. They had no idea what I was saying, so I jumped over a little two-foot high chain and ran down the tarmac, hoping that someone would see me and stop. This WAS 1985 and security was different. I was trying to get a 737 to stop. What was I thinking? The pilot couldn't hear me. He had no side mirrors. By the way, I had on cowboy boots and a Stetson hat and was carrying a briefcase.

About that time I heard, "STOP."
I kept after the plane. "STOP OR I"LL SHOOT!!"
THAT got my attention.

I didn't take another step. I turned around and there was a Texas Ranger with a pistol about two feet long over his head. I tried explaining our situation to him but to no avail.

"Sorry about that sir, you'll just have to make other arrangements." As we walked back to the charter office I took one more glance at the aircraft. Guess what? The plane turned right and taxied back to us.

As we took our seats on the plane we took a lot of abuse. My seat was beside Harry Rainey, who managed the University Stores. He immediately began giving me grief. "You had a lot of nerve chasing this plane down the tarmac. Did you really think you could stop it?" About that time, Odell Mayberry, from Pulaski, Virginia, leaned over from behind me and loudly said, "Yes, but the hell of it was, HE DID!!"

That 1985 team had just two freshmen, Kevin Strickland, from Mt. Airy, NC, and Billy King, from Sterling, Va. Billy was a great defender. In 1988, in the East Regionals at the Meadowlands, Duke was matched up against John Chaney's Temple Owls, and the leading scorer in Division 1 basketball, Mark Macon. By his senior season, King was nationally known as a 'lock-down' defender. He drew the task of defending Macon. King hounded Macon into his worst game of the season.

Number one, there was a lot of film that the coaches had us watch, and I was watching at home, as well. I realized that he always went left when he went to shoot the ball, and so I tried to force him back to his right hand.

In the game, it was man-to-man, so I had him by myself most of the time, but Temple also set a lot of screens for him. If I knew I was going to get picked off, I'd yell at Quin (Snyder) to switch, or Danny (Ferry) to switch out to make sure he didn't get open shots. The guys did a great job of getting me through and being there if they did try to help.

Even though Billy was a great defender, he could be a scorer, too.

I was when I was in high school, and I figured out ways to score once I got to Duke. I knew, going into games, that people weren't going to guard me so I'd shoot the ball early and be aggressive, and then teams would change their philosophy. I usually took the first four shots of a game and scored, and then they would change up. Against N.C. State, Coach Valvano put (Charles) Shackleford on me, so I drove around him and scored, and he switched back.

After earning his Duke degree, King went to work with the Philadelphia 76ers in June 1997, as Vice-President of basketball administration. In one year, he was promoted to General Manager, and five years after that, Billy was named President of the 76ers, as well as keeping the General Manager duties.

The 1986 Duke seniors were five of those six precocious freshmen who came into Krzyzewski's program in the fall of 1982 to build it up.

JOHNNY DAWKINS, JAY BILAS, MARK ALARIE, BOB & WELDON WILLIAMS FINAL FOUR IN DALLAS 3/86

In addition, Mike had recruited two freshmen who made significant contributions in '86. Quin Snyder and Danny Ferry got lots of playing time because of their immense talents, and their abilities to play defense. Danny was the more-highly recruited, because he was the son of former NBA player and General manager Bob Ferry, and because he played for Morgan Wooten at DeMatha High. In a ferocious recruiting war, Ferry picked Duke over UNC. I was so happy that day that Phyllis and I joined the Iron Dukes.

The 1985 inaugural pre-season NIT tournament started an eight-games-in-17-days stretch. I flew with the team to Houston for the NIT on Wednesday for the Thursday night Lamar game. Friday morning, I flew back to Durham to broadcast the Duke-UNC football game on Saturday afternoon. The game was a classic, as Steve Sloan beat Carolina for his only win over the Heels. Sophomore QB Steve 'Snake' Slayden and WR Doug Green hooked up on a TD pass with time running out and Duke pulled off a 23-21 upset. Doug made a twisting catch with his toes nailed down just in bounds in the end zone.

First thing Sunday morning I was on a plane to Houston again for Duke's win over UAB. Tuesday was a drive to Williamsburg and back for the William and Mary game. The Semis and Final of the NIT were Friday and Sunday in Madison Square Garden. Duke squeaked out a 71-70 win over St. John's, then won the title over Kansas, 92-86. We helped dedicate the Dean E. Smith Center in January but couldn't spoil it for the Heels.

In a rare Saturday night/Sunday afternoon combo in February, Johnny Dawkins played some of his best basketball. He was fouled with just seconds remaining in a tie game and promptly made both free throws to beat N.C. State in Raleigh. The next afternoon in Cameron, with a national audience watching, Johnny deflected a David Rivers game-winning attempt, as Duke beat Notre Dame. Duke beat Carolina in Cameron in the last game of the regular season, 82-74. It was Duke's first place finish in twenty years.

Coach K got his first ACC Tournament championship to go with the regular season title the next weekend in Greensboro with wins over Wake Forest, Virginia and Georgia Tech.

Duke came back to Greensboro five days later for the first round of the NCAA Tournament. Lafayette Stribling brought his Mississippi Valley State Delta Devils to the Coliseum. Stribling was dressed in white, from his suit down to his cowboy boots. Maybe the smallest crowd of the season witnessed a sluggish first half, but Dawkins didn't let this be HIS last college game. As we were leaving the Coliseum, most of the Mississippi Valley State players were asking for autographs from the Duke Players. It was great to see the respect and appreciation the players gave each other. A second round win over Old Dominion sent Duke to the Regionals in the Meadowlands. The Blue DEVILS beat Ray Meyer's DePaul Blue DEMONS to advance.

David Robinson and Navy were all that was between Duke and the Final Four. Dawkins set the tempo early by getting his 6'4" body OVER the 7'1" Robinson for a dunk. With a few minutes left, the students began chanting "Abandon Ship, Abandon Ship."

'Big D--little A--double L--AS.' That's where Duke was headed. They were joined there by No. 2 Kansas, No. 7 Louisville and unranked LSU.

On Friday before the Semi-Finals, Phyllis and I drove out to find Dealey Plaza. This is a 'must-see' sight in Dallas. It doesn't look like it did on November 22nd, 1963. Several famous signs are no longer where they were. They paved the parking lot behind the fence. There is a commemorative plaque on the grassy knoll. To stand and look at the Texas Schoolbook Depository where Lee Harvey Oswald, and possibly others, fired the shot(s) that killed President John F. Kennedy and wounded Texas Governor John Connally, was unbelievable. Yes, I DO believe Oswald did NOT act alone.

Back to the Final Four. Duke had a rematch with Kansas in their first game and it resembled the Championship game of the Preseason NIT. That was a portend of things to come in this one. Again, it was a physical game that wore down both teams. Duke won, 71-67, and I got to broadcast my second NCAA championship game.

During this era, the NCAA and the Final Four hosts usually held a big outing for the teams, their 'official parties' and the media on Sunday. Dallas threw a Texas Barbeque at South Fork Ranch where the TV series, 'Dallas' was made. Phyllis and I were invited and what a time we had. As soon as the team knew they were going to the Final Four, David Henderson just knew he was going to get to sit in J.R. Ewing's chair. We were included in the team's private tour of the house, and I discretely told our guide about David's wish and asked if it would be possible, and he said it would not be a problem. The guide said there would be a photo op at J.R.'s desk, and he called for a volunteer. Henderson nearly jumped into the chair. To make the picture more memorable, I had him wear my Stetson. Yes, the one that was in the plane-chasing scene in Houston.

BOB & DALLAS COWBOYS CHEERLEADERS

Picture this: David in a Stetson, reared back in J.R.'s chair, with a smile that would have taken two pages of this book if I had put it in. There was also a photo op with the Dallas Cowboy Cheerleaders at the ranch, and as you can see, I took advantage of that, and Phyllis didn't mind. She took this picture.

Later on we all enjoyed some great Texas-style BBQ. It is not as good as North Carolina 'Q' since it was beef and not pork. We were entertained by B.J. Thomas and the Forrester Sisters. To this day, that was the best event of its kind at any of the Final Fours I attended.

BOB & PHYLLIS @ SOUTH FORK RANCH

Most of the media comments during the Final Four talked about the players, and the way they conducted themselves.

Come Monday night, the Blue Devils kinda ran out of steam. They played so hard, but the shots just didn't drop, and I really feel that the physicality of the Kansas game led to much of that. Louisville won the Championship. In the post-game news conference, Krzyzewski was so proud of his kids and talked about Coach Crum and his team and the excellent game they played. Mike said he would not change a thing if they played again. Coach K's teams are build around honesty, trust, and no excuses. That IS Duke Basketball.

Two years later, Duke went back to the Final Four with a team that was led by Danny Ferry, Alaa Abdelnaby and freshman Christian Laettner. They lost in the Semi-Finals to Kansas.

Even as a freshman, Laettner was an outstanding free throw shooter. He missed two in a very memorable game for me. In the final seconds of the Arizona game in the Meadowlands in February, Christian was fouled and went to the line for two free throws. He missed both. Retired Greensboro News-Record sportswriter Wilt Browning recalls.

In long careers of covering sports, only the most avid writers and broadcasters can remember precious few of the games that seemed so important as they were going on. But occasionally, there are events that set those games apart.

Such was the case at the end of the day on February 26, 1989. Duke played Arizona in a basketball game in the Meadowlands across the river from New York City. A still youngish Mike Krzyzewski worked the sidelines while prematurely silver-haired Lute (I Don't Get No Respect) Olson handled the strategy for Arizona.

Sitting mid-court and about halfway up among the crowd in the lower level seats - on the Duke side - was Richard Milhous Nixon. He laughed and talked with people around him as the game went on and, like the rest of us, fell silent when tall, smooth-faced Christian Laettner, still a rookie though it was late in his freshman season, went to the free throw line.

It was a tenuous thing, putting a game such as this in the hands of a freshman, even one with the upside most people envisioned for Laettner. A mere 10 seconds remained on the big clock overhead. Arizona led, 77-75. Duke, therefore, would need both free throws to tie. If Laettner missed even one of the two he had been awarded, Duke's chances of victory seemed remote at best.

We had our answer quickly. He missed the first. Then the second - then with little meaning at all - clanked off the iron. And just that quickly, the game was over. A dejected Laettner hurried away, his teammates and coaches in his wake, to the sanctity of the dressing room.

Bob and I would be along soon to do the things broadcasters and writers do in such situations. We would ask the hard questions and the not-so-hard. No one had to tell us that these are the toughest dressing rooms. Blowouts are easier than to come this close.

I went to the locker room for my post-game interviews with Coach and a player. Browning was the only other person in the hallway.

Bob and I waited outside the doors to the Duke dressing room that seemed more silent than I had expected. It would be a while before Bob and I - the only two people from North Carolina covering the game, as I recall - would be allowed inside, and we stood talking for a time when a familiar figure appeared far down the long hall leading to the dressing room.

I turned to see who it was. I looked back at Wilt and said, "Is that who I think it is?"

"It sure looks like him," he replied.

It was the former President, a man who once studied law at Duke. He seemed only to be strolling, in no rush, but clearly coming in our direction. He walked up to me, stuck out his hand and said, "Hi, I'm Richard Nixon."

"Yes, Mr. President. I know who you are. I voted for you twice." I wasn't old enough to vote for him when he ran unsuccessfully in 1960. The voting age then was 21. Browning again.

"Tough loss," he said to us as he joined the group of three. Bob agreed. And we were silent for a moment.

"Mr. President," I said, "I am a little surprised that you came alone, not surrounded by Secret Service escorts."

"Oh," he said softly, "nobody cares about an old president any more."

We talked for a few minutes with him asking all the questions. He wanted to know all about my job, and I told him. President Nixon said, "You know that I graduated from Duke Law School and I still pull for the Blue Devils."

I told him that I was well aware of that fact, and that I thought Duke should have jumped at the chance to house the Nixon Presidential Library.

He said, "you know Bob, I used to think I had the best job in America. Now, I believe you do."

I told him I'd always felt that way, and was glad to hear him say it too. I asked if he would consent to an interview before I had went in to do Coach's post-game. He agreed. We were in a commercial break and on the wireless mic I told my color man/engineer, "Give it to me as soon as this break's over, and tell Phyllis to get down here quickly."

"What's the hurry?"

"I have President Nixon with me."

This guy was a very strong and vocal advocate of the opposing party, and we had decided to never talk politics. His retort was, "So?"

I shot back, "He's a Duke Law grad and a former President of the United States. Now SEND IT TO ME!!"

He did, and the interview went great. Phyllis had gotten there just as we finished and I introduced her to President Nixon and we had him autograph both of our media credentials. His interview is on the CD.

He then asked if I thought that he might have the opportunity to speak with 'the young man who missed those free throws.' I tapped on the door and told the assistant that President Nixon wanted to come in if possible. Within a minute President Nixon was taken into the Duke locker room and Coach K asked him to speak to the team. He did, and then walked over and sat down with Laettner. It caught the freshman by surprise.

> *It was really weird because we were all disappointed over the loss, and Coach K mentioned that President Nixon would be coming in. That kinda lifted our spirits immediately, and made us forget about the loss for a few minutes. Nixon walked in and that was real cool. And he just said something like, 'Keep your heads up. I've missed a few shots here and there.' He said something like, 'It's not how many times you fall off the horse, it's how many times you get back on.' It was a good little distraction in a time of disappointment for us.*

President Nixon then added, "I'll guarantee you that you're going to make some really big shots to win some big games for Duke before you graduate." How prophetic!!

Wilt Browning again.

> *Bob and I continued to wait. It would be longer now, but neither of us had the pressure of deadline. And finally, the former President reappeared.*

"May I ask what you told the team?" I inquired. "I was anxious to have a word with Christian Laettner," Nixon said. "He will be a great player, and I just told him that everything would be all right and that I should know; I've lost a few myself."

Then he was gone, walking alone once again down that cold hallway.

Even if some of the fine detail is eroded by the years now, it remains one of the memorable moments in a long, long career.

Bob Harris has been a friend and an associate for close to 30 years now. I came to North Carolina too late to have spent much time listening to the legendary Add Penfield doing Duke football and basketball, but Bob and I are contemporaries. Not only contemporaries, but fellow members of the board for the North Carolina Sports Hall of Fame, the group of men and women whose basic charge is to preserve the state's sports heritage by annually ushering in new classes of inductees. Bob became one of those inductees in 2006 and wears the ring proudly. kindness. As what we writers sometimes refer to as a "talking head," Bob has stood out. But his has been a challenge only those closest to Duke athletics could best appreciate. Bob has done it with style and professionalism.

WILT BROWNING
Sportswriter - Greensboro, Charlotte, Asheville & Atlanta

Another Duke graduate sought the Presidency and was 'testing the waters' at the 1999 NCAA Tournament First Round in Charlotte. Former Duke Homecoming Queen, Elizabeth Hanford Dole was in attendance and agreed to chat with me on our pre-game show. We talked about her under-graduate days on the 'Methodist Flats'

BOB INTERVIEWS PRESIDENTIAL CANDIDATE & FORMER DUKE HOMECOMING QUEEN, ELIZABETH DOLE
(**Blue Devil Weekly Photo**)

and her other positions of leadership to that point. She wasn't successful in her bid for the Republican nomination, but later became one of the U.S. Senators from North Carolina

CHAPTER EIGHTEEN

ABOUT ONE IN A MILLION

One of Duke's better known, and successful recent football coaches is Steve Spurrier, the Heisman Trophy winner from Florida. He took the Blue Devils to an ACC Championship and the All-American Bowl in 1989, and had three winning seasons in a row.

Spurrier wanted to get into coaching after his NFL career ended in 1976. Steve was quarterbacks coach at Florida in 1978, and after a year doing the same thing at Georgia Tech, Red Wilson brought 'the Ball Coach' to the Methodist Flats as his Offensive Coordinator.

We never knew what to expect from Spurrier's offenses. My duties at the radio station kept me from attending practices before the game at Maryland in 1982. I wanted to get together with Steve on the plane or in the hotel, but he was recruiting and we didn't touch base. I caught up with him as he came to the coach's box next to our broadcast booth about ten minutes before kickoff. I asked him what new stuff he had for the Terps.

"Aw shoot, Bobby, we didn't put anything new in. Same old stuff."

I believed him until our FIRST possession. The team came off the far sideline to the ball and snapped it. Bennett threw a pass that picked up about 25 yards. They ran to the ball and snapped it again. Another 15-20 yard completion, Third play, same thing. Fourth play, same thing for a touchdown. They kicked the extra point and I took a commercial break and looked to my right into the coach's box and everyone of them were laughing their heads off at me trying to keep up with Steve's 'hurry-hurry' offense.

The lure of pro ball called him away from Durham for a while. He was head coach of the Tampa Bay Bandits of the USFL for three years. In 1987, Tom Butters, who not only loved winning football games the 'Spurrier Way,' but also playing golf with the multi-talented Tennessean in the off-season, lured Steve and Jerri back to Duke as his head coach.

Steve Slayden, Anthony Dilweg, Billy Ray and Dave Brown appreciated it too. They were record setting Duke quarterbacks in the Spurrier system. In 1988 A.D., who had been the mop-up QB and an outstanding punter for three years came into his own. He threw for almost 4,000 yards and 24 touchdowns.

> *Being part of a team that won 7 games my senior was very meaningful, especially after Frank Dascenzo told me before the Carolina game that if we defeated UNC we would be the first Duke football team in 25 years to win 7 games in a season. He also asked me to sign his game day program if we beat Carolina. After we defeated Carolina 35-29 without our head coach on the sideline, I signed his program.*
>
> *Beating Tennessee in Knoxville was a HUGE highlight in my career. I'll never forget Ben Bennett challenging me the week of the game to, one, beat Tennessee, and two, in typical BB style, beat his Tennessee game day stats. Thanks to incredibly stout line play and a sticky handed receiver named Clarkston Hines, we defeated the Vols in front of a shocked Rocky Top crowd of 95,000 under the September lights. Oh, I also beat Ben's personal stats that night - icing on the cake.*

Dilweg was named ACC Player of the Year in 1988. He threw for 475 yards against Wake Forest that year. All of this was the result of playing for a former Heisman Trophy winner who loved daring quarterbacks, and Dilweg was daring.

> *I loved playing for Steve - he was an extremely demanding coach*

and always expected his QBs to be well prepared for every opponent and situation, as well as intimate with his potent game plan. He was an extraordinary game day coach that was always quick to formulate an explosive, impromptu offensive play between series to pierce an opponent's exposed weakness. He allowed me to change any play at the line of scrimmage as long as it was going from good to great. If you screwed up he was brutally tough on you in a way that makes far more sense to me today than it did when I was a 23 year old. He ALWAYS wanted to know what a QB was thinking when the QB went through his pass progression on any offensive play. Steve told me the reason he did that was to make sure the QB was thinking "right". Although Steve's delivery could be perceived as harsh at times, the content of his message was priceless. My personal focus was not how Steve said something, but what he said.

Late in that 1988 season, Duke was 6-3 and rode into Carter-Finley Stadium for a shootout with N.C. State. Dilweg and Company hung 43 points on the Wolfpack that afternoon. Unfortunately, State hung 43 on the Blue Devils. A late penalty cost Duke a win, and ultimately, a bowl game. Spurrier was as mad as I've EVER seen him. I went down to the field after the broadcast to tape the TV show. With cameras rolling for the first segment of the show, Steve blew a fuse and lambasted the officiating and said, in no uncertain terms, that the 'refs cost us this game.' We finished that segment and I looked at Johnny Moore, the executive producer with raised eyebrows and said, "I guess we'll have to do THAT one again. The 'Ball Coach' said, "Why?" I said, If we leave it like that, you'll be suspended."

Johnny told me that he'd already said all that and more to the writers and TV cameras in the post-game news conference. Okaaaaay. This would be interesting.

Sure enough, Spurrier was suspended for one game on Monday. Guess what? We only had one more game on the schedule. UNC was our final opponent, and it was in Wallace Wade. Spurrier was barred from the stadium. Duke won 35-29 without him in the stadium.

In the '89 season, Dave Brown, in his third start after Billy Ray was injured, threw for 479 in the season finale at Carolina. But it had not been all 'peaches and cream.'

It was an interesting year for me personally because I was supposed to be in the running for starting QB with Billy Ray. I started the year being a big disappointment. Spurrier was on me for not playing well and he indicated at the end of spring practice that he didn't think I was ready to play. He said, "I'm gonna play you in the South Carolina game (the season opener) at least one series, but I'm telling you that Billy is the starter." I went home for the summer, and I took it pretty hard. I questioned a lot of things about the way I was doing things.

I think that, by getting a taste of what things were like in that first game, and playing in the fourth quarter of that Virginia game two weeks later when we were getting blown out, and I threw three touchdown passes, the light bulb just went off and I thought, "Boy, it took a lot of hard work to get to this point, but it was worth it." It was a growing experience for me.

On the rushing front, Randy Cuthbert ran for 234 yards against Georgia Tech in 1989 and Roger Boone piled up 201 against Northwestern that same season. "Cutty' had 1,023 yards for the season in that bowl year of 1989, including six 100-yard games.

Entering the 1989 season, Spurrier and his team had some pretty lofty goals.

Back then we had started meeting before the season with the seniors and the captains, Bubba Metts and Hollywood Howell, and said, "What kind of goals do you want to set for the year?" Normally, our goals were a winning season, going to a bowl and winning a bowl game, and beat North Carolina. So after we went through the usual things, Bubba Metts said, "Coach, we've been talking and we think we can win the ACC." And I said, "Now, wait a minute. Let's don't put a goal on there that's unrealistic." I'd always wanted to put things that I thought were realistic, and Bubba said, "We've got N.C.

State, Georgia Tech, and Clemson at home and we think we've got a shot at it." So I said, "OK I'll put it on there but lets not tell anybody in public. We'll just keep this within the team." So that was one of our goals, and after the big upset of Clemson we got on that good roll we knew that goal was within reach.

I really admire the entire team for getting ready to play every week, and achieving that goal right there.

The Blue Devils started the 1989 season 1-3 after a 49-28 loss at Virginia, leaving Clarkston Hines and his teammates really down.

I was depressed! We definitely did not start the way we all thought we would. Things just weren't clicking. We couldn't put our fingers on it, but looking back, we played some really good teams. We played at South Carolina, Tennessee and Virginia. It was an angry Tennessee team, by the way, who was thinking about our coming out to Knoxville in '88 and upsetting them, 31-26. It was tough on us, and we definitely had some confidence issues after beginning the year 1-3. I felt that I wasn't contributing like I wanted to contribute.

Spurrier, though, wasn't thinking about reassessing the team's goals for the season.

We didn't really talk about re-thinking our goals, we just talked about what we had to do to get better and win a game or two. We changed our entire defense. We went to Virginia playing our normal zones, the cover 2s and cover 3s, and occasionally some man-to-man, and we just couldn't stop anybody with the normal defense. We had an outstanding offensive line with those three fifth-year seniors (Metts, Chris Port and Brett Tulacro), All-American wide receiver Clarkston Hines. Billy Ray and Dave Brown were pretty good quarterbacks and two tight ends; Dave Colonna and Bud Zuberer were very good.

We needed to change our defense and get the other team off the field some how or another. The only way to do it was to put eight, even nine men up around the line of scrimmage and force the other team to throw the ball, because they were just moving it up and down the field on us. So, the Clemson game, we put in an all-out blitz package of eight guys up there, and Wyatt Smith and Quinton McCracken, our two little cornerbacks, they had to play their guy all over the field. We were hopin' they could hold up, and they did it. They did it the whole year very well. That's what gave us a chance to start winning some games, and, of course, that big win against Clemson just gave us tremendous confidence that, if we go play like this, we've got a chance against everybody. And that's the way it turned out. We beat everybody after that.

The post game news conference of that Virginia game is more memorable than the game. Duke was headed home to take on the No. 7 team in the country, Clemson, the next Saturday. A writer asked Spurrier what he thought Duke's chances of beating the Tigers might be. He thought for a minute and replied, "Oh, probably about a million-to-one."

Yeah, I was really frustrated that we did not force a punt at Virginia. They never punted the entire game. They had the ball eight possessions. I will never forget that. They scored seven touchdowns and we actually forced a field goal that hit the upright, and that was their eight possessions. They had seven touchdowns and a field goal that hit the uprights and bounced backwards. That's how they got their 49. We ended up with 28. I was really upset and thought to myself that we didn't have much of a chance this year, we just can't stop anybody. That's when we went back and changed our defense. I told Jim Collins and Bob Sanders that we had to do something different on defense, so that's what we did. We changed it completely, and that was the key for us. It gave us a chance to win.

Hines felt a weight lifting from his shoulders.

I know that I was relieved and it took the pressure off us. We had nothing to lose. All we had to do was give it our best effort and let whatever happens, happen. Usually when you have a Top

10 team coming in, there is some nervousness and the stage is big and you want to do really well, and that puts pressure on you. With Coach making his 'one-in-a-million' statement, we were loose. We had nothing to lose.

I never thought about Coach trying to 'psych-out' the media or the other team, but maybe that's what he had in mind. Obviously, Clemson didn't have their best game. Maybe they took us for granted, and maybe they should have. We were 1-3 and, despite the fact that we played them tough the year before, I don't think they had their best game.

That was the subject of many columns and TV and radio stories all that week. Saturday dawned gray and dreary. There was a misty rain most of the day, making Spurrier's 'Airball' offense rely on a ground attack that had been less than effective in the first four games. The Blue Devils had put 96 points on the board in the first four games, but most had come off the strong right arm of Billy Ray, the Alabama transfer. Hines agrees.

It wasn't a big passing game like we had later in the year. It was efficient and we got several good passes in. I remember catching a touchdown pass and one sideline pass, but there were lots of passes to the running backs.

Duke literally pushed the winning touchdown across the Clemson goal line, with 'Cutty' getting blocking and pushing from Dave Colonna, Bubba Metts, Chip Nitowski, Chris Port, Bret Tulacro, and Wes White. Defensive stalwarts George Edwards, Quinton McCracken, Wyatt Smith, John Howell and Erwin Sampson kept the Tigers in check and Duke upset Clemson, 21-17. Was this the defining moment for this team? Dave Brown says, partially.

The Clemson game is the obvious one, but I think that game was a culmination of things. It was the seven days leading up to the game after getting blown out at Virginia, and the comments by George Welsh, that we don't play a real style of football, we just play two-hand touch. I think those things got the team upset. Then, to go out and beat the #7 team in the nation, I think that just catapulted our team. We knew we were good but we didn't have the confidence we should have had. That game gave us the confidence to know we could play with anybody.

They rattled of six more wins to close out the regular season 8-3, and win the ACC championship. This was the goal of the '89 team. As Clarkston Hines recalls, the team was anticipating this.

We were confident. We were coming off a 7-3-1 season and we felt we should have gone to a bowl game in '88. We had beaten some really good teams and started the '88 season 5-0. We felt that, if we could get good quarterback play from Billy Ray, who was replacing ACC Player-of-the-Year Anthony Dilweg, we would be good. Our confidence was high. We had a good preseason camp and had a lot of continuity and so we were anticipating having a good season.

I have been taping daily radio shows to run every Monday through Friday on our network stations since the mid-80s. The routine is, tape the Monday show after the game on Saturday. See the coach on Monday and tape the Tuesday and Wednesday shows. See him again on Wednesday to tape the Thursday and Friday shows. EVERY Wednesday when I went to see Steve, he was at his desk, drawing plays. The dialogue was almost always the same.

"Come here, Bobby. Look at this play. You think this'll score?"

"Did you draw it, coach?"

"Yep."

"It'll score. You've never designed a play to pick up two or three yards, have you?"

"Nope."

The Blue Devils went to Chapel Hill for the last game of the season, and blistered the Tar Heels 41-0. That sent Mack Brown's team to its second straight 1-10 season. As I said on the air at the beginning of the broadcast, "A crowd of 46,000 is on hand today, but the vast majority are dressed as aluminum bleachers." There might have been 20,000 fans in the stands on that bitterly cold day.

Spurrier said that the game plan for UNC was only one thing.

Game planning was simply to win the game, not let it get away. I think our guys had a good week of practice and we were favored pretty well over North Carolina, because they were struggling that year. We did not play real sharp that game. I think (UNC QB) Chuckie Burnette threw us six interceptions, and we made over 600 yards of offense and only got 41 points. We had a chance to score in the 60s that game, but we messed up three, four, or maybe five times in the red zone. We were down there the whole game and, 41 sounds pretty good, but getting six turnovers and over 600 yards of offense, we should have scored a lot more. But we were happy to have won the conference championship. That was the main thing, just to beat 'em. We weren't talking about a big score.

A Duke highlight of the game was Cuthbert racing around the right end and heading down the sideline. Freshman cornerback Cliff Baskerville 'hunkered-down' to block 'Cutty's' path to the end zone. Being all of five-feet-eleven-inches tall and weighing 164 pounds, he was no match for the six-three, 235-pounder who had a full head of steam. When the collision occurred, Baskerville went down hard. Randy kept on going. I asked Tony Haynes on the sidelines what happened, since the 'meeting' had happened right in front of him. He was laughing so hard he could barely get out the words 'split his pants.' The impact had split Baskerville's pants from his belt in the back, to his crotch. He needed a seamstress.

Dave Brown only saw the collision from the back of the play.

It's funny because I played against Baskerville in high school. He was a quarterback and it was great to see him playing defense and getting run-over by Cutty. That was the highlight of that game. I didn't see his pants actually split until our season-ending party and they showed it over and over and over in slo-mo, and that's when we knew just how hard Cutty had hit him.

I think Tony has now stopped laughing long enough to talk about that game from his vantage point on the Duke sidelines.

Everyone remembers 41-0, and for years, UNC moaned about Spurrier running up the score. Well, of course he did. Duke was trying to break a number of ACC passing and offensive records that day, and I believe Randy Cuthbert was trying to get over 1,000 yards for the season. Well, throughout the game, Spurrier kept asking me about total yards, passing yards and how many yards Cuthbert had. Not only did he want to kill Carolina, he wanted to break all those records in their yard and wanted me to update him on the stats. It was 41-0, but Spurrier was annoyed most of the game because he really thought Duke should have beaten them worse.

Steve's answer to the Tar Heel fans...

Now in the fourth quarter when it was out of hand, we had the game won, there were some goals we wanted to get. We wanted to average 500 yards of offense a game. Carl (Franks) upstairs said we

CLYDE CUPPLES, WES CHESSON, GOV. JIM MARTIN, BOB, JOEL STUTTS
1989 ALL AMERICAN BOWL - BIRMINGHAM

needed 26 more yards to average 500 a game for the season. I'd never had a team average 500 yards of offense a game, so I said, "well, we might as well try to get it if we can, so we got that.

Several photos were taken of the team sprawled out in front of the scoreboard that read, 'Duke 41 – UNC 0.' Since that day, the scoreboards have been cut off at the final horn if the Heels lose. Spurrier explains why the picture was taken.

The reason we took the picture was not to rub it in on North Carolina. When we beat Maryland at Maryland, 46-25, for Duke's first win there since 1960, and this was 29 years later, we made a picture there. Jim Collins' wife, Geri, has been on the sidelines forever, taking pictures and giving them to the players and coaches. I said, "Geri, we're going get the team together under that scoreboard and take a picture." Maryland left the lights (scoreboard) on too, and I've got that picture in my office here (in Columbia) right now, Bob. The guys loved it. When we got into the locker room, I told the guys, "Now, if we win the rest of our conference games, we're going to take a picture at North Carolina, if we win the conference championship." We had to win all the games to do that.

So, when the game was over, we went to our locker room and had a few comments and said The Lord's Prayer together, and then I said, "Hey, we've got to take a picture under that scoreboard." And we went back out and made it. There were a lot of people down there taking pictures of that.

Spurrier gave the team a couple of weeks off as they got ready for the All American Bowl in Birmingham, Ala. That game was played on December 28 at Legion Field. This was Duke's first bowl bid in 27 years, and Dave Brown relishes the fact that he was a part of it.

It is such a great thing. We have a bond, and I still idolize Spurrier to this day. He's a guy I looked up to all my life and playing here, he taught me so much, and helped me make it to the next level.

I'm a South Carolina fan now. I enjoy watching them play. I was a Florida fan when he was there. If you're a successful coach, your players always want to be around you.

Rumors of Spurrier leaving Duke for Florida had already begun to swirl. Steve didn't deny them, nor did he validate them. Everyone knew that Florida was his alma mater, and he loved Gainesville, and Ben Hill Griffin's money would be hard to turn down, too.

QB Billy Ray had sufficiently recovered from the shoulder injury he suffered in the final minutes of the win over Georgia Tech. Now, Duke had TWO proven signal-callers. Dave Brown had filled in more than adequately. In his first start at Wake Forest, the Deacons, and everyone else watching the game, knew 'Brownie' was going to handoff several times just to get the butterflies settled down. Spurrier had hinted that's what he would do for most of the week.

We actually had great confidence in Dave Brown. He was ready to play. Billy had played pretty well and so we didn't make any changes. But, when Billy Ray sprained his shoulder in the Georgia Tech game, a guy landed on it, it was obvious that Dave Brown was going to start the next game. I guess we just didn't announce it too much. Dave was our last man. Todd Decker was our next quarterback and he just wasn't ready to play at that time. Dave Brown went the distance the last three games. We had tremendous confidence in him to run our offense. As you know, he set all kinds of school records during that three-game stretch.

The Blue Devils began their first offensive possession on their 24-yard line. Wake Forest crowded the line of scrimmage. Dave Brown had something else in store for the Deacons.

We had talked the whole week about how Wake was going to be keying on Randy Cuthbert, and they should have been. He was on a tear at that time. At breakfast that Saturday morning of the game, we sat down at the table and Coach actually got some Cheerios and put them on the table and he drew up exactly what he thought was going to happen. I was going to fake to Randy up the middle and Clarkston Hines would be on a 'read-route.' He was going to run a corner route if they were in 'cover two.' Anything else they were in, he would run a 'go route.' The play call was 'Jones' probably because of Cedric Jones, a wide receiver in the early 80s. Spurrier would always name plays after players who made good plays on it.

So after the fake, Hines was wide open on the left sideline and I hit him in stride. He went 76-yards for the touchdown. That was a great way to get going in my first career start. Clarkston had a great game. I think he only caught five passes, but they went for 251 yards and three touchdowns. There was a 97-yarder late in the game. My thought was 'Clarkston, go run and get it, and I'll throw it as far as I can." It was nice to have a guy that could do that. I was kinda nervous because Clarkston was such an established guy and an All-American. And to be a young guy throwing to him was different because I hadn't had the reps with him since he was a starter. I wanted to make sure that since the play was designed for him, I was going to find him and make him like me in the process. So I was feeding him the ball at will.

Hines looks at that play and the day from his perspective.

On that first play, something very much went wrong in the Wake Forest secondary. I don't know if they had their calls in sync, but it appeared to me that a coverage breakdown ensued, and I was wide open. Brownie just threw it out there and there was no one around. I could have walked into the end zone, that's how open I was. That was just an incredible game. It was a great way for him to come out in his first start.

Here's 'The Ball-Coach's take on it....

I don't know if I was eating Cheerios or not, but I think we shifted to a two-tight end formation, hoping that Wake would maybe mess up a little bit, and we might hit Clarkston down the sidelines. And sure enough, he hit him on the dead run down the sidelines and he went about 80 yards for a touchdown.

Later in the game, he had a 97-yarder. He had 251 yards for the day. What was neat about that was Wake Forest had an excellent offensive game too. 52-35, so it was a game where we needed to score a bunch of points to win.

Texas Tech coach Spike Dykes had his Red Raiders ready and they took control early. Runningback James Gray scored four touchdowns and gained 280 yards for the night as Texas Tech blasted Duke 49-21.

BOB & 'THE BALL COACH'

We taped the Duke Football TV Show after the game in the locker room. During that taping, Spurrier confirmed that the loss WAS his last game as coach of the Blue Devils. He was headed to Florida and six SEC titles and the 1996 National Championship.

'Airball' was fun. It was fun for the players, it was fun for the fans, and it was fun for the broadcasters.

CHAPTER NINETEEN
1990 SETS THE STAGE

How could the largest loss in NCAA Final Four history lead to a National Championship? It did. UNLV embarrassed Duke in the 1990 championship game in Denver, 103-73.

Duke graduated three starters from that team, but the two who returned were Coach's base for two years that will never be forgotten. There's not a Duke fan on the planet who can't tell you where they were and what they were doing when Laettner made the winning basket with two seconds to play in the East Regional final game against Kentucky in 1992. He is on almost every 'greatest collegiate basketball player' list. Christian is one of the most competitive people in everything he did that I have ever met. There have been only four players in NCAA history to play in four straight Final Fours. The other three are Greg Koubek, Clay Buckley and Brian Davis. Christian is the only one to have started in all four.

Bobby Hurley didn't actually look like the 'face' of Duke Basketball. But, just toss it up and see what happened. He played in three Final Fours, won two NCAA championships and was MVP in 1992. He still holds the NCAA assist record with 1,076.

I still say, if I had to go into any kind of fight, and I could pick two people to go with me, it would be those two. They would win.

As with all his teams, Mike had to develop team chemistry. None of Mike's Duke teams have ever been alike. Things like style of play and attitude have always been staples, but every team has to find its identity.

Just like the 1986 season, 1991 began by playing in the Pre- Season NIT. I love spending Thanksgiving in New York City. The Macy's Parade down Broadway kicks off the Christmas season. The Marriott Marquis on Times Square has always hosted the four teams, and fans of the four teams who want to watch the parade can do it either of two ways. They can get to a street-side position in front of the hotel around 6am, or stay in the hotel and watch, in the warmth of a glassed-in balcony, and see the whole thing. There is a continuous brunch and you can go and come at your leisure. Some years we have opted for bundling up with our big coats and everything else that's warm and standing on the street. I always start humming Mel Torme's 'The Christmas Song' about this time."Chestnuts roasting on an open fire, Jack Frost nipping at your nose, Yuletide carols being sung by a fire, and folks dressed up like Eskimos." You can finish up with a visit to Radio City Music Hall and take in their 'Christmas Spectacular.'

Right before Christmas, Duke took a two-game road trip, beginning in Cambridge, Ma. to play Harvard, and then on to Norman, Ok. I got really smart and packed a group of cold weather clothes for Cambridge, and a warm weather group for Oklahoma. Just my luck!! It was in the 70s in Cambridge, so I wore warm weather outfits and planned to get them cleaned in Norman. The plan changed for my benefit when we stepped off the plane in Oklahoma City. It was very cold and snow was blowing so hard I could barely see to drive to Norman!!! Am I lucky or what?? The clothing arrangement was perfect. The Sooners had not lost in 51 games in the Lloyd Noble Center, and the 12,000 fans that came couldn't believe the streak was over that night.

The ACC opener was against the Cavaliers at Virginia and Duke headed back to Durham with an 81-64 loss. I'm glad I wasn't on that bus for that four-hour ride.

According to reports, Coach told the team, as the bus rolled into campus, to go to the locker room and get on practice gear and hit the floor. The practice was a rough one. Coach wasn't worried about the Blue

Devils' skills, he was concerned about their attitude.

Did I say the practice was rough? Grant Hill was on the receiving end of an errant elbow from his own roommate, Tony Lang. He missed two games with a broken nose and had to wear a mask for several games after he came back. Last I heard, Grant still has the mask and told me he thought he looked like some sci-fi monster. This practice may have been the turning point of the season. Five blowout wins later, the Blue Devils made the No. 5 Tar Heels number six.

I think the LSU game in Cameron was one of the best that year. The match up between Christian Laettner and Shaquille O'Neal was awesome. Shaq was the biggest man I had seen since shaking hands with Wilt Chamberlain when he came to Charlotte as a player-coach for the Conquistadors in the ABA.

Shaq had a miserable day. Laettner made shots from all over the court, and O'Neal had a tough time getting the ball. It wasn't just Laettner vs. O'Neal, it was Duke vs. the guys in purple and gold. Duke's perimeter and passing-lane defense was at its best. After the 88-70 pasting, I told George Laettner, "I think your son just added several million dollars to his first pro contract." That draft was still over a year away.

The kids played one of the toughest schedules in the country and saw a lot of it by playing the best teams in the nation. Duke beat Carolina at the Smith Center in Chapel Hill for the second time that season, 83-77, and took the regular season ACC Championship. That's title number one.

Title number two was supposed to be the ACC Tournament in Charlotte, but a funny thing happened on the way to picking up that trophy. Duke lost to UNC in the Championship game, AND, they didn't get a number one seed in the East.

If the players were expecting Mike to be mad in the locker room, they were wrong. His message to them was, "We have gotten the bad game out of our system, and we are going to learn from it and put it behind us." And then he made a very prophetic statement, "We are going to win the national championship in three weeks."

CHAPTER TWENTY
COULD THIS BE THE YEAR?

Duke wouldn't even think about championship rings. There was this little matter of winning six games in the next three weekends. Every team in the field of sixty-four had a 'chance' to win it all. OK, maybe not the four No. 16 seeds. None of them has ever won a first round game, much less anything else. But after the first round, upsets are almost as common as blowout wins.

Let me set the record straight right here about this thing called "March Madness." TV did NOT coin the phrase for the NCAA tournament. It was first used to describe the Atlantic Coast Conference Tournament. Prior to the expansion of the NCAA Tournament field, the only way to get a bid to the NCAA Tournament was to win your conference. Not all leagues had tournaments. Actually, MOST didn't. The ACC Tournament was so successful AND lucrative, that others began to use the ACC as a blue print. An ACC school could go undefeated in the regular season, but they still had to endure those three "maddening days" at the ACC Tournament; those "maddening March" days; the days of "March Madness." That is your history lesson for now .

Duke was sent to the Midwest Region as the No. 2 seed, and the first two games were in the Metrodome in Minneapolis. Louisiana-Monroe and Iowa were sent home. On to Pontiac, Mi. to play in the Silverdome. The Sweet Sixteen game was a rematch against UConn. We had eliminated them from the 1990 Tournament, thanks to Christian's FIRST last second winning basket. This one wasn't close, Duke won 81-67.

The ACC played the Big East again in the Midwest Final, and another 1990 rematch. Lou Carnesecca's St. John's team was coming off an upset win over No. 1 seeded Ohio State. In the 78-61 Duke win, Hurley had twenty points, seven rebounds, four assists, and just one turnover, earning him the Regional MVP award.

The Blue Devils were on their way to a fourth straight Final Four in the Hoosier Dome in Indianapolis. Can you say rematch No. 3? Knock, Knock, Knock. Guess who? It was the "Runnin' Rebels" of UNLV. I'll share a bit of locker room stuff with you. After the win over St. John's, Mike Krzyzewski started his very BEST psychological maneuver ever. He told the players before going the news conference, "Do NOT believe anything you hear me say outside our locker room between now and tip off next Saturday in Indianapolis." After the usual recap of the St. John's game, Mike started singing the praises of UNLV. He wondered out loud if ANYONE could beat them.

The 1991 NCAA Championship had already been awarded to UNLV by the media. They were the top team in the country in the first poll of the season, and held No. 1 all year. They were unbeaten. Jerry Tarkanian had coached his teams to a 45-game win streak, dating back to the '90 season. Only two games had even been close.

I was at almost all of Mike's interviews from that one until we taped our pre-game show for the Vegas game. He did not waiver from his plan. He was so good that I almost started to believe him, but when that thought did get into my head, I remembered his Silverdome talk to the team.

The Final Four had a distinct 'Old North State' flavor. Kansas and North Carolina were on the other side of the bracket. Roy Williams coached Kansas. He hails from the North Carolina mountains and was Dean Smith's assistant for ten years. This was a classic 'student vs. mentor' match-up.

The NCAA and CBS got what they wanted; the 'Invincibles' vs. the 'Little Private Guys,' and Dean vs. Roy. Would there be a fourth meeting of the year between the Blue Devils and Tar Heels? Duke has never played UNC in the NCAA Tournament, and to play our "15-501" enemies for the 'World Championship' of college basketball would have been a huge thing for the ACC. I don't agree with that line of thinking. I have always felt that an NCAA Championship meeting would destroy the greatest rivalry in all of sport. If Duke would win, UNC could never top it, and vice versa. I believe Duke would have beaten Carolina in that Final Four but we didn't get the chance. Kansas sent them back to Chapel Hill.

An Indianapolis Final Four was exciting. The city went all out to put out the welcome mat for everyone. Krzyzewski wanted his team to feel the carnival atmosphere of Indy. He felt that it wouldn't be a distraction. His team was ready. There were mandatory practices, meetings, press conferences, and many other things they had to do, so why not give them some free time?

Jerry Tarkanian looked at it differently. He kept his team on the outskirts of town and kept fans and others away from them. They practiced at a local high school and reportedly had the windows covered to keep anyone from peeking in. All four teams were there with the same purpose, to win a championship. There was just more pressure on the undefeated Rebels to repeat. The Duke team was the opposite. They got to 'experience the Final Four' with certain limits. Mike gave the team some time after the Friday night team meal to be with their families.

Phyllis and I enjoyed Market Square and all of the activities as well. We even ordered a piece of the 'Final Four Floor' before the games started. Pretty fortuitous, eh? We had a great dinner at one of my favorite restaurants, St. Elmo Steak House.

Final Four Friday can be fun. All four teams had a hour for an open practice in the Hoosier Dome, and more than 30,000 fans came to watch a great display. The Tar Heels had the court first, with the Jayhawks second. Both teams kept it close to the vest and basically used it as a shoot-around. The third team on the floor was the 'Invincibles.' The 1990 champions took the court almost arrogantly, as if this practice was an annoyance. It was a business trip for them, and they wanted to play the games, win the trophy again and head home. These Vegas 'cats' were not your typical student-athletes. These were older men. A few of their youngest were older than our oldest players, and they could have held their own against a lot of pro teams.

When it was the Blue Devils' turn, they hit the floor with energy and the Hoosier Dome crowd loved it. Coach brought the Blue Devils out with a dunking drill that had all of the fans in awe. I saw, in that ten-minute period, more variations of dunks than I'd ever seen. The fans loved it and the guys were all smiles.

We often hear the champions from the previous year referred to as the 'defending' champions. That is a misnomer. Their championship is for the previous year, and they are forever the champion of that particular year. There is nothing to defend. Their record for the following year and forever has nothing to do with that title. Boxing has a champion who puts the title on the line and if he is defeated, the challenger becomes the champ.

I always record the pre-game 5-minute segment with Mike an hour and a half before tip-off. Early in his career we taped it the day before a game. Around 1985, I had a station commitment for the entire day and asked when he wanted to tape. He suggested about 45 minutes before tip off. I agreed. After that game he asked if I wanted to tape the show at that time for every game. He said it gave him something to do while the players were warming-up. That has been the routine since.

At halftime of the first Semi-Final, I went to the locker room to tape the show. One of the assistants told me that Mike was showing some tape to Hurley. I was talking with some of the players and noticed that they were really loose. At one point, Thomas Hill hopped up and left the room. The other guys were all laughing. I asked what was up and the players told me to watch the TV monitor. CBS' Leslie Visser was getting ready to do a report 'outside the Kansas locker room.' It wasn't the Kansas door at all; it was a door to a section of the DUKE locker room. As Leslie began her report, the door behind her opened just enough for Thomas' head to appear behind her. He grinned, gave a quick wave, and shut the door. He came running back into our room and the team went nuts.

After taping the show, I started down the hallway toward the floor. Just at that moment, the big roll-up door opened, and off the bus came the UNLV team. As they passed by me, they looked like they were going to a funeral.

When I got back to the press table where we were setup to broadcast, I told Phyllis, "We're going to win this game."

BOB & STATISTICIAN PHYLLIS AT COURTSIDE IN INDY

"What on earth makes you think that?" was her question.

"Just a gut feeling, I just saw the most unbelievable contrast in moods ever," I told her.

That first Semi-Final game was a bit of a surprise as Roy Williams sent his Jayhawks straight at the Tar Heels, and won. Coach Smith was ejected from the game (the only one of his career) in the final minutes after being 'teed-up' a second time.

Kansas was going to play for the Championship on Monday night. Most everyone expected them play Vegas, except the group in the Duke locker room. The Blue Devils executed Mike's game plan to near-perfection; keep it close enough to win at the end. UNLV had not felt game pressure in so long they didn't know how to handle it. Duke had.

No one in the Duke locker room had any doubts about winning this game. Coach K reminded the team at their Friday night dinner that "there will come a time in the game tomorrow that UNLV will look in your eyes and what they see will be what will determine who will win the game."

It was tip-off time and, as usual, a lot of the media were not on press row. They, of course had gone to the media room to hear the post game remarks from the coaches and their players. They also wanted to find out just why Dean had been ejected. We also found out later that UNC assistant coach Bill Guthridge went after Peter Pavia, the referee who called the second technical on Coach Smith and sent him to the locker room. This all took place in the corridor outside the locker rooms and Guthridge had to be restrained.

Back to the game. The opening tip-off was headed towards a UNLV player when Grant Hill grabbed it and put in an easy lay-up. This game had one of the more memorable finishes of my career. With just over two minutes left, Duke was behind by five. Bobby hit a three-pointer to cut the lead to 76-74. It wasn't just a three-point basket, it set up Duke's win. Afterward, Coach said it was the biggest play of the game. Brian Davis drove the baseline and was fouled. Basket good, one free throw coming. Brian's free throw put Duke up by one. The Blue Devils turned the ball over, UNLV tied the game 77-all.

With fifteen seconds left. Thomas Hill took a shot that bounced off the rim to Laettner. He was fouled on his put-back attempt. Coach K called a time out. In the huddle, he looked at Christian. Before Mike could say anything, Laettner smiled and said, "I got 'em coach." He made two, and Duke led by two. With less than ten seconds left UNLV tried to inbound the ball but couldn't. They used their last time out. Coach told the players, "when the buzzer sounds there will be NO celebrating on the floor. We still have 40 minutes to play."

A desperation shot bounced off the rim right to Bobby. As he grabbed the ball, the horn sounded and the Blue Devils took the best punch that one of the greatest teams that has ever played the game could muster, and beat the UNLV Runnin' Rebels 79-77.

BOB @ FINAL FOUR

My call at the buzzer went like this. "The Blue Devils have just pulled off the biggest upset in Duke history with a 79 to 77 victory over the 'Runnin' Rebels of UNLV. They'll play for the NCAA Championship on Monday night here in Indianapolis." Several players almost forgot Coach's directive about celebrating, but Hurley put the game ball under his arm and escorted his teammates off the floor. Bobby told me later:

A big part of me was super excited and happy, but the other part of me knew that if we didn't get the job done on Monday night that none of it was going to matter that much or be that important. It was all about winning that national title, and that's what we set out to do.

As Coach K was being interviewed by CBS, he said, "We still have one more game to play. The theme for the trip to Indianapolis was 'eighty minutes,' not just the forty we just played." The other forty minutes would be against Kansas.

When we got back to the hotel after all the media requirements, it was total chaos. Everybody wanted to shake hands with, or hug, every player on the roster. Coach K told the kids to go and spend some time with their families. He immediately assembled his staff to start on the game plan for Monday night. Was Duke a better team than Kansas? Maybe, but Mike knew that Kansas could beat Duke, and that DUKE could beat Duke. It was now a mental thing.

Duke and Kansas had one day to prepare for the title game. Mike Krzyzewski has proven to be one of the greatest at preparing his teams to play on very short notice. A lot of times the Semi-Final games in any tournament may really pit the best two teams. With such a short turn-around time, the team that has to win a hard fought, emotional game can be at a disadvantage. An emotional Semi-Final win can just as easily cost a team the championship, if they are not mentally prepared. A great example was the 1986 Final Four. Duke was definitely the best team in the country with Kansas second. Those two beat the heck out of each other in the Semi-Finals and Louisville won the title on Monday night.

Coach got the team together when they got on the Hoosier Dome floor for the closed practice that Sunday afternoon. He told them "We're National Champions as long as you keep your focus."

Another concern now was not emotional, but physical. Laettner and Hurley had played the entire UNLV game. There was no doubt they were spent. Had the 48 hours been enough to rejuvenate them? The answer came very early in the championship game.

Game time! Duke got the opening tip and Greg Koubek popped in a three-pointer and followed it up with a two. After a Kansas free throw,

Hurley lofted a pass to the baseline that looked like it might end up ten rows back in the seats. 'Superman' Grant Hill leaped a tall building in a single bound, locked his right hand around the ball and jammed it for a 7-1 Duke lead. It was a lead that the Blue Devils would never relinquish. The outcome was probably sealed right before the half. Down 39-34, Kansas tried to hold the ball for the last shot but Bobby stole the ball and flipped it to Thomas Hill who jacked up a three. Up eight at half time? It was an omen. After 11+ minutes of the second half Duke led by14. KU forced a couple of turnovers and cut their deficit to 70-65 with a half-minute left.

In their sixth Final Four under Coach K, Duke won their first NCAA basketball championship, 72-65. 'How Sweet It Is!!!!'

What did I do? As long as CBS was on the air, I couldn't go on the floor for interviews. I did the next best thing. I wormed my way behind the Duke bench with my wireless microphone and headed straight for Max Crowder. He had been with Duke at every Final Four.

"Max, you're finally going to get that Championship ring," I said. Max was all choked up. I had never seen him like that. The Duke players all huddled around us chanting, "King Kong! King Kong! King Kong!"

What was that all about? I didn't ask, but found out the next Sunday night on Coach's last call-in radio show. He explained that since Duke had not won in their eight previous Final Fours, it had to be Max's fault. Mike said, "If I had a monkey on my back, then Max had a gorilla." Max wasn't in Minneapolis for the 1992 Final Four. He passed away in the summer of 1992.

The Blue Devils of Duke University finally had their NCAA Championship. The team hotel was a mob scene with friends, family, former players, and fans on hand to celebrate with the team. Mike was beaming like a brand new father. He would finally get to enjoy the moment. We all did.

CHAPTER TWENTY-ONE

IS TWO-IN-A-ROW TOO MUCH TO ASK?

With a national championship comes some 'side effects.' Fans came out of the woodwork. Everyone wanted in on the elation. People were calling the basketball office for signed memorabilia, and asking for the coaches and players to speak here and appear there. The flood was overwhelming. It was a great feeling, but it was almost more than the program could stand. Coach told me a year later that the players were signing five to six times more memorabilia than before, but they had to turn down ten times as many things as before. It was unbelievable.

The Blue Devils were no longer the 'hunter.' Now they would be the 'hunted.' Duke now had a huge bulls-eye on their collective backs.

The first thing Coach K told his team at the first team meeting for the 1992 season was, "We are NOT defending a national title. We are PURSUING a national title. I don't want to hear anyone use the word defend."

The 1992 Duke Blue Devils were ranked number one in all the preseason magazines. No team won back-to-back national titles since UCLA in 1973.

By the way, the NCAA Tournament was not a 64-team field until 1980. It was an eight-team tournament from 1939 until 1950. In 1951 it was doubled to 16. There were 22 teams in 1953, and from '54 until '74 the numbers varied from 23 to 25. In 1975 it was expanded to 32. Forty teams participated in 1979. Those champion UCLA teams never had to play beyond the Rocky Mountains until the Final Four, and two wins put them there. This is not to take away from what Coach Wooden did. He competed according to NCAA pairings procedures during those times. I think it is a lot harder to win the NCAA title now than then.

The season began on Saturday afternoon at 4pm with a nationally televised exhibition against the Soviet National Team at Cameron. I remember all of this because the Duke football team played at noon in Chapel Hill. Football games last about three hours. We had a shortened post-game and I had a Highway Patrolman escort me to Cameron. The pre-game show hit the air as soon as the football post-game was over, and I was RUNNING up the steps to the Crows Nest as Dr. Art Chandler was introducing the starting lineups. We won by 20.

Harvard visited Durham on November 30th. This was our top scoring game of the season with 118 points. I didn't broadcast that game, I was 7,660 miles west of Cameron Indoor Stadium in the Tokyo Dome in Japan. The Duke football team played Clemson in the Coca-Cola Japan Bowl game on Sunday afternoon, and the time slots matched wonderfully. We took the air from Japan at the end of the Saturday night game in Durham thanks to a 14-hour time difference. The Tigers beat the Blue Devils, 33-21.

WES CHESSON, TROY WILLIAMSON & BOB
TOKYO DOME 11/91

Krzyzewski scheduled a game with Canisius in Buffalo, New York as a homecoming game for Laettner. Christian played at the Nichols School there. This was the last basketball trip that trainer Max Crowder made.

He entered Duke Medical Center the next week for tests that showed the presence of Mesothelioma.

A game at Mathews Arena on the campus of Boston University saw the Blue Devils get a 10-point win, and two radio guys sweat our buns off IN MID-JANUARY. Tony Haynes was especially hot because of setting up all the equipment.

> *Mathews Arena was a hockey arena, and they had this device that sent all the heat up to the ceiling when they were converting from hockey to basketball. The Terriers had played hockey there on Friday night and the basketball game was at 1:00 Saturday afternoon. The temperature up in the booth made Cameron seem like a refrigerator. Setting up the equipment was so difficult and I was sweating like crazy. You and I eventually went to the souvenir stand and bought two t-shirts, and we did the game wearing them, not shirt and tie.*

On February 8th, the Blue Devils played the Tigers of LSU in the Maravich Assembly Center in Baton Rouge. It wasn't just a rematch of the Tigers and Blue Devils, but another battle of the titans, Shaquille O'Neal and Laettner.

As intimidating as Shaq was, and is, I had an even scarier meeting prior to the game. As per usual, I was headed to the Duke locker room 90 minutes prior to tip-off to tape Coach's pre-game show. Just as I started into the tunnel, the security guards stopped everyone because the LSU team was coming onto the floor. I backed up against the wall (I thought) to let them go by. I moved as far back as I could when I saw O'Neal. About that time, I thought the wall was 'breathing.' Something was. I turned around, and there to my horror, about 12 inches from my face, was the face of Tigers' mascot, Mike V (No. 5). Mike the Tiger was a Bengal tiger that weighed about 500 pounds, and his presence that close to me may have been the initial cause of my later heart problems! You've heard the old adage, 'caught between a rock and a hard place?' Well, that's child's play compared to being caught between Shaq and Mike the Tiger. Thankfully, Shaq could leave that area, and as soon as he did, so did I. I'm just glad Mike didn't let out one of his famous roars while I was face-to- face with him. I would be writing this book posthumously!

Grant Hill replaced Bobby at the point and scored 16 points. Hurley had broken his foot. Laettner had another great game, scoring 12 points in the second half. Duke beat LSU for the second straight year, 77-67.

Duke held the No.1 spot in the polls all season long, despite two losses. The reason for this was that the other four teams in the top 5 lost during the week as well.

On February 26th, the Devils secured first place in the ACC regular season race with a win over Virginia, and it was the night that Duke retired Christian Laettner's jersey No.32.

Two days later we headed to the west coast to play the No. 4 UCLA Bruins in Pauley Pavilion. We arrived in Los Angeles on Saturday and went to Pauley to practice. We had to park the bus about a block from the venerable arena and walk. The UCLA students were lying in wait. They formed a human gauntlet, four and five deep in places. They were heckling and cursing every player and coach by name. I was walking between Laettner and Davis, and they were smiling and waving to the students, but under their breaths it was a different story. I was laughing too. The next day Duke left L.A. with a 75-65 victory.

Seniors Christian Laettner, Brian Davis and Ron Burt wore their Duke jersey for a final time in Cameron Indoor Stadium against North Carolina. Saying goodbye to these three seniors made it all the more special. Duke finished the game with an 18-6 run and beat UNC 89-77.

CHAPTER TWENTY-TWO

THE GREATEST GAME EVER!!

The ACC Tournament was played in the Charlotte Coliseum in 1992. Duke beat Maryland, Georgia Tech and Carolina, by 20, to take the title. Laettner earned the Tournament's Everett Case Award as the most outstanding player. He had 25 points in the title game. Duke cut down the nets and looked toward the NCAAs.

It had been ten years since a team went wire-to-wire in the number one position. The last two were Indiana in 1976, and UNC in 1982.

Duke earned the overall No. 1 seed and went to the East Region. The best thing about the East Regional was that Greensboro hosted the first two rounds. Duke would get a chance to play, basically, a 'home game.' Up first was Campbell University, a small Baptist college located in Buies Creek, NC. The media immediately made it a David versus Goliath match-up. At the open practice session the night before the first games, we were expecting a big crowd but nothing like the more than 5,000 that showed up. I got a pleasant surprise in the media area. I started to introduce myself to Campbell coach Billy Lee to get a pre-game interview for the next night. He looked straight at me and said, "Bob, I know who you are. I've been listening to you for a long time." Billy was a lot of fun to interview with his great sense of humor.

Campbell played with a lot of heart. But, so did the Blue Devils. They played with as much heart as their opponents from 'the Creek,' as Lee always referred his school. Duke won, 82-56. Two days later the Devils played Iowa, and just like the game in the '91 Regionals, Duke won.

The Spectrum in Philadelphia was the next stop. Duke played Seton Hall, and there was an added 'family' aspect in this game. Bobby Hurley and his younger brother, Danny, would be on the same floor for the first time since they were teammates at St. Anthony's High School. Bobby had a difficult game.

> *It was a real conflict for me. I liked to try and attack my opponent, and being that he was my brother and my best friend, it was difficult to be in an attack mode against him. I was really happy when that game ended. A lot of the other guys on the team performed well. I didn't really play any good in that game. It was difficult emotionally playing it. Maybe I played worse games in my career, but I couldn't compete like I normally did against Danny. It was just something, you know, growing up with him, to want to beat him.*

Bobby was two of seven from the field for four points and had seven assists. Danny was zero for four, and only played 18 minutes. The final score was 81-69 and Duke was going to play Kentucky for the right to go to the Final Four in what many experts still consider the greatest college basketball game ever.

The game brought together two of the best basketball programs in the country, and two of the nations top coaches, Mike Krzyzewski and Rick Pitino, would go head-to-head. Kentucky was still reeling from a major recruiting scandal.

Duke had played Kentucky in other NCAAs. The Blue Devils lost to the 'Cats in St. Louis in 1978, and in the 1966 national semis. In the 1980 Midwest Regional, the Devils won by a point IN RUPP ARENA. When I play in the Children's Charities of the Bluegrass celebrity golf tournament each June in Lexington, KY, I still remind Kyle Macy about that game. None of that mattered. It was March 28th in Philadelphia, and THESE two teams had never met

Four seniors, Sean Woods, Richie Farmer, Deron Feldhouse, and John

Pelphrey, were to be commended for staying at UK despite the NCAA probation. Freshman Jamal Mashburn gave them a potent lineup.

Kentucky came after Duke like an offensive buzz saw. They jumped out a 20-12 lead, but the Devils came right back with offense of their own and took a 27-22 lead. For the rest of the first half, the lead seesawed back-and-forth with Duke taking a 50-45 lead to the locker room at half time.

Tom Clark was one of the three NCAA officials working the game. He worked a total of 26 years in the Big-10 and other midwestern conferences, but this was his first regional final.

I realized the importance of this game. I was already sweating when we walked out on the floor, and I have NEVER been known as one who sweats. I knew I was in something special from the 'git-go.' A close game like this one always kept me more focused. I would rather work a close game than a blowout. This one was close. I believe there were about nine lead changes in the last four minutes of regulation. Every possession meant something, and you certainly didn't want to be the one to call something that would make a difference, that potentially might not have been the right call.

The second half started just like the first as Kentucky took it to Duke. The intensity level was ratcheted up a few notches because of an incident midway through the half that fans and sportswriters STILL discuss.

Laettner went up for a shot. UK freshman, Aminu Timberlake fouled him. Laettner came down off balance and stepped lightly on Timberlake's chest. One of the officials hit him with an intentional technical foul. The Kentucky fans were outraged and wanted him tossed out of the game as well. Clark explains the situation from the officials' perspective.

I live in the midst of Kentucky fans here in Cincinnati, and I get the question all the time when I'm making talks to school kids and civic clubs. I was not even involved in that call. I didn't even know what transpired until after the game. But, from what I have seen, and I've watched the film hundreds of times, I definitely believe that they (Tim Higgins and Charlie Range) made the correct call. I tell the Kentucky fans, and any others who mention it, that he did NOT stomp on Timberlake. He simply placed his foot on Timberlake's chest. It wasn't anything that was blatant nor was he trying to hurt him. Timberlake actually looks up at Christian and smiles, kinda laughs at him, and points his finger at him. If Timberlake had gotten up and pushed Christian or started a fight, we would have ejected them both. He didn't do anything except lay on the floor and point his finger at Laettner and laugh at him. Was it a flagrant technical foul? I definitely do not believe that. Was it an intentional technical foul, which they gave? It definitely was.

The foul was Christian's fourth and Coach pulled him off the floor and chastised him for doing something stupid. Duke had the game under control and he lost his focus. The Wildcats went on a 9-0 run and took the lead on a three pointer. Duke seized the lead 93-91, and UK hit a lay up with 33 seconds left to tie it at 93-all. Duke had the ball, and with it, the last shot. Bobby Hurley dribbled down court, and just missed a runner as regulation ended. The game went to overtime, 93-93. Krzyzewski summed up the entire game by telling me....

The best thing about this game was that a lot of great players made great plays. I'll always marvel at how many great plays that so many kids made. That's what made it such a special game. It is the best game I've ever been involved in.

With Jamal Mashburn sitting on the UK bench after his fifth foul, the Wildcats again took the lead, but Duke came back to tie. Did Mashburn's absence draw the Wildcats closer? Tom Clark was right there.

No, they were already so focused on the game, as were Duke AND the officials. I don't think that they could have put more effort than they did for the entire game. Obviously Mashburn was the one they leaned on, but I don't think they could have played any harder or better than they did at that time. Both Duke and Kentucky were the epitome of teamwork, hustle, intensity, focus and attention; it couldn't have been any better.

Duke was leading 102-101 with 7.2 seconds left. Pitino called a time out to set a play. Sean Woods took the inbounds pass, drove down the lane and banked a shot off the glass over Laettner's out-stretched arms. It was so high, I thought he had thrown it over the backboard. Kentucky wins?? Nope, 2.1 seconds are still on the clock. Not every one saw that shot. Duke's Thomas Hill was one of them.

In real time I didn't see the shot. I was so focused on my guy who was kinda spaced out (not THAT kind of spaced out, creating space for a shooter!!); trying to make sure he didn't get a shot. By the reaction of the crowd, I knew something positive had happened for Kentucky. The next thing I did was look at the scoreboard and I saw that they were up. When he hit it, I just thought, 'Let's get to the huddle and draw something up and execute it."

Referee Clark saw the shot AND what happened immediately.

I was center official, and I think most everyone was stunned when he TOOK that shot, much less, that it went in. The thing that was amazing to me was, and I was ready for it, when that ball cleared that basket, four of the five Duke players immediately signaled timeout. That's why they were winners. Instead of saying, 'Oh my gosh, we've lost,' or 'I can't believe this,' they had the presence of mind and the preparation to get the clock stopped immediately. I don't think the ball was two centimeters out of that net before four of those five had their hands up to get the time out right now. I was ready for it and blew my whistle to stop the clock at that moment. It didn't stop automatically in 1992 like it does today.

Just as Clark was prepared for this scenario, so were Krzyzewski's players....

That wasn't by accident. Back then, the clock didn't stop on a made basket like it does today. They had to act quickly and they did. They were very aware if the situation, and knew they had time do something if they got the clock stopped. We work on those things all the time. You've seen us work on every imaginable end-of-half and end-of-game situation over and over in our practices. You don't want to leave any situation to chance.

As soon as the team got to the Duke bench, Mike looked at them and said, "We are going to win." He wasn't just trying to bolster their confidence, he knew that he had to instill the mindset of winning.

When they sat down in front of me, I again looked at every one of them and I repeated it. 'We're going to win.' At first I was the only one who believed it, but as we talked, I could see in their eyes and on their faces that they were beginning to believe it too.

I then said, 'Here's what we're going to do.' I began diagramming the play I wanted to run. I looked at Grant and asked him, 'Can you throw the ball 75 feet?' And he said, 'Yes.' I wanted to get a positive response from him. I then told him that he would make the in-bounds pass. 'If they put someone in front of you, just step back to throw it.' Hill was 6'8" and could see over most of them. The other four on the floor, Christian, Bobby, Thomas and Tony all knew what they had to do and they did it.

They had worked all year to be in this very position. From Bobby Hurley's perspective, it went like this:

Coach kinda felt that everyone was shocked, and it WAS a really difficult shot that Woods made. He just wanted to bring us back to the moment, and let us know that we could get this done. Luckily, Grant believed and Christian, obviously, believed and it worked out. I had my doubts until after the shot, but those guys got it done on that play.

Thomas Hill had no doubts the play would work.

No doubts whatsoever. Seriously, those are game situations that we practiced every day. For me, at that point, I had done it for three years. At no point was I nervous or unsure or had any doubt that we'd at least have a good play drawn up.

Laettner chimes in with his recollections of the moment.

He looked at us and said, 'We can win this game.' And then he started to infuse some positive thinking into our heads. That's what he's good at. He's very well schooled at thinking positively and moving on to the next play. Immediately he started to put positive thoughts in our heads. After that he drew up the play and he said, Grant, can you make the pass?' Grant said 'yes.' Right away, he has us all thinking positively like 'do this little thing. Do that little thing, and maybe a big thing can happen. Maybe a really great thing can happen if we do these small things first.'

'Grant, can you make the pass?' 'Yes.'

'Christian can you make the catch?' 'Yes.'

Then he said, 'Let's go out there and run our play that we had practiced.' We tried it in the Wake Forest game a month before but didn't do the little things right.

I still think that's one of the biggest, most important things he did for that stretch from when Woods hit his shot until I made mine.

When Duke called the time out, we took a commercial break on the radio. I leaned back in my chair, locked my fingers together behind my head and looked up at the scoreboard. I said to myself, "If we don't get a shot, or we miss it, it will be 103-102. The Final Four string will be broken and Kentucky is going. Maybe it's not our year. If we make it, it's 104-103. 104-103, 104-103." I made sure that I had the final scores in my mind. In the huge upset win over UNLV in '91, I had fluffed the score. Maybe no one listening noticed, but I did and I didn't want that to happen this time. I never even considered a three-pointer.

While the teams and radio announcers planned strategies for the final two seconds, the officiating crew was gearing up for WHATEVER was to happen.

We were having trouble hearing the horn for most of the second half. Even at the 12-minute timeout Tim Higgins came over to me and said, 'Tom, with this noise, if this goes down to a last second shot, we're gonna be in trouble because we can't hear the horn.' He laughed about it. We couldn't even hear the warning horn at that point. What would it be like if that did happen now? Tim just said, 'Let's just make sure if it's good or not.'

Now it was time to put it into practice.

The buzzer sounds. The time out is over.

Krzyzewski set up a play they had worked on in practice all season, and had even tried once during the regular season.

It was a variation of that end-of-game play. At Wake Forest, Grant threw a wicked curve ball to Christian, and he had trouble with it and stepped out of bounds. I asked him later if he had ever pitched in a baseball game. With that kind of curve ball, he would be vicious. A right-handed batter couldn't touch it, and a lefthander would get hit with it if he didn't get out of the way.

It was 'do-or-die' and Grant Hill and Christian Laettner had to make it work. Hill would inbound the ball with a three-quarter-court pass to Laettner. He was to roll up from the far left corner and end up just inside the top of the key and get the pass.

If Kentucky prevented this, Grant's second option was Bobby Hurley at mid-court.

I was coming across near half-court, and just thank God that the first option worked out and we didn't need the second option. I don't think I ever made a game winning shot in my career, so I don't know if I wanted the ball in my hands in that spot.

Where was T. Hill, and what was he to do?

I was running the opposite wing, and the play was designed that, if Christian couldn't get a shot off look for Bob or me running the sideline for a wing jump shot or whatever we could get off. If you notice in the video, it looks like I was standing out of bounds, but I was just watching the shot as it was going through the net at that point.

Pitino didn't put a defender in front Grant and his pass to Christian was right on the money. Coach K had prepared them for this possibility....

That didn't surprise me all that much. Rick had done so much with that program following the probation and the defections. I knew he had a plan for whatever we did. We figured that they'd do that and double Christian. After all, he WAS 19 for 19 up to that point. He had made all ten free throws and all nine from the floor. They probably knew we would try to get the ball to him.

Even with the double-team, you never want to foul the shooter in that situation. You don't want to put a guy who hasn't missed from the line all night back on the line with the game hanging in the balance.

Grant was taken aback momentarily, but it turned out to be a huge positive...

Initially, when I came out of the timeout huddle, the first thing that came to mind was that no one was on the ball. I'm thinking, 'It's almost a confidence booster.' Certainly, Bob, you remember, previously when we played Wake Forest earlier in the year and we had the same situation, and they put somebody on the ball, I kinda made a bad pass, and I had that in the back of my head as I came out of the huddle. But, as I got to the line, I saw that they were going to put everybody down the floor, I felt like, 'Wow, I can really do this. I can just loft it up there to Laettner and let him do what he does.' I had some confidence, maybe there's a chance.

I certainly saw the line of the shot, so it looked good, but the way he had been playing, I knew when he caught it, he was going to make a play. I'm thinking, 'Just get it to him.' He had two men on him, but I still was going to go to him, and they kinda didn't guard him. They at least let him catch it. And then when he took a dribble, I'm thinking, "No. No. No, don't dribble." But he had the presence of mind to know that in two seconds you can have time to make a little shimmy, a dribble, and get the shot up. But I could see it, and I could see the angle, and it looked good from the time it left his hands.

Here it is from Christian's perspective.

I set up in the corner nearest our bench. I wasn't worried about Grant's pass at all. It didn't even enter into my mind. I knew he was going to throw a good pass. In the Wake game, he didn't throw a good pass and he felt bad about that. We practiced it quite a bit all season long. There was a lot of room for him to back up if needed. What I was worrying about the whole time, I was saying to myself, 'Man, I've really got to get the ball in my hands, I've gotta catch the ball.' In that situation, a lot of times, the play never even develops, because the pass doesn't get in the offensive player's hands. I told myself to 'go up big and strong and once you get the ball, you have two seconds and you don't have to rush it and settle for a blind, spinning bad shot.'

I knew I had time to make a fake or to take a dribble and set myself up to make a move. If you're doing something that is a little more rushed or just a fling up there it's not really a move. I faked one way, and went the other way. Grant threw a tremendous pass and I was lucky enough to get the ball in my hands. The Kentucky players froze just a bit, because the one thing you don't want to do is to foul in that situation.

Once I got the ball, they didn't play enough defense and they let me get a good look and I was very schooled at those types of shots, or hitting shots with the buzzer going off, not because of all the game situations, but because of all the practice time. When I was at Duke with (Coach Pete) Gaudet, we would work for twenty extra minutes after practice. When we were getting to the end of the sessions, after I had made so many of those shots, he would say, 'OK, last shot.' He would make me run to half-court and then run back to the shooting area, and he'd say, OK, five, four, three, two, one.' We must have practiced that a hundred times. I didn't do the Kentucky move a hundred times, but I was used to shooting under pressure when I was tired, trying to create pressure in practice.

I went up and got a good look at the basket, and I made the shot, and after that, as you know Bob, it was just pandemonium.

Let's get a sixth view of 'The Shot' from Tom Clark.

Tim Higgins had the throw-in responsibility and Charlie Range had the baseline. I had the mid-court, which meant an additional responsibility, the clock. I knew I had to be able to see the clock as well as the shot, if there was one. I also had to make sure the player that got the pass didn't travel or get fouled. I really thought Kentucky wouldn't allow Duke to throw the ball long, and that Hurley was going to take a shot from the mid-court area. I tried to get in position to get a perfect line with the potential shooter and the clock on top of the backboard. I was really concerned with that, and the fact that I wasn't going to call a foul unless they 'have to put him in the Naval hospital.' I'm not calling a 'ticky-tack' foul.

When I saw Hill throw it deep, I looked around and saw no one that close to Laettner. If you look at that famous picture (the one taken by Chuck Liddy), I'm as close to Christian as any of the Kentucky players are. I had always been taught, in this situation, to think, 'release, clock,' meaning see the release of the shot and the time on the clock simultaneously. There was two-tenths of a second on that clock when the ball left Laettner's hand. I was so happy that he got it off before the 0:00 showed; that he didn't travel; that no one fouled him. I was kinda stunned when I saw it go in.

I looked over to the scorer's table where Bob Dibler, the standby official, was holding his hands out as if to say, 'Did it count or not?' I had NO doubt about it. The shot was good.

"They throw it the length of the floor, Laettner catches, comes down, dribbles, shoots, scoooooooooooooooooores. Christian Laettner has hit the bucket at the buzzer; the Blue Devils win it 104 to 103. Look out Minneapolis, here come the Blue Devils."

This IS a "HOW SWEET IT IS!!" moment.

How about a seventh view of 'THE SHOT' from Mike Krzyzewski's vantage point, or lack thereof....

I knew when I saw Christian catch the ball and make that move to turn and shoot it that it was going in. I never saw the shot go in. All of our guys were standing as he shot it, and began jumping around and screaming, so I knew it went in and we had won. What I DID see was Richie Farmer just fall to the floor right in front of our bench. I saw both ends of the emotional spectrum right there. Our team was so happy, and Kentucky's players were crushed. They had played the game of their lives, and still lost.

From the Duke perspective it was a glorious moment. Christian was running down the court with his arms up over his head. Thomas Hill had his hands on his head, crying, "Oh, my God, oh my God."

It's funny because, for four years of scoring and all that other stuff, that's what I am recognized for. But I'll take whatever I can get, I guess. It's such a good thing to be a part of Duke basketball history. To have been a part of this game is very special. The older I get the more I appreciate that experience and really understand what that game was for us, what it meant for our Duke program.

All the others ended up in a pile on the floor. One thing the TV cameras failed to show was Coach K's reactions. Richie Farmer was getting up from the floor right in front of the Duke bench. Mike stopped Richie and put is arms around him. This was a fine young man who had just played his final college game. With all of the pandemonium surrounding them, Mike was the epitome of a true sportsman.

After shaking hands with Pitino and the others, Coach walked over to the Kentucky Radio Network location. He congratulated Cawood Ledford, the 'Voice of the Wildcats,' who was finishing up his final career broadcast. He asked if would be possible to say a few words.

After seeing Richie Farmer just collapse to the floor in front of our bench, I realized the magnitude of this loss for them; even with everything that group had done for Kentucky basketball. I went across the court to the Kentucky radio location and asked if I might go on with them for just a minute. Cawood Ledford was such a legendary broadcaster, and I had so much respect for him. I knew a lot of their fans would be listening to his broadcast.

As Cawood handed the headset microphone to him, Mike talked to the Wildcats fans....

I just told the fans how much empathy we had for them. I told them how honored I was just to be a part of such a great game, played at such a high level. This is one of the greatest games I have ever been a part of. It was a great game that you hate to see end, and one that, really, you hate to see either team lose. You should be very proud of your team. Give them the welcome home they deserve. They've represented you in the best possible way.

Ledford, summed up Mike's gesture wonderfully, "His action just reeked of class. It was what college basketball should be all about." A banner honoring Cawood hangs in the Rupp Arena rafters with all of the retired UK jerseys. It says 'Cawood Ledford' and has a microphone on it. He was inducted into the Naismith Memorial Basketball Hall of Fame in 1994, and is among the finest play-by-play commentators in the history of sports. He was my friend.

When we finished our post-game, I did something I had never done before, and never since. I went into an opponent's locker room. I sought out Richie, Sean, John and Deron and told each one of them how proud I was that they had stayed for four years and helped the Kentucky program to 'rise from the ashes.' All they could do was just nod or, with a choking throat, whisper, "Thank you."

CHAPTER TWENTY- THREE

TWO-IN-A-ROW IS NOT TOO MUCH TO ASK

Five straight years in the Final Four. That was amazing in that era.Duke was off to Minneapolis to play in the Metrodome again. The Semi-Final opponent was Indiana. The media always hunts for story lines, and they had another goodie; Bobby Knight versus Mike Krzyzewski. Mentor versus protégé.

Give Mike a week to prepare between games and he is 'money in the bank.' Some surmised though, that the Blue Devils, read that Laettner, would be spent after the Kentucky game. W-R-O-N-G!

After a slow start, Bobby Hurley led Duke on a run that cut the deficit to 42-37 at halftime. The second half was just the opposite of the first. The Blue Devils blew the Hoosiers' doors off, outscoring them 28-5 through the first ten minutes. Indiana's first field goal didn't go down until over six minutes had been played. Even though Indiana cut the Duke lead to 78-75, Duke hung on to advance to the title game, 80-78.

The post-game was a real downer for Mike as he walked to half court to shake hands with his mentor. Knight gave him a quick 'dead fish' handshake and walked right over to Col. Tom Rogers and hugged him. Col. Rogers had been Knight's assistant at West Point. Talk about a slap in the face! Coach K took the high road in the media room. He praised his ex-coach and the Hoosiers for a great game. He also credited Bobby Hurley for turning the game around in the final minutes of the first half.

The Blue Devils were now forty minutes from being the first back-to-back NCAA champions in nearly two decades, but Michigan's Fab Five stood in the way. They were downright cocky. They were also downright talented. They had been listening to all of the media hype about how they were 'destined to win four NCAA titles in their careers.' The Wolverines started taunting Duke players during pregame warm-ups with things like, "It's payback time," (referring to their overtime loss to the Blue Devils that December) and other unprintable comments. The Blue Devils just ignored them.

The game started a bit sluggishly for the Devils. Could it be that the emotional ride they had been on for two weeks had caught up with them? Christian had one of his worst halves of his career. He turned the ball over seven times and scored just five points. Coach K sat him down three times. Duke wasn't the 'Lone Ranger' in this malady. Each team managed only two points in the last three minutes of the first half. As Duke left the court and climbed up the stairs to the dressing room the scoreboard read: Michigan 31- Duke 30.

The Metrodome was built for football and baseball, not basketball. The court was, thankfully, placed near one end zone and aluminum bleacher seats were installed on the opposite side. Most all of the seats had a good line of sight. The teams left the court and had to go a little way before ascending a long flight of stairs that led to the pro teams' locker rooms.

Being the number one seed has its perks. Duke dressed in the Minnesota Twins' locker room. The players all had nice-sized lockers, and the coaches picked lockers away from the players. Guess what the name was on Coach K's locker. None other than Kirby Puckett. Coach had used the same locker the year before in the Regionals.

A side story to this.... In July of 1992, Calvin Hill, Grant's father, got tickets for Phyllis and I to take the family to Baltimore for a weekend series between the Orioles and the, you guessed it, Minnesota Twins. I had a media field pass to interview several players prior to the game. I went to the Orioles dugout first and interviewed Cal Ripken. When I got to the Twins dugout, I got comments from Carl Willis, a pitcher from Yanceyville, NC, and Puckett. After we did his interview, we talked a bit about Duke and my job. He said, "I need to ask you about something that I heard. Did Coach K REALLY use my locker?" "Absolutely, both years," I replied. His reaction was astounding. "I can't believe that Coach K used my locker. Wait till I tell the guys."

I asked him if he would possibly autograph a baseball for Coach. "You gotta be kiddin' me. Would he really want one?" I assured him that he would, and not only did Kirby sign a ball for Coach, he signed one for me too. What a bonus!!!

A photographer was sitting on the dugout steps and snapped a couple of pictures of Puckett, and I heard him mutter, "If I did that, they'd yank my credential." I didn't have a clue what he was talking about until I got back to our seats in the stands. I was reading the back of the pass and noticed the line, 'Media shall not ask any player(s) for autographs. Failure to comply will result in revocation of the pass and expulsion from the stadium.' Oops!!! I watched the games and Coach K and I have our Kirby Puckett autographed baseballs. End of story.

In the locker room, Mike blistered them. He didn't give them the old 'I know you're tired' speech. He called them out, one by one, and told each just how poorly he was playing, and it certainly didn't appear that were playing for the national title. That was it. Door slammed, he was gone. This wasn't an out-of-control Mike. He knew exactly what he was doing. As I have said many times, Mike is a master motivator. This time, he was leaving it up to the team. They responded. Hurley took the floor and continued to call them out individually.

> *I just think Christian was worn down. He had been through a lot the weekend before, going through a game like the Kentucky game, and producing like he did. He just wasn't all the way there, and Thomas (Hill) and I kinda got after him and, I think, motivated him to reach a little deeper and he came out in the second half and had a good half against Michigan.*

Laettner, Davis, and Ron Burt were getting ready for the last half of college basketball they would ever play. Those three and Christian Ast wouldn't wear a Duke jersey again.

With just under seven minutes left in the game, Coach called a time out. They needed that two-minute rest for two reasons, to recoup, and to let Coach set up the play that turned the game.

Again, Grant Hill was to throw the ball into Christian. New wrinkle, he was to throw it back to Grant, then another quick pass back to Laettner for the three-point shot. Have I lost you yet? OK, that was the plan. The first two passes worked, but when Hill sent it back to Laettner, he fumbled the ball. Here's where the mind of a wily veteran wins games. Christian drove to the basket and, oh no, fumbled it again. Disaster? No. Christian twisted free under the basket and made a fantastic shot.

As Dr. Art Chandler would say, "Here comes Duke!" With just over ninety seconds to play, the Blue Devils were up by 13. Coach K put the subs in to finish the game.

The final horn sounded and Duke was the 1992 NCAA National Champion. The Fab Five would never win a championship. For Duke, can you say BACK-TO-BACK NCAA Championships?

CHAPTER TWENTY-FOUR
A BROKEN ARM, A FINAL 4 AND KOUFAX

Not very many Duke fans probably will remember the 1992 football season. Barry Wilson's third Blue Devils squad won only two games and dropped nine. The ninth loss that season came at home to UNC. That game is very memorable to our sideline reporter, Tony Haynes. It was not the game itself, but an injury in the second quarter.

> *I broke my elbow in that game at Wallace Wade Stadium. Tar Heels' QB Jason Stanicek was running an option toward the Duke bench and was tackled. As he went down, one of the Duke safeties veered away from the pile to avoid a penalty for a late hit. Duke Orthopedic Physician, Dr. Frank Bassett was standing directly in front of me and saw the guy coming. He jumped out of the way and I got drilled. You guys saw me go sprawling on the track. I said I was okay, and thought I was. But I did notice my elbow stiffening up and told Dr. Bassett. He took me upstairs into the Finch-Yeager Building for X-Rays at halftime. Finch-Yeager is home to Duke Sports Medicine 360 days a year, and the football press box for five Saturdays. They still have the ability to take players up to the third floor for X-Rays and preliminary diagnoses.*
>
> *By the time I got back on the sidelines, Frank was looking at the X-Rays. He said, 'You broke it.' I said, 'Broke what?' He said*

'Your elbow.' I couldn't believe it. He said, 'If you want to continue broadcasting the game I'll give you a couple of Tylenol and a sling.' I said, 'Heck yea, I'm not going anywhere...this game is too good.' Duke lost a heart-breaker, 31-28.

The 1992-93 Blue Devils basketball team beat Michigan in the second game of the year. Chris Webber and company came into Cameron Indoor Stadium December 5th with all the swagger of a No. 1 squad. A Duke fraternity had a little swagger too. They put on a skit for the crowd with four of the ball boys donning shirts with the names of the Michigan starters on their backs. They went through a segment of antics mocking the Wolverines' stars. The fifth 'player' on the floor wasn't a ball boy. He had a tee shirt with the name 'Webber' on the back. He was about two and a half feet tall, and just two years old. The video of that performance is in the Harris household because that short 'Webber' was our grandson Tripp Winkler. He bounced the ball and threw it about as high as his head as he attempted 'shots.' When the skit was over, he would not leave the floor. He became the star, running away from the guys who were trying to get him off the floor. The teams were coming back out for warm ups. Bobbi finally grabbed him just before the 'real' Webber came out of the Michigan locker room.

As the third seed in the Midwest at the Rosemont Horizon in Chicago, we beat Southern Illinois in the first round, but lost, in the second round to California. The Bears took advantage of what I thought was a bad call. Jason Kidd had possession of the ball, lying on the end line with part of his upper torso out of bounds. The Final Four streak was broken at five.

After we left the air, our crew sat courtside watching our feed from the media room, and saw Mike fighting back the tears as he recapped the game and season. He made sure the media knew that his tears were not because of the loss. They were because he would never have the privilege of coaching Bobby Hurley again. There was always a special bond between Mike and his point guards, but Hurley was like a son. He played the way Mike did at Army, passing, defending, and leaving everything on the floor.

After graduation, Bobby played for the Sacramento Kings in the NBA for five years. It might have been 15 years, but for a drunken driver who rammed Bobby's car, nearly killing him. Hurley was chosen as one of the top fifty players in ACC history on the ACC's 50th Anniversary. He is now an assistant coach for his brother Danny at Wagner. He also owns Devil Eleven Stables and raises thoroughbred racehorses. What on earth possessed Bobby to turn to raising horses?

I guess you never know which direction your life is going and how things play out. When I was finishing playing in the NBA, I met some people that were involved with horses and racing. I thought it would be something fun to do, and I got hooked and I had a couple of good winners right away and it evolved quickly into a business.

'Song and a Prayer' has been great for me, and he's been our meal ticket, really. He's a stud in Kentucky and doing very well, and he makes up for a lot of mistakes we make along the way. He's something special.

Is there a correlation between playing basketball and owning racehorses?

You just want to try and get athletes. I played with great athletes so I kinda know what great athletes look like, and that's what I try to do when I'm evaluating the horses to see who could be that horse that could take us to the next level.

After losing in the second round of the 1994 ACC Tournament, Duke again circled the wagons for the NCAA Tournament. We traveled to St. Petersburg and beat Texas Southern and Michigan State. That night held two surprises. Boston College eliminated UNC and Marquette sent Kentucky packing.

In the Sweet 16 in Knoxville, Tn, the Marquette Warriors were 59-49 victims. Top-ranked Purdue was next. National Player of the Year candidate, Glenn Robinson came into the game averaging 31 points per game, but Grant Hill held the 'Big Dog' to 13 points in a 69-60 win.

Two days before we played them, we watched them beat Kansas after we beat Marquette, and I think he had 42 against them, 30 in the first half. We were like, "Man, he's good." Cherokee Parks and I were roommates that year, and the night before our game, we kinda had a game plan, and Tony Lang and I were going to guard him. We felt that he hadn't seen guys as tall and as athletic as we were, who could guard him on the perimeters. We were really going to get in to him and kind of funnel him to Cherokee. So, Cherokee and I were in the hall doing defensive slides up and down the hotel hallway. We were really excited and looking forward to the challenge of trying to contain him.

The Blue Devils headed back home to Durham to prepare for a bus trip to the Final Four, being held for the second time ever in North Carolina. The city of Charlotte went all out for the event. Three weeks earlier, 24,000 fans in the Coliseum saw Duke get bounced from the ACC Tournament.

The Semi-Finals had No. 2 Arkansas taking on No. 9 Arizona, and Duke, ranked No. 6, playing No. 14 Florida. Arkansas was the only top seed left in the tournament. Duke and Arizona were both No. 2 seeds, and Florida was No. 3 in the East.

The Final Four was crazier than normal because President Bill Clinton decided he wanted to come to cheer on his Razorbacks. With all of the Secret Service, it took forever for fans to get into the Coliseum. Even the media were held up. We had to unpack all of our gear, and our engineer, Tony Haynes, had to explain what every little piece was, and why we had it.

I went down to the Coliseum early in the day to work on editing some tape for the pre-game. Of course, about 30 minutes in, they made everyone leave the building because the secret service had to run the bomb-sniffing dogs through the place because the Clintons would be attending the game. It was a major inconvenience, but no one was going to deprive him of seeing his beloved Razorbacks. If

Duke would have been playing anyone else, there's no way he would have been there.

As far as I know, he was the first President to attend a Final Four. Arkansas defeated Arizona 81-72. Duke earned a fourth championship game in five years, beating the 'Gators 70-65.

On Monday night the favored Razorbacks had to come from behind to win in the final seconds. Scottie Thurman hit a three-pointer from the right wing. I still contend that if Tony Lang hadn't clipped his fingernails on Sunday, he would have blocked that shot. But the Hogs prevailed, 76-72.

What does a baseball Hall of Famer have to do with Duke basketball? I'll tell you.

Sandy Koufax was born in Brooklyn, and was better known for basketball than for baseball. Koufax attended the University of Cincinnati on a basketball scholarship, but in the spring of 1954, he made the college baseball team, where a scout for the Brooklyn Dodgers saw him and signed him. He played his entire major league career with my Brooklyn/Los Angeles Dodgers, from 1955 to 1966.

In the early 90's, Sandy bought a house in Pinehurst and started coming to Duke basketball home games. He would wait until after the game had started to come in and would leave before it was over. He didn't want to be the center of attention and cause any problems. I had always heard how shy he was, but he was the most reclusive super star I had ever seen.

At that Final Four in 1994 in Charlotte, I was talking with Doug Collins on the patio of the team hotel, I looked over to a corner and there sat Sandy Koufax. I mentioned to Doug that I would really love to meet Sandy but didn't want to interrupt him. Doug said that he knew Koufax and introduced us. We chatted for several minutes before I excused myself and went back to my room to finish preparation for that night's National Championship game broadcast.

The morning after the game, I went to the desk to check out and

Sandy was doing the same thing. We talked about Duke's heartbreaking loss to Arkansas, and then he asked me which route was I was going to take to Durham. He wondered what the best route might be to get back to Pinehurst. I gave him the most direct route, through Albemarle, and we said our goodbyes. I wished I had brought a baseball to get signed.

The next year, I started carrying a baseball, just in case I might run into him again. Luck was with me at the ACC Tournament in Greensboro. Sandy had connections with CBS and got press passes for several events. Arriving very early for the Saturday session, I spotted Sandy sitting alone at the end of the court. I pulled the ball and a pen out of my bag and went to see him. After we talked a few minutes, I asked if he'd mind signing the ball for me. He looked all around the Coliseum to see if anyone else was around, and the few media people there were all busy getting ready for the game. He asked me why I had a baseball at a basketball tournament, and I told him that I didn't want to miss another opportunity like I did in Charlotte. Not only did he sign and personalize the ball to me, he gave me his address in Vero Beach, Florida to send some of my baseball cards for him to sign. What a guy!

As I went back to my seat to 'hide' my treasure, a Durham sportswriter stopped me and asked if that was Koufax that I had been talking to. He was looking for a column and I knew that Sandy didn't want to do any interviews. By the time I got through hemming and hawing, the writer grabbed his pad and turned to the end of the court only to find it empty. Koufax was gone. He thanked me later. By the way, I have a nice signed picture of the last pitch of Sandy's first no-hitter in my office. I still carry a baseball in my briefcase because you never know who you might run into.

Later in that spring, I had a great football experience. When Fred Goldsmith was hired as Duke's 18th head football coach in 1994 he had to change the atmosphere of Blue Devils football. He showed up at 6am on the first morning of off-season conditioning in a camouflage outfit. It was boot camp!! He got the players' attention quickly. Barry Wilson's last Duke team was 3-8, but a good number of players were returning for '94.

Before the spring game, Fred decided to have a 'celebrity head coach' for each team on the sidelines. I was selected to coach the Blue team. I actually got to call several plays during the game, from a 'recommended' list, of course. I WANTED to run a double-reverse-pass, but the assistants wouldn't let me. I even diagrammed several single wing plays that I remembered from Coach Toby Webb's playbook in Albemarle. No dice!

What the hay, we had a lot of fun and I got to know the players a lot better than before. What's more, my Blue team won!!! Don't believe me? The players don't carry a losing coach off the field on their shoulders, do they? Check out the picture.

"THE WINNING COACH" 1994
DUKE SPRING GAME

That's running back Robert Baldwin holding my left leg. I coached him so well in the spring game that he gained 1,187 yards and scored 12 touchdowns in the fall and led Duke to the Hall of Fame (Outback) Bowl in Tampa, Fla.

The Blue Devils opened the '94 season with Maryland at home. Duke was a slight favorite, but Baldwin had a field day. He ran for 238 yards against the Terps. That's STILL the Duke single-game rushing record. The Blue Devils dined on 'turtle stew' that afternoon, 49-16. Duke won seven straight games out of the gate and were ranked 16th in the country when they rolled into Tallahassee to take on the No. 9 Seminoles. It wasn't pretty. Bobby Bowden's boys ran and passed Duke dizzy in a 59-20 whipping.

Duke recovered enough to beat Virginia the next Saturday by three, but lost consecutive one-point games to N.C. State and UNC to finish the season 8-3.

That was good enough to get Goldsmith's first Duke team to Tampa to play the humongous Badgers of Wisconsin. The Blue Devils had a disastrous start, but Baldwin had a TD and Tom Cochran kicked two field goals and an extra point to tie the game 13-13 in the third. The Badgers then outscored the Devils 21-7 for the 34-20 victory. Goldsmith earned National Coach of the Year honors for his turning around of the program. Unfortunately, it didn't stay turned. In Fred's other four years, his teams went 3-8, 0-11, 2-9 and 4-7. Goldsmith was released after the 1998 season.

The 1997 season provided some fireworks. Duke and Virginia were tied, 10-10, late in the 4th quarter when Chris Combs sacked the quarterback to take UVa out of field goal range. But then the referee penalized Combs 15-yards for saluting to the crowd after the sack, and Virginia eventually kicked the game-winning field goal. In the postgame, Tony Haynes was standing outside the locker room with several writers, waiting to do the coach's interview.

> *Goldsmith comes barreling through the door, but Sports Information Director Mike Cragg pulls him back in the locker room, knowing that he wasn't yet in a good enough mental state to go on the air. A few minutes later, he comes out and is ready, or so I thought. I knew I had to ask him a question about the controversial play, but do it in a way that wouldn't get him suspended. So, I asked, 'Coach, did you get an explanation on the unsportsmanlike penalty?'*
>
> *He yelled, 'I got an explanation and it was unsatisfactory!' Cragg and assistant Mike Sobb were standing behind him with a 'deer in the headlights' look, not knowing what he might say next. I was about to ask another question (Sobb was urging me to do so), and Goldsmith yelled, 'I want to speak to Bradley Faircloth (ACC Supervisor of Officials) right now!' He then took a few steps back, grabbed a cup of water, calmed down and came back, saying something like, 'but that's not what lost us the football game.*

CHAPTER TWENTY- FIVE

'K' IS DOWN, BUT NOT OUT!!

When teams are as successful as the Duke basketball program had been since 1986, some fans began to think that Final Fours and such were almost their birthright. The Final Four and national championship are always Duke's goal. Only UCLA, from 1964 to '75, had ever had any success like that. There is an old saying, 'sometimes you get the bear, and sometimes the bear gets you." In 1995 the bear got Duke.

For the Blue Devils AND Coach K, it started out bad and got worse. Krzyzewski had planned a trip to Australia for his team, but a lack of academic excellence by several freshman players got it cancelled. Basketball at Duke is ultra-important, but classroom performance is more important anything else. Duke players ARE '***student***-athletes.'

Mike also began having pain in his back and leg that summer. The pain got worse. He couldn't sit for a long period of time and he seemed to be in constant discomfort and pain.

The Duke medical staff found that Mike had a severe back problem. Mike possesses a tremendous 'mind-over-matter' ability. In late October, just after practice began, he had surgery. Less than two weeks later, against the doctor's suggestion to take six to eight weeks off, Mike was back at practice. The doctors relented, as long as he was careful and used a special ergonomic "stool/seat" that allowed him to lean in a sort of sit/ stand position. He used it in the office and on the practice court. Soon he was exhausted. His body was doing its best to heal but Mike kept going in spite of the pain. Duke was scheduled to play in the Rainbow Classic between Christmas and New Years. I chose to accompany the football team to the Hall of Fame Bowl. I spent that week with the team at all of their functions. I used a cell phone for the very first time that week, as I called in 'on the scene' reports for WDNC radio.

TONY HAYNES, BOB & WES CHESSON 11/06

We sent our sideline reporter, Tony Haynes, to Honolulu to broadcast the Rainbow Classic. He left Hawaii right after the final game and flew to Tampa to provide sideline coverage the next day. Tony told me that, because of the pain, Mike had to stand almost the entire flight over and back. He coached just twelve games.

After a loss to Clemson at Cameron, Coach K told his assistants that he was going to resign the next day. He felt that 'Duke deserved the best and he was no longer able to do his best.' This wasn't a leave of absence, it was retirement.

The assistant coaches thought he might be acting too quickly and wanted him to take some time to think about it. Mike's wife, Mickie, told them, "I know Mike better than anyone, and after all he has accomplished, I'm not going to let him go out like that." He took their advice, and that of Tom Butters, and took some time off. Pete Gaudet became Interim Coach, with Mike Brey and Tommy Amaker handling the talk shows and TV shows.

When I met the team at the Raleigh-Durham airport for the flight to Atlanta, Coach wasn't with them. That's when I learned of his leave of absence.

Something humorous made the Atlanta trip a little better. Haynes loves to tell this story on Tech coach Bobby Cremins.

On Monday before Duke was to play at Tech, we all listened as Cremins talked to the media during the weekly teleconference.

During the 15-minute interview, you could clearly hear the sound of water moving around. Bob and I talked about it on the way down, wondering if he was doing the teleconference from the bathtub. After we got to Tech, Sports Information Director Mike Finn took us to Bobby's office so I could do a pre-game interview. Before we started, Bob asked me if I wanted to ask coach about the teleconference. I was embarrassed and shyly said, 'Naa, that's not necessary.' By then though, it was too late. Cremins knew something was up and said, 'What, what are you talking about?' I then asked him, 'We just wanted to know if you did the teleconference from the bathtub?" His face turned beet red, and he looked at Finn in a panic. Finn said, 'Yea coach, everyone knows.' We all laughed, but Cremins was clearly embarrassed.

The Blue Devils went 4-15 the rest of the way, ending up with a 13-18 over-all record. Most all of the losses were close. Fifteen were by seven or less.

A very memorable moment occurred in the Duke-Carolina game in Cameron. The Tar Heels were No. 2 in the country, and the Blue Devils were 0-7 in the ACC. Duke had no business even being IN the game in the last few minutes, but they tied the score to force overtime. With the final seconds of OT ticking away, Jeff Capel brought the ball across mid-court and let it fly. The shot went into the basket, the Duke fans went into orbit, and the game went into a second overtime. Duke lost 102-100, but it was a classic.

From a game official's viewpoint, veteran Larry Rose offers his insight.

I had the ESPN game with Duke and Carolina in February 1995 when Jeff Capel hit the half court shot that put the game into a second overtime. That game is now an ESPN classic. I remember thinking; "There is no way that we can afford to blow a call in a game like this." Cameron was hot; the fans were loud; the coaches were on their feet; and we were running, running and running. It was one the most enjoyable games of my career.

One of Rose's partners that night was another ACC veteran, Duke Edsall.

I really don't remember a whole lot about the game itself, although it was a great game up until the end. The place was loud, it was hot, and we were lucky that the game was so well played we didn't screw it up. We were in the 1st OT and Duke was down to the last shot. I was in the lead position and when Jeff let it go I had a great look at the flight of the ball. My only thought was, 'We're going to have to play another 5 minutes.' What a game!

Rose was one of the most respected referees in the ACC, but he had to earn that respect.

Early in my career, in the late eighties, I worked a game that was another Duke-type game, a hard and well-played game. I had a lot of tough calls that night and Coach K, in his usual way, had made several comments to me about my decisions. Finally, reality hit him. He was not going to change me, or my calls. He came storming down the sideline during a timeout to tell me. He told me, in no uncertain terms, that I would never call another Duke game. Of course I gave him a technical, and he REALLY got mad. He called Mr. Barakat (ACC Supervisor of Officials) after the game, or the next day, and told him he did not want to see me again. The next week, I was back at Duke, again in a tough game. During a timeout late in the game, he came down to the end of his bench. I was standing on the end line. I was thinking, 'I am going to have to throw him out if he starts in again.' He started toward me, and as he did, he said, "You are a better man than I am, to come back and work like you worked tonight. I have total respect for you.' Since that incident Coach K and I have shared a great respect for each other.

A February 26 game in Pauley Pavilion was NOT one of those narrow losses, it was 100-77, but a very memorable event took place on that trip. It was during the O.J. Simpson murder trial, and Tony, team photographer Jimmy Wallace and I had a rental car and were doing some Hollywood sightseeing. Tony wanted to see the O.J. house. So Jimmy, who was the navigator, found it on the map and we drove over to Rockingham Drive and looked around, along with several other 'curiosity-seekers.' Tony suggested that we try to find Bundy Drive, the murder scene. Again, Jimmy gave us directions, and off we went, with Tony timing our trip.

I think it took us only 12 minutes. Later on in October, when the not guilty verdict was rendered, the jurors said they didn't think he had time, in an hour, to commit the murders and get back to his house. Of course, we knew that was bunk because it took us only 12 minutes to drive from the two locations.

Only 12 minutes on a late Saturday afternoon and having to cross a very busy thoroughfare without benefit of a stoplight, and we were following a map and didn't really know where we were going.

A healthier Coach K was on the sidelines for the Blue Devils in 1995-96. Duke started fine and won the Great Alaska Shootout.

This brings to mind a favorite story that always gets Tony Haynes to laughing. Everyone from the 'lower 48' must include a trip to Eklutna when they travel to Alaska. Eklutna is a native village just outside Anchorage. It is just off the Glenn Highway, at the head of the Knik Arm of Cook Inlet. It is a rather small community of about 70, but many of the tribal members live in the surrounding communities.

Eklutna is the last of eight villages that existed before the American colonists first showed up in the region, around 1915. It was settled more than 800 years ago. With the arrival of Russian Orthodox missionaries in the 1840s, there was a mixing of Orthodox Christianity and native practices. Visitors can still view the brightly colored spirit houses at the Eklutna Cemetery, built in 1650. Almost all of the residents of Eklutna are either Alaska Native or part Native. (This was gleaned from the brochures and Internet information.)

Before Duke's first visit to the Great Alaska Shootout in 1996, I was looking through all of the material from the Alaska Travel & Tourism office to find things for all of us to do when we had free time during the week we would be there. In addition to Denali Park, Mt. McKinley, Cook Inlet, the Kenai Peninsula, and the glaciers, Eklutna jumped out at me.

I had Phyllis and Tony all excited about visiting the village. I thought the pictures I had seen in the publicity pictures were of normal-sized houses and churches. When we arrived, all we saw were these small spirit-houses, and not much else. I turned around twice and drove back through it just to make sure we weren't missing something. Three dejected Duke folks made our way through the snow, back to Anchorage. When Duke went back in 1999, David Modlin filled in as our engineer, and Tony had built it up so much that 'Mod' couldn't wait to get there. We didn't let on about our let down the first time there, and waited to see his reaction. It was the same as ours had been three years before. The Blue Devils played in the event for the final time in 2004. We didn't go to Eklutna.

Things turned sour for the team as they were 8-8 in the ACC, tied for fourth place, and lost to Maryland in the first round of the ACC Tournament. Duke lost in the first round game of the NCAA Tournament to Eastern Michigan. Pack up the equipment, this season is history.

On the annual trip to Tallahassee in 1997, the team went to the Silver Slipper restaurant for dinner the evening before the game. Tony Haynes and I usually found a table away from the team for our meal. On this particular evening, we had company, the driver of the team bus. He was a very engaging gentleman, and we asked him to join us. The conversation covered the gamut of world events, and the team's successes, but Tony still breaks up when talking about this incident.

We were talking about natural disasters because there had just been a massive earthquake in Japan. The driver said, 'The thing that really scares ME are those volcanoes, and all that saliva coming out.' Bob and I avoided eye contact for most of the meal, knowing we would bust out laughing if we looked at each other. Of course we let several of the players in on the comment after we got on the bus to go back to the hotel. They relayed it to the row behind them until everyone was aware of it. It was like a domino effect as the players heard the story and busted out laughing.

Duke teams from 1998 to 2001 showcased some of the finest players in Blue Devils annals. In that period, Duke lost only 11 games, just two in the ACC regular season, and won 48. They won two ACC Tournament titles. The 1997-1998 team lost to Kentucky in the regional championship game in St. Petersburg.

I have seen many great players at Duke, but one who played with a lot of verve was Steve Wojciechowski. He came in the year that Mike had his back problems. 'Wojo' was probably the player who missed Coach K the most that year.

As the point guard at Duke, you're an extension of the coach. When he's gone, it really knocks you back, because you can always look to him for stability and strength, or get direction. Usually, if you don't know what to do, you just follow his directions and you're going to be in really good shape. Not having him there in '95 left a huge leadership void in the program at that point. In hindsight, it was an amazing lesson for me and for some of the other guys, because, one, it made you a lot tougher. It made us even hungrier.

The program changed at that time. I equate it to Coach running an amazing 'Mom & Pop' shop for the first years of his career where everything the program did plugged into him. After the back injury, the program went in a different direction. It's like he runs a 'Fortune 500' company now.

During his junior and senior years, the point guard started every game, and earned the 1998 National Defensive Player of the Year. He is currently an Associate Head Coach.

Duke won the Maui Classic right out of the gate in 1998 by beating the 1997 National Champion Arizona Wildcats. They jumped to No. 1, and then Elton Brand broke his foot in the first practice after the Christmas break. He was 'supposed' to be out for the season. Coach changed strategy by featuring the perimeter game. Duke was 20-1 heading into the game with No. 2 UNC.

In that stretch, the Blue Devils played Maryland for the second time in the season. Tony Haynes remembers Gary Williams much more that the final outcome.

Duke was hosting Maryland at Cameron on January 29. Seven minutes into the game, Gary Williams, going nuts as usual, was ejected after picking up two technicals. At halftime, Assistant SID Mike Sobb told us that Williams was stewing in the locker room, and was being forced to listen to us because there was no TV down there. You and I laughed, knowing it must have been murder for him to be forced to listen to the Duke radio crew while his team was getting drilled 86-59. As an after-thought to that, we all know how much he hated to lose to Duke. The first year I was at State and did a pre-game interview with Gary, he looked at me and asked, 'You're not at Duke anymore?' I told him, that I had switched over to State last summer. He said, 'Glad you finally saw the light.

After the first meeting in College Park, we had something happen that I couldn't believe. I got a phone call from the hotel security at the Greenbelt Marriott where we always stay. The officer asked me if I was the person driving a van that was loaded with, what appeared to him to be, radio equipment. I told him that I was, and he told me to meet him in the lobby because someone had broken into it. I called Tony and woke him up and we met the guard in the lobby.

My phone rang at about 1:30 in the morning (never a good sign) and it was Bob telling me that someone had tried to break into the van and steal our radio equipment. As it turned out, hotel security had seen the guy and called the police. As I recall, the police turned the dogs loose on the guy and chased him into the woods behind the hotel. One of the dogs bit the guy in the rear-end and he surrendered. We didn't lose any equipment, although the rental van was damaged. The guy broke out the window on the driver's side and lugged a couple of cases up through the van and out. He wasn't smart enough to open the back door and take it out the easy way.

In the first meeting between Duke and Carolina in 1998, it was No. 1 Duke playing No. 2 Carolina.. The game was played in Chapel Hill and the Tar Heels beat Duke 'like a drum' 97-73. As usual, the Carolina loss just jacked up the team. Wojciechowski has seen the Duke-Carolina rivalry from three perspectives; as a Duke player, as our analyst in the booth, and as Mike Krzyzewski's assistant coach. He defines it well.

As a player, it's the most competitive and intense that you'll play in. The Duke-Carolina rivalry is something that you dream about when you're a little kid playing in the backyard. It captures the attention of the country. As a player you always dream about playing on that type of stage. And you're going to compete against a great school, with great kids, and great players. You always want to try yourself against the best.

It's the same coaching, because you're coaching against great coaches and competing against them on the court and recruiting, because they're eight miles down the road.

From a broadcaster's standpoint, I can't tell you how much I appreciate it. After being a player and a coach, I think broadcasting is harder than both, for me at least. In coaching, I'm still right in the

BOB, STEVE WOJCIECHOWSKI, JOHN ROTH & JOHN BROCKWELL
NCAA TOURNAMENT CHARLOTTE 3/99

mix of the action. It's tough for me to step away from the sidelines. I have all the respect in the world you guys who do that.

Referees enjoy working a Duke/Carolina game too. Duke Edsall is a part of the lore.

I've been so lucky to have many great experiences with Duke Basketball and in my visits to Cameron Indoor Stadium. Just to be a part of some of the classic Duke/Carolina games over the years has been a highlight of my refereeing career. I've been involved in 3 of the twelve overtime games in the history of the series. Five of those twelve were during my years in the ACC.

That leads us to the last game of the regular season against the Tar Heels, this time at home. With a little more than ten minutes to play UNC was up 64-47. Coach K called a time out and told the guys to 'just relax and play the game that you wanted to play.' Carolina made only two baskets the rest of the game. Duke won, 77-75. As the final buzzer sounded, Wojo eluded everyone on the floor to find his coach.

Senior night is always a special night because it's a culmination of four years of hard work and playing in front of the greatest fans in the country and playing with some great teammates who have become lifelong friends. It's your final chance to play, and for us, we were competing for a regular season championship against the University of North Carolina. We had an outstanding team and so did they. Right out of the gate they jumped on us pretty good. When you have guys like Vince Carter and Antawn Jamison, that can happen. It was so emotional, and at times you can be too emotional, and they took advantage of it.

We did not play well in the first half and they were up 17 with about 10 minutes to go in the game. From that point, things just started clicking. I remember that Cameron was as hot as it's ever been, and as loud as I can remember. We finally caught a rhythm to our game. We picked up the defensive intensity and got some buckets.

We had a huge boost from Elton Brand who was coming off foot surgery. Roshown McLeod had a huge game and we were able to fight and won the game 77-75.

Certainly, one of MY best moments was to share that victory and that ACC championship with Coach K directly after the horn. Coach and I have a really special relationship. My career really came full circle. My freshman year he was out with the back surgery, and we really had a tough year. From that point, going 13-18, to the point of winning the ACC championship and being No. 1 in the nation and winning 32 games, there are a lot of steps you have to take to go from the bottom to the top. He was there with me and my teammates, every step of the way. I was so fortunate to have played for him.

Duke became the first team to win 15 ACC games in a single season.The students stormed the floor to celebrate two things, the win over UNC, and Coach K's 500th win. Tony Haynes, remembers something else.

Another epic Duke – Carolina basketball game had just concluded with the Blue Devils rallying from 17 points down over the last eight minutes to beat their arch rivals, thus sending raucous Cameron Indoor Stadium into a frenzy. Up in the crows' nest, Bob Harris was getting emotional; he was in fact, choked up and unable to fully convey to his listeners what had just transpired. Privileged to be his color man that day, it dawned on me what Bob was truly all about: no one had more passion for Duke or more love for his job than this man. For our remaining days and beyond, there will only be one "Voice of the Blue Devils."

I have three favorite sites for the ACC Tournament, Greensboro, Greensboro, and Greensboro. I'm not putting down any of the other sites but, Greensboro and the ACC Tournament go hand-in-hand. It is centrally located within the ACC's geographical footprint, and the ACC offices are there. The Greensboro Sports Council and the Coliseum staff work so diligently to put on the tournament and they do an amazing job every time we are there.

The one thing that Greensboro has that the other sites don't is presence. When the ACC Tournament comes to Greensboro, it is THE only game in town. The tournament, the schools, the players and the coaches command the media attention.

Charlotte is my second favorite. When the event is in Atlanta, Tampa, and Washington they have so many other things going on ALL the time that the ACC is relegated to the latter pages of the sports section. In Atlanta you have to share with pro basketball, hockey and even NASCAR. In D.C., I wonder if anyone even knows the tournament is there, other than the fans. In Tampa, they don't even know what the ACC is.

Duke and Carolina were number one seeds for the NCAAs, as UNC went to the East and Duke went to the South. The Blue Devils had to play two games in Rupp Arena and a lot of the fans were angry that the Wildcats weren't there and Duke was. The ghost of Christian Laettner was there. Most of the crowd was hoping for an early departure for the Blue Devils, but we beat Radford and Oklahoma State to earn a trip to the Sweet Sixteen in St. Petersburg.

Syracuse was our first victim there. Then came Kentucky, with the winner going to the Final Four in San Antonio. Duke lost a 17-point lead, and the game.

Orlando 'Tubby' Smith was the coach of the Wildcats. I am so old that I actually broadcast a game in 1973 that Tubby played in. He was a standout guard at High Point College, and played at Pfeiffer when I was broadcasting some of their games for WZKY in Albemarle. I also broadcast games that Rick Barnes of Texas (he went to Lenoir Rhyne), Cy Alexander (Catawba College), formerly of South Carolina State, and John Lentz of Lenoir Rhyne (he also played at LR) played in.

I ran into Tubby after he finished his media duties following the game. I congratulated him on the win and wished him 'good luck' at the Final Four. Before we said our 'goodbyes' I told him that the Wildcats WOULD win the NCAA championship. He looked at me very skeptically. I assured him that I was serious.

Tubby hasn't let me forget that prediction to this day. They did beat Utah, 78-69 in San Antonio.

CHAPTER TWENTY-SIX
MOVING TO MOORE

In July 1998, I made a great career move. I quit WDNC and daily radio to join Moore Productions and devote all my time and energies to the Duke broadcasts, coaches' TV shows and daily radio shows. I met Johnny Moore, the owner of the company, in 1977 when he came to Duke. He was fresh out of Guilford College where he was Sports Information Director as a student. Johnny was a Triangle guy, having grown up in Garner, and he and his family were life-long Duke fans.

Tom Mickle hired him at Duke and that was the birth of the 'M&M Boys.' They were the best sports info duo in the ACC. The writers and broadcasters loved them. Johnny was also Promotions Director for the athletic department, as well as helping in fund-raising. With those jobs, he established a foundation for publishing Blue Devil Weekly and eventually the broadcast rights-holder for Duke football and men's and women's basketball.

He has always had the attitude that, "You don't work FOR me, you work WITH me." That was his secret for success. Johnny has always been more than an employer. He's been my friend.

For over 30 years Duke fans have been able to know exactly what happens within the Duke football and basketball programs and at the games through the eyes of Bob Harris. They have been able to feel the emotion of last second shots and then find out just how that player felt when he hit that shot through his interviews. Bob has been so connected to the fans that he has basically become an extension of them in the radio booth, giving him the ability to communicate those very special moments in Duke athletic history with feeling. It is that feeling and connection with the fans, coaches and players that has made Bob Harris the unique "Voice of the Blue Devils."

Johnny Moore, President/ Executive Producer
Duke Radio Network

Moore Productions was not a large company. I was just the seventh full-time staff member, and my title was Vice President/Radio. John Roth was the editor and chief writer of ***Blue Devil Weekly***, but is now host of the football and basketball pregame and halftime shows. He is our analyst for men's basketball broadcasts. He still finds time to produce the TV shows for the football and basketball coaches, and hosts the Kevin White radio show. In his 'spare' time, John wrote T***he Encyclopedia of Duke Basketball***, THE definitive resource for any researcher. John is the most knowledgeable person on Duke athletics that I know.

I was watching a movie on 9/11 when the screen went dark for the announcement of a major news development. It was one of those "we interrupt this program" moments that I will never forget. I was 18 years old and this was pre-World Trade Center terrorism — 9/11 of 1976. This movie was on the big screen in Page Auditorium at Duke, one of my first Saturday nights on campus as a college freshman. The interruption was to inform all of us youthful Blue Devils that our football team had just upset Tennessee at Neyland Stadium in the season opener — big news indeed.

Had I been listening to the radio instead of attending the movie, I would have heard Bob Harris' first play-by-play broadcast of a Duke football game. I am pretty sure he did not punctuate the triumph with his now familiar audio signature, "HOW SWEET IT IS!" From what I've been told, he was more preoccupied with getting off the air so he could find a restroom! But even though Bob and I didn't know each other at the time, I have come to relish the symmetry of sharing such a special occasion with such an admired colleague — Bob's first football game as the Voice of the Blue Devils and mine as an official Dukie were one and the same.

Since joining Bob's radio broadcasting team in 1998-99, one of my favorite experiences has been going mobile with our pregame show, particularly at Wallace Wade Stadium. With headphones in place and wireless microphone in hand, I move across the concourse and through the crowd encountering some of Duke's most loyal fans during their most optimistic moments. So many of them stop to offer me a greeting of some kind: a wave, a handshake, a pat on the back, a quick chat. It's a little bit of a rush and truly rewarding — not necessarily being recognized, but feeling the warmth of such a friendly, extended Blue Devil family.

The vast majority of these encounters end the same way, with folks asking me to pass along some pleasantry to Bob. "Tell Bob I said hey." "Tell Bob to have a good game." And that brings me to my main point here — virtually everyone with a royal blue allegiance knows Bob, and Bob seems to know all of them. I can easily imagine what it would be like if Bob accompanied me on these pregame walks; we would hardly be able to move, as Bob would be delivering his trademark hearty handshake to a steady stream of Blue Devil partisans, each of them enjoying his undivided attention.

Literally thousands of Duke fans have grown up listening to Bob and they love the way he speaks to them through his broadcasts. But I think they love the way he speaks to them in person even more. They feel a genuine affection for him, as evidenced by the number of people who stop by the radio booth to present Bob with hot dogs and peanuts, send photos and memorabilia to his office, invite him to charity golf tournaments or welcome him at stadiums throughout the ACC. We arrived early for a game in Charlotte one time and a man in an orange windbreaker gave me a big wave and hello from across the arena. I asked Bob if he knew the guy, and of course he did. "Oh, that's Elwood from Wadesboro," Bob said, waving back to a man who had been a regular caller on our postgame talk show.

I have enjoyed countless highlights broadcasting Duke games with Bob. From beginning to end, the 2001 basketball season in particular was an unforgettable ride, especially the two stunning comebacks against Maryland. The postgame show following an ACC championship contest is always a personal thrill, with me anchoring on press row, Bob hustling up interviews on the floor and our engineer John Rose ensuring a seamless production. Those are the times when live radio can provide emotion, energy and information better than any other medium, so it's very satisfying to look back and realize that Bob and I have done some of our best work together in those situations. I know we are both deeply grateful to the Duke basketball program for giving us so many of those opportunities, that's for sure!"

Our sales manager was a very unique and charming gentleman. The majority of his career had revolved around the national advertising for Chrysler. When the Chrysler advertising account moved from one agency to another, Russ Hamilton went with it. Lee Iacocca INSISTED on it. We all called him 'Mr. Russ.' I think Carolyn hung that moniker on him and it stuck. When he decided to retire, he wanted to relocate, and because he had worked with the Elkins family and their Chrysler dealership in Durham, he selected 'the Bull City' for he and June to retire to. Johnny also convinced him to become the 'part-time' sales manager for our company, and he brought a number of national advertisers to ***Blue Devil Weekly***, the coaches' TV shows and the Network. His health situation forced him to have a third retirement party in 2006. Hey, I'd just like to have ONE retirement party.

Russ took me to lunch on my first day in the office. He said it was tradition. I love tradition, especially when good food and good people are involved. For the seven years 'Mr. Russ' and I worked across the lobby from each other, we had a unique relationship. We both loved sports of all kinds and constantly were telling sports stories to each other and reminiscing of the great teams, players and games gone by. If either one of us got stuck for a name or event, the other one usually could fill in the blanks. We both love jokes, him hearing them and me telling them.

Unsung heroes? We had two of them. Carolyn Smith has been with the company since its infancy. Nettie Brogdon became a part-time employee about a year before I joined the company. She retired in 2009. They took care of the majority of the subscriptions and renewals for ***Blue Devil Weekly***, and made sure the proper people got their calls, messages and visitors. After 'Mr. Russ' left us, they 'got' to hear my jokes. They were great laughers, even for the corny ones. I have worked in many varied workplaces in my career, but this one was unique. There were no required hours for any of us. We all did whatever it took to accomplish the project. Unlike some of my previous situations, there was never an attitude or ego problem at Moore. No one took credit for making something happen. No one got upset that another might have gained recognition for an accomplishment. EVERYONE got the job done

During the latter years at WZKY, I wondered if I 'had what it took' to work for a network or in a major market. I knew one of the greats, ABC's Chris Schenkel, through the National Sportswriters and Sportscasters Association. At an NSSA function in Salisbury, NC, I asked Chris for some career advice. He told me of his ascension to ABC, and then shared a piece of information that caused me to re-consider my plan. He said he had spent relatively few nights at home since the new year had begun because of all the travel. He told me this in APRIL!! This was the very reason I left Goodyear in 1967.

The National Sportswriters & Sportscasters Association is recognizes sportscasters and sportswriters from all over the United States for their leadership, devotion and contributions. Salisbury, North Carolina serves as the headquarters for the NSSA, and it is responsible for the organizing and counting of all the ballots for the winners of the National, State, and Hall of Fame awards. It began there in 1959 as the brainchild of restaurateur

BOB & ABC's BOB COSTAS AT NSSA AWARDS 4/92

Pete DiMizio to honor regional sportscasters and sportswriters whom he had met at the Greensboro Open Golf Tournament. Its first Annual Awards Program was held on April 12, 1960. I was fortunate to win the North Carolina Sportscaster of the Year Award in 1988 and 1991.

I was a board member and officer of the North Carolina Association of Sports Broadcasters from its inception in 1967 through 1977. In the early 70s, our state association entered into an alliance with NSSA, and we urged a dual membership payment through NCSASB for our members. As part of the pact, our officers would present the 50 NSSA broadcasters' plaques at their April banquet in Salisbury. Since I lived 30 miles down U.S. 52, it was easy for me to be a part of the banquet each year. It was at this two-day event that I had an opportunity to meet and interview many luminaries of my field.

Mel Allen, the veteran 'voice' of the New York Yankees, visited NSSA for a number of years and I really wanted to interview him. I finally got my chance in the clubhouse of the Salisbury Country Club. Sitting alone on a couch in a small room, he told me he only had about ten minutes for the interview. I had a 60-minute cassette tape in the recorder and I started my questioning. Mel talked. And he talked. I heard my recorder click off and he was still going. I quietly flipped the cassette over to side 2 and hit 'record'. When side 2 ran out, he was still regaling stories of the 'Bronx Bombers.' I didn't have the heart to tell him to stop. We must have talked for well over an hour, and I had 60 minutes of one of the best ever.

I still believed I could make it at a larger station, but I had stipulations. The Duke position was perfect. I have had an opportunity to live in a great area, have a career that I honestly love, and still have time for my family. That is the attitude that prevailed at Moore Productions. Family atmosphere? You bet. I saw Johnny's two small daughters grow up and graduate from college, and John's three children, and Carolyn and Nettie's grandchildren grow up. They have had the same experiences with Tripp and Meredith.

As of July 1, 2009, Moore Productions was no more. The Duke Radio Network, coaches TV shows and Blue Devil Weekly are now under the banner of ISP Sports of Winston-Salem. ISP Sports is a nationwide company that owns multimedia rights to properties at over 60 major college conferences and universities. Eight of the 12 ACC schools fly the flag of ISP. ISP is truly "America's Home for College Sports."

Blue Devil Weekly is now a monthly magazine with a new name, a new look and a new focus. It is called **GoDuke The Magazine** and is published monthly from August through June.

CHAPTER TWENTY- SEVEN

SETTING THE STAGE – PART II

The 1998-1999 Duke Blue Devils started the season No.1 in the polls. They ended the year 37-2, and lost only one regular season game, and played for the NCAA National Championship. The only loss during the season was in the Great Alaskan Shoot-Out championship game to Cincinnati. A Bearcat player went the length of the court for the winning basket at the horn. Duke didn't lose again until March.

The Blue Devils reeled off 32 consecutive wins. Twenty-eight of them were by ten or more points. Duke's margin of victory for THE SEASON was 24 points per game.

The starters, Cory Maggette, Elton Brand, William Avery, Chris Carrawell, and Trajan Langdon led this juggernaut. Shane Battier was a part-time starter. Five of them were named All-ACC, something that had never happened before. This team was never really tested except for that Cincinnati game and an overtime win over St. John's.

Duke beat Virginia, N.C. State and Carolina to win the ACC Tournament in Charlotte. A week later the Blue Devils were back in the Coliseum in the East Region. They took care of Florida A&M and Tulsa to get back to the Sweet Sixteen in the Meadowlands. The Southwest Missouri State Bears went down by 17, and then Duke took out Temple by 21, and advanced to the Final Four at Tropicana Field in St. Petersburg, Fl.

Some members of the media had all but given the championship to

Duke. The No. 1 Blue Devils, No. 2 Michigan State, and No. 3 UConn were all in attendance for a chance at the NCAA title, plus Ohio State. The Blue Devils faced Michigan State for the second time that season and Mike Krzyzewski's squad took care of business and advanced to the Monday night game to face the Huskies.

Former neighbors, William Avery and Ricky Moore, went head-to-head. They grew up ten houses apart in Augusta, Georgia. Duke led 39-37 at half, but it got a lot tougher in the second period. UConn's defense was as good as Duke had faced in quite some time. With 25 seconds left Connecticut was up, 75-74. Langdon brought the ball up court for the last shot but never got it off. He was called for traveling. Two Huskies free throws made the final margin 77-74.

The Duke locker room was a mess. There were lots of tears because they all knew that they had let a championship slip away. This game just solidified my feeling that the best team in the country doesn't always win the National Championship.

It was decision time for a lot of Duke players. Avery, Brand and Maggette all opted for the 'play-for-pay' life in the NBA, and Chris Burgess followed his father's wishes and transferred to Utah. Elton's decision was a hard one. He and his mom sought advice from Coach K and he urged Elton to do what he felt in his heart was best for his career.

Mike has always been honest and up front with his players who are considering the early jump to the pros or transferring to another school. He wants what's best for his team, but NOT at the expense of his players. They come first. I don't think that Mike felt that Avery's and Maggette's opting for the NBA was in their best interest at that time.

There was another change came that year. Former player and assistant coach Quin Snyder took the head-coaching job at Missouri.

Let's switch sports for a minute. In the fall of 2000 I received a call from a longtime friend, Kelly Adams. I knew Kelly was a Shriner but didn't realize that he was on the Shrine Bowl Committee. As mentioned earlier, one of my first sports memories was listening to the 1947 Shrine Bowl game and waiting to hear my Dad yell at me from the stands on the radio broadcast. The Shrine Bowl of the Carolinas matched the best high school football seniors from North and South Carolina in Charlotte's Memorial Stadium on an early December Saturday afternoon. It was complete with a parade through downtown Charlotte with every Shrine unit in the two Carolinas. They would parade all the way down to the stadium and all of the musical units, clowns and others would parade on to the field for pre-game and halftime activities. In a word, it was the highlight of the high school football season. It was a high honor to be selected to play, coach or officiate in the game. I had no idea that phone call would make me a part of this great spectacle.

Kelly was moving through the stations of the Shrine toward Potentate. He asked me if I would like to be the play-by-play announcer for the 2000 game. My mind raced back over the games that I had a specific memory for. That 1947 game which featured Albemarle's Bob "Goo Goo" Gantt, the 1958 game that was coached by Bulldogs legend Toby Webb, the 1967 game when Albemarle's Rick Russell played in sun, rain, sleet and snow in one afternoon, the 1972 game when Rod Broadway of West Stanly was the Defensive Player of the Game, and the 1997 game that Phyllis and I attended. Now, I was being given the opportunity to broadcast the game

I quickly checked the Duke basketball schedule and to my joy, the Blue Devils didn't have a game that Saturday. I jumped at the chance. He asked if I needed a crew or not. I asked if I could bring Wes to do color, and Clyde Cupples to spot. He agreed and I called the two of them to see if they were interested. They both accepted without hesitating. Kelly had the engineering and stats covered, so we were set.

I headed to Maiden, NC on Thursday of game week and watched the North Carolina team practice and talked with the coaches. Tom Brown of Maiden High was the head coach and Gary Merrill of Northern Durham was one of his assistants. Another assistant was Hickory High's David Elder. I had broadcast games for him when he was head coach at South

Stanly and I was at WZKY.

On Friday, I watched the South Carolina squad practice, and then headed to the host hotel for the Players' Banquet that night. One of the first Shriners I ran into there was an old college classmate, Phil 'Tank' Raiford. He had been the Executive Director in 1998. We reminisced about the days in West Raleigh.

Game day dawned gray, and rainy. That might be an understatement. It POURED; so much, that most of the Shrine units didn't march in the parade downtown. It put a real damper on the crowd too. I don't remember what the announced attendance was, but by the start of the 4th quarter, there weren't 1,000 people in the stands. It didn't help that the Sandlapper squad was kicking the North Carolina team all over the field. The 66-14 S.C. win set records for the most combined points and the largest margin of victory. There were twelve players on the two rosters that Wes, Clyde and I would see for four more years on ACC rosters. Lance Johnson and John Paul Kimbrough came to Duke the next fall while 4 players went on to UNC, 3 to NCSU, and one each to Clemson, Maryland, and the Naval Academy.

Even with the lopsided game played on a miserable day, I was honored to have been asked to broadcast the 64th and last North Carolina/South Carolina High School Shrine Bowl football game that was played in Memorial Stadium in Charlotte. The next year it was moved to Rock Hill, South Carolina, and eventually to Wofford College in Spartanburg in 2004.

Back to roundball. The 2000 season really surprised the 'experts.' Everyone expected it to be a rebuilding year, but no one told Mike Krzyzewski and his staff. They were busily getting ready to win.From the results of the first two games, one might not have suspected that. Duke lost the first two games of the season for the first time since Hal Bradley's 1958-59 team began 0-3. In the ensuing months, Duke set the all-time record for consecutive ACC wins at 28, breaking N.C. State's record of 27, set during the 1973, '74 and '75 seasons.

The Blue Devils beat Carolina on the final day of the season, giving them first place in the ACC regular season. Remember, there was no such thing as the regular season championship at that time, even though Dean Smith insisted there was when HIS teams finished first.

The Blue Devils smacked Clemson, Wake Forest and Maryland to win the ACC Tournament in Charlotte, and headed off to the NCAA Tournament with a No. 1 seed and a No.3 national ranking. The first two games East Region games were in Winston-Salem against Lamar and Kansas, with Roy Williams on the Jayhawks' bench. The Blue Devils won, 69-64.

Duke moved into the Sweet Sixteen in Syracuse against Florida. They lost 87-78, and were on the chartered plane the next morning heading back to Durham.

CHAPTER TWENTY-EIGHT

2001 – AN NCAA CHAMPIONSHIP ODYSSEY

It had been nine years since Duke won back-to-back National Championships. They were oh so close in 1994, 1998 and 1999 but came up short all three years. In 2001, the Blue Devils tried again. And they were successful again.

Duke started the '01 season No. 2 in the nation, behind Arizona, and participated in the pre-season NIT again.. The second game was against Villanova in Cameron and Coach K picked up his 500th win. After the game the team and coaches were brought back onto the floor to see Duke University name the playing surface 'Coach K Court.'

Another trip to Madison Square Garden saw Duke beat Texas and Temple to bring home the NIT trophy.

After the semester exam break, Duke headed out to the 'left coast' to play Portland in the Rose Garden. On the trip out, we had a harrowing experience. Our charter flights always make sure that they serve hot chocolate chip cookies after the evening meals, and I went to the back galley to get a second one and was leaning over the back seat talking with Jason Williams and one of the flight attendants. Jason was sitting on the aisle across from the attendant. I had a cookie in one hand and a Coke in the other. We were just north of Denver, Co, when all of a sudden I heard a rumble at the front of the plane. Then it began moving toward the back where we were. The attendant grabbed the Coke out of my hand and pulled me down to the seat near Jason and yelled for me to buckle up.

About that time, we dropped about 1,000 feet, VERY quickly. I looked at Jason and he looked scared. I was too. Before the pilot could explain what had happened, the attendant told Jason and me that we had just encountered 'clean-air turbulence.' It's a phenomenon that occurs when you're flying west over the Front Range portion of the Rocky Mountains and the air is clear and cold. According to experts, clean air turbulence is very problematic because, first of all, it cannot always be foreseen, so there is no warning for anyone. It is also felt mildly in the flight deck and is more severe in the aft section. That's where we were. Clean air turbulence can also occur when no clouds are in sight. Even worse for occupants, aircraft radars can't detect it. Our attendant said she had experienced it several times in similar situations, but Jason and I hadn't, and we never want to again!

The morning of the Portland game, I was sitting in my hotel room with the phone to my ear, as Bobbi was getting ready to receive her diploma at the Campbell University graduation ceremonies. She called me on her cell phone as she lined up to receive the sheepskin and we talked a bit as she described what was going on. I heard them call her name, and then a voice said, "Bobbi, what on earth are you doing with that phone?" It was Dr. Jerry Wallace, who was an assistant to the President at Campbell. Then I heard, "Congrat....." And Bobbi said, "Here, talk to my Daddy, he's in Portland with Duke." The next thing I heard was, "Bob, I just want you to know how proud we are of Bobbi and what she has accomplished with all she has had to go through for the last two years. Get those Blue Devils to win another one tonight." It was the President of Campbell University, Dr. Norman Wiggins. We had known each other for about 20 years, and had it not been for that, I don't think she could have gotten away with that. Cell phones were a 'no-no' at graduation. Bobbi said he had an odd look on his face as she handed him the phone. He had been caught off guard.

After the win over Portland, we then flew down the coast to play Stanford in the Pete Newell Classic in Oakland. Duke lost by one at the buzzer, but I don't think the presence of Stanford alums, Tiger Woods or Condoleezza Rice, had any effect on the game..

With the record at 18-1, we flew to College Park to play Maryland, and this game became an 'instant classic' the minute it was over. With 70 seconds remaining, Duke was trailing by ten points. Now began a performance for the ages. Things were going badly for Duke, and the Maryland fans were lickin' their chops for a blow out. Jason Williams was having an horrific game. In the first eight minutes, he had ten turnovers, but in the last 13 SECONDS of the game he scored eight points.

It's still a blur, to this day. I was having one of the worst games of my life. Chris Collins and I joke about it all the time. He says, "Man, you might have been the first guy to have a quadruple-double as far as points, rebounds, assists and turnovers. It was just one of those days when nothing was going right. From the jump, Steve Blake had just owned me with his wingspan and Juan Dixon helping off his man. I was always seeing him out of the corner of my eye when I would drive to the basket. And shots weren't going down and the Maryland fans were getting to me. I was frustrated and I was a little tired, I was winded. It was just one of those scenarios where it was just a horrible death.

The one thing I can say about our team that year is that we had great leaders. Nate James was phenomenal. He was a man of few words. He just always played hard. He always gave you that effort. Shane Battier was the leader of our team vocally, just saying not to quit. I remember that we'd called a timeout and Coach looked at us and said, "Don't any of you guys quit on me." We were getting our butts kicked but we'll fight to the end on this one. We came out of the huddle and Chris Duhon was in the game with Shane, Nate, Mike Dunleavey, and we all got in a huddle and, I just remember the fans chanting, 'Overrated, overrated.'

I don't know what it was after that point, but I just made a promise to myself that I was going to foul somebody really, really hard, and send him to the line, or I was going to get a steal. That possession I came down and scored on a lay-up, we went to a full-court press, and Drew Nicholas was the guy I was guarding, and I was going to face guard him on the throw-in. Then I thought, "I'm going to let him catch the ball, because I was angry. I just wanted to foul the heck out of him. I just wanted to chop him so hard that his arms would come off. He got the ball and Shane came over to double-team him, and we pushed him to the corner. When you see the video, it's funny, I raked down so hard on him with my right hand, and I got all ball. The ball popped out and I caught the ball, and I thought I was out of bounds. I was just going to catch it and shoot. I did, and I made it, and now we're down only five.

Maryland called timeout and we came back on the floor, and Duhon said, "Let him catch the ball again. He's the one we want." We let him catch the ball again and then we fouled him and he goes to the free throw line. As he gets ready for the free throws, I'm on his right at the top of the lane and Chris is behind him at the top of the circle. We're both talking to him. "This one is going to be short, this one is going to be long." He misses both shots and Chris grabs the rebound and gives it directly to me and he runs to the corner. I tug on the front of my jersey to call the 'LA' set to run the 'screen and roll.'

I was still angry and I said to myself, "I'm shooting this shot, no matter what." I came around the screen and the guy doesn't step out and I let it fly with a three, and all of a sudden, we're down two. It was one of the most memorable experiences of my life. And then, Nate goes to the line and makes two clutch free throws and we send it to overtime. They just had this look of defeat on their faces, and ever since we hit those threes, I knew we were going to be able to own them for the rest of that game. We had some epic battles with Maryland that year, but I'll remember this one for the rest of my life because we had the will not to quit.

I am now so fortunate to be able to broadcast games on ESPN. Sometimes a team will get down eight or ten points with a minute to play, and my partner will say, 'Aw, this one is over.' I always say, 'No it isn't. The game is never over until that horn sounds.' I still remember 10 points in 70 seconds at Maryland.

Nate James made two free throws that sent the game into overtime and kept the Terrapin fans quiet. The overtime period was all Duke, and we won a thriller 98-96. Ten points in seventy seconds is worth revisiting. Listen to it on the CD.

The Blue Devils were two games behind UNC in the ACC race after they lost at Virginia on Valentines night. Duke had finished first four straight years but now they were in a precarious position. They responded with wins against Georgia Tech the night Shane Battier's number 31 jersey was retired, and Wake Forest. Then, lo and behold, the cavalry came to the rescue. It was the last-place Clemson Tigers. They beat UNC, IN CLEMSON OF COURSE, since they haven't won in Chapel Hill since Methuselah was a toddler. Now the Devils were just one game back.

The Terps came to Cameron, and Duke lost...... twice. The score was 91 – 80, but in the locker room, it was worse, Carlos Boozer was now out with a broken foot. That was Duke's last loss of the season.

Mike never wavered. He had faced similar situations in the past. At practice the next afternoon, he told them that they 'would win the national championship at the end of the season, IF they did what he told them to do on the court.' Their goal was still within their grasp.

It was adjustment time, and Mike and his staff decided on a 'center by committee' strategy. Casey Sanders, Matt Christiansen and a walk-on from the football team, Reggie Love rotated as game situations dictated. The most important change may have been senior captain Nate James' selfless act. He told Coach K that he felt the team would be better served with him coming off the bench. Coach installed freshman Chris Duhon as the point guard, and the team headed for Chapel Hill.

Duke had to beat the Tar Heels to share the regular season title with them. Duke won, 95-81, and the two would see each other again in a week in Atlanta in the ACC championship game. The Blue Devils beat N.C. State in the first round, and everybody wanted to know why were we wearing our black road uniforms instead of home white ones, since we were the higher seed? Well the answer is easy. The equipment managers forgot to pack the whites. That was highly irregular. Duke basketball has had the most competent, hard-working managerial staff I've ever seen. These young men and women seem to always be on the job, preparing for practices and games, and they are there long after the practices and games are over. For ANYTHING to be overlooked is grounds for the earth to spin in reverse!

Semi-Final Saturday saw Duke dodge a bullet out of the rifle of Maryland's Juan Dixon. Thankfully, his three-point throw from mid-court at the buzzer clanged and Duke advanced.

The championship game on Sunday was the 'dream game,' Duke against Carolina – round three. Sunday afternoon was Duke time. It was a 26-point blow out, and Coach K's 600th victory. It was Shane Battier's 70th ACC win, the league record for all time ACC wins by an individual.

Heigh Ho, Heigh Ho, it's off to the East Region we go. For the third year in a row, Duke was No. 1 seed, and five other ACC teams made the 65-team field. Hello, Greensboro! Duke is back. Monmouth College lost by 43 points, and in the second round, Quin Snyder's Missouri Tigers played a great game but lost, 94-81. The Sweet Sixteen had a slot for the Blue Devils for the 12th time in sixteen years. We played in the First Union Center in Philadelphia against UCLA. Devils 76 - Bruins 63. Another team from Los Angeles, Southern Cal lost by 10, and Duke won their ninth regional championship in ten tries. Final Four number thirteenth was just around the corner, and it was a familiar corner.

It can get as cold in Minneapolis in March as any other location in the Lower 48. Duke's Semi-Final game on the final Saturday in March, in the Metrodome, nearly generated enough heat to melt glaciers. Shhhhh! Don't tell those 'global warming' people. They'll try to blame THAT on Duke too.

Guess who's coming to dinner on Saturday night? Gary Williams and that crowd from Maryland. Duke had already faced Maryland three times, but four in the same season? Duke had played an ACC team four times in a season seven times, but the fourth was never in the NCAA Tournament.

When the Terps built a 22-point lead in the first half, Coach called a time out and told the players, "Just go out and play the way you know how to play. No more set plays. What are you afraid of, that you will lose by 40? Follow your instincts; be the players I know you are."

Duke cut the lead to 11 at the end of the half, and then scored on five of their first six possessions to start the second half. Boozer's two free throws with just under five minutes remaining gave Duke the lead for good. Final -- Duke 95, Maryland 84 in one of the greatest comebacks in Final Four history.

Mike Krzyzewski was now preparing his seventh Duke team to play in an NCAA Championship game. Seven in 21 seasons? Not too shabby. As the Blue Devils sought their third NCAA title, the Arizona Wildcats were prepping for their second in the last five years. They beat Michigan State in the game before ours on Saturday.

BOB INTERVIEWS CHRIS DUHON AFTER 2001 CHAMPIONSHIP

CBS' BILL WALTON INTERVIEWS BOB @ 2001 FINAL FOUR

The Wildcats were number one in the preseason polls, and ended the year number two. Defense was the name of this game and Duke clung to a two-point edge at halftime.

Mike Dunleavey's three three-pointers on three successive possessions early in the second half catapulted the Blue Devils to a lead that Arizona could not overcome. Duke had an 82-72 win and that third NCAA

BOB INTERVIEWS COACH K AFTER 3RD NCAA TITLE 4/01

Championship. There is nothing in the world like being on the floor right after a victorious championship game and seeing the emotion of the players and coaches. I LOVE those kinds of interviews. It was another HOW SWEET IT IS!!! moment.

When I started the Duke job in 1976, I had no dreams of what my future might be like. Certainly, my thoughts never included national championships and bowl games or longevity.

2001 was a year that we all will remember for many things. Duke won the NCAA basketball championship for a third time, I celebrated my 25th year as 'Voice of the Blue Devils', and it was the year that 3,030 people died and another 2,337 were injured as a result of the terrorist attacks on 9/11.

My wife has always been able to surprise me by keeping secrets. She has a flair for announcements of these surprises. Pregnancies, new jobs, birthdays and anniversaries were just a few. 2001 would be one of the biggest surprises of all.

In 1999, Phyllis wanted to find a visible remembrance of my forthcoming 25th anniversary with the Network. After several months of scouring catalogues and websites, she found the perfect item, a 9" tall, Waterford crystal microphone.

She found one and had it engraved with:

BOB HARRIS
VOICE OF THE BLUE DEVILS
25th ANNIVERSARY

Phyllis asked Coach K if it might be presented at the halftime of the Duke-Carolina basketball game, but Krzyzewski said, "No. Bob has meant too much to Duke and our teams. We couldn't share in the experience at a game. Let's do it at the team banquet." Phyllis agreed and delivered it to Coach's office

THE FAMILY CELEBRATES WITH ME AT TEAM BANQUET 4/01

three days before the banquet.

The Duke basketball banquet is not your average, run-of-the-mill sports banquet. It is always a first-class affair with a different theme each year. I have emceed the banquet for years and we have a run-through rehearsal with the players on the afternoon of the event. I had the script and order of events, and nothing was different from previous years, except the players' names.

I always get the banquet started with some announcements and introduce the team on stage, then call for the person who will have the invocation. Dinner follows and then the second half begins with my introduction of the Athletic Director. My night's work is finished. Not on this night. Athletic Director Joe Alleva made his remarks and introduced Coach K. He made a few remarks and asked me to come back to the stage. This was different. As I approached the podium, Coach began talking about my 25 years, and what it had meant to him personally and to the teams and the fans. One of the senior cheerleaders came on stage with the crystal microphone, and gave it to Mike. He presented it to me and told me to say a few words. I think I got out something about 'being the luckiest person in the world to do something that I love.' Then I choked up and could only say, "Thank you." I got a standing ovation that lasted several minutes. As I came back to our table, I understood why Bobbi, Tripp and Meredith were seated there, and that no one had really 'backed out, so they were invited.'

After the banquet, I realized that several hundred friends had been invited and were in the upper arena for the program. They all came down on the floor to help me celebrate the crowning touch to a wonderful basketball season, and the FIRST 25 years as the "Voice of the Blue Devils."

Phyllis and Bobbi had also written to many of my friends who couldn't be there and asked them to write letters about their experiences with, and thoughts about me. They assembled the letters in a nice book and presented it to me after the banquet with all of the friends who had attended looking on. I couldn't sleep that night until I had read every letter, and had written a note to each person. This was another 'HOW SWEET IT IS!!' moment.

2004 was another memorable year. One of the highlights of the regular season was the trip to Chapel Hill in early February, and the Blue Devils came home with an 83-81 overtime win over the Tar Heels.

Chris Duhon made his last trip to the Smith Center a memorable one as he went the length of the floor with time running out to hit the game-winning lay-up. Referee Duke Edsall remembers it too.

> *Yes, I remember chasing Chris Duhon down the court when he went coast to coast to win the overtime game at Carolina in 2004. The funny thing is, I was in the trail position going to the lead position, and had a half court head start. He just blew by me, and everybody else on the floor. Another great finish.*

Duke made it to the finals of the ACC Tourney in Greensboro, but the five-year streak as champions was snapped by Maryland.

The Blue Devils did win the ACC title for the next two years, giving them an unprecedented seven ACC Tournament titles in eight years.

BOB & COACH K AFTER ACC CHAMPIONSHIP 304

In spite the loss in the ACC title game, we were the No. 1 seed in the Atlanta Region. Krzyzewski's squad won the regional title, beating Alabama State, Seton Hall, Illinois, and Xavier.

The Final Four was in San Antonio in '04, and Duke drew UConn in the semis. It looked like the Devils were going back to the finals when they were ahead by eight points with three minutes left, but they went ice-cold and didn't make a single basket in the last in the last four and a half minutes. Chris Duhon made an unbelievable three-pointer at the horn, but the Huskies prevailed, 79-78.

I have had the pleasure of witnessing greatness on the court over my Duke broadcasting career, and one youngster who possessed that was J.J. Redick. J.J. came in with a reputation being a fabulous three-point scorer. Early on he showed just that. When he came back to campus to begin his junior season, he was in the best shape of his life, thanks to listening to his Mom's nutritional advice. He also took control on the court. His precocious maneuvers through the lane to get open for a shot got him beat up too. I interviewed him in our post-game show many times with blood oozing from his scratches and early signs of bruising. Guess what? He never gave an inch. 'Amazing' is a timeworn term, but he was simply amazing.

DUKE LEADING SCORER J.J. REDICK

J.J. set the Duke single season scoring record that had lasted for five years. He also broke Dick Hemric's ACC career scoring mark of 2,769 points at Georgia Tech February 22, 2006. Redick held twelve Duke records when he graduated in 2006 and was the ACC Player of the Year Award in 2005 and '06, As a senior, he earned the Naismith, Wooden, Robertson and Rupp Awards. No.4 was honored with his jersey retirement in 2006.

CHAPTER TWENTY-NINE
TITLE NUMBER 4

This book was supposed to be released before the annual Duke-Carolina basketball game in Cameron Indoor Stadium on March 6, 2010. I already had a book signing set up for Krzyzewskiville for Friday night before the game. Several delays in the original schedule caused those things to be cancelled. There was a reason. There would be one more chapter to write. This chapter began on Friday, October 16th with the first 'Countdown to Craziness" and ended with the 2010 Blue Devils standing on the stage in Indianapolis on April 5th watching 'One Shinning Moment" as National Champions. The events and stories in between those dates beckoned another chapter to this book.

In November, Duke made its sixth appearance in the early season NIT event, and beat Coastal Carolina and Charlotte in the first two games in Cameron, and then beat Herb Sendek's Arizona State Sun Devils and Jim Calhoun's UConn Huskies in Madison Square Garden for the title. Former Clemson coach Cliff Ellis was coaching Coastal Carolina, and I played in their charity golf tournament in June. They always have several items for a live auction, and Cliff asked me if I would auction off four tickets that were right behind the Chanticleer's bench in Cameron. I was delighted to see a Duke fan bidding against a Coastal fan for them. When you get two or more bidders who really want something, you can get a handsome price for the item. The bidding finally got to $2,200.00 and the Duke fan won out. He asked me during the bidding if he could come up to the Crows Nest the night of the game to see our vantage point if he bought the package. I agreed, he won, and he came up at halftime.

It snowed on us in New York City on the Saturday before Christmas when Duke played Gonzaga in the Garden. The game was no contest. The 7th-ranked Blue Devils ran the Zags out of the arena, 76-41. Most of the players left for their Christmas break with families directly from New York. We were one of the last two planes to get out of Newark because it was snowing sideways. The Los Angeles Lakers plane was the other. They had beaten the Nets across the Hudson River, and needed to get out too. Kyle Singler and his family had to rent a car and drive to Chicago to get a flight to Oregon, but they made it safely.

Wednesday nights in Raleigh are sometimes no fun at all. January 20th was no exception. N.C. State was 12-6 overall and just 1-3 in the ACC; on that night they stunned Duke 88-74. After the loss at N.C. State, Coach K and the team closed ranks. A 'no weak link' mantra was taken on and the team avoided their first 0-4 slide on the road since 1981-82 and Duke held No. 17 Clemson to their lowest point total at home in seven years with a 60-47 win. ESPN College Game Day broadcast from Littlejohn and about 4,000 orange-clad early risers turned out 10 hours before tip-off. A sign held up in the crowd before game told of the Tigers' attitudes: "Breathe if you hate Duke." The 'Duke-haters' rear their ugly heads yet again. There's been a lot of that going around in the last 20 years

The Blue Devils stepped out of conference for a January 30th trip to the nation's capitol, but what happened on the Verizon Center floor that Saturday afternoon was less than capital!! With the President and Vice President of the United States looking on, the No. 7 Hoyas blew No. 8 Duke out of the arena. A few minutes before the start of the game, I asked Referee Ed Corbett if he had ever worked a game in front of a President and he said, "No, and I hope I never do again. It took Bryan (Kersey, one of the other officials) and I FORTY-FIVE minutes to get from the parking area to our locker room." It WAS utter chaos with all the security checking every body and every thing going into the building. Next play!!

When Duke gathered for their next practice several changes were made. The most notable was a slight modification of the offense. Until the Georgetown game, most of the half-court offense was run out of sets. The staff felt that more motion was needed in order to get open looks for Singler. From that point forward, Kyle averaged 19.4 points a game to finish the season.

Any and every time the Blue Devils and Tar Heels go head-to-head, no matter what the competition, nor the perceived strengths of each side, it will be a war. This first meeting of the basketball season was no exception. UNC came into the game on a three game losing streak. They had lost seven of nine in the calendar year. Both teams had been in the Top 10 in the last four meetings, but North Carolina had dropped from the Top 25 two weeks prior to this game. The Heels had been No. 6 in the pre-season poll and a co-favorite, with Duke, for the ACC title. Duke got a 10-point win in Chapel Hill and the Tar heels' misery continued as they dropped near the bottom of the league standings. It was a very gratifying win for the Blue Devils, because it was Carolina, and they had lost six of the last seven meetings with UNC.

February 13th was a monumental day for Duke basketball. It was Mike Krzyzewski's 1,000th game in 30 years at Duke, his 63rd birthday, and the celebration of 70 years of Cameron Indoor Stadium. Mike became the eighth Division I coach to reach that milestone at one school."I could not have had a better place to coach," Krzyzewski said. He added that the school "was more of who I want to be. I'm not saying I'm like Duke, but I want to be like Duke."

From 'Lefty' Driesell to J.J. Redick, over 100 former players, coaches and staff came back to Cameron to celebrate. The weekend got off to a great start on Friday night at the Washington-Duke Inn with a reception. Given my penchant for autographs, I viewed this as a 'mother lode' for a project. When the athletic department decided to replace the original playing floor of Cameron Indoor Stadium in the summer of 1977, I stumbled onto a treasure. I happened to be in Cameron and watched as the workers were taking up the old floor. They did saw out and save the two sections that had the Blue Devil mascot painted on them. They had been located at the base lines at both ends of the floor. Other than that, they had bobcats in there just ripping up boards. I got a bright idea and asked the foreman what they were going to do with all the other wood. His answer broke my heart. "We'll just take it over to the trash pile and probably burn it." BURN HISTORY??? No way!

I asked if I might have a piece or two. He told me to get all I wanted. I'm sorry I didn't have a semi-truck to save all of it for posterity (not to mention all the money it would bring with today's memorabilia market). I gathered up six pieces that were four to six feet long, relatively in tact, and had some markings on them. I brought them home and have saved them for over 30 years.

I carried a 3-foot piece to the reception and managed to get 35 signatures on it. All decades, from the 40s to the 70s were represented. Dick Gilbert and Curtis Beall were there from 1944, Ed Koffenberger from 1947, Bucky Allen, Hayes Clement and 'Lefty Driesell' were three from the 50s. Other headliners were Howard Hurt, Hack Tison and Mike Lewis from the 60s, and Pete Kramer, Kevin Billerman and Kenny Dennard from the 70s. Coaches Vic Bubas, Neill McGeachy, Bucky Waters and Lou Goetz signed the floor for me. This is now another item, as Connie Francis sang, "Among My Souvenirs."

The game? Well, it ended like ¾ of Mike's other victories with a huge win, 77-56. It was Brian Zoubek's 'coming-out-party.' The 7'1" bearded behemoth had 16 points and 17 rebounds as Zoub made his first start of the season, and Krzyzewski called him "the difference." The thing I remember most was my post game interview with Zoub. As he answered my questions, I saw one of the most wonderful expressions on his face that I've ever seen on a player. It was a look of pride, satisfaction and accomplishment. As I told his parents several weeks later, "That was a look I will NEVER forget." As I have said several times in this book, I will NEVER have a favorite Duke player. Every player who has worn a

Duke uniform since 1976 is special to me.

After the game, Duke President Richard Brodhead and Athletic Director Kevin White presented Coach with a framed Duke jersey, with the number 1,000. The players all put on T-shirts that had Coach's silhouette on them while the Crazies sang "Happy Birthday" to him.

Later in the afternoon, Krzyzewski addressed the reunion gathering in Scharf Hall and thanked them for their wonderful support of the program. He headed off the rumors that the New Jersey Nets were interested in him. "The guy's Russian, right? You think he'd hire a Polish guy?" Krzyzewski quipped in reference to Mikhail Prokhorov, the Russian billionaire and the Nets' prospective buyer. Then, he added with a laugh: "No one's contacted me, and if they do, I think 'nyet' would be easy for me to say."

The loss at Maryland on March 3rd may have been the most difficult loss to accept. A mere 18 days before, Duke had manhandled the Terps in Cameron by 21 points. On senior night, before their usual belligerent crowd, Grevis Vasquez put on a show in his home finale. He scored 20 points, including a desperation heave at the basket with 37 seconds left, and No. 22 Maryland beat No. 4 Duke 79-72.

Also as usual, at the buzzer, fans stormed the court. Thanks to some BRAVE Maryland security folks, the teams were allowed to shake hands before heading to the locker rooms. Those guys locked arms to prevent the unruly mob of students from making a scene. Since we were broadcasting right beside the Duke bench area, we were in danger of being jostled around, but more importantly, losing some expensive broadcast equipment. Had it not been for our conscientious and feisty engineer, John Rose, the equipment would have been knocked to the floor like several students were. John put his body between the onrush and the equipment, and we were saved. Three students that I watched weren't so lucky. They were either knocked town or tripped over other students and hit the floor about five feet from where the three of us were now standing to make sure nothing further happened. Their fellow classmates had NO concern for them and just stepped on them and kept on going to the center of the floor to try and get five seconds of 'face-time' on TV. One writer, who was located in the end zone watched as a small boy was knocked down in his line of sight. He told me after the game that the look of horror on the kid's face was awful, and NO ONE made an attempt to help the little fellow get up or to see if he was hurt.

Senior night at Cameron 2010 saw Scheyer, Thomas and Zoubek, along with 5th year grad student Jordan Davidson received the accolades they so richly deserved before playing Carolina. None of those four, or anyone else in the building will forget that night.

After taping Coach K's pre-game interview an hour and a half before tip off, I went through the players' lounge to get a couple of bottles of orange juice to take to the Crows' Nest for my 'in-game throat lubrication' that night. Associate Coaches Chris Collins and Steve Wojciechowski were sitting on the couch and I just looked down at them and said, "I would like to see a 30-point win for these seniors tonight." I didn't get a verbal response, but the grins on their faces led me to believe they wanted the same thing.

Marcus Ginyard made one of two free throws after he was fouled by Lance, and that gave UNC their ONLY lead of the night, 1-0, fifteen seconds into the game. The score was more than doubled, 53-26 as both teams retired to their locker rooms, and the second half was just pure misery for the Tar Heels as Duke was up by 36 with 11:13 left in the game. Every player on the roster played, and the seniors all received standing ovations as Coach subbed for them, one at a time.

Coach K told me in the locker room, "That was one of the best games we've played all year. The three veterans on the perimeter really set the stage in the first half with how they passed and moved with one another. I think we would have been tough to beat by anybody tonight."

The 82-50 rout was Duke's most one-sided home win in college basketball's fiercest rivalry and gave the Devils a share of their 12th ACC regular-season title. The Tar Heels were serenaded by the Crazies throughout the second half with chants of 'NIT.' After the game the team got a surprise in the locker room. They were all given tee shirts with 17-0 on the front. Below the numbers were the words, OUR HOUSE, and below that was '09-'10. There was a silhouette background of basketball pictures from the season to that point. They were designed by Kyle Singler as a tribute to the team and the leadership of the seniors.

Not only was this the final game in Cameron for the seniors, it was the final game at the microphone for the man who put glasses on me in 1982, Dr. Art Chandler. Art had been the public address announcer for 40 years and never took a penny for his efforts. It was a labor of love. He missed the last half of the 1991 season because he was deployed as a Colonel in the Army Reserve, as the Chief of Medicine, 312th Field Hospital, with headquarters about a mile south of the Iraqi border, about 40 miles west of Kuwait. Most of their time was spent treating U.S. soldiers as well as Iraqi civilians and soldiers with eye injuries in the Middle East during Desert Storm. Coach sent him a "care" package after the National Championship to let him know he wasn't forgotten. Art was honored at halftime of the Tulsa game with a video message from Coach K and a Duke rocking chair.

"I have loved this. It has not been a chore at all. It's been an honor to be part of it all these years," Chandler told me about two weeks after the Final Four. "I'm at peace with the situation right now, but I know it's really going to be hard when the season starts next year."

The 77-year old Chandler graduated from Duke School Of Medicine in 1959. He did his internship here in 1960.

"Here Comes Duke" will never sound the same.

The 2010 Atlantic Coast Conference Basketball Tournament

returned to its rightful home, the Greensboro Coliseum, for another hectic weekend. Thursday proved to be 'Upset City' as Georgia Tech was the only 'higher' seed to survive. I had the pleasure to team with former Wake Forest head coach, and 35-year friend, Dave Odom to broadcast the first game of the Tournament, No. 8 seed Boston College against No. 9 seed Virginia. No one knew that would be Al Skinner's swan song at B.C. He was released in early April.

Frank Haith's Miami Hurricanes then had the largest margin of victory of the entire weekend as they walloped the Demon Deacons of Wake Forest by 21. Dino Gaudio coached in a win and a loss in the NCAA Tournament and HE was fired in early April.

In the first game of the night session, the '09 National Champion North Carolina Tar Heels were unceremoniously shone the exit by the No. 7 seeded Georgia Tech Yellow Jackets, 62-58.

N.C. State beat Clemson as coach Oliver Purnell lost his last regular season game, this one and a first round NCAA game, and then signed a seven year deal to coach the DePaul Blue Demons. That's three coaches gone in one post season.

The Duke Blue Devils opened the Friday afternoon session with a noon meeting with Virginia, and the Blue Devils pulled away 57-46. Coach K likened Scheyer to, "That guy that you want on your baseball team who goes 0 for 4, then in the bottom of the eighth, he gets a double, and knocks in the winning run. He goes onto the next play really well." Duke became the winningest team in tournament history with its 85th win. This would be their 12th semifinal berth in 13 years.

Duke beat Miami on Saturday afternoon, 77-74, and readied for Georgia Tech. By Sunday's tipoff, Duke fans had found plenty of tickets from fans of losing schools and that put plenty of royal blue in the seats. It was a home-court advantage for the Devils and made Georgia Tech's job even tougher.

Duke held a one-point lead in the final seconds. I left my center-court broadcast location with the wireless microphone and took up residence at the corner of the court next to the Duke bench during the 'under 4 minute' timeout. I had to be in position to get to the coaches and players as soon as the game was over. I had a straight line-of-sight for Scheyer's last shot with 18 seconds left. He curled around a screen, took a pass and launched a 3-pointer that dropped perfectly through the net and Duke won 65-61. The Blue Devils' 18th ACC championship was in the bag, putting them in a great position to pluck a No. 1 seed in the NCAA tournament. Singler earned the Everette Case Award that signifies the MVP of the Tourney. Duke now has the most ACC tournament titles ever. Krzyzewski's 12th title moved him within one of Dean Smith for the most in league history.

Singler had a nasty red scratch about 4 inches long on the back of his right shoulder after the game. In his zealousness to retrieve a loose ball, he went diving over a press table, taking out ESPN's Dan Schulman and ending up on the floor between press-row tables late in the first half. By the way, Dan's partner, Dick Vitale, was heading the other way when he saw Kyle flying toward him. No Zoubek he. He'd rather 'flee than fight.'

Several hours after the Blue Devils cut down the nets in Greensboro, they found out what their NCAA Tournament path would look like on the NCAA Selection Sunday show. When the four No. 1 seeds were announced at the top of the show, the Blue Devils were delighted to see their name pop up as the top seed in the South Region. They would begin their odyssey in Jacksonville, Florida on Friday night against the winner of the play-in game between Winthrop and Arkansas-Pine Bluff.

Almost immediately, the national media and 'talking heads' began their 'Duke bashing' that continues through this writing. 'Duke shouldn't be a No. 1 Seed.' 'Duke doesn't deserve to be a No. 1.' 'Duke was GIVEN the easiest road to the Final Four,' Ad Nauseum!!!!! Duke DID deserve to be a No. 1 seed. They played one of the toughest schedules in the country. All of the Sagarin, Pomeroy and RPI ratings had Duke in the top three. Why wouldn't they be a No. 1 seed?

One thing is different during the NCAAs, talk show interviews. The requests certainly pick up during this time over the number of requests for my time during the season. In the five days between the South Region championship in Houston and our Semi-Final game in Indianapolis, I was on 17 talk shows from Charleston, SC on the east coast to San Francisco on the west. I had to turn down several because they wanted me at a time that I already had one scheduled for another station.

Our charter flight left RDU on Wednesday evening for Jacksonville. Thursday's media day and open practice sessions were about par for the course. The crowd for the practice session was not large, but they were appreciative of the teams' efforts. Duke players rewarded some of our fans with souvenir tee shirts that they threw into the crowd.

The 'upset bug' had already sent several favorites home from the tournament on Thursday and in the early games on Friday afternoon. The Blue Devils opened their South Regional effort with a blowout 73-44 victory over No. 16 seed Arkansas-Pine Bluff. UAPB was playing their second game of the tourney, having had beaten Winthrop in the play-in game on Tuesday night. I watched that game with the Duke coaches because I had to record Coach K's Wednesday radio show as soon as it was over. Chris Collins was in charge of the scouting for this game. He and 'Wojo' always alternate games and it was Chris' turn. Good thing too. Steve and his wife, Lindsey, had welcomed their second son, Charlie, into the world early that morning.

The Blue Devil mascot's headband for the game read: "Played In, Blown Out." The Blue Devils made him a prophet. Duke never trailed in the game, and advanced to play California and former Duke player Jamal Boykin. The win gave Mike his 11th 30-win season in 30 years at Duke. When told it was his 11th year with 30 wins he told the media: "That's a lot of wins. The best thing is to have 31 and move on."

Golden Lions coach George Ivory played on a heavy underdog team that gave No. 1 Duke a scare in the 1st round in Greensboro 24 years before. As a player, Ivory was a sophomore starter for 16th-seeded Mississippi Valley State.

Saturday was another media obligation. This media day was not like the one two days ago. I was only concerned with Cal. The other two surviving teams in Jacksonville were Cornell, and Wisconsin, but they were in the East Region.

On Sunday evening the Blue Devils earned another trip to the Sweet 16 after beating California 68-53. Coach said of his stifling man-to-man defense, "I don't know if we'll go any further this year, but this is a better team because it can play total defense. Some people say, 'in the past they relied on the 3-point shot too much.' Well, what else were we going to rely on? We relied on it enough to win 30 games. Just because you lose, doesn't mean those kids underachieved. They maxed. This team is better. It's not a great team, but it's an excellent defensive team that hopefully can be a little bit better offensively as we go forward."

We returned to Durham late Sunday, and on Monday I immediately started preparing for the Houston games. Purdue would be my first priority because they had beaten Texas A&M. The other two teams that would be in Reliant Stadium were Baylor and upstart St. Mary's of California. I had to complete and print my score sheets for all three of them as well as write broadcast openings and compile all of the stats and bio information for all of the players we might face.

Just like last week, we departed RDU on Wednesday evening. The Houston schedule for everyone would be a carbon copy of the Jacksonville agenda. We hoped the results would be the same. Duke pulled away in the second half for a 70-57 win over Purdue.

Before I go any further, I need to set the scenario for you for this Regional and for the Final Four. At this site, Reliant Stadium, the floor was raised three feet above the football stadium's normal surface. Press row was on that football surface. My belt buckle was below the basketball court. I have a 'bird's-eye' view in Cameron, but I had a 'worm's-eye' view of this game. We could NOT see the three-point line from the foul line to the base line on the side of the floor opposite our position. We were on the front row of the media, across from the Duke bench. Mike coached the game from a stool on the raised floor, three feet above the Duke bench and his assistants who he relies on so much during the games. He was uncomfortable about that the entire weekend and the next, too.

Duke, now 32-5, had lost in the Sweet 16 in three of the previous five years. There were rumblings about whether the once powerful Blue Devils had lost their edge. Rumblings dispelled!! Duke kept on playing while other high seeds were falling by the wayside. They and Kentucky were the only No. 1 seeds left after Kansas and Syracuse were upset.

Kyle had 24 points and Scheyer popped in 18. Did somebody say something about a shooting slump? Yes they did. Jon jokingly said, "I haven't lost my shot. I know right where it is. It's in Houston, waiting for me to get there."

Jon knew that just winning in the Sweet 16 for this group of seniors' first time wasn't something to sit back and boast about. "It feels good, but we really can't relax at all. It's really important to refocus. We can't enjoy wins right now. After the season, we can look back and enjoy them." Eleven days later they began to look back and enjoy.

When I watched the Baylor team at the open practices on Thursday, I just knew we'd have a tough time matching up with their athletic front line. They were 6'10", 6'10", and 7'0" with VERY quick guards. Add to that a strong bench, and that put some doubts in my mind.

After we beat the Boilermakers, I tried to block out those Thursday apprehensions. Then I remembered that THEY would have match-up problems with Duke.They had no answer for Nolan Smith, who, along with Scheyer exploited Baylor's zone, and combined for 49 points to give Duke to a 78-71 South Regional win and a trip to the Final Four

The Baylor game was special for Nolan. He got a text message from his mom, Monica Malone, that morning, reminding him what was at stake. It just said, 'If you win, you go back to Indy, where your father played for a championship.' Nolan had known from the Selection Sunday show that if Duke continued to win they would play in the Final Four in Indy. Before leaving the Houston Hilton Sunday, he watched an ESPN program, "Outside The Lines," that was shown last year about him and his dad, Derek Smith. Nolan had but a precious few years with his father. Derek died at age 34 of a heart attack in 1996. Nolan was only 8 years old.

Thirty years before, in 1970, in Indianapolis, Derek Smith helped Louisville win an NCAA Championship by beating UCLA, 59-54.

Nolan has watched his DVD of that game a lot. He remembers the fearless, determined look in his father's eyes. That Sunday evening, fans in Houston saw that same look in Nolan's eyes.

Earlier, Sunday morning, he Twittered, "This one is for you Dad!! I love you!" Nolan wanted to honor his father, and he did it just the way Derek would have wanted it. It was possibly the best game of his life.

Duke was headed to Indianapolis for its first Final Four in six years and would meet West Virginia, the No. 2 seed from the East Regional.

Another late night flight back to Durham and quickly to the preparation on Monday morning. Again, it would be a short stay at home as Duke followed the same travel schedule as the two previous weeks. The team had to be in Indianapolis for media days Thursday and Friday.

I was able to get Phyllis on the team plane with our radio crew. This would be HER 12th Final Four as well as mine. We both remembered the excitement of our first one in 1978, and the other ten as well. We drove to campus on Wednesday afternoon and left our car there, in HOPES of a victory celebration if we won the Championship. How fortuitous! There were three busses going to the airport. The first left at 4:30 and carried the cheerleaders and band with all their instruments. The second and third busses left Cameron at 5pm. Our staff bus went straight to RDU, while the team bus went to the University Club, as they always do, for the players' meal. After all, they had just finished practice and were hungry. They would arrive about forty-five minutes after we did. This certainly helped the boarding procedure. The security crew at RDU's General Aviation terminal is the best! They are all so friendly and they understand our situation as well as we do theirs.

Once we arrived in Indianapolis, we boarded our assigned vehicles. The team and staff busses went to the Hilton downtown. The band and cheerleaders were housed at a hotel north of town. The police escort got us to the hotel in short order, and we had quite a crowd to welcome us there.

Thursday was the first media day, with coaches and selected players meeting with reporters and getting used to the Final Four atmosphere.

After all of that was completed, they had a closed practice in the stadium.

That evening brought on one of my long anticipated meals. We headed to St. Elmo Steak House, about a five-block walk from the Hilton. I made sure to remind Phyllis, John Roth and John Rose about the 'heat' of the sauce on the shrimp cocktail. They didn't want a whole one so I ordered one for the table and we shared it, all but Phyllis 'shrimp are used for bait' Harris. She just won't eat them. I ate her portion.

On the walk back to the hotel we held a 'reunion' at the corner of Maryland and Illinois Streets. As we were waiting for the light to change, up walked Bobby Cremins and his wife Carolyn, along with their son, Bobby III. While we were catching up on things with them, Jay Bilas, wife Wendy and youngsters Victoria and Anthony came up and we had a gabfest for quite a while right there in the middle of downtown Indy.

Friday was another media day as well as the open practices. Nearly 30,000 fans showed up for the early portion. That's natural, because the hometown team, Butler, was the first to hit the floor. After the Bulldogs finished, about 15,000 of them left. That was the first time I've ever seen that kind of mass exit on Friday. Our broadcast crew had network duties on Friday. Rose had to set up all of our equipment. That, in itself, is a two-hour job. As he worked on that, Roth and I were back in the media area most of the time, getting interviews for the Saturday night broadcast, and listening to the coaches and players from all four schools answer questions from the media.

During the Duke practice time, I went up to the 7th level of Lucas Oil Stadium to be a guest on ncaa.com's tournament broadcast. As I looked down on the court from that perch, the host asked me if I could identify the players. I looked down and said, "Well, that's....uh...and over there is....uh. No, I really can't." I could not believe people actually paid good money for those seats. The game was a rumor from there!!! I guess that saying you were at the Final Four means a lot to some people. I'm glad that Duke's successes got the three of us second row courtside media seats. By the way, they were not free. ISP Sports paid a handsome sum for us to broadcast the games. Westwood One Network pays the

NCAA a rights fee for all the broadcast rights to the entire tournament. They charge each school a fee for each game their team plays. Our fees are based on the number of radio stations on our network. A flat rate is charged for the 'flagship' station and a lesser flat rate for each of the other stations. As I said, the seats were not cheap.

Saturday finally arrived and the town was buzzing. This was the biggest event in a while with the local favorites' campus just 5.6 miles from the Final Four site. Butler was the talk of the town, everywhere except in the Duke and West Virginia camps. They were concerned about each other.

West Virginia was one of the nation's best rebounding teams, but they simply couldn't keep 'Zoub' off the boards. He yanked down 10 rebounds and dished out three assists. That's not a misprint; it's a result of Duke's 'rebound-and-kick' strategy. That and 20 assists, with just six turnovers, sparked Duke to a 78-57 victory over the Mountaineers.

In the post-game media interview, Krzyzewski credited Nolan and Jon. "Our care for the ball was excellent. These two (pointing to them) had 12 assists and no turnovers." Scheyer credited all of this to preparation by the coaching staff, "I thought we were really well prepared, and we felt comfortable no matter what they did." Zoubek was a major reason why Duke was headed to the Championship game. "Teams haven't seen me as much. They see a 7-foot-1 white guy who can't move extremely well, and can't jump that high."

As he explained, "It's a process; a lot of days in the gym, a lot of sweat, and a lot of hatred toward 'Wojo' for all the stuff he put me through (laugh goes here). But it was all worth it. It's hard to see the future in all the work you put in and how's it going to help you, and is it worth it? It is. This really proves that."

The Blue Devils were in the championship game for the 10th time in school history. Speaking of point differentials, I got into a habit of prediction the margins of victory with a media friend of mine, and I must brag a bit. I explained about calling for a 30-point win over UNC at home, and it was 32. In the first two rounds in Jacksonville, I said the margin over Arkansas-Pine Bluff would be whatever Coach wanted it to be. It was. I forecast a 13-point win over Cal. It was 15. In Houston, I said Duke would beat Purdue by a dozen and it ended up 13. I was antsy about the Baylor pick for the Elite Eight game, but gave an 'iffy' 3-point win to the Blue Devils. The final was 7. Then came the Final Four. I thought this West Virginia game would be closer than it was. I picked 7. If I am going to miss it by 14, I'd rather miss it low. I also told this one to Horizon League Commissioner, Jon LeCrone, whom I have known for 30+ years. I went a step further and predicted his Butler Bulldogs would beat MSU by 2. BINGO!!!! Hear the quarters falling out of the machine??

When we met in the media room prior to the Championship game, Jon and I simply wished each other 'Good Luck and have a great game.' No prediction TO HIM. To my media buddy, I got really carried away with my successes and said it would be a minimum of 15. OH, so now you DON'T want me to go Vegas with you, eh??

Why did I miss this one so badly? The Bulldogs were better than advertised, and they played, probably, their best game of the year on Monday night, April 5th, starting at 9:21pm.

The Sunday afternoon media events were more about "David and Goliath" or "Cinderella" or any other analogy the media could come up with to describe the little guys against the behemoths. They were not David. They hadn't used a sling all year. They weren't Cinderella. She hadn't had 25 beaus before the Prince. They HAD won 25 consecutive basketball games, and had been ranked all year. They were GOOD!

A crowd of 70,390 filled Lucas Oil Stadium for the Championship game. With Michigan State and West Virginia out, there were tons of tickets for sale Saturday night after the games, Sunday and Monday, and the hometown Butler fans bought up the majority. They were treated a game that ended one of the most memorable tournaments in NCAA history.

Duke, as usual, won with defense. They hounded the 'Dogs on every possession. Butler, though, gave up 60 points for the first time since February. Duke won with clutch shooting.

Butler cut a five-point deficit to one and had a chance to win it with about 13 seconds left. Gordon Hayward got the ball at the top of the key. He managed to get to the baseline, but Zoubek forced him to take an off-balance shot from 15 feet, which he missed. Brian got the rebound and was fouled immediately with 3.6 seconds on the clock. He made the first of two free throws to give Duke a two point lead. He missed the second one intentionally. Why??? Butler had no more timeouts. If Brian had made the free throw, the clock would not have started until it was touched in bounds. That would have given the Bulldogs more time to get the ball into an advantageous position to possibly make a game-winning basket.

The Bulldogs had their chance to win it now. Hayward rebounded the miss and got it quickly up the floor. His desperation shot at the buzzer from just inside the mid-court line, near the right sideline, caromed off the glass and the rim, and the Blue Devils were NCAA National Champions for the 4th time, all on Mike Krzyzewski's watch.

"MISSION ACCOMPLISHED!!! THE DUKE BLUE DEVILS HAVE WON THE 2010 NCAA BASKETBALL NATIONAL CHAMPION-SHIP. THE TROPHY NOW RESIDES IN DURHAM! HOW SWEET IT IS!!!!"

The exploding fireworks and constant deluge of streamers and confetti from the rafters of the stadium heralded the accomplishments of this gritty Duke team. It gave celebration to the leadership of the four seniors. It gave me a chance to get to the floor to do post-game interviews with the players and Coach K, and to watch the faces of the Duke players and coaches as they hugged each other, screamed and jumped up and down. I was also given the same Championship t-shirt and cap that the players all put on. I wore my cap doing the

BOB WITH TROPHY

interviews, but put the shirt in my pocket for safekeeping. It is great to be a part of this team and program.

The Blue Devils stopped Butler's 25-game winning streak, and won another Championship for Krzyzewski. It was his first since 2001, but this one tied him for second place on the all-time list with Adolph Rupp.

"Both teams and all the kids on both teams played their hearts out," Krzyzewski said in my interview with him on the floor. "There was never more than a few points separating us, so a lot of kids made big plays for both teams. Neither team lost this game. We just had two more points than Butler did when the horn sounded."

Here is the TRUE (as I believe it to be) reason why Hayward's final shot was just a bit to the right of the mark. The majority of the Butler fans in the lower arena were on the left side of that basket, behind the Bulldog's bench. The vast majority of the Duke fans were on the right side. With all of the air being expelled from the Butler fans' lungs, as they were shouting, "Yessssss," and all of the Duke fans' air being sucked IN by their gasps, the shot had no chance. Kenny Dennard taught me all the 'Laws of Physics and Other Matters Relevant to Basketball' back in 1980 after the ACC Tournament. (See page 228 for his detailed explanation)

After the game and all the media requirements were finished, Coach and I went into the small section of the locker room that was for the Duke coaches, and taped two daily radio shows for Tuesday and Wednesday's use. In the season wrap up show I asked Mike when he first had a feeling this group could win a National Championship. And I quickly interjected, "And don't say 'right after the horn sounded.'" He laughed and related this story for the fans.

I'll share a moment that I had with our Athletic Director, Kevin White. Mickie and I host a wine-tasting celebration for the V Foundation every August in Napa Valley, California. It raises two to three million dollars each year to fight cancer. One of those nights we were having a glass of wine, or maybe two, and I told him that we were going to have a great group of kids. We're gonna be really good, and I think we might have a chance to win a National Championship. And He reminded me of that this week because I had forgotten it. Maybe I had more than one or two glasses that night, and maybe that's why I said it. But it proved to be true.

As far as when I had that feeling during the season, it was early in February. I knew after the Georgetown game that there were some changes that we needed to make in our offense. We had a few days to practice and we made those changes.

By the way, this Duke-Butler NCAA championship game matched the highest preliminary television rating since 1999, for the Connecticut-Duke game. Duke's 61-59 win over Butler earned a 16.0 overnight rating and 25 share. That's up 34 percent from the 11.9 and 19 of last year.

About an hour and a half after the final buzzer, we boarded the team bus and headed back to the Hilton. When we got within sight of the hotel our bus driver, Bob Elliott, blew the horn continuously until we pulled under the canopy. Many of the overflow crowd of happy Duke fans and former players couldn't get into the hotel and waited outside. The players departed the bus first, then the coaches and then the rest of us. The lobby was jam-packed and the hotel management and security did a great job of cordoning off a four-foot wide corridor for us to use to get in and to a special presentation downstairs from the lobby. Everyone was cheering and straining against the ropes, just trying to shake hands, get a 'hi five' or take a picture. I think I might have set a personal record the six days we were in Indy for posing for pictures and signing autographs. I shutter to think of what it was like for the players.

We were ushered down to the lower level for a 'families only' gathering. Of course it wasn't just the players' families. It was the 'Duke basketball family.' The purpose of the gathering was the presentation of the National Basketball Coaches Association crystal basketball, emblematic of the National Championship. Jim Haney, the Executive Director of NABC, presented it to Coach K, and after a few acceptance remarks he gave all the picture-takers in the audience a chance to get a shot of him kissing the ball. I talked with several former players for a short while, grabbed some food from the buffet table, and went to our room to celebrate with Phyllis. We had an early wake up call and it was already 2:30am.

The flight home from Indianapolis on Tuesday morning was delayed about an hour by the meticulous TSA staff at the Indianapolis airport. They went through EVERY piece of carry-on with a 'fine-tooth-comb' and wanded every person more than Newark and Miami ever did.

Touchdown at RDU came at 1:05pm. The Welcome Home Celebration in Cameron was supposed to have begun at 1pm. Oops! As we taxied toward our awaiting busses at General Aviation, the Captain came on the intercom to tell us to look out both sides of the plane as we made the final turn off the taxiway. We were welcomed home by the RDU Fire Department with a 'Victory Spray' from their trucks. As we de-planed we could see the balcony of the terminal was packed with well-wishers. Quite a few G.A. employees were at the busses to personally congratulate the team. Those busses had already been painted with the words "DUKE BLUE DEVILS -- 2010 NATIONAL CHAMPIONS."

We had an escort by the Durham County Sheriff's Department from RDU to Cameron. There were four squad cars and three motorcycle units who handled traffic getting out of the airport, moving traffic over on I-40 and along Durham streets to campus. One of the local TV stations had its news helicopter over our busses all the way. Motorists were honking horns and waving to the motorcade as we passed by. Once we arrived at the back entrance to the Schwartz-Butters Athletic Center that adjoins Cameron, we were greeted by a great group of athletic department staff, including Coach David Cutcliffe and his wife Karen.

We were ushered down to the hallways outside the locker room and were briefed on the program plans. An area beside the stage was reserved for families, and Phyllis joined that group. Bart Smith, Director of Promotions, handed me the 'Order of Service' for the program that

I was going to M.C. The crowd in Cameron was watching the last minutes of the Championship game and we could hear them cheering just as if the game was being played in the building. When it finished, I walked up on the stage alone, and the sight and sounds were unbelievable. Cameron was PACKED!!! The noise was ear splitting. I just stood there for several moments. I was not waiting for them to quiet down. I was soaking in all of this. I had never been in this situation.

WELCOME HOME '10 BOB @ PODIUM
(CREDIT DAVE BRADLEY)

I apologized for our 'slight' delay, and thanked them all for coming and being patient. And then I said, " I only have one thing to say..... HOW SWEET IT IS!!!!!!!!!!!!!" They went nuts again and the team, coaches and staff joined me on stage and the crescendo was deafening. I

WELCOME HOME FROM BEHIND TEAM
(CREDIT JON GARDINER - DUKE PHOTO)

then introduced Coach K to take care of the rest of the program. He talked of the successes of this team and the individuals who made it all happen, and pointed to the place where the 2010 National Championship banner would hang, right beside the other three. He then thanked everyone for being the best fans in the world. He introduced the three seniors and they echoed Coach's comments. He then asked Nolan to speak, and shyly, he did. He brought Kyle to the mic amid chants of 'One More Year.' Singler gave that boyish grin and talked about this team, and how special it was.

I knew you'd agree that another chapter was needed.

As you can see, life truly has been a series of choices for me. Most choices were small and didn't change my life to a large degree, and some choices may have seemed insignificant at the time, but had a huge effect on my path. My life's course changed many times and was not always exactly as I had anticipated, but we all have to be ready for the changes that come along each day and see them for the opportunities they are. I really thought this book was headed to the printer in late 2009, but it didn't. I kept wondering why things were not advancing like I had planned, and then the reason was made clear. It was not my plan, it was God's.

Four small words...but a lifetime of meaning...

HOW SWEET IT IS!!!

<u>**COMPACT DISC PROGRAM**</u>

1 - INTRO

ALBEMARLE VS. LEXINGTON HIGH SCHOOL FOOTBALL 10/73

2 - FIRST DUKE NETWORK AIRTIME - DUKE VS. CLEMSON 10/18/75

3 - FIRST DUKE PLAY-BY-PLAY - DUKE @ TENNESSEE 9/11/76

4 - UNC 39 -- DUKE 38 11/20/76

5 - DUKE 21 -- UNC 17 11/20/82

6 - BENNETT TO MILLITELLO TO BEAT STATE 11/12/83

7 - BENNETT SETS NCAA RECORD @ UNC 11/19/83

8 - OVERTIME @ VIRGINIA 10/9/99

9 - JETS VS. EAGLES RALEIGH 8/89

10 - HALL OF FAMER ENOS SLAUGHTER 1975

11 - HOMERUN KING HANK AARON AFTER #713 9/29/73

12 - CINCINNATI ALL-STAR JOHNNY BENCH 7/72

13 - YANKEES BROADCASTER MEL ALLEN 1972

14 - EDDIE FEIGNER (KING & HIS COURT) 5/5/72

15 - BRAVES MANAGER CLYDE KING 7/27/74

16 - HALL OF FAMER BOB FELLER 8/9/88

17 - DODGERS' HALL OF FAMER DUKE SNIDER 11/12/93

18 - NEW YORK YANKEE REGGIE JACKSON - 3/25/93

19 - GERTIE DUNN AAWPBL 7/94

20 - FIRST DUKE BASKETBALL PLAY-BY-PLAY 1/2/76

21 - DUKE 92 - UNC 84 1/14/78

22 - DUKE PLAYERS INTRODUCE THEMSELVES 3/4/78

23 - BILL FOSTER FINAL FOUR PREGAME 3/27/78

24 - BANKS' SHOT VS. UNC 2/28/81

25 - KRZYZEWSKI FINAL FOUR POSTGAME 3/31/86

26 - KRZYZEWSKI PREGAME 2/20/92

27 - DUKE 77 - UNC 75 2/28/98

28 - 10 POINTS IN 70 SECONDS 1/27/01

29 - I REALLY DO LIKE REFEREES

30 - HORACE 'BONES' McKINNEY -COUGARS' POSTGAME

31 - RED SKELTON 9/4/82

32 - ARCHIE CAMPBELL & BOB SING @ DUKE CHILDREN'S CLASSIC

33 - ROGER MARIS PROMO 5/81

34 - BIG ANNOUNCEMENT 10/18/90

35 - BIG ANNOUNCEMENT II 8/31/93

36 - TRACK PLAY-BY-PLAY 4/76

37 - 'THE GREATEST' 10/8/76

38 - RICHARD NIXON 2/26/89

39 - MONTAGE OF PLAY-BY-PLAY CALLS & CLOSE

PHOTOGRAPHY CREDITS

Bobby Bogle

Blue Devil Weekly

Dave Bradley

Coastal Classic Golf Tournament - Aline F. Lasseter, Exec. Dir, New Hanover Regional Medical Center Foundation

Robert Crawford Photography

Duke University Photography

Jim Elkins - Elkins Chrysler-Plymouth

John Elkins Photography

Bob Harris personal photos

Hugh Morton & UNC ARCHIVES

National Sportscasters & Sportswriters Association

David Page

Andy Park

"Stanly County Remembers" - Margaret Snyder, Event Co-Chair

Bill Straus Photography, Inc

Jim Wallace

AUDIO CREDITS

NCAA & Host Communications - Mike Dodson, V.P.